The *Essential* Handbook of Eating Disorders

The *Essential* Handbook of Eating Disorders

Edited by

Janet Treasure
Institute of Psychiatry, London, UK

Ulrike Schmidt
Institute of Psychiatry, London, UK

Eric van Furth
Robert-Fleury Stichting, Leidschendam, The Netherlands

WILEY

Other Wiley Editorial Offices

John Wiley & Sons Inc., 111 River Street, Hoboken, NJ 07030, USA

Jossey-Bass, 989 Market Street, San Francisco, CA 94103-1741, USA

Wiley-VCH Verlag GmbH, Boschstr. 12, D-69469 Weinheim, Germany

John Wiley & Sons Australia Ltd, 33 Park Road, Milton, Queensland 4064, Australia

John Wiley & Sons (Asia) Pte Ltd, 2 Clementi Loop #02-01, Jin Xing Distripark, Singapore 129809

John Wiley & Sons Canada Ltd, 22 Worcester Road, Etobicoke, Ontario, Canada M9W 1L1

Wiley also publishes its books in a variety of electronic formats. Some content that appears in print may not be
available in electronic books.

Library of Congress Cataloging-in-Publication Data
The essential handbook of eating disorders / edited by Janet Treasure, Ulrike Schmidt, Eric van Furth.
     p.   cm.
     Includes index.
     ISBN 0-470-01463-6
     1. Eating disorders–Handbooks, manuals, etc.   I. Treasure, Janet.   II. Schmidt, Ulrike, 1955–
III. Furth, Eric van.

     RC552.E18E85   2005
     616.85′26—dc22   2004027086

British Library Cataloguing in Publication Data
A catalogue record for this book is available from the British Library

ISBN 0-470-01463-6

Typeset in 10/12pt Times by TechBooks, New Delhi, India
Printed and bound in Great Britain by Antony Rowe Ltd, Chippenham, Wiltshire
This book is printed on acid-free paper responsibly manufactured from sustainable forestry
in which at least two trees are planted for each one used for paper production.

To Tom, Jean and Sam.

To David and Lukas
U.S.

To Machteld, and our children,
Annick, Wytze and Bram
E.v.F.

Contents

About the Editors

Janet Treasure, *Department of Psychiatry, 5th Floor, Thomas Guy House, Guys Hospital, London, SE1 9RT, United Kingdom*
Professor Treasure is a psychiatrist who has specialised in the treatment of eating disorders for over 20 years. She trained with Professor Gerald Russell at the Maudsley Hospital and the Institute of Psychiatry. The clinic provides treatment for a population of 2 million in south-east London and is a national referral centre. The unit is active in research and development.

Ulrike Schmidt, *Section of Eating Disorders, Institute of Psychiatry, De Crespigny Park, London, SE5 8AF, United Kingdom*
Dr Ulrike Schmidt is a Consultant Psychiatrist in the Eating Disorders Unit at the Maudsley Hospital and Reader in Eating Disorders at the Institute of Psychiatry. Her research interests include all aspects of eating disorders, but in particular brief psychological and self-help treatments. She has co-authored two self-help books and accompanying clinicians' guides.

Eric van Furth, *Robert-Fleury Stichting, National Centre for Eating Disorders, PO Box 2260, AK Leidschendam, The Netherlands*
Dr Eric van Furth is a psychologist-psychotherapist in the National Centre for Eating Disorders at the Robert-Fleury Stichting (Robert-Fleury Foundation), a general psychiatric hospital in Leidschendam, The Netherlands. He is Honorary Lecturer at the Department of Psychiatry of Leiden University and Honorary Senior Research Fellow at the Department of Psychiatry at St. George's Hospital Medical School, London (UK).

Contributors

Eia Asen, *Marlborough Family Service, London, UK*

Núria Bará-Carril, *John Conolly Wing, West London Mental Health NHS Trust, Uxbridge Road, Southall, Middlesex UBI 3EG, UK*

Beatrice Bauer, *Università Luigi Bocconi, Via Bocconi 8, 20135 Milan, Italy*

Helen Birchall, *University of Leicester, Brandon Mental Health Unit, Leicester General Hospital, Gwendolen Road, Leicester LE5 4PW, UK*

Tijs Bruna, *GGZ Zoetermeer, Brechtzijde 20, 2725 NS Zoetermeer, The Netherlands*

Padmal de Silva, *Eating Disorders Unit, Institute of Psychiatry, De Crespigny Park, London SE5 8AF, UK*

Ivan Eisler, *Adolescent Eating Disorder Service, Maudsley Hospital and Psychotherapy Section, Institute of Psychiatry, De Crespigny Park, London SE5 8AF, UK*

Jaap Fogteloo, *Department of General Internal Medicine, Leiden University Medical Centre, PO Box 9600, 2300 RC, Leiden, The Netherlands*

Wolfgang Herzog, *Ruprecht Karls Universität, Medizinische Klinkum, Bergheimer Strasse 58, 69115 Heidelberg, Germany*

Hans Wijbrand Hoek, *Department of Psychiatric Residency and Research, Parnassia, The Hague Psychiatric Institute, Albardastraat 100, 2555 VZ The Hague, The Netherlands*

Helen Kennerley, *Oxford Cognitive Therapy Centre, Department of Clinical Psychology, Warneford Hospital, Oxford OX3 7JX, UK*

Daniel le Grange, *Eating Disorders Program, Assistant Professor of Psychiatry, The University of Chicago, 5841 S. Maryland Avenue, MC 3077, Chicago, IL 60637, USA*

Bernd Löwe, *Ruprecht Karls Universität, Medizinische Klinkum, Bergheimer Strasse 58, 69115 Heidelberg, Germany*

Søren Nielsen, *Psychiatric Youth Centre, Storstrøm County Psychiatric Services, Ringstedgade 61, DK-4700 Næstved, Denmark*

Bob Palmer, *University of Leicester, Brandon Mental Health Unit, Leicester General Hospital, Gwendolen Road, Leicester LE5 4PW, UK*

Paul Robinson, *Royal Free Eating Disorders Service, Department of Psychiatry, Royal Free Hospital, Pond Street, London NW3 2QG, UK*

Ulrike Schmidt, *Eating Disorders Unit, Institute of Psychiatry, De Crespigny Park, London SE5 8AF, UK*

Jacob Seidell, *Department for Chronic Diseases Epidemiology, National Institute of Public Health and the Environment, PO Box 1, 3720 BA Bilthoven, The Netherlands*

Roz Shafran, *Oxford University, Department of Psychiatry, Warneford Hospital, Oxford, OX3 7JX, UK*

Rick Stein, *Department of Psychiatry, Weight Management and Eating Disorders Program, Washington University School of Medicine, 660 South Euclid, Campus Box 8134, St. Louis, MO 63110-1093, USA*

Janet Treasure, *Department of Psychiatry, 5th Floor, Thomas Guy House, Guys Hospital, London SE1 9RT, UK*

Daphne van Hoeken, *Department of Research, Parnassia, The Hague Psychiatric Institute, Albardastraat 100, 2555 VZ The Hague, The Netherlands*

Glenn Waller, *Department of Psychiatry, St George's Hospital Medical School, University of London SW17 0RE, UK*

Peter Webster, *Hayes Grove Priory Hospital, Bromley, Kent, UK*

Robinson Welch, *Department of Psychiatry, Washington University School of Medicine, 660 South Euclid, Campus Box 8134, St Louis, MO 63110-1093, USA*

Denise Wilfley, *Washington University School of Medicine, Department of Psychiatry 660 South Euclid, Campus Box 8134, St. Louis, MO 63110-1093, USA*

Anthony Winston, *Eating Disorders Unit, Woodleigh Beeches Centre, Warwick Hospital, Lakin Road, Warwick CV34 5BW, UK*

Stephen Zipfel, *Medizinische Universität, Klinik Psychosomatische, Medizin und Psychotherapie, Silcherstr. 5, 72076 Tübingen, Germany*

Preface

From the second edition of the very popular *Handbook of Eating Disorders,* we have selected 14 essential chapters. Our aim was to create a concise 'pocket handbook' that should be of use to most practitioners in the field, providing them with the key information that they need.

The drive behind the first edition of the Handbook was to honour the retirement of Professor Gerald Russell and many of the chapters were written by the diaspora of clinicians and scientists emanating from his academic and clinical leadership. Within the decade since that edition was conceived, developed and executed there have been changes in the balance of clinical and academic connections. A European school has started to emerge. In part EEC funding has facilitated this but, in addition, curiosity into the contrasts and similarities between countries and the willingness and ability to communicate has cemented this approach. Thus the second edition represents a European perspective. There have been marked advances in knowledge and understanding of the eating disorders over this time. Also the spectrum of what is called 'eating disorders' has gradually expanded into obesity as new conditions such as binge eating disorder have been introduced into the diagnostic system. The dialectical process of synthesis between the body of knowledge from the obese and the lean end of the spectrum can enrich our understanding. We also used a rather unique method to foster a synthesis and consensus approach. We tried whenever possible to pair authors on the chapters with colleagues in other schools, countries or disciplines.

This meant that all of the chapters in the second edition were rewritten. However, we did not want to lose sight of the original edition, which had provided a coherent, readable and authoritative overview of this rapidly developing field.

There are inherent paradoxes in such a task. How can you satisfy the quality demands of evidence-based science with the need by clinicians, carers and users for clear, concise, coherent models? We hope that we have been able to fulfil this task. Thus, for the clinician, there is a strong practical emphasis with a problem-based approach, which means that this book has a richness of detail and wisdom that will be valued by all of the professional disciplines involved in caring for people with an eating disorder.

J.T.
U.S.
E.v.F.

CHAPTER 1

Concepts of Eating Disorders

Bob Palmer

*University of Leicester, Brandon Mental Health Unit,
Leicester General Hospital, UK*

The nosology of mental disorders inevitably dithers between the wish to delineate useful categories and the hope of discovering natural kinds. It would be good to achieve both but each aspiration alone is elusive enough. Indeed, some would reckon the second hope to be forlorn and there has been a tendency to emphasise the pragmatic and the descriptive. The current classifications—ICD-10 and DSM-IV—are the offspring of this tendency (WHO, 1992; APA, 1994). Yet there is a nagging feeling that there are 'real' disorders out there to be discovered rather than merely defined.

Within the field of eating disorders, anorexia nervosa crystallised out as a separate and distinct disorder over the course of the last century (Mount Sinai, 1965). It had the advantage of one criterion that was both undisputed and easy to measure, namely low weight. However, it was the description of the characterising beliefs and behaviours that led to the disorder being separated off from other states with weight loss. Furthermore, it was the description of similar beliefs and behaviours in people of unremarkable weight that led to the definition of bulimia nervosa and its relatives. However, it is arguably when the definition of mental disorder relies upon the mental state—as it almost inevitably should—that classification becomes more difficult. Can we really measure people's thoughts and feelings reliably and is it reasonable to expect that they should fit neatly into categories? Even classifying behaviour is problematic enough. However, if we do observe that people come to suffer in similar ways and with similar beliefs then this may give clues not only about sociological generalisations but also, perhaps especially, about innate and probably biological mechanisms which may underpin their disorder.

People may come to be more similar when they are stuck within a morbid process than when they are well because the range of their behaviour and experience is at least in part constrained by potentially definable processes in which such biological mechanisms are playing some limiting part. Tolstoy wrote, 'all happy families resemble one another, but each unhappy family is unhappy in its own way'. This is questionable even with regard to families and unhappiness, but with individuals and disorder it seems likely that the reverse is true. The range of what is morbid is narrower than the range of the non-morbid. Anti-psychiatrists tend to emphasise the prescriptive nature of 'normality' and to portray the person who is 'labelled' mentally disordered as something of a free spirit. However, the

The Essential *Handbook of Eating Disorders.* Edited by J. Treasure, U. Schmidt and E. van Furth.
© 2005 John Wiley & Sons, Ltd.

psychiatric perspective is different. The patient suffering from a mental disorder is seen as constrained and trapped by forces that are outwith his or her control. It is the sufferer who is the tram compared with the normal person who resembles the bus in having much more freedom. Both the bus and the tram are limited by their physical attributes but the tram is additionally constrained by the rails. Study of the patterns of disorder could give clues as to the nature of these 'rails'.

So what is the status of our current attempts at classification? What patterns can we discern in people with eating disorders? How well do our conventional diagnoses map these patterns? And do any of these patterns suggest the presence of plausible mechanisms of aetiological significance? Do our categories promise to be more than convenient pigeonholes? Are there 'real' disorders out there?

What follows is a clinician's view of our present classifications and some speculation about what mechanisms and natural kinds might lurk beneath the surface of their syndromes and diagnostic criteria.

CURRENT CLASSIFICATION

An ideal classification should consist of categories that are mutually exclusive and collectively exhaustive. Its entities should be discreet and together they should cover the ground. The classification of eating disorders measures up to these standards rather poorly. The canon contains only two major categories—anorexia nervosa (AN) and bulimia nervosa (BN). Anorexia nervosa has low weight as an essential criterion. Bulimia nervosa has binge eating as a necessary criterion. The two disorders share the criterion of what in broad terms might be described as an over-concern about body weight and size although some would see a major difference in degree or emphasis in the typical ideas held by sufferers from AN and BN. In DSM-IV, AN takes precedence over BN in the sense that the presence of the former bars the diagnosis of the latter. In contrast in the earlier version, DSM-III-R, it was possible to make the dual diagnosis of both AN and Bulimia Nervosa (APA, 1987). There is in DSM-IV, however, a new subclassification of AN into binge–purging and pure restricting subtypes. The rules in both of these sets of criteria represent different responses to the fact that low weight and bingeing occur together commonly and that, hence, the cardinal features of AN and BN are closely related even in cross-section. When longitudinal course over time is considered then the overlap becomes even more striking. In many series, a substantial minority of BN sufferers have a past history of AN. The reverse transition from BN to AN is less common, but does occur. Thus, AN and BN are far from being entirely discreet disorders and can be made to seem so only by dint of a certain sophistry. However, if the classification of the eating disorders fails to meet fully the ideal of providing discreet entities, it fails even more in respect of the second criterion, that of covering the ground. Many people present with eating disorders that fulfil criteria for neither of the two main disorders. How are these to be classified?

DSM-IV does provide two additional diagnoses, namely binge eating disorder (BED) and eating disorder not otherwise specified (EDNOS). Binge eating disorder is included only as a provisional category 'for further study'. It is strictly a variety of EDNOS within DSM-IV although, in practice,it has come already to be accorded the status of a diagnosis in its own right. However in general, EDNOS is defined essentially by exclusion, that is as being any clinical eating disorder that does not fulfil criteria for AN or BN.

THE PROBLEM OF EDNOS

The classification of the eating disorders achieves the standard of being collectively exhaustive only through having the 'rag bag' or residual category of EDNOS. The EDNOS category has only one positive criterion and one negative criterion. The positive criterion is that the individual being thus diagnosed should be deemed to have an eating disorder of clinical severity—a disorder that matters. The negative criterion is that the disorder should not fulfil criteria for AN or BN.

The EDNOS category thus defined is common. In many clinical series of people presenting to eating disorders services it is the single most common diagnosis and in some forms the majority of cases. Furthermore, as with AN and BN, the longitudinal perspective is illuminating but complicating. Many cases of the two main disorders change their characteristics over time so that those who have suffered from either at one time come later to suffer from neither but continue to have a clinically significant eating disorder (Sullivan et al., 1998; Fairburn et al., 2000). They can then be diagnosed only as being in a state of EDNOS. It is less clear whether people commonly move from a time of sustained EDNOS into one of the classic disorders.

A weakness of the EDNOS category resides in the limitations of its two criteria. The positive criterion is not defined. Where is the line to be drawn that defines a state as an *eating* disorder and of *clinical* significance? This is a matter of judgement. For instance, someone who is eating little and has lost a great deal of weight through severe major depression or because of delusions of poisoning would clearly have a disorder of clinical significance but would still not be diagnosed as EDNOS. The diagnosis is not appropriate because the state is not construed as an eating disorder. There is an implicit further criterion operating here; that is, that EDNOS should be diagnosed only if no non-eating disorder diagnosis is adequate. The positive criterion is further tested when there is uncertainty about whether an individual with eating disorder symptoms, such as maladaptive weight concern or self-induced vomiting, is affected to an extent that constitutes a disorder of clinical significance. Interestingly the judgement may sometimes depend upon the degree not only of the eating disorder symptoms but also of the associated non-specific symptoms. Thus, if the person has important associated anxiety and depressive symptoms or major problems of self-esteem— albeit not amounting to diagnosable syndromes in their own right—this may contribute to the decision that a diagnosis of EDNOS is appropriate. However, DSM-IV does not set out how these judgements should be made.

The negative criterion is also questionable when an individual fails narrowly to fulfil just one criterion for one of the major disorders. For instance, amenorrhoea is a difficult symptom to evaluate and yet some criteria demand that it should be present for the diagnosis of AN in females. The use of an oral contraceptive pill can complicate the issue and, furthermore, there is evidence to suggest that the presence or absence of this symptom makes little difference. Should someone who shows an otherwise typical picture of AN really be denied the diagnosis because of continuing menstruation? The ICD-10 system makes the sensible provision for a diagnosis of so-called 'Atypical AN' (or indeed 'Atypical BN') in cases where an individual narrowly misses fully meeting criteria but is clearly in a state very closely akin to one of these main disorders. However, once again these categories are not really defined and the atypical categories merely provide a buffer zone between the full disorders and others. There is still disputed territory at the other margin. In epidemiological work, the term 'partial syndrome' is often used to describe these sorts of states. The decision about whether to count a subject as a 'case' in a survey may require a different kind of judgement to that of the clinician who must decide whether a patient fits a diagnosis. In the former case, the decision may affect aetiological inference; in the latter, the decision may influence the nature of the treatment offered. Sometimes whether or not treatment will be offered at all may be at stake. These things can be important.

Thus the EDNOS category inevitably includes some less severe cases that nevertheless pass the test of being of clinical significance. Many of these will be 'partial syndromes' of a kind that just miss out on fulfilling criteria for one of the main disorders. They will often do so in ways which may be quantitative—the bulimic who does not binge quite often enough—or qualitative, that is, their difference does not seem to threaten the essence of the disorder—e.g. the previously cited case of the female 'anorectic' whose periods persist surprisingly despite important weight loss. However, there will also be people who have disorders which are diagnosed as EDNOS but who seem to be caught up in patterns of difficulty that are qualitatively different in ways which do seem to be significant.

ATYPICAL BEHAVIOURS

Some unusual cases differ in terms of the behaviour that they show. A not uncommon clinical picture is that of the person who is at an unremarkable weight and does not binge. She is thereby barred by definition from being diagnosed as having either AN or BN. She nevertheless induces vomiting after almost every meal. This pattern is one of the examples of EDNOS cited in the DSM-IV manual. A similar behavioural variant would be the person who eats nothing at all because of fear of weight gain but sustains a fair body weight entirely through the consumption of calorific fluids. Another important condition is eating disorder associated with insulin-dependent diabetes mellitus which may sometimes be severe without involving either weight loss or bingeing. Omitting or using insulin erratically in the service of weight control may constitute a clear eating disorder and be life threatening without even approximating to either classic AN or BN (Peveler, 1995). All such states are truly atypical but nevertheless they seem to be sufficiently akin to the typical eating disorders that it does not offend our clinical sensibilities to include them as interesting variants. We seem to feel that in essence they are the same. Is this because we feel that the essence of the eating disorders lies in the beliefs and ideas of the sufferer? But what of people who are atypical in their ideas?

ATYPICAL IDEAS

Controversies about details notwithstanding, both AN and BN include among their necessary criteria the issue of what, for the sake of brevity, might be called 'weight concern'. The different systems use different words but they all clearly refer to ideas which are at least similar. Furthermore, these ideas are held to be the central psychopathology of the disorders. They are deemed to be of the essence and to provide the motivation for the eating restraint which seems to be a key to the pathogenesis of AN and probably of BN too. And yet, there seem to be eating disordered people who do not have them or at least do not talk about them. Every clinician has come across many sufferers who initially deny concern about body weight and shape. Some later reveal that they had had such ideas but that they had been wary and kept quiet about them. Others continue to deny having such weight concerns. Some convince some clinicians that this is truly the case. But is it possible to have, say, anorexia nervosa without weight concern? The diagnostic criteria would say not. However, the clinicians who first described anorexia nervosa in the nineteenth century did not emphasise weight concern. Indeed, the early accounts by Gull and Lasegue do not mention it even though their clinical descriptions are in other respects both vivid and thorough (Mount Sinai, 1965). Likewise, colleagues working in China describe many young women who otherwise seem to have anorexia nervosa but who lack evident weight concern (Lee, Ho & Hsu, 1993). So sure are they that these are cases of 'anorexia nervosa' that they are so designated in the papers which describe them. So much for diagnostic criteria. But then, surely, Lee and his colleagues are following what most would regard as clinical common sense. Perhaps, such common sense rests upon an as yet unmentioned third attribute of a good classification—along with discreet entities and covering the ground—namely that of utility in practice. The Chinese patients without weight concern probably need to be managed in much the same way as their more typical equivalents. But what does such pragmatism do to ideas about the essence of eating disorders?

MOTIVATED EATING RESTRAINT

It is possible to make only a modest change to the diagnostic criteria for the eating disorders and thereby encompass some of the non-weight concerned sufferers. If eating restraint is promoted to be a central or even necessary component of the mechanism of the eating disorders, then weight concern may be seen as one motivation for such restraint among many that are possible (Palmer, 1993). For, instance, restraint may be motivated by religious ideas, ideas of fitness, ideas of asceticism and so on. Many clinicians will recognise some patients for whom such ideas seem to occupy the same position as ideas of weight concern in more typical cases. They reflect the same 'entanglement' between ideas of weight and eating control and wider personal issues such as self-esteem and emotional control. Such atypical ideas may be more common in atypical sufferers such as males.

It is not difficult to think that motivated eating restraint might occupy a central position in the pathogenesis of the eating disorders. Restraint in some sense is clearly involved in AN. Furthermore, it may be plausibly invoked in BN via the kind of rebound effect that has been called 'counterregulation' (Herman & Polivy, 1984; Palmer, 1998). However, such explanations seem to require that the sufferer is fighting her natural urges to eat. She is seen as not having lost her appetite but rather as attempting not to give in to it—'successfully' in the case of the AN sufferer; unsuccessfully in the case of the BN sufferer. Indeed it may be thought an advantage of accounts of eating disorders which give a central place to eating restraint that they are parsimonious in having no need to postulate some primary disorder of appetite or drive to eat. The effects of eating restraint upon individuals with an intact appetite are well documented (Herman & Polivy, 1984; Polivy & Herman, 1995). Restraint leads to distortion. Indeed, a story can be told about these effects that can be spun into a plausible account of the eating disorders. However, although parsimony of explanation may be a virtue, the simplest accounts are not always true. There could be a place for some more primary abnormality of appetite. Surprisingly there is a deal of uncertainty about appetite in eating disorders.

THE VEXED QUESTION OF APPETITE

Hunger or appetite in eating-disordered people have received rather little systematic study. There remains considerable uncertainty. This seems to be for at least three reasons. Firstly, there are inherent difficulties in measuring the subjective strength of hunger or appetite. Secondly, ratings of hunger are likely to be unreliable in people who have complex and distorting ideas about what they should be eating. The sufferer may mislead others, and perhaps even herself, when putting her subjective experiences into words or filling in a rating scale. On the other hand, for obvious reasons, what an eating-disordered individual actually eats cannot be taken as a simple behavioural indicator of the drive to eat. Lastly, clinicians and other experts may assume that they know about hunger and the like in eating-disordered subjects. However, various experts have various views. Especially with respect to AN, some claim that they 'know' that sufferers characteristically experience an enhanced urge to eat which is kept under tight control (see many of the present author's writings). Others say that the drive to eat must be less than normal if the subjects are to 'successfully' stop themselves from eating in the face of gross self-deprivation (Pinel, Assanand & Lehman, 2000). Many are impressed—or perhaps bewildered—by the variety of accounts which their patients give to them.

With regard to the problems of measurement or even description, there are conceptual as well as technical difficulties about what hunger or appetite or drive to eat may be taken to mean as definable terms. These terms do not seem to be used consistently or reliably and may need to be thought of as far from synonymous. For instance, an eating-disordered person may say that she is never hungry but may nevertheless acknowledge a strong urge to eat. It is as if the term hunger had too positive a connotation for it to be used about such a problematic experience.

In principle, hunger or the drive to eat might be abnormal in being reduced or increased. In practice, in many cases in which hunger is *reduced*—i.e. where there is true anorexia—a diagnosis of an eating disorder is not seriously considered. For instance, weight loss associated with physical illness with loss of appetite or depressive illness with true anorexia is not appropriately described as anorexia *nervosa*. The 'nervosa' implies that the relationship between the person's eating and their weight loss is more complex—more entangled with wider personal issues—than that of being simply 'off their food'. Once again, there is some lack of clarity here. Even those who would claim that AN sufferers do have a diminished appetite would want to reserve the diagnosis for those people who seem to be not eating for broadly 'psychological' reasons and who have relevant and related ideas often about weight concern. For instance, a sufferer may couch her immediate aversion to eating in terms of bloating or discomfort, but also have wider ideas of guilt or whatever. At the extreme, it is certainly conceivable that a person could present at low weight who was without both 'weight concern' and motivated eating restraint and who seemed to have some true anorexia. Under what conditions, if any, should she (or he) be considered for a diagnosis of AN? Strictly, such a patient should be diagnosed as EDNOS if no other diagnosis fits. Such people probably do exist although they seem to be scarce (perhaps they present to other kinds of clinician). However, their apparent rarity in practice may suggest that their characteristics should not be considered as threatening refutation of hypotheses about the nature of AN itself. Perhaps they are truly different. At the other end of the dimension of appetite or urge to eat, it seems likely that those who suffer from Binge Eating Disorder (BED) might also have an unusual—this time increased—appetite which is not based upon the distortions of restraint.

A primary *increase* in appetite or drive to eat might possibly be present in AN where it would trigger the restraint as a reaction. However, there seems to be little evidence for this. Such a primary increase is more plausible as a component of the mechanisms of BN and even more so for BED. In BN, the model of restraint acting upon an intact but unremarkable appetite is plausible. Most BN subjects report that the onset of attempted restraint preceded the onset of binge eating. However, this is not the case for a small but interesting minority of BN sufferers and for most of those who suffer with BED. Characteristically BED subjects either do not consistently restrain or the onset of their bingeing precedes that of restraint (Mussell et al., 1995, 1997). The different average outcome of BN and BED in terms of weight change at follow-up provides further support for a possible primary problem of increased appetite in the latter group. Fairburn et al. (2000) have shown that a community group of BED sufferers put on an average of 4.2 kg over the five-year follow-up period and that the rate of obesity rose from 22% to 39%. This weight gain occurred whether or not they continued to have BED. In contrast, BN sufferers gained on average only 3.3 kg from a lower base line and only 15% were obese at follow-up. Thus, many sufferers from BED are or become obese. Perhaps most are grappling with a drive to eat which is truly increased and which destines them for obesity, all other things being equal. Perhaps those who have a more 'straightforward' psychology become straightforwardly obese in the face of this increased drive to eat rather than becoming caught up in BED.

SET POINTS OR SETTLING POINTS?

Restraint-based models of eating disorder tend to go along with models of eating control which emphasise regulation of body weight. This may be seen as involving a regulation of weight around a set point or at least a set range that is variable across individuals but relatively constant for any one individual (Keesey, 1995). Some people regulate around a low weight, some around a high weight and most, by definition, around an average weight. Or so this story goes. The chief drive to eat is thought of as resulting from a biology in which even minor deprivation triggers the urge to eat in order to restore the well-fed state. Such set point models have an intuitive appeal. Furthermore, they can have an ideological utility in simplified form as the basis of a way of talking about eating disorders (Palmer, 1989). However, they have been criticised as not adequately accounting for important phenomena (Pinel, Assanand & Lehman, 2000). Especially, such models seem to overestimate the degree of the inherent stability of people's body weight, especially with regard to the evidently widespread vulnerability to weight gain and obesity. Although there are anecdotes about Sumo wrestlers and evidence from studies that sometimes weight gain is difficult, for many people much of the time weight gain is all too easy (Sims & Horton, 1968). This seems to apply even to weight gain to levels that carry significant disadvantages for health (Pinel, Assanand & Lehman, 2000). The degree to which the bodies of many people 'defend' an upper limit around any set point seems to be less than the models would predict. There seems to be at least an asymmetry between the lower and upper limits. Any dieter knows this. Set point ideas seem to have merit with regard to downward deviations in weight but are rather less good in accounting for weight gain above 'normal' levels. In as much as an eating disorder involves low weight and restraint, set point models may be useful. However, this may not be the case with respect to eating disorders at normal or above normal weight.

Set point ideas are often dressed up with evolutionary stories. It is suggested that regulatory mechanisms would have evolved which tended to keep an individual within a range which was optimal for survival and reproduction. However, a criticism of set point theory suggests that in the ancestral environment, where food would have been scarce, mechanisms would have been favoured that allowed an animal to eat more food when it was available than would be necessary for its immediate needs. Storage of potential energy and substance—putting on weight—would be advantageous in circumstances of erratic food supply in a way that would not be the case for strong satiety mechanisms which cut consumption when immediate needs were met. Furthermore, it is plausible that such permissive mechanisms might be more advantageous for younger females of reproductive age and, indeed, some sexual difference in satiety mechanisms can be observed (Goodwin, Fairburn & Cowen, 1987). But if restraint models are not fully adequate, what other models are available? One is that of so-called positive-incentive theory. This emphasises the rewards of eating, including its hedonic properties. Feeding is intrinsically rewarding and this is especially the case with respect of foods which might well have been valuable but scarce in the ancestral environment such as sweet foods, fatty foods and salty foods. Eating such foods was—and of course still is—especially rewarding. In the past this meant they were especially sought out despite the difficulty in finding them. Now that they are readily available, they are eaten to excess. Positive-incentive theory may hold more promise in explaining aspects of those eating disorders in which restraint seems to play little or no part and which occur at normal or high body weight. There may be complex entanglement between the hedonics of eating and emotion in people with binge eating. And less dramatically the positive incentives may be relevant to obesity.

Pinel, Assanand and Lehman (2000) have proposed a tentative theory of anorexia nervosa in which they suggest that the under-eating characteristic of that disorder may reflect a change of the usually positive incentive of eating towards the negative. However, it is not clear that such an interpretation fits the facts. Thus, as mentioned above, there is controversy about the nature of the subjective urge to eat in AN. Furthermore, it seems highly plausible that deprivation might well be the key drive to eating in those who are at a low weight and hungry and that the positive incentive to eat might well take over when the animal or human is well fed. Sensory specific satiety is a real phenomenon and bread and butter may well suffice when one is deprived, but it takes chocolate pudding to override that full feeling after two or three previous courses. While it may seem more parsimonious to invoke either a set point theory or a positive incentive theory, perhaps both kinds of ideas are required; the first in discussing states of deprivation and weight loss and the second in discussing the regulation of eating in times of plenty and higher weight. It is at least as easy to tell evolutionary stories around such a dual mechanism as it is around a simpler model.

The notion that there is a mechanism that regulates body weight around a set point may be contrasted with the idea that any apparent stability of body weight reflects a settling point which is the net result of two or more mechanisms that may have quite different functions. The implication for intervention may well be different, perhaps especially for the treatment of obesity where the idea of a set point that is defended even when it is problematically high tends to promote therapeutic pessimism (Garner & Wooley, 1991).

CONCLUSIONS

Our cherished diagnoses of AN and BN are here to stay. They clearly describe many patients in the clinic and are useful. Furthermore, the use of definite diagnostic criteria has made an important contribution to research. However, an undue concentration upon individuals who fulfil diagnostic criteria may lead to a somewhat blinkered view. The testing out of new formulations such as that of BED is useful although it would be a pity if such categories invented 'for further study' were routinely and prematurely reified as diagnoses. We need ideas to inform our observations but to be sufficiently open-minded to be able to notice the unexpected.

The view from the clinic can potentially provide suggestions about where it might be profitable to look for more basic physiological and pathological mechanisms.

Returning to the metaphor used above, it may be possible to guess at the location of some of the 'tramlines' that constrain our patients. The following are some summary comments based upon the view through this particular pair of eyes.

1. In looking for mechanisms underlying the eating disorders, ideas which invoke essentially normal regulatory mechanisms which have been pushed out of kilter are to be preferred as more parsimonious if they are adequate.
2. Models based upon eating restraint seem to have merit and may even be adequate for most cases of AN and BN.
3. 'Motivated eating restraint' is a more inclusive and arguably better formulation than 'weight concern' as the criterion for the core psychopathology of most eating disorders.
4. The 'normal mechanisms' invoked may need to include positive-incentive ideas as well as or instead of ideas of restraint if eating disorders at normal or high weight are to be adequately explained.
5. True abnormalities of appetite or drive to eat may play a part in some cases of BN, in BED and in obesity. Likewise, some cases of restricting AN may have some primary change in appetite although this is more speculative. Such variation of appetite may be genetically determined.
6. There should be more research into the difficult topic of the phenomenology of appetite in the eating disorders.
7. Such research should go hand in hand with biological research into the complex mechanisms that are doubtless involved in normal and pathological feeding in animals and human beings.
8. Whenever practical, research should include atypical (EDNOS) cases as well as the typical.
9. A future classification may include a major divide between 'disorders of restraint' and 'disorders of increased appetite'.
10. All true eating disorders—disorders with 'nervosa'—are characterised by an 'entanglement' between the relevant basic weight and eating control mechanisms and the sufferer's interpretation of the meaning of the effects of these within his or her own

individual experience. And, although some generalisations can be made, such interpretations are likely to be varied or even idiosyncratic and to defy neat classification.

REFERENCES

APA (1987) *Diagnostic and Statistical Manual of Mental Disorders* (3rd Edition) Revised. Washington, D.C.: American Psychiatric Association.

APA (1994) *Diagnostic and Statistical Manual of Mental Disorders* (4th Edition). Washington, D.C.: American Psychiatric Association.

Fairburn, C.G., Cooper, Z., Doll, H.A., Norman, P. & O'Connor, M. (2000) The natural course of bulimia nervosa and binge eating disorder in young women. *Archives of General Psychiatry*, **57**, 659–665.

Garner, D.M. & Wooley, S.C. (1991) Confronting the failure of behavioural and dietary treatments of obesity. *Clinical Psychology Review*, **11**, 729–780.

Goodwin, G.M., Fairburn, C.G. & Cowen, P.J. (1987) Dieting changes serotonergic function in women, not men: Implications for the aetiology of anorexia nervosa. *Psychological Medicine*, **17**, 839–842.

Herman, C.P. & Polivy, J. (1984) A boundary model for the regulation of eating. In A.J. Stunkard & E. Stellar (Eds), *Eating and its Disorders*. New York: Raven Press.

Keesey, R.E. (1995) A set-point model of body weight regulation. In K.D. Brownell & C.G. Fairburn (Eds), *Eating Disorders and Obesity: A Comprehensive Handbook*. New York: Guilford Press.

Lee, S., Ho, T.P. & Hsu, L.K.G. (1993) Fat phobic and non-fat phobic anorexia nervosa: A comparative study. *Psychological Medicine*, **23**, 999–1017.

Mount Sinai (1965) Evolution of psychosomatic concepts—anorexia nervosa: A paradigm. *The International Psycho-Analytic Library* No. 65. London: Hogarth Press.

Mussell, M.P., Mitchell, J.E., Weller, C.L., Raymond, N.C., Crow, S.J. & Crosby, R.D. (1995) Onset of binge eating, dieting, obesity, and mood disorders among subjects seeking treatment for binge eating disorder. *International Journal of Eating Disorders*, **17**, 395–410.

Mussell, M.P., Mitchell, J.E., Fenna, C.J., Crosby, R.D., Miller, J.P. & Hoberman, H.M. (1997). A comparison of binge eating and dieting in the development of bulimia nervosa. *International Journal of Eating Disorders*, **21**, 353–360.

Palmer, R.L. (1989) The Spring Story: A way of talking about clinical eating disorder. *British Review of Anorexia Nervosa and Bulimia*, **4**, 33–41.

Palmer, R.L. (1993) Weight concern should not be a necessary criterion for the eating disorders; a polemic. *International Journal of Eating Disorders*, **14**, 459–465.

Palmer, R.L. (1998) The aetiology of bulimia nervosa. In H.W., Hoek, J.L. Treasure & M.A. Katzman (Eds), *Neurobiology in the Treatment of Eating Disorders*. Chichester and New York: John Wiley & Sons.

Peveler, R.C. (1995) Eating disorders and diabetes. In K.D. Brownell & C.G. Fairburn (Eds), *Eating Disorders and Obesity; a Comprehensive Handbook*. New York: Guilford Press.

Pinel, J.P.J., Assanand, S. & Lehman, D.R. (2000) Hunger, eating and ill health. *American Psychologist*, **55**, 1105–1116.

Polivy, J. & Herman, C.P. (1995) Dieting and its relation to eating disorders. In K.D. Brownell & C.G. Fairburn (Eds), *Eating Disorders and Obesity; A Comprehensive Handbook*. New York: Guilford Press.

Sims, E.A.H. & Horton, E.S. (1968) Endocrine and metabolic adaptation to obesity and starvation. *American Journal of Clinical Nutrition*, **21**, 1455–1470.

Sullivan, P.F., Bulik, C.M., Fear, J.L. & Pickering, A. (1998) Outcome of anorexia nervosa: a case-control study. *American Journal of Psychiatry*, **155**, 939–946.

WHO (1992) *The ICD-10 Classification of Mental and Behavioural Disorders: Clinical Descriptions and Diagnostic Guidelines*. Geneva: World Health Organisation.

CHAPTER 2

Epidemiology

Daphne van Hoeken
Parnassia, The Hague Psychiatric Institute, The Netherlands
Jacob Seidell
Department of Nutrition and Health,
Free University of Amsterdam, The Netherlands
and
Hans Wijbrand Hoek
Parnassia, The Hague Psychiatric Institute, The Netherlands and
Department of Epidemiology, Mailman School of Public Health,
Columbia University, New York, USA

SUMMARY

- The average prevalence rate for young females is 0.3% for anorexia nervosa and 1% for bulimia nervosa. The overall prevalence of obesity may be in the order of 5–10%. The overall incidence is at least 8 per 100 000 person-years for anorexia nervosa and 12 per 100 000 person-years for bulimia nervosa. No reliable incidence data are available for obesity. The standardized mortality rate in the first 10 years after detection is 9.6 for anorexia nervosa, 7.4 for bulimia nervosa. For obesity it is assumed that mortality is elevated by about 50–150% in most adult populations.
- The incidence rate of anorexia nervosa has increased during the past 50 years, particularly in females 10–24 years old. The registered incidence of bulimia nervosa has increased, at least during the first five years after bulimia nervosa was introduced in the DSM-III. The prevalence of obesity is increasing in most of the established market economies. Without societal changes a substantial and steadily rising proportion of adults will succumb to the medical complications of obesity.
- Risk factor research is still sparse, both for eating disorders and for obesity. There is a need for prospective, follow-up designs using initially healthy subjects at high risk for developing an eating disorder or obesity. Depending on the question to be answered, these could be matched on sex, age and socio-economic status with initially healthy intermediate- and low-risk groups.
- Detailed and reliable registration of case definition, demographic and other characteristics of the patient, symptoms and concomitants the disease or disorder remain of the utmost importance to advance evidence-based treatment and prevention.

The Essential *Handbook of Eating Disorders.* Edited by J. Treasure, U. Schmidt and E. van Furth.
© 2005 John Wiley & Sons, Ltd.

INTRODUCTION

As defined by Regier and Burke (2000) 'mental disorder epidemiology is the quantitative study of the distribution and causes of mental disorder in human populations'. Populations are groups sharing a common feature, and the features distinguishing a population with a higher disease rate from another with a lower disease rate serve as clues to aetiology. Incidence and prevalence rates are the basic measures of disease frequency.

In this chapter the incidence and prevalence of eating disorders and obesity are discussed. In eating disordered patients, there is a weight continuum from underweight in anorexia nervosa through normal weight in normal weight bulimics to overweight in the majority of binge-eating disorder patients. It is likely that a number of obese persons have an underlying eating disorder. Traditionally, however, epidemiological research in the fields of obesity and of eating disorders have been two separate lines of study. By addressing the epidemiology of eating disorders and the epidemiology of obesity together in one chapter, a preliminary step is made to share ideas and knowledge.

- *Prevalence*: The prevalence is the total number of cases in the population. The point prevalence is the prevalence at a specific point in time. The one-year period prevalence rate is the point prevalence rate plus the annual incidence rate. The prevalence rate is most useful for planning facilities, as it indicates the demand for care. Prevalent cases reflect the disease itself as well as coexisting factors.
- *Incidence*: The incidence is the number of new cases in the population in a specified period of time (usually one year), and is commonly expressed per 100 000 of the population per year. Incidence rates of eating disorders represent the situation at the moment of detection, which is not necessarily the same as the true start of the disorder.

Studies on the incidence of eating disorders in the general population are lacking, and the incidence rates available have been based on cases presenting to health care. Very few studies have attempted to calculate the incidence rate of obesity. The criterion for obesity is a matter of definition on a gliding scale from low to high weight. It is difficult and probably not meaningful to define at what moment overweight becomes incident obesity.

Incidence rate differences between groups are better clues to aetiology than prevalence rate differences, because they refer to recently started disease (Eaton et al., 1995).

Mortality

Mortality rates are common measures in health statistics. They are often used as indicator for the severity of a disorder. The standard measures are the crude mortality rate (CMR) and the standardized mortality rate (SMR). The CMR is the fraction of deaths within the study population. The SMR is the fraction of the observed mortality rate (CMR) compared to the expected mortality rate in the population of origin, e.g. all young females.

Risk Factors

Population differences in morbidity or mortality rates point out risk factors. A risk factor is a measurable characteristic of a subject that precedes the outcome of interest and which dichotimises the population into a high- and a low-risk group. When it can be changed, and manipulation of the factor changes the outcome, it is a causal risk factor (Kraemer et al., 1997). A risk factor may be an individual characteristic, or a characteristic of the subject's context. The method of choice for assessing the impact of individual characteristics is a prospective follow-up study. Risk factors can be identified by comparing initially healthy subjects who have developed an unfavourable outcome at follow-up with those who have not.

Methodological Aspects

Epidemiological studies have to counter a number of methodological problems (see Szmukler, 1985, and Hoek, 1993, for overviews). Problems specific to the eating disorders are their low prevalence and the tendency of eating disorder subjects to conceal their illness and avoid professional help (Hsu, 1996). These make it necessary to study a very large number of subjects from the general population in order to reach enough differential power for the cases. This is highly time- and cost-intensive. Several strategies have been used to circumvent this problem, in particular case register and other record-based studies, two-stage studies, and studies of special populations.

The limitations of record-based studies are considerable (Hsu, 1996). Register-based frequencies represent cases detected in inpatient, and occasionally outpatient, care. Treated cases represent only a minority of all cases. Findings from case registers/hospital records are of more value to treatment planning than for generating hypotheses on the aetiology of disease, because there is no direct access to the subjects and the additional information that is available is usually limited and of a demographic nature only.

At present a two-stage screening approach is the most widely accepted procedure for case identification. First a large population is screened for the likelihood of an eating disorder by means of a screening questionnaire, identifying an at-risk population (first stage). Then definite cases are established using a personal interview on subjects from this at-risk population as well as on a randomly selected sample of those not at risk (second stage) (Williams et al., 1980). Methodological problems of two-stage studies are poor response rates, sensitivity/specificity of the screening instrument and the often restricted size of the interviewed groups, particularly of those not at risk (Fairburn & Beglin, 1990).

Studies of special populations address a particular segment of the general population, selected *a priori* for being at increased risk, such as female high school/university students, athletes or a particular age cohort. The major methodological problem associated with this type of study is the specificity of the findings to the selected subset of the general population.

Both two-stage studies and studies of special populations have the potential for providing information relevant to the aetiology, because there is direct access to the subjects and the availability of additional information is not restricted by a predetermined registration system. Register-based prevalence studies and prevalence studies of eating disorders using only questionnaires will not be discussed in this chapter.

There are several types of risk. One is the risk one runs as a member of a particular group. This is usually assessed by comparing prevalence or incidence rates between demographic subgroups (relative risks or risk ratios). Another is the risk one runs because of individual characteristics. A common approach for this has been to use a case-control design. In studies of this type one looks for premorbid differences between prevalent cases and a control group of subjects, usually matched on age, gender and social class. Methodological difficulties centre around the interpretation of the results. The issues are the directionality (cause/consequence) of the findings and the reliability of information gathered retrospectively on premorbid differences. Whether the differences found represent true risk factors that precede—not follow or accompany—the onset of disorder and which developmental mechanisms are operant can only be uncovered in prospective follow-up studies. In such studies, risk factors can be identified by comparing initially healthy subjects who have developed a disorder at follow-up to those who have not. Thus, the preferred method for assessing individual risk is a study with a prospective follow-up design.

EATING DISORDERS

Classification

In the paragraphs on anorexia nervosa and bulimia nervosa only studies using strict definitions of these eating disorders (meeting Russell, DSM or ICD criteria) are discussed. Another category, the Eating Disorders Not Otherwise Specified (EDNOS) is a mixed category. It includes a heterogeneity of patients who do not meet all criteria for anorexia nervosa or bulimia nervosa but who do have symptoms severe enough to qualify them as having a clinically significant eating disorder. This heterogeneity makes it a difficult category for the search on possible aetiologic factors. Hardly any reliable epidemiological information is available. Therefore the EDNOS is not included in this overview. In DSM-IV (APA, 1994) a provision was made for a separate eating disorder category to be researched further, the Binge Eating Disorder (BED). Only limited epidemiological information is available on this category to date.

   The epidemiology of eating disorders has been reviewed before, e.g. Hoek (1993), Hsu (1996), van Hoeken et al. (1998). The section on eating disorders is an adaptation and update of the review by van Hoeken and colleagues.

ANOREXIA NERVOSA

Prevalence

The current standard for prevalence studies of eating disorders are studies employing a two-stage selection of cases. Table 2.1 summarizes the two-stage surveys of anorexia nervosa in young females.

   All studies have succeeded in obtaining high response rates of 85% or more, except Meadows et al. (1986), who reached a response rate of 70%. Those two-stage surveys that identified cases found a prevalence rate of strictly defined anorexia nervosa of between 0.2 and 0.8% of young females, with an average prevalence of 0.3%. These rates are possibly minimum estimates. Most studies found much higher prevalence rates for partial syndromes of anorexia nervosa.

   Two other studies are discussed here because they are not confined to high-risk populations and give prevalence figures for the entire population. A drawback is that these studies did not use a two-stage procedure for case finding. In a general practice study in the

Table 2.1 Two-stage surveys of prevalence of anorexia nervosa in young females

Study	Subjects			Methods		Prevalence
	Source	Age	n	Screening[a]	Criteria	%
Button and Whitehouse (1981)	College students	16–22	446	EAT	Feighner	0.2
Szmukler (1983)	Private schools	14–19	1331	EAT	Russell	0.8
	State schools	14–19	1676	EAT	Russell	0.2
King (1989)	General practice	16–35	539	EAT	Russell	0
Meadows et al. (1986)	General practice	18–22	584	EAT	DSM-III	0.2[b]
Johnson-Sabine et al. (1988)	Schoolgirls	14–16	1010	EAT	Russell	0
Råstam et al. (1989)	Schoolgirls	15	2136	Growth chart + questionnaire	DSM-III	0.47
					DSM-III-R	0.23
Whitaker et al. (1990)	Highschool girls	13–18	2544	EAT	DSM-III	0.3
Whitehouse et al. (1992)	General practice	16–35	540	Questionnaire	DSM-III-R	0.2
Rathner and Messner (1993)	Schoolgirls + case register	11–20	517	EAT	DSM-III-R	0.58
Wlodarczyk-Bisaga and Dolan (1996)	Schoolgirls	14–16	747	EAT	DSM-III-R	0
Steinhausen et al. (1997)	Schoolgirls	14–17	276	EDE-S	DSM-III-R	0.7
Nobakht and Dezhkam (2000)	Schoolgirls	15–18	3100	EAT	DSM-IV	0.9

[a]EAT—Eating Attitudes Test; EDE-S—Eating Disorders Examination, Screening Version.
[b]Not found by screening (EAT score below threshold).

Netherlands, Hoek (1991) found a raw point-prevalence rate of 18.4 per 100 000 of the total population (95% CI 12.7–26.8) on 1 January 1985. Lucas et al. (1991) used a very extensive case-finding method. It included all medical records of health care providers, general practitioners and specialists in the community of Rochester, Minnesota. They also screened records mentioning related diagnostic terms for possible non-detected cases. They found an overall sex- and age-adjusted point prevalence of 149.5 per 100 000 (95% CI 119.3–179.7) on 1 January 1985.

A main explanation for this difference can be found in the inclusion of probable and possible cases by Lucas et al. Definite cases constituted only 39% (82 out of 208) of all incident cases identified in the period 1935–1989 (Lucas et al., 1999). Applying this rate to the point prevalence of 149.5 gives an estimated point prevalence of 58.9 per 100 000 for definite cases in Rochester, Minnesota, on 1 January 1985. The remaining difference with the point prevalence reported by Hoek (1991) could be explained by the greater variety of medical sources searched by Lucas et al. (1991).

Incidence

The incidence studies of anorexia nervosa have used psychiatric case registers, medical records of hospitals in a circumscribed area, registrations by general practitioners or medical records of health care providers in a community. Table 2.2 summarizes the results of the

Table 2.2 Incidence of anorexia nervosa per year per 100 000 population

Study	Region	Source	Period	Incidence
Theander (1970)	Southern Sweden	Hospital records	1931–1940	0.10
			1941–1950	0.20
			1951–1960	0.45
			(1931–1960)	(0.24)
Willi et al. (1983, 1990); Martz et al. (2001)	Zurich	Hospital records	1956–1958	0.38
			1963–1965	0.55
			1973–1975	1.12
			1983–1985	1.43
			1993–1995	1.17
Jones et al. (1980)	Monroe County	Case register + hospital records	1960–1969	0.37
			1970–1976	0.64
Kendell et al. (1973)	NE Scotland	Case register	1960–1969	1.60
Szmukler et al. (1986)	NE Scotland	Case register	1978–1982	4.06
Kendell et al. (1973)	Camberwell	Case register	1965–1971	0.66
Hoek and Brook (1985)	Assen	Case register	1974–1982	5.0
Møller-Madsen and Nystrup (1992)	Denmark	Case-register	1970	0.42
			1988	1.36
			1989	1.17
Lucas et al. (1999)	Rochester, MN	Medical records	1935–1949	9.1
			1950–1959	4.3
			1960–1969	7.0
			1970–1979	7.9
			1980–1989	12.0
			(1935–1989)	(8.3)
Hoek et al. (1995)	Netherlands	Gen. practitioners	1985–1989	8.1
Turnbull et al. (1996)	England, Wales	Gen. practitioners	1993	4.2

studies on the incidence of anorexia nervosa that report overall rates for a general population sample.

The overall rates vary considerably, ranging from 0.10 in a hospital-records-based study in Sweden in the 1930s to 12.0 in a medical-records-based study in the USA in the 1980s, both per 100 000 population per year.

Incidence rates derived from general practices on average represent more recently started eating disorders than those based on other medical records. There were two studies of this type (Hoek et al., 1995, and Turnbull et al., 1996). In the study by Hoek and colleagues, general practitioners using DSM-III-R criteria have recorded the rate of eating disorders in a large (1985: $N = 151\,781$), representative sample (1.1%) of the Dutch population. The incidence rate of anorexia nervosa was 8.1 per 100 00 person years (95% CI 6.1–10.2) during the period 1985–1989. During the study period 63% of the incident cases were referred to mental health care, accounting for an incidence rate of anorexia nervosa in mental health care of 5.1 per year per 100 000 population. Turnbull et al. (1996) searched the UK General Practice Research Database (GPRD), covering 550 general practitioners and 4 million patients, for first diagnoses of anorexia in the period 1988–1993. A randomly selected subset of cases was checked with DSM-IV criteria, from which estimates for adjusted incidence rates were made. For anorexia nervosa they found an age- and sex-adjusted incidence rate of 4.2 (95% CI 3.4–5.0) per 100 000 population in 1993.

Lucas et al. (1991, 1999) used the most extensive case-finding method (see the section on prevalence). Over the period of 1935–1989, they report an overall age- and sex-adjusted incidence rate of anorexia nervosa of 8.3 per 100 000 person-years (95% CI 7.1–9.4).

Age and Sex

Incidence rates of anorexia nervosa are highest for females 15–19 years old. These constitute approximately 40% of all identified cases and 60% of female cases. For example, Lucas et al. (1999) report an incidence rate of 73.9 per 100 000 person-years for 15–19-year-old women over the period of 1935–1989, with a continual rise since the 1930s to a top rate of 135.7 for the period 1980–1989.

Although it is clear that anorexia nervosa occurs in men as well as in women, and in younger as well as in older people, few studies report incidence rates for males or for people beyond the age of 35. This makes it difficult to evaluate the size of the problem for them. The majority of male incidence rates reported was below 0.5 per 100 000 population per year (e.g. Turnbull et al., 1996). In those studies where it is reported, the female to male ratio usually is around 11 to 1 (e.g. Hoek et al., 1995). On an overall female rate of 15.0 per 100 000 population per year, Lucas et al. (1999) report a rate of 9.5 for 30–39-year-old women, 5.9 for 40–49-year-old women, 1.8 for 50–59-year-old women, and 0.0 for women aged 60 and over.

Time Trends

There has been considerable debate whether the incidence of eating disorders is, or has been, on the increase. Since the 1970s, the number of incidence studies has increased. Case register studies prior to the 1980s show at most a slight increase over time of incident anorexia nervosa cases (Hoek, 1993). The studies in the 1980s show widely diverging incidence rates. Most likely, there is a methodological explanation for these differences. The main problem lies in the need for long study periods. This results in a sensitivity of these studies to minor changes in absolute incidence numbers and in methods, for example variations in registration policy, demographic differences between the populations, faulty inclusion of readmissions, the particular methods of detection used, or the availability of services (Williams & King, 1987; Fombonne, 1995).

From the studies that have used long study periods, it may now be concluded that there is an upward trend in the incidence of anorexia nervosa since the 1950s. The increase is most substantial in females 15–24 years of age. Lucas et al. (1999) found that the age-adjusted incidence rates of anorexia nervosa in females 15–24 years old showed a highly significant linear increasing trend from 1935 to 1989, with an estimated rate of increase of 1.03 per 100 000 person-years per calendar year. In 10–14-year-old females a rise in incidence was observed for each decade since the 1950s. The rates for men and for women aged 25 and over remained relatively low.

All record-based studies will grossly underestimate the true incidence, because not all cases will be referred to mental health care or become hospitalized. The increase in incidence rates of registered cases implies at least that there is an increased demand for health care facilities for anorexia nervosa.

Mortality

Sullivan (1995) conducted a meta-analysis on crude mortality rates (CMR) for anorexia nervosa in 42 published studies. The CMR found was 5.9% (178 deaths in 3006 patients), translating into 0.56% per year or 5.6% per decade. In the studies specifying cause of death, 54% of the subjects died as a result of eating disorder complications, 27% committed suicide and the remaining 19% died of unknown or other causes.

Nielsen (2001) has conducted an update of a previous meta-analysis on standardized mortality rates (SMR). The overall aggregate SMR of anorexia nervosa in studies with 6–12 years follow-up is 9.6 (95% CI 7.8–11.5) and in studies with 20–40 years follow-up 3.7 (95% CI 2.8–4.7). Thus in the long run subjects with anorexia nervosa have an almost four-fold risk of dying compared to healthy people the same age and sex.

BULIMIA NERVOSA

Prevalence

In 1990 Fairburn and Beglin gave a review of the prevalence studies on bulimia nervosa. This landmark review yielded the generally accepted prevalence rate of 1% of young females with bulimia nervosa according to DSM criteria. Table 2.3 summarizes two-stage surveys of bulimia nervosa in young females that have been published since the review by Fairburn and Beglin.

Despite the different classifications used (DSM-III versus DSM-III-R) and different types of prevalence rates provided (lifetime prevalence, e.g. Bushnell et al., 1990, versus point prevalence, e.g. Rathner & Messner, 1993), the aggregated prevalence rate according to

Table 2.3 Two-stage surveys of prevalence of bulimia nervosa in young females

Study	Subjects			Method		Prevalence
	Source	Age	N	Screening[a]	Criteria	%
Whitaker et al. (1990)	Highschool girls	13–18	2544	EAT	DSM-III	4.2
Bushnell et al. (1990)	Household census	18–24		DIS	DSM-III	4.5
		25–44				2.0
		(18–44)	(777)			(2.6)
Szabó and Túry (1991)	Schoolgirls	14–18	416	EAT, BCDS, ANIS	DSM-III	0
					DSM-III-R	0
	College girls	19–36	224	EAT, BCDS, ANIS	DSM-III	4.0
					DSM-III-R	1.3
Whitehouse et al. (1992)	General practice	16–35	540	Questionnaire	DSM-III-R	1.5
Rathner and Messner (1993)	Schoolgirls + case register	11–20	517	EAT	DSM-III-R	0
Wlodarczyk-Bisaga and Dolan (1996)	Schoolgirls	14–16	747	EAT	DSM-III-R	0
Santonastaso et al. (1996)	Schoolgirls	16	359	EAT	DSM-IV	0.5
Steinhausen et al. (1997)	Schoolgirls	14–17	276	EDE-S	DSM-III-R	0.5
Nobakht and Dezhkam (2000)	Schoolgirls	15–18	3100	EAT	DSM-IV	3.2

[a]EAT—Eating Attitudes Test; DIS—Diagnostic Interview Schedule; BCDS—Bulimia Cognitive Distortions Scale; ANIS—Anorexia Nervosa Inventory Scale; EDE-S—Eating Disorder Examination, Screening Version.

DSM criteria remains 1%. The prevalence of subclinical eating disorders is substantially higher than that of full-syndrome bulimia nervosa (e.g. Whitehouse et al., 1992: 1.5% for full-syndrome, and 5.4% for partial syndrome bulimia nervosa).

The results of three studies not using a two-stage procedure for case finding are also reported here, because they address the prevalence for the entire population and not just for the high-risk group of young females. In a study of incident cases reported by general practitioners, Hoek (1991) reports a point-prevalence rate of 20.4 per 100 000 of the total population. Garfinkel et al. (1995) assessed eating disorders in a random, stratified, non-clinical community sample, using a structured interview for the whole sample. They reported a lifetime prevalence for bulimia nervosa of 1.1% in women and of 0.1% in men aged 15–65, using DSM-III-R criteria. In a study by Soundy et al. (1995) no attempt to determine prevalence rates for bulimia nervosa was made because they considered the information about how long symptoms had persisted and the long duration (mean 39.8 months) of symptoms before diagnosis to be too unreliable.

Incidence

There have been only few incidence studies of bulimia nervosa. The most obvious reason is the lack of criteria for bulimia nervosa in the past. Most case registers use the International Classification of Diseases (currently ICD-10; WHO, 1992). The ICD-9 (WHO, 1978) and previous versions did not provide a separate code for bulimia nervosa. Bulimia nervosa has been distinguished as a separate disorder by Russell in 1979 and DSM-III in 1980 (APA, 1980). Before 1980 the term 'bulimia' in medical records designated symptoms of heterogeneous conditions manifested by overeating, but not the syndrome as it is known today. Therefore it is difficult to examine trends in the incidence of bulimia nervosa or a possible shift from anorexia nervosa to bulimia nervosa, which might have influenced the previously described incidence rates of anorexia nervosa.

Three studies are reviewed here: those of Soundy et al. (1995), Hoek et al. (1995) and Turnbull et al. (1996). Soundy and colleagues used methodology similar to that in the long-term anorexia nervosa study by Lucas et al. (1991), screening all medical records of health care providers, general practitioners and specialists in Rochester, Minnesota, over the period of 1980–1990 for a clinical diagnosis of bulimia nervosa as well as for related symptoms. Hoek and colleagues studied the incidence rate of bulimia nervosa using DSM-III-R criteria in a large general practice study representative of the Dutch population, covering the period 1985–1989. Turnbull and colleagues screened the General Practice Research Database (GPRD), covering a large representative sample of the English and Welsh population, for first diagnoses of anorexia nervosa and bulimia nervosa in 1993. Another general population study by Pagsberg and Wang (1994) is not discussed here, because the population under consideration is relatively small (<50 000 inhabitants from the island of Bornholm, Denmark).

The three studies under consideration all report an annual incidence of bulimia nervosa around 12 per 100 000 population: 13.5 for Soundy et al., 11.5 for Hoek et al., and 12.2 for Turnbull et al.

Age and Sex

Soundy et al. (1995) report an incidence of bulimia nervosa of 26.5 for females, and of 0.8 for males per 100 000 population, yielding a female to male ratio of 33:1. Hoek et al. (1995) report similar rates of 21.9 for females and 0.8 for males per 100 000 population, yielding a female to male ratio of 27:1. For the highest risk group of 20–24-year-old females rates close to 82 per 100 000 are found: 82.7 for Soundy et al. and 82.1 for Hoek et al. Hoek and colleagues report a rate of 8.3 per 100 000 for women aged 35–64. Turnbull et al. (1996) report an annual incidence of 1.7 per 100 000 people (men and women) aged 40 and over.

Time Trends

Soundy et al. (1995) found yearly incidence rates to rise sharply from 7.4 per 100 000 females in 1980 to 49.7 in 1983, and then remain relatively constant around 30 per 100 000 females. This would seem to be related to the publication, and following implementation in the field, of DSM-III in 1980, introducing bulimia nervosa as an official diagnostic category. Hoek et al. (1995) report a non-significant trend for the incidence rates of bulimia nervosa to increase by 15% each year in the period 1985–1989. Turnbull et al. (1996) noted a highly significant, three-fold increase in bulimia nervosa incidence rates for women aged 10–39 in the period 1988–1993, increasing from 14.6 in 1988 to 51.7 in 1993.

These incidence rates of bulimia nervosa can only serve as minimum estimates of the true incidence rate. The reasons are the lack of data, the greater taboo around bulimia nervosa and its smaller perceptibility compared to anorexia nervosa.

Mortality

Combination of the results of the meta-analyses of the crude mortality rate (CMR) by Keel and Mitchell (1997) and Nielsen (2001) yields a CMR of bulimia nervosa of 0.4% (11 deaths in 2692 patients). No information is available as to the distribution of causes of death.

Nielsen (2001) has conducted an update of a previous meta-analysis on standardized mortality rates (SMR). The overall aggregate SMR of bulimia nervosa in studies with 5–11 years follow-up is 7.4 (95% CI 2.9–14.9). Longer follow-up periods are not yet available. However, as suggested by Nielsen (personal communication), there may be serious publication bias in this rate. When mortality information of all 42 bulimia nervosa cohorts is used, not just that of the 5 cohorts reporting SMR, the SMR changes to 1.56 (95% C.I. 0.8 –2.7).

Thus, within the first 10 years after detection, subjects with bulimia nervosa run an increased risk of dying compared to healthy people of the same age and sex. But it is still open to debate as to whether this risk is only moderately increased (1.5 times) or, with a seven-fold increase, is close to the risk (more than nine-fold increase) of anorexia nervosa.

BINGE EATING DISORDER

The Binge Eating Disorder (BED) has the status of 'Diagnostic Category in Need of Further Research' in the 1994 version of the *Diagnostic and Statistical Manual of Mental Disorders* (DSM-IV; APA, 1994). A general problem with the comparison of studies of BED—and bulimia nervosa for that matter—lies in the diagnosis of a binge. Studies may differ in the way the boundaries of a binge were set, resulting in subject groups that are not fully comparable.

As for anorexia nervosa and bulimia nervosa, the focus here is on prevalence studies using a two-stage case identification procedure in the general population. Cotrufo et al. (1998) were the only researchers to use a two-stage procedure. They identified two cases of BED in a group of 919 13–19-year-old females, giving a prevalence rate of 0.2%. The low rate may be due to the relatively young age of the investigated population. Also the sample size is rather small for a low-frequency disorder.

Hay (1998) conducted interviews to determine the prevalence of bulimic type eating disorders on all subjects in a large general population sample (3001 interviews). The mean age of the cases was 35.2 years. Using DSM-IV criteria, a (point) prevalence for BED of 1% was found. Using a broader definition by Fairburn and Cooper (1993), the prevalence was estimated at 2.5%. A weakness of the study was that diagnoses were based on a very limited number of questions (two gating questions, and three further probes). No information was given regarding the sensitivity/specificity of the instrument.

No reports on crude or standardized mortality rates have been located for BED.

RISK FACTORS

Context of the Individual

Social Class

Most psychiatric disorders show a higher prevalence in the lower socio-economic classes. It is difficult to determine whether this is the result of the social selection process, or whether it is caused by social factors (Dohrenwend et al., 1992).

For anorexia nervosa, there has been a traditional belief of an upper social class preponderance. In reviewing the evidence, Gard and Freeman (1996) concluded that the relationship between anorexia nervosa and high socio-economic status is unproven, due to data collection biases including sample size, clinical status and referral patterns. A recent study on a large comprehensive clinical database, covering 692 referrals to a UK national specialist centre over a time lapse of 33 years, challenges this conclusion: McClelland and Crisp (2001) found referrals for anorexia nervosa from the two highest social classes to be almost twice as high as expected. They present evidence that their findings are unrelated to differences in clinical features or in access to their service.

For bulimia nervosa, Gard and Freeman (1996) conclude that—similar to most psychiatric disorders—there seems to be a preponderance in the low socio-economic groups.

Level of Industrialization

It is commonly thought that anorexia nervosa is a western illness: there appears to be a developmental gradient across countries, with a predominance in industrialized, developed countries, linking the disorder to an affluent society (Hoek, 1993). This gradient has been hypothesized to be connected with the sociocultural theory, which holds that eating disorders are promoted by a 'western' culture favouring slimness as a beauty ideal for females. By consequence, eating disorders would be less prevalent in underdeveloped, non-western cultures. Unfortunately, up to date few developing countries have the facilities and means needed to arrive at reliable epidemiological data.

Some recent publications cast doubts on the validity of the sociocultural theory, at least for anorexia nervosa. For example, Hoek et al. (1998) found an incidence of anorexia nervosa on the Caribbean island of Curaçao within the range of rates reported in western countries. A methodological problem of this type of study is the definition and assessment of what typifies a culture as 'non-western'. For more discussion on this matter, the reader is referred to Chapter 8 in this book and Nasser et al. (2001).

Level of Urbanization

Hoek et al. (1995) report that the incidence of bulimia nervosa is three to five times higher in urbanized areas and cities than in rural areas, while anorexia nervosa is found with almost equal frequency in areas with different degrees of urbanization. The drift-hypothesis, relating urbanization differences to migration for educational reasons, is rejected because the differences remain after adjusting for age. Other social factors involved might be an increased pressure to be slender and decreased social control in urbanized areas. If these hold true, this would imply that anorexia nervosa is less sensitive to social factors than bulimia nervosa, has a more biological origin, and is more driven by other factors such as a tendency towards asceticism and compulsive behaviour.

Occupation

Some occupations appear to run a greater potential risk of being linked to the development of an eating disorder (Vandereycken & Hoek, 1993). Typical examples of these are professions within the world of fashion and ballet. We do not know whether this is a causal factor or the result of disturbed attitudes around body and shape. In other words, are pre-anorexics attracted by the ballet world, or are the requirements of the profession conducive to the development of anorexia nervosa?

Individual Characteristics

The method of choice for assessing individual risk is a prospective follow-up study. Unfortunately, none of the few prospective studies reported employs a two-stage case identification procedure and they address only a subsample of the general population. Wlodarczyk-Bisaga and Dolan (1996) re-interviewed a high- and a low-risk group of 14–16-year-old schoolgirls, defined by their scores on the EAT, 10 months after initial assessment. No clinical cases were detected at either measurement point. Patton et al. (1999) conducted a cohort study over three years with six-month intervals in students initially aged 14–15 years. All new cases of eating disorder developed during the study had partial/subclinical syndromes of bulimia nervosa. Both dieting and psychiatric morbidity were implicated as risk factors, but from this study it is not clear whether this also holds for full-syndrome eating disorders.

Although case-control studies in general are not discussed here because of their methodological drawbacks, an exception is made for the studies by Fairburn and colleagues (1997, 1998, 1999). They compared subjects with bulimia nervosa (1997), binge eating disorder (1998) and anorexia nervosa (1999) with each other, with healthy control subjects without an eating disorder (general risk factors), and with subjects with other psychiatric disorders (specific risk factors), recruited from general practices in Oxfordshire, England. After screening with self-report questionnaires, a retrospective risk-factor interview was carried out that addressed the premorbid period. This interview focused on biological, psychological and social factors thought to place persons at risk for the development of eating disorders. For anorexia nervosa and bulimia nervosa, the great majority of the risk factors found were general risk factors, separating eating disorder cases from healthy controls. For BED only a few general risk factors were identified.

Some specific risk factors, separating eating disorder cases from other psychiatric cases were also found. For anorexia nervosa subjects they were personal vulnerability factors, particularly childhood characteristics of negative self-evaluation and perfectionism. For bulimia nervosa these were dieting vulnerability factors, such as parental obesity, childhood obesity and negative comments from family members about eating, appearance and weight. The results suggest that both bulimia nervosa and binge eating disorder are most likely to develop in dieters who are at risk of obesity and psychiatric disorder in general (Fairburn et al., 1997, 1998). This result is in line with the conclusions of Patton et al. (1999).

OBESITY

Classification

The epidemiology of obesity has for many years been difficult to study because many countries had their own specific criteria for the classification of different degrees of overweight. Gradually during the 1990s, however, the body mass index (BMI = weight/squared height) became a universally accepted measure of the degree of overweight, and now identical cut-points are recommended. In the most recent classification of weight in adults by the World Health Organization (WHO, 1998a), four levels over overweight are defined. The first three each cover 5 units of BMI, from pre-obese starting at a BMI of 25.0, through obese class I at 30.0 and obese class II at 35.0 to the highest level of overweight (obese class III) at a BMI of 40.0 and upwards. The associated health risks are deemed to increase accordingly from increased at pre-obese to very severely increased at obese class III.

The BMI is used because it is highly correlated with body fat percentage and is unrelated to stature. The correlation between BMI and body fat percentage is usually in the range of 0.7 to 0.9 in adults aged 25–65, but lower in subjects at other ages. The level of body fatness for a given BMI varies greatly by age, sex and ethnicity (Deurenberg et al., 1991). This may necessitate sex-, age- and ethnic-specific criteria for the use of the BMI. This issue is currently under intense debate in the obesity research community. Already researchers in Asian countries have criticized the WHO cut-off points. The absolute health risks seem to be higher at any level of the BMI in Chinese and South-Asian people, which is probably also true for Asians living elsewhere. This implies that for Asians the cut-off points to designate overweight or obesity should be lowered by several units of BMI. Because China and India alone each have over a billion inhabitants, small changes in the criteria for overweight or obesity potentially increase the world estimate of the number of obese people by several hundred million (currently estimates are about 250 million world wide).

Much research over the last decade has suggested that for an accurate classification of weight with respect to health risks one needs to factor in the abdominal fat distribution (e.g. Lean et al., 1998). In June 1998 the National Institute of Health (National Heart, Lung and Blood Institute) adopted the BMI classification and combined this with waist cut-off points (NIH, 1998). In this classification the combination of overweight (BMI between 25 and 30 kg/m^2) or moderate obesity (BMI between 30 and 35 kg/m^2) with a large waist circumference (≥ 102 cm in men or ≥ 88 cm in women) is proposed to carry additional health risk.

Prevalence

In many reviews it has been shown that obesity (defined as a body mass index of 30 kg/m^2 or higher) is a prevalent condition in most countries with established market economies (Seidell, 1997), and there is wide variation in prevalence of obesity between and within these countries: e.g. Toulouse in France with a prevalence of obesity of 9% in men and 11% in women and Strasbourg in France with 22% of the men and 23% of the women meeting the obesity criterion. In industrialized countries obesity is usually more frequent among those with relatively low socio-economic status. In cross-sectional surveys the prevalence increases with age until about 60–70 years of age after which the prevalence declines (Seidell & Flegal, 1997). For an explanation of the age effect a combination of selective survival, cohort effect and general weight loss after the age of 60 has been proposed.

There is uncertainty about most national prevalence estimates of obesity due to a lack of solid data, large differences between regions within the same country and secular trends. The numbers corresponding to the midpoint of the estimates add up to about 250 million obese adults, which is about 7% of the total adult world population. It does not seem unreasonable that the true prevalence of obesity is in the order of 5–10%. In most countries the prevalence of overweight (BMI between 25 and 30 kg/m^2) is about two to three times as large as the prevalence of obesity. This means that as many as one billion people may be overweight or obese.

Time Trends

In most of these established market economies it has been shown that the prevalence is increasing over time (Seidell & Flegal, 1997). Figures 2.1 and 2.2 show the changes in the prevalence of obesity (BMI $\geq$ 30) in men and women aged 35–64 years in several centres participating in the WHO MONICA project. In this project cardiovascular risk factors were monitored through independent cross-sectional population surveys over a 10-year period. The surveys included random samples of at least 200 people of each sex for each 10-year age group for the age range 36–64 years (Molarius et al., 2000).

There is a rapid increase in the prevalence of obesity in most centres from countries in the European Union, particularly in men. In centres in countries from central and eastern Europe the prevalence at follow-up of obesity in women remains among the highest in Europe, even though it may have stabilized or even slightly decreased over time.

The study by Molarius et al. (2000) also showed that social class differences in the prevalence of obesity are increasing with time. Obesity increasingly seems to be becoming an almost exclusive lower class problem in Europe.

Regional Differences

The most recent (1988–1994) estimates of obesity prevalence in adults in the USA are about 20% in men and 25% in women (Seidell & Flegal, 1997). In other parts of the world obesity is also frequent. Martorell et al. (2000) recently described the prevalence of obesity in young adult women aged 15–49 years. It was on average 10% in countries from Latin America and 17% in countries in North Africa and the middle east. Obesity is uncommon in Sub-Saharan Africa, China and India, although in all regions the prevalence seems to be increasing, particularly among the affluent parts of the population in the larger cities (Seidell & Rissanen, 1997). In these countries we quite often see the paradoxical combination of increasing under- and overnutrition. This is quite obviously related to growing inequalities in income and access to food in these regions. In addition, as already mentioned, classification criteria based on white populations might not be appropriate for Asian populations.

Incidence

Very few studies have attempted to calculate the incidence rate of obesity. The criterion for obesity is a matter of definition on a gliding scale from low to high weight. This makes it difficult to determine at what moment overweight becomes (incident) obesity and to separate incident from prevalent cases at the moment of registration. In one report a four-year incidence rate of obesity was calculated from data collected in a mixed longitudinal study carried out between 1980 and 1984 in young adults aged 19–31 years in The Netherlands (Rookus et al., 1987). The incidence was determined to be 0.9% per 4 years (95% CI: 0.1–3.4%) in men and 2.5% in 4 years (95% CI: 0.9–5.5%) in women aged 29–31 years of age. It increased with age, particularly in women.

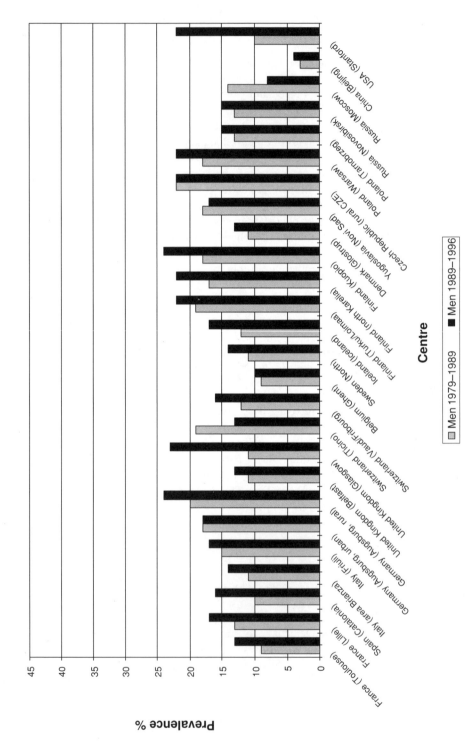

Figure 2.1 The WHO MONICA project: Changes in the prevalence of obesity over 10 years in men aged 35–64 years

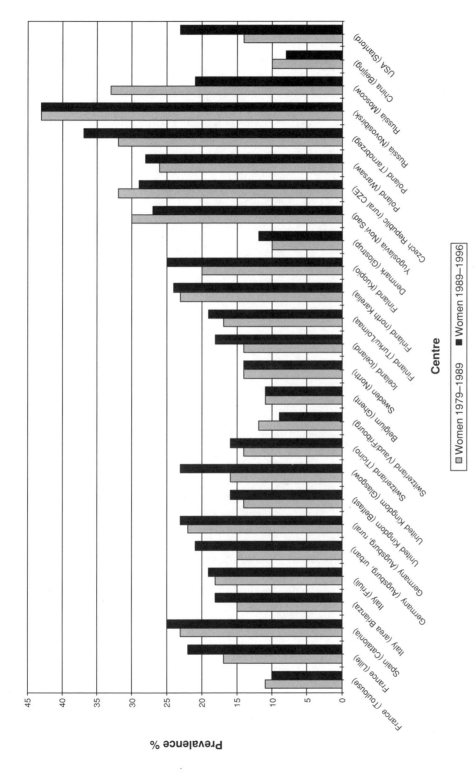

Figure 2.2 The WHO MONICA project: Changes in the prevalence of obesity over 10 years in women aged 35–64 years

Mortality

The relation between high body mass index and mortality has been studied for many decades in many populations. Available evidence shows that obesity is clearly associated with an increased risk of mortality. For instance, recently pooled analyses of six large American prospective studies showed that the number of deaths attributable to obesity is in the order of 300 000 per year in the United States alone (Allison et al., 1999). It is difficult and probably not meaningful to give a single figure for a standardized mortality rate (SMR) in the obese. Research has shown that the SMR for obesity is strongly dependent upon sex, age and ethnicity. In addition, the SMR strongly depends upon the presence of covariates such as smoking habits. It is generally assumed that mortality is elevated by about 50–150% in most adult populations (Seidell et al., 1999). Obesity is a major cause of mortality in most affluent countries. More important, however, is that obesity is associated with a dramatic increase in morbidity and impairment of quality of life. In essence, the true burden of obesity is measured by the increase in number of unhealthy life-years rather than by the reduction in total life-years.

Risk Factors

Context of the Individual

The relation between obesity and social class is highly variable across cultures. In most industrialized countries obesity is more common in people with relatively low socio-economic status. This phenomenon is generally more pronounced in women than in men. The exact reasons for this social class gradient are unknown but generally are assumed to result from both sociocultural perceptions of body shape in combinations with obesity-promoting lifestyles (high consumption of high fat foods and relatively low consumption of fruits and vegetables as well as relatively low physical activity level during leisure time). The reason why this is more pronounced in women than in men probably reflects the stronger emphasis on thinness among women with high education and income. In non-industrialized countries, however, obesity is usually much more common among those with relatively high socio-economic status. In these circumstances obesity is usually being regarded as a sign of material wealth and is thus considered to be a desirable trait. In many countries undergoing an economic transition and industrialization, the relations between social class are subject to change and can vary greatly by region. In rural China, for instance, obesity is still more common among those with relatively high socio-economic status but an inverse association between social class and obesity is observed in large cities such as Beijing (Seidell & Rissanen, 1997).

Individual Characteristics

On an ecological or population level the time trends in the prevalence of obesity are not too difficult to explain although exact quantification of different factors is almost impossible.

On the one hand there is an increase in the average energy supply per capita. The World Health Report (WHO, 1998b) has estimated that the average energy supply per capita in the world has risen from 2300 kcal in 1963 to 2720 kcal in 1992, with an estimated 2900 kcal in 2010. These increases are obviously not evenly distributed across the world's population and, sadly, many remain undernourished. In Asia (particularly China and India) and most of Latin America undernourishment is declining. The number of people with access to at least 2700 kcal has increased from 0.145 billion in 1969–1971 to 1.8 billion in 1990–1992 and is estimated to grow to 2.7 billion in 2010. Even when corrected for the increase in the world's population this implies a more than ten-fold increase in the number of people with access to high calorific diets. The globalization of agricultural production and food processing has not only affected the quantity of energy available per capita but also the energy density.

On the other hand, there is a decrease in the average energy expenditure per capita. Increasing sedentary behaviour has been proposed to be another main reason for the increase in the prevalence of obesity in countries with established market economies. Large and important differences can be seen in the number of hours spent at sedentary jobs and behind television or computer screens during leisure time. Also, the type of transportation is almost certainly a factor. For example, 30% of short trips in the Netherlands are done by bicycle and 18% by walking. In the UK these percentages are 8% by bicycling and 12% walking and, in the USA, 1% by bicycle and 9% by walking (Pucher, 1997).

Given the changes in lifestyles and resulting changes in energy balance over the last decades in many parts of the world it is not surprising that, on average, people gain weight. With small changes in average body weight the prevalence of obesity increases rapidly. For every unit increase in average BMI there is an increase in the prevalence of obesity of 5% (WHO, 1998a).

CONCLUSIONS

For anorexia nervosa an average prevalence rate of 0.3% was found for young females. Although Soundy et al. (1995) caution for the possibility of unreliable information, figures of an average prevalence rate of bulimia nervosa of 1% in women and 0.1% in men seem accurate. A tentative conclusion is that the prevalence of binge eating disorder (BED) is more likely to be 1% than 4% or more. The true prevalence of obesity may be in the order of 5–10%.

Assuming that even the studies with the most complete case finding methods yield an underestimate of the true incidence, as state of the art we conclude that the overall incidence of anorexia nervosa is at least 8 per 100 000 population per year and the incidence of bulimia nervosa is at least 12 per 100 000 population per year. The incidence rate of anorexia nervosa has increased during the past 50 years, particularly in females 10–24 years old. The registered incidence of bulimia nervosa has increased, at least during the first five years after bulimia nervosa was added to the DSM-III. For BED and obesity not enough incidence information is available for an accurate summary.

Risk factor research is still sparse, both for eating disorders and for obesity, and some group and individual characteristics, particularly related to dieting, have been tentatively identified as carrying with them an increased risk.

COMMENTS

The value of epidemiology lies in its particular methodology that gives rise to population-based disease rates and ratios. When properly established, these rates and ratios provide a scientific basis on the community level for treatment planning and aetiologic model building. Epidemiological information is needed to examine and extend on clinical observations.

The basic epidemiological measures are incidence and prevalence rates. For the purpose of treatment planning, there is an ongoing need for prevalence information at the local level. For reasons of time- and cost-efficiency, this is best done by monitoring existing health care consumption registers. Attention must be paid to the interpretation of changing consumption rates in relation to changes in health care recruitment and admission policy. When the adequacy or accuracy of case definition and registration is questioned, efforts are needed to improve registration.

For the purpose of aetiological model building, the mere determination of prevalence and incidence rates is not enough. Although more is becoming known on general and specific risk factors for the onset of an eating disorder, there still is an impressive gap. Furthermore, the developmental mechanisms of these factors are largely unknown. The general conclusion is that dieting behaviour plays a role in the pathogenesis of anorexia nervosa, bulimia nervosa and binge eating disorder. For more information on this matter, see also Chapter 9 in this book. However, not all dieters proceed to develop an eating disorder. A prospective follow-up study of initially healthy dieters sampled from the general population may shed light on the mechanisms that turn dieting into an eating disorder.

To circumvent the power- and cost-problems caused by the relatively low rates of eating disorders in the general population, a few suggestions for the design of economically feasible studies providing generalizable, reliable results on risk factors and mechanisms are given:

- There is a need for prospective, follow-up designs using initially healthy subjects at high risk for developing an eating disorder, such as young females, dieters and participants in weight-restricted sports including ballet dancing. Depending on the question to be answered, these could be matched on sex, age and socio-economic status with initially healthy intermediate- and low-risk groups.
- For lower risk groups, such as males or older persons, a prospective design is too cost-inefficient and a case-control design is more appropriate. Cases should be collected at as low a level of entry into the health care system as possible, preferably primary care. As controls, same-sex siblings and other same-sex persons matched for age and socio-economic status could be of use. To facilitate hypothesis testing and the exchange of knowledge and ideas, the formation of a multi-centre database of these rare cases would mean a great improvement.
- For both prospective follow-up studies and case-control studies of eating disorders, a comprehensive assessment of biological, psychological, familial and social variables is needed. The factors and mechanisms studied should be based on findings from previous research such as that by Fairburn et al. (1997). To decide on the effect of weight- and shape-centred beauty ideals on the frequency of eating disorders, studies are needed that compare the distribution of eating disorders between groups differing in weight- and shape-related attitudes.

Finally, an issue to be solved for epidemiological studies on eating disorders is the reliance on a categorical approach of caseness, particularly for the 'newer' diagnoses of bulimia nervosa, the eating disorders not otherwise specified, and BED. By focusing on incident clinical cases and ignoring atypical or subclinical cases, aetiological reasoning may miss the crucial developmental elements in what have been called 'broad spectrum' disorders.

Obesity is a complex disorder with biological, sociological and psychological dimensions. The fundamental causes of the increase in obesity rates are sedentary lifestyles and high-fat, energy-dense diets. The rising rates reflect the profound changes in society and in the behavioural patterns of the communities, although some individuals may become obese partly because they have a genetic or other biological predisposition to gain more readily when they are exposed to an unfavourable environment. Identifying environmental, behavioural, and biological factors that contribute to an individual's weight gain is particularly difficult.

The World Health Organization has concluded that the global epidemic of obesity is so serious that public health action is urgently required. It is thus essential to develop new preventive public health strategies which affect the entire society. Without societal changes a substantial and steadily rising proportion of adults will succumb to the medical complications of obesity. Indeed, the medical burden of obesity already threatens to overwhelm health services. The spectrum of problems seen in both developing and developed countries is having so negative an impact that the World Health Organization considers obesity to be regarded as today's principal neglected public health problem (WHO, 1998b).

Unless a miracle occurs, it will not be possible to predict an individual's risk at developing an eating disorder or becoming obese, let alone arrive at evidence-based successful preventive measures, for quite a few years.

REFERENCES

Allison, D.B., Fontaine, K.R., Manson, J.E., Stevens, J. & VanItallie, T.B. (1999) Annual deaths attributable to obesity in the United States. *Journal of the American Medical Association*, **282**, 1530–1538.

APA (1980) *Diagnostic and Statistical Manual of Mental Disorders* (3rd Edition). Washington, D.C.: American Psychiatric Association.

APA (1994) *Diagnostic and Statistical Manual of Mental Disorders* (4th Edition). Washington, D.C.: American Psychiatric Association.

Bushnell, J.A., Wells, J.E., Hornblow, A.R., Oakly-Browne, M.A. & Joyce, P. (1990) Prevalence of three bulimia syndromes in the general population. *Psychological Medicine*, **20**, 671–680.

Button, E.J. & Whitehouse, A. (1981) Subclinical anorexia nervosa. *Psychological Medicine*, **11**, 509–516.

Cotrufo, P., Barretta, V., Monteleone, P. & Maj, M. (1998) Full-syndrome, partial-syndrome and subclinical eating disorders: An epidemiological study of female students in Southern Italy. *Acta Psychiatrica Scandinavica*, **98**, 112–115.

Deurenberg, P., Weststrate, J.A. & Seidell, J.C. (1991) Body mass index as a measure of body fatness: Age- and sex-specific prediction formulas. *British Journal of Nutrition*, **65**, 105–114.

Dohrenwend, B.P., Levav, I., Shrout, P.E., Schwartz, S., Naveh, G., Link, B.G., Skodol, A.E. & Stueve, A. (1992) Socioeconomic status and psychiatric disorders: The causation-selection issue. *Science*, **255**, 946–952.

Eaton, W.W., Tien, A.Y. & Poeschla, B.D. (1995) Epidemiology of schizophrenia. In J.A. Den Boer, H.G.M. Westenberg & H.M. Van Praag (Eds), *Advances in the Neurobiology of Schizophrenia* (pp. 27–57). Chichester: John Wiley & Sons.

Fairburn, C.G. & Beglin, S.J. (1990) Studies of the epidemiology of bulimia nervosa. *American Journal of Psychiatry*, **147**, 401–408.

Fairburn, C.G. & Cooper, Z. (1993) The Eating Disorder Examination (12th Edn). In C.G. Fairburn & G.T. Wilson (Eds), *Binge Eating: Nature, Assessment and Treatment* (pp. 317–360). New York: Guilford Press.

Fairburn, C.G., Cooper, Z., Doll, H.A. & Welch, S.L. (1999) Risk factors for anorexia nervosa. Three integrated case-control comparisons. *Archives of General Psychiatry*, **56**, 468–476.

Fairburn, C.G., Doll, H.A., Welch, S.L., Hay, P.J., Davies, B.A. & O'Connor, M.E. (1998) Risk factors for binge eating disorder. A community-based, case-control study. *Archives of General Psychiatry*, **55**, 425–432.

Fairburn, C.G., Welch, S.L., Doll, H.A., Davies, B.A. & O'Connor, M.E. (1997) Risk factors for bulimia nervosa. A community-based case-control study. *Archives of General Psychiatry*, **54**, 509–517.

Fombonne, E. (1995) Anorexia nervosa. No evidence of an increase. *British Journal of Psychiatry*, **166**, 464–471.

Gard, M.C.E. & Freeman, C.P. (1996) The dismantling of a myth: A review of eating disorders and socioeconomic status. *International Journal of Eating Disorders*, **20**, 1–12.

Garfinkel, P.E., Lin, E., Goering, P., Spegg, C., Goldbloom, D.S., Kennedy, S., Kaplan, A.S. & Woodside, D.B. (1995) Bulimia nervosa in a Canadian community sample: Prevalence and comparison of subgroups. *American Journal of Psychiatry*, **152**, 1052–1058.

Hay, P. (1998) The epidemiology of eating disorder behaviors: An Australian community-based survey. *International Journal of Eating Disorders*, **23**, 371–382.

Hoek, H.W. (1991) The incidence and prevalence of anorexia nervosa and bulimia nervosa in primary care. *Psychological Medicine*, **21**, 455–460.

Hoek, H.W. (1993) Review of the epidemiological studies of eating disorders. *International Review of Psychiatry*, **5**, 61–74.

Hoek, H.W., Bartelds, A.I.M., Bosveld, J.J.F., van der Graaf. Y, Limpens, V.E.L., Maiwald, M. & Spaaij, C.J.K. (1995) Impact of urbanization on detection rates of eating disorders. *American Journal of Psychiatry*, **152**, 1272–1278.

Hoek, H.W. & Brook, F.G. (1985) Patterns of care of anorexia nervosa. *Journal of Psychiatric Research*, **19**, 155–160.

Hoek, H.W., van Harten, P.N., van Hoeken, D. & Susser, E. (1998) Lack of relation between culture and anorexia nervosa: Results of an incidence study on Curaçao. *New England Journal of Medicine*, **338**, 1231–1232.

Hsu, L.K.G. (1996) Epidemiology of the eating disorders. *The Psychiatric Clinics of North America*, **19**, 681–700.

Johnson-Sabine, E., Wood, K., Patton, G., Mann, A. & Wakeling, A. (1988) Abnormal eating attitudes in London schoolgirls—a prospective epidemiological study: Factors associated with abnormal response on screening questionnaires. *Psychological Medicine*, **18**, 615–622.

Jones, D.J., Fox, M.M., Babigian, H.M. & Hutton, H.E. (1980) Epidemiology of anorexia nervosa in Monroe County, New York: 1960–1976. *Psychosomatic Medicine*, **42**, 551–558.

Keel, P.K. & Mitchell, J.E. (1997) Outcome in bulimia nervosa. *American Journal of Psychiatry*, **154**, 313–321.

Kendell, R.E., Hall, D.J., Hailey, A. & Babigian H.M. (1973) The epidemiology of anorexia nervosa. *Psychological Medicine*, **3**, 200–203.

King, M.B. (1989) Eating disorders in a general practice population. Prevalence, characteristics and follow-up at 12 to 18 months. *Psychological Medicine*, Suppl. **14**, 1–34.

Kraemer, H.C., Kazdin, A.E., Offord, D.R., Kessler, R.C., Jensen, P.S. & Kupfer, D.J. (1997) Coming to terms with the terms of risk. *Archives of General Psychiatry*, **54**, 337–343.

Lean, M.E.J., Han, T.S. & Seidell, J.C. (1998) Impairment of health and quality of life in men and women with a large waist. *Lancet*, **351**, 853–856.

Lucas, A.R., Beard, C.M., O'Fallon, W.M. & Kurland, L.T. (1991) 50-Year trends in the incidence of anorexia nervosa in Rochester, Minn.: a population-based study. *American Journal of Psychiatry*, **148**, 917–922.

Lucas, A.R., Crowson, C.S., O'Fallon, W.M. & Melton, L.J. (1999) The ups and downs of anorexia nervosa. *International Journal of Eating Disorders*, **26**, 397–405.

Martorell, R., Khan, L.K., Hughes, M.L. & Grummer-Strawn, L.M. (2000) Obesity in women from developing countries. *European Journal of Clinical Nutrition*, **54**, 247–252.

Martz, J. (2001) Entwickling der Inzidenz und andere Aspekte von Anorexia Nervosa im Kanton Zurich, 1956–1995. Doctoral dissertation, Zurich University.

McClelland, L. & Crisp, A. (2001) Anorexia nervosa and social class. *International Journal of Eating Disorders*, **29**, 150–156.

Meadows, G.N., Palmer, R.L., Newball, E.U.M. & Kenrick, J.M.T. (1986) Eating attitudes and disorder in young women: A general practice based survey. *Psychological Medicine*, **16**, 351–357.

Molarius, A., Seidell, J.C., Sans, S., Tuomilehto, J. & Kuulasmaa, K. (2000) Educational level and relative body weight and changes in their associations over ten years—an international perspective from the WHO MONICA project. *American Journal of Public Health*, **90**, 1260–1268.

Møller-Madsen, S. & Nystrup, J. (1992) Incidence of anorexia nervosa in Denmark. *Acta Psychiatrica Scandinavica*, **86**, 197–200.

Nasser, M. (1997) *Culture and Weight Consciousness*. London: Routledge.

Nasser, M., Katzman, M.A. & Gordon, R.A. (Eds) (2001) *Eating Disorders and Cultures in Transition*, London: Brunner Routledge.

NIH (1998) *Clinical Guidelines on the Identification, Evaluation, and Treatment of Overweight and Obesity in Adults. The Evidence Report*. National Institute of Health, NHLBI.

Nielsen, S. (2001) Epidemiology and mortality of eating disorders. *Psychiatric Clinics of North America*, **24**, 201–214.

Nobakht, M. & Dezhkam, M. (2000) An epidemiological study of eating disorders in Iran. *International Journal of Eating Disorders*, **28**, 265–271.

Pagsberg, A.K. & Wang, A.R. (1994) Epidemiology of anorexia nervosa and bulimia nervosa in Bornholm County, Denmark, 1970–1989. *Acta Psychiatrica Scandinavica*, **90**, 259–265.

Patton, G.C., Selzer, R., Coffey, C., Carlin, J.B. & Wolfe, R. (1999) Onset of adolescent eating disorders: Population based cohort study over 3 years. *British Medical Journal*, **318**, 765–768.

Pucher, J. (1997) Bicycling boom in Germany: A revival engineered by public policy. *Transportation Quarterly*, **51**, 31–46.

Råstam, M., Gillberg, C. & Garton, M. (1989) Anorexia nervosa in a Swedish urban region: A population based study. *British Journal of Psychiatry*, **155**, 642–646.

Rathner, G. & Messner, K. (1993) Detection of eating disorders in a small rural town: An epidemiological study. *Psychological Medicine*, **23**, 175–184.

Regier, D.A. & Burke, J.D. (2000) Epidemiology. In B.J. Sadock & V.A. Sadock (Eds), *Comprehensive Textbook of Psychiatry* (pp. 500–522). Philadelphia: Lippincott Williams & Wilkins.

Rookus, M.A., Burema, van 't Hof, M.A., Deurenberg, P. & Hautvast, J.G.A.J. (1987) The development of the body mass index in young adults, II. Interrelationships of level, change and fluctuation, a four-year longitudinal study. *Human Biology*, **59**, 617–630.

Russell, G.F.M. (1979) Bulimia nervos: An ominous variant of anorexia nervosa. *Psychological Medicine*, **9**, 429–448.

Santonastaso, P., Zanetti, T., Sala, A., Favaretto, G., Vidotto, G. & Favaro, A. (1996) Prevalence of eating disorders in Italy: A survey on a sample of 16-year-old female students. *Psychotherapy and Psychosomatics*, **65**, 158–162.

Seidell, J.C. (1997) Time trends in obesity: An epidemiological perspective. *Hormone and Metabolic Research*, **29**, 155–158.

Seidell, J.C. & Flegal, K.M. (1997) Assessing obesity: Classification and epidemiology. *British Medical Bulletin*, **53**, 238–252.

Seidell, J.C. & Rissanen, A. (1997) World-wide prevalence of obesity and time-trends. In G.A. Bray, C. Bouchard & W.P.T. James (Eds), *Handbook of Obesity* (pp. 79-91). New York: M. Dekker Inc.

Seidell, J.C., Visscher, T.L.S. & Hoogeveen, R.T. (1999) Overweight and obesity in the mortality rate data: Current evidence and research issues. *Medical Science Sports Exercises*, **31**, 597–601.

Soundy, T.J., Lucas, A.R., Suman, V.J. & Melton, L.J. (1995) Bulimia nervosa in Rochester, Minnesota, from 1980 to 1990. *Psychological Medicine*, **25**, 1065–1071.

Steinhausen, H.C., Winkler, C. & Meier, M. (1997) Eating disorders in adolescence in a Swiss epidemiological study. *International Journal of Eating Disorders*, **22**, 147–151.

Sullivan, P.F. (1995) Mortality in anorexia nervosa. *American Journal of Psychiatry*, **152**, 1073–1074.

Szabó, P. & Túry, F. (1991) The prevalence of bulimia nervosa in a Hungarian college and secondary school population. *Psychotherapy and Psychosomatics*, **56**, 43–47.

Szmukler, G.I. (1983) Weight and food preoccupation in a population of English schoolgirls. In G.I. Bargman (Ed.), *Understanding Anorexia Nervosa and Bulimia: Report of 4th Ross Conference on Medical Research* (pp. 21–27). Ross, Columbus, Ohio.

Szmukler, G.I. (1985) The epidemiology of anorexia nervosa and bulimia. *Journal of Psychiatric Research*, **19**, 143–153.

Szmukler, G., McCance, C., McCrone, L. & Hunter, D. (1986) Anorexia nervosa: A psychiatric case register study from Aberdeen. *Psychological Medicine*, **16**, 49–58.

Theander, S. (1970) Anorexia nervosa: A psychiatric investigation of 94 female patients. *Acta Psychiatrica Scandinavica*, Suppl. **214**.

Turnbull, S., Ward, A., Treasure, J., Jick, H. & Derby, L. (1996) The demand for eating disorder care. An epidemiological study using the General Practice Research Database. *British Journal of Psychiatry*, **169**, 705–712.

Van Hoeken, D., Lucas, A.R. & Hoek, H.W. (1998) Epidemiology. In H.W. Hoek, J.L. Treasure & M.A. Katzman (Eds), *Neurobiology in the Treatment of Eating Disorders* (pp. 97–126). Chichester: John Wiley & Sons.

Vandereycken, W. & Hoek, H.W. (1993) Are eating disorders culture-bound syndromes? In K.A. Halmi (Ed.), *Psychobiology and Treatment of Anorexia Nervosa and Bulimia Nervosa* (pp. 19–36). Washington DC: American Psychopathological Association.

Whitaker, A., Johnson, J., Shaffer, D., Rapoport, J.L., Kalikow, K., Walsh, B.T., Davies, M., Braiman, S. & Dolinsky, A. (1990) Uncommon troubles in young people: Prevalence estimates of selected psychiatric disorders in a nonreferred adolescent population. *Archives of General Psychiatry*, **47**, 487–496.

Whitehouse, A.M., Cooper, P.J., Vize, C.V., Hill, C. & Vogel, L. (1992) Prevalence of eating disorders in three Cambridge general practices: Hidden and conspicuous morbidity. *British Journal of General Practice*, **42**, 57–60.

WHO (1978) *Mental Disorders: Glossary and Guide to their Classification in Accordance with the Ninth Revision of the International Classification of Diseases*. Geneva: World Health Organization.

WHO (1992) *The ICD-10 Classification of Mental and Behavioural Disorders: Clinical Descriptions and Diagnostic Guidelines*. Geneva: World Health Organization.

WHO (1998a) *Obesity: Preventing and Managing the Global Epidemic*. Geneva: WHO (WHO/NUT/NCD/98.1).

WHO (1998b) *The World Health Report 1998. Life in the 21st Century—A Vision for All*. Geneva: WHO.

Willi, J., Giacometti G. & Limacher, B. (1990) Update on the epidemiology of anorexia nervosa in a defined region of Switzerland. *American Journal of Psychiatry*, **147**, 1514–1517.

Willi, J. & Grossman, S. (1983) Epidemiology of anorexia nervosa in a defined region of Switzerland. *American Journal of Psychiatry*, **140**, 564–657.

Williams, P. & King, M. (1987) The 'epidemic' of anorexia nervosa: another medical myth? *The Lancet*, **i**, 205–207.

Williams, P., Tarnopolsky, A. & Hand, D. (1980) Case definition and case identification in psychiatric epidemiology: Review and reassessment. *Psychological Medicine*, **10**, 101–114.

Wlodarczyk-Bisaga, K. & Dolan, B. (1996) A two-stage epidemiological study of abnormal eating attitudes and their prospective risk factors in Polish schoolgirls. *Psychological Medicine*, **26**, 1021–1032.

CHAPTER 3

Cognitive-Behavioural Models

Roz Shafran
Department of Psychiatry, Warneford Hospital, Oxford, UK
and
Padmal de Silva
Eating Disorders Unit, Institute of Psychiatry, London, UK

INTRODUCTION

In keeping with the rest of this handbook, this chapter not only focuses on the two most widely research eating disorders—anorexia nervosa and bulimia nervosa—but it also includes obesity. The relationship between these eating disorders and obesity is described in other chapters and it is notable that a personal or family history of obesity is a specific risk factor for the development of bulimia nervosa (Fairburn, Cooper, Doll & Welch, 1999). The strong relationship between anorexia nervosa and bulimia nervosa is well documented with over one-quarter of patients with bulimia nervosa having experienced an episode of anorexia nervosa (Braun, Sunday & Halmi, 1994; Bulik et al., 1995). It is therefore no surprise to see some overlap in the cognitive-behavioural accounts of anorexia nervosa, bulimia nervosa and obesity. Despite the similarities, there are also important differences that must be taken into account by cognitive-behavioural models of these disorders.

This chapter begins by describing the purpose of cognitive-behavioural models and introducing general principles that guide cognitive-behavioural models of disorders. An important distinction is drawn between models of the aetiology of these disorders and their maintenance. It is argued that the cognitive-behavioural models of the maintenance of these disorders are more likely to lead to developments in the effective treatments than models of aetiology. A critical review of cognitive-behavioural models of each of these disorders is provided. Experimental and treatment outcome data are used to evaluate the models. The chapter ends by calling for further research to directly evaluate the models and their derived cognitive-behavioural treatments.

THE PURPOSE OF COGNITIVE-BEHAVIOURAL MODELS

In this context, the term 'models' is used to describe theoretical schemes for ordering information in a broad and comprehensive way (Gelder, 1997). Cognitive-behavioural models

The Essential *Handbook of Eating Disorders.* Edited by J. Treasure, U. Schmidt and E. van Furth.
© 2005 John Wiley & Sons, Ltd.

can have many functions, depending on whether they are accounts of the development of the disorder or the maintenance of the disorder. They have two main purposes. First, they provide a means of understanding the development or maintenance of the most important cognitive and behavioural aspects of the phenomenology of the disorder. In anorexia nervosa, the cognitive aspects that need to be explained include (but are not limited to) the determination to actively maintain a low weight, negative self-evaluation, body image disturbance, preoccupation with eating, shape and weight, and the egosyntonicity of the disorder. The primary behaviour in need of explanation is dietary restriction. Other behaviours that may require explanation are episodes of binge eating, excessive exercise and self-induced vomiting or taking of laxatives (American Psychiatric Association, 1994).

In bulimia nervosa, the cognitive aspects are similar to those of in anorexia nervosa but the additional behaviours that require explanation include the objective episodes of binge eating and the resultant compensatory behaviour (APA, 1994). In obesity, the cognitive aspect that needs to be explained is debatable but may relate to beliefs about the positive effects of eating and the negative consequences of not eating. In addition, people with obesity who are trying to control their weight have to impose control over their energy intake/expenditure (Wilson, 1993). The behaviour that needs to be explained is over-eating and, for a minority of patients, binge eating.

The second purpose of cognitive-behavioural models is to improve the treatment of the disorder. Put succinctly, 'some of the most effective psychological treatments for emotional disorders have been developed by constructing a model of the development and maintenance of the disorder and then devising a set of treatment procedures that focus on the core pathology and reverse the maintaining factors' (Clark, 1997, p. 121). There is often overlap between factors leading to the development of a disorder and their maintenance (e.g. dieting). Nevertheless, it is important to draw the neglected distinction between development and maintenance (see Cooper, 1997) since it is the maintenance mechanisms that need to be reversed if the therapeutic intervention is to be effective. Understanding the development of a disorder may give some *clues* as to the processes that might reverse the development of the disorder, and may give a good indication of how to prevent relapse. However, better information regarding intervention is obtained by understanding the mechanisms that maintain the disorder since reversing these maintaining mechanisms will result in an effective treatment intervention. This has been shown to be the case for the anxiety disorders (e.g. panic disorder; Clark, 1997) and bulimia nervosa (Fairburn, 1997).

The two purposes of the cognitive-behavioural model are connected. Understanding the phenomenology of the disorder allows for treatment interventions, and treatment interventions based on the model can help inform our understanding of the disorder. This is the case in a general way but the same principle applies within therapy. Presenting a patient with a model that makes sense of the development or maintenance of their disorder is important in engaging the patients (particularly those with anorexia nervosa) and in providing a cognitive-behavioural formulation of the problem to guide a specific treatment intervention (see Persons, 1989).

GENERAL PRINCIPLES OF COGNITIVE-BEHAVIOURAL MODELS

As their name suggests, cognitive-behavioural models combine two approaches. First, models incorporating behavioural theories and therapies which were proposed by Watson early in the twentieth century (Watson, 1925). Behavioural theories and therapies were based on the principles of learning and were effective in the treatment of anxiety disorders (Wolpe, 1958). The majority of existing therapies for obesity are behavioural (e.g. Wing, 1998; Wadden et al., 1998). Dissatisfaction due to the lack of advancement in theorising about behaviour therapy and the lack of success in dealing with depression led to the development of cognitive theories and therapy in the 1970s (see Rachman, 1997).

Second, models incorporate cognitive theories, such as those of Beck (Beck, 1976, 1985), that propose that one's emotions are influenced by one's thoughts, and that emotional disorders result from particular interpretation of events. For example, if clothes feel tight and this is interpreted as 'I'm fat' then such an interpretation is likely to result in low mood and body dissatisfaction; if the person interprets the tightness of the clothes as 'these have been shrunk by the drycleaners', then the resulting emotion may be anger. Cognitive therapy uses the cognitive model to identify and correct cognitive distortions and deficiencies by encouraging the patient to use rules of evidence and logic, and to consider alternative explanations (Beck, 1976). For example, a patient with an eating disorder who thinks 'I'm fat' can be encouraged to distinguish between the thought 'I think I am fat', the feeling 'I feel fat' and the real situation 'I am significantly overweight' (Fairburn, Marcus & Wilson, 1993).

Pure behavioural or pure cognitive models are rarely postulated nowadays as providing explanatory accounts of complex behaviours. What are commonly found instead are cognitive-behavioural models, where cognitive and behavioural concepts are integrated and used as major elements. There have been detailed theoretical discussion of these issues (e.g. Brewin, 1988; Williams et al., 1988; Wolpe, 1993). Similarly in treatment, cognitive and behavioural techniques are interwoven, most notably in the form of behavioural experiments that the patient uses to gather evidence to examine the validity of the patient's thoughts or assumptions (Beck, 1995). For example, the negative automatic thought, 'If I eat an extra biscuit a day for the next week, I will gain at least three kilograms' can be tested behaviourally by determining the amount of weight gain (if any) that results from eating the extra biscuit for a week.

SPECIFIC VS GENERAL COGNITIVE-BEHAVIOURAL MODELS

Beck's cognitive model of emotional disorders (Beck, 1979) was originally postulated to account for depression. It also provides a general framework for understanding the development and maintenance of emotional disorders. Beck proposes that different types of thinking (termed 'negative automatic thoughts', 'dysfunctional assumptions' and 'core beliefs') are characterised by cognitive distortions such as 'all-or-nothing thinking' (e.g. 'I'm either fat or I'm thin') or 'discounting positive information' (e.g. 'She's only saying I look nice because she feels sorry for me') (see Beck, 1995).

Some of the cognitive-behavioural models described below (e.g. Garner & Bemis, 1982, 1985; Wolff & Serpell, 1998) stick closely to Beck's framework and make particular use of Beck's general cognitive-behavioural techniques. Other models take the principle that cognitive-behavioural processes maintain the disorder but are specific to the disorder. For example, the leading model of bulimia nervosa (Fairburn, 1997) proposes that the central cognitive maintaining process is the judging of self-worth largely, or even exclusively, in terms of shape or weight. In this type of approach, the particular cognitive-behavioural model of maintenance indicates a specific cognitive-behavioural intervention. Given that the most successful psychological treatment interventions have derived from specific models of the maintenance of the disorder (e.g. panic disorder, Clark, 1986; bulimia nervosa, Fairburn, 1985), it is our view that specific models of maintenance are likely to generate more treatment advances than the generic models.

ANOREXIA NERVOSA

Models of Development

For the reasons stated above, it is important to separate models of the development and maintenance of disorders, although the two overlap. Cognitive-behavioural (and other) models of the development of anorexia nervosa are usually multifactorial in nature (see Garner & Garfinkel, 1997). The origins of the disorder are likely to be related to numerous predisposing and precipitating factors including individual variables such as perfectionism (Dally & Gomez, 1979; Fairburn et al., 1999; Lilenfeld, 1998), environmental factors, and genetic factors (see Lilenfeld & Kaye, 1998). Issues such as adolescent conflict, family problems, a negative comment about shape and weight, the sense of failure and loss of control can all serve as precipitating factors (Beumont, George & Smart, 1976; Garfinkel & Garner, 1983; Gilbert, 1986).

Models of Maintenance

Behavioural Models

The earliest behavioural theories suggested that the 'impairment of food intake in anorexia nervosa can be viewed as a specific learned behavior, perpetuated by environmental reinforcements' (Blinder, Freeman & Stunkard, 1970, p. 1093). The individual engages in excessive dieting. The resultant weight loss may be positively reinforced (at least initially) by the reactions of peer groups and negatively reinforced by the absence of being overweight (which can be met with disapproval and even peer rejection). This over-simplistic model leaves many questions unanswered. Some suggest that general societal pressure are too remote to act as an immediate reinforcer for dietary restriction; other positive reinforcers that have been suggested are attention (Allyon, Haughton & Osmond, 1964), stimuli in the environment (Bachrach, Erwin & Mohr, 1965), an empty stomach (Gilbert, 1986) or an endogeneously produced substance (Szmukler & Tantam, 1984). Avoiding anxiety associated with eating and weight gain has also been suggested to negatively reinforce dietary restriction (Leitenberg, Agras & Thomson, 1968).

Slade's Functional Analysis

In one of the most fully developed accounts of the origins and maintenance of anorexia nervosa, Slade (1982) proposes that general dissatisfaction with life and oneself arises from a combination of interpersonal problems and conflicts of adolescence. Such dissatisfaction is proposed to interact with perfectionism to give rise to a need to control and achieve success in some aspect of life. If dieting is triggered, for example by the critical comments of a peer, this need for control and achievement becomes focused on the dieting behaviour. The dieting is reinforced positively by feelings of success and satisfaction, and is negatively reinforced through the fear of weight gain and avoidance of stressors, which preceded the onset of the disorder. These reinforcers intensify the dieting behaviour and weight spirals downwards. Together with the endocrine disturbance, which may be a direct effect of stress or indirect effect caused through weight loss, this eventually leads to anorexia nervosa.

Vitousek's Approach[1]

Hilde Bruch (1973, 1982) was critical of the purely behavioural approach and, despite being a psychoanalyst in orientation, she stressed the importance of these patients' thinking style (Bruch, 1973) and the person's idiosyncratic interpretation of the meaning of events. Bruch's ideas were subsequently refined and extended by Garner and Bemis in two key articles (Garner & Bemis, 1982, 1985) in which they applied to anorexia nervosa the principles of Beck's cognitive theory and therapy of depression (Beck, 1979). Their cognitive-behavioural view has since been elaborated by Vitousek and colleagues in a series of articles that have focused on the role of self-esteem (Garner & Bemis, 1985), information processing (Vitousek & Hollon, 1990), self-representation (Vitousek & Ewald, 1993), personality variables (Vitousek & Manke, 1994) and motivation respectively (Vitousek, Watson & Wilson, 1999). This is the leading cognitive-behavioural account and it 'holds that anorexic and bulimic symptoms are maintained by a characteristic set of beliefs about weight and shape' (Vitousek & Orimoto, 1993, p. 193). They propose that the core cognitive disturbance can be understood in terms of 'schema' (organised cognitive structures) that unite the views of the self and the culturally derived beliefs about the virtue of thinness for female appearance (Vitousek, 1996; Vitousek & Hollon, 1990; Vitousek & Manke, 1994). Such schema give rise to the belief that the solution to a view of the self as unworthy, imperfect and overwhelmed is thinness and weight loss, which are therefore pursued relentlessly.

According to this account, anorexic beliefs and behaviour are reinforced in four main ways. First, they are positively reinforced by feelings of success, achievement, moral superiority and control that result from successful dietary restriction. Second, they are negatively reinforced by the avoidance of being fat. Over time, the margin of safety needed to avoid 'fatness' increases, which is proposed to explain the need for an ever-decreasing target weight. Third, self-worth is defined in terms of shape and weight which gives rise to a series of cognitive processing biases that maintain the anorexic beliefs and behaviour. Finally, the effects of starvation contribute in various ways to the maintenance of the disorder, for example, by increasing concrete thinking. Additional reinforcements include social reinforcement for being slim, concern and attention from family members as weight loss increases and the development of an anorexic identity in which the individual becomes increasingly isolated so that her dysfunctional thinking and behaviour comprise the essence of her personality.

Other Cognitive-Behavioural Models emphasising Weight and Shape

Other cognitive-behavioural perspectives have emerged (see Cooper, 1997, for a review) including that of Kleifield and colleagues (Kleifield, 1996), Williamson et al. (1990) and the Maudsley unit (Wolff & Serpell, 1998). These models differ slightly but have the same focus on the central anorexic premise of the importance of weight and shape. For example, typical

---

[1] Also known as Bemis's approach.

anorexic assumptions are described as 'If I'm thin, I'm special, if I'm fat, I'm worthless' (Wolff & Serpell, 1998, p. 406). Other examples of cognitive distortions are:

- Selective abstraction (selecting out small parts of a situation while ignoring other evidence, and coming to conclusions on that basis), e.g. 'Other people will like me more if I am thin.'
- Dichotomous reasoning (thinking in terms of extremes and absolutes), e.g. 'If I am not thin, then I am fat.'
- Overgeneralisation (deriving a rule from one event and applying it to other situations or events), e.g. 'I was unhappy when I was at normal weight. So I know that putting on weight is going to make me unhappy.'
- Magnification (exaggerating the significance of events), e.g. 'Gaining two pounds has made me unattractive.'
- Superstitious thinking (assuming causal relationships between unrelated things), e.g. 'If I eat this, it will be converted into fat on my stomach immediately.'

The account by the Maudsley group incorporates advances in the role of cognitive theory. The result is a model that includes metacognitions ('thoughts about thoughts'), safety behaviours (behaviours designed to protect the individual from 'threat' but that actually serve to magnify the perception of threat (Salkovskis, 1996)) and the Interacting Cognitive Subsystems model (Teasdale, 1993) in which weight/shape are linked with self-esteem (Wolff & Serpell, 1998). In this account, particular emphasis is placed on the patients' 'pro-anorexia' (p. 411) beliefs about the disorder as a factor in its maintenance, e.g. 'if I didn't have anorexia, my whole world would fall apart, I wouldn't be able to cope' (p. 412).

Guidano and Liotti (1983)

The cognitive-behavioural model of Guidano and Liotti (1983) proposed that the central feature of anorexia nervosa was a deficit in cognitive structures relating to personal identity rather than weight and shape. They suggested that the personal identity in anorexia nervosa comprises beliefs of ineffectiveness, failure, and the futility of disclosing personal views or emotions. The difficulties with personal identity are suggested to arise from a failure to develop autonomy in childhood and lack of individuality during development. Such patients are suggested to use dieting and weight loss as inappropriate means of coping with the difficulties in personal identity.

Fairburn, Shafran and Cooper (1999)

The model of Fairburn, Shafran and Cooper (1999) proposes that the core psychopathology of anorexia nervosa is a need for self-control that becomes focused on controlling eating, shape and weight. This model suggests that dietary restriction is maintained in three ways. First, dietary restriction is maintained by positive reinforcement from a temporary increase in feelings of self-control and self-worth. Dietary restriction is suggested to become an index of self-control and self-worth. Second, the physiological sequalae of starvation are suggested to be interpreted as a threat to perceived control over eating, or a failure of control over eating. For example, feeling full after eating only a small amount (heightened satiety) is hypothesised to lead to the interpretation 'I've eaten too much' i.e., a perceived failure of control over-eating. As a consequence, dietary restriction may result. These two mechanisms are culturally independent.

The third mechanism suggested to maintain dietary restriction in patients with restricting anorexia nervosa proposes that controlling one's shape and weight is used as an index of self-control in general in western cultures. This third mechanism concerns the over-importance of shape and weight, and addresses behaviours such as frequent weighing and checking of one's body shape. It is hypothesised that frequent weighing or checking of one's body shape results in a perceived failure of control over eating, shape and weight as any perceived imperfections are likely to be magnified by such frequent body checking or weighing. Active avoidance of body checking or weighing is suggested to maintain the perception of a failure of control over eating, shape and weight as the person has no means by which to disconfirm her view that she is 'too large'. This model is currently being evaluated but has been somewhat superseded by a 'transdiagnostic' cognitive-behavioural model which attempts to account for eating disorder psychopathology across all the eating disorders, i.e. anorexia nervosa, bulimia nervosa and atypical eating disorders (Fairburn, Cooper & Shafran, in press).

Evaluation of Models

Some of the above models generate testable hypotheses and predictions that are open to empirical investigation (see Vitousek & Hollon, 1990), while others are less amenable to such evaluation. Empirical data evaluating the models has been considered in terms of self-report questionnaire data, experimental data and data on treatment outcome.

Self-Report and Interview Data

While self-report may be particularly vulnerable to bias and distortion in this population (Vitousek, Daly & Heiser, 1991), an abundance of studies have shown that patients with anorexia nervosa have a distinct set of cognitions regarding eating, shape and weight (e.g. Clark, Feldman & Channon, 1989; Cooper, Todd & Cohen-Tovee, 1996; Cooper & Turner, 2000; Mizes, 1992). Such studies provide support for the prediction deriving from the cognitive-behavioural models that patients with anorexia nervosa have 'negative automatic thoughts', 'underlying assumptions' and 'core beliefs' related to eating, shape and weight (see Vitousek, 1996, and Cooper, 1997, for reviews). However, since such cognitions are consistent with all the cognitive-behavioural models, the studies cannot provide particular support for any one model.

Experimental Data

Information-processing tasks have been used to test predictions deriving mainly from Vitousek's cognitive-behavioural account (e.g. Vitousek & Hollon, 1990). Cognitive-behavioural theories predict that attention will be biased towards stimuli related to body fatness and to fattening food since these stimuli are threatening to people with eating disorders (Williamson et al., 1999). Studies of attention have been conducted using the Stroop colour-naming task (Stroop, 1935) and patients with anorexia nervosa are slower to colour-name words relevant to their concerns than normal controls (e.g. Ben-Tovim et al.,

1989; Channon, Hemsley & de Silva, 1988; Cooper & Fairburn, 1992a; Green, McKenna & de Silva, 1994; Long, Hinton & Gillespie, 1994). (For reviews, see Vitousek, 1996, and Williamson, Mathews & McLeod, 1996.) Data from these Stroop experiments are difficult to interpret; they may be assessing state-like salient concerns instead of stable attentional biases and they do not provide definitive evidence of biases in attention (Vitousek, 1996). Nevertheless, they are at least consistent with the cognitive-behavioural theories described above. There have been no studies with patients with anorexia nervosa using the dichotic listening task or lexical decision tasks although such studies have been done in people with bulimia nervosa (Schotte, McNally & Turner, 1990; see later) and women with body dysphoria (Fuller, Williamson & Anderon, 1995).

Cognitive-behavioural theories suggest that personally salient information concerning shape and weight will be more readily encoded and recalled than neutral stimuli. People with 'body dysphoria' have been shown to recall more body-related words and difficulty recalling thinness words than those low in 'body dysphoria' (Baker, Williamson & Sylve, 1995; Watkins et al., 1995). A memory bias for words concerning 'fatness' was found in a mixed group of patients with eating disorders (Sebastian, Williamson & Blouin, 1996) and an explicit memory bias for anorexia-nervosa related words was recently demonstrated in a small sample of patients with anorexia nervosa compared to non-dieting controls (Herman et al., 1998). This finding could not be attributed to the valence of the words.

In summary, such experimental data have provided support for the leading cognitive-behavioural model of anorexia nervosa (Garner & Bemis, 1985; Vitousek & Hollon, 1990). However, as with the case of the questionnaire studies, the experimental data do not provide particular support for any one specific model as opposed to another.

Treatment Outcome Data

It is worth noting that an effective cognitive-behavioural treatment that is derived from a cognitive-behavioural model does not 'prove' that the model is correct since the treatment could be effective for a number of other, non-specific reasons. Such data can only be taken as being consistent with the cognitive-behavioural model and providing indirect support for it. It is, however, possible to conclude that the maintenance model is incorrect if the therapy reverses the proposed maintaining mechanisms yet the disorder persists.

Based on the early behavioural accounts, operant paradigms were implemented consisting of (a) isolating patients from reinforcers and (b) providing the reinforcers in response to specified criteria such as weight gain or calorie intake. At least 60 publications describing operant techniques for anorexia nervosa were published in the 1960s and 1970s and the literature has been thoroughly reviewed elsewhere (Halmi, 1985). Reviews indicate the effectiveness of operant conditioning in the short-term but the technique has questionable utility for long-term improvement (see Bemis, 1982). More recently, behaviour therapy plus education has been shown to be successful in a recent controlled study (Treasure et al., 1995), indicating the promise of this type of therapy.

Cognitive-behavioural therapy, however, is considered to be indicated for AN in adults by 90% of clinicians (Herzog et al., 1992). As with the cognitive-behavioural models, the leading account of the cognitive-behavioural treatment of anorexia nervosa is that proposed by Garner and Bemis (1982, 1985). To date, the descriptions of this treatment have tended to be schematic rather than detailed, although two recent publications have provided rather more information (Pike, Loeb & Vitousek, 1996; Garner, Vitousek & Pike, 1997).

There have been three controlled studies of a cognitive behavioural treatment (Channon et al., 1989; Halmi et al., 2000; Pike, 2000) for anorexia nervosa but all have methodological limitations. In the first study (Channon et al., 1989), no group could be considered clinically recovered by the end of the study period and it is unclear whether the treatment did derive directly from the cognitive-behavioural theory of Garner and Bemis (1982). In the second study (Halmi et al., 2000), the drop-out rate from all conditions was extremely high, which makes the results difficult to interpret. In the third study, the best to date, CBT was compared to nutritional counselling and found to be more effective (Pike, 2000). However, this sample of patients were weight-restored patients with 'anorexia nervosa'. The effectiveness of this intervention in a sample of underweight patients with anorexia nervosa is unknown.

In summary, the treatment outcome data neither support nor refute any of the proposed cognitive-behavioural models. At present, there is no generally accepted treatment and anorexia nervosa 'is one of the most frustrating and recalcitrant forms of psychopathology' (Vitousek, Watson & Wilson, 1998).

BULIMIA NERVOSA

Behavioural Models

As was the case in anorexia nervosa, purely behavioural models were developed first to account for the maintenance of the disorder. One of the earliest behavioural accounts proposed that purging was positively reinforced because it reduces anxiety associated with binge eating (Rosen & Leitenberg, 1982). This purely behavioural model can, at best, account for only part of the maintenance of bulimia nervosa and does not address psychosocial and cognitive factors. Furthermore, the theoretical model on which it is based (the two-stage fear-reduction model of Mowrer, 1960) has been shown to be an inadequate explanation for a range of disorders (see Rachman, 1984, for a critique of this model).

Fairburn's Cognitive-Behavioural Model

At the same time as the behavioural model was proposed, Fairburn (1981) described a cognitive-behavioural model of bulimia nervosa. This cognitive-behavioural model attempts to explain the core cognitive and behavioural components of the disorder, in particular low self-esteem, overconcern with shape and weight, rigid dietary restriction, binge eating and purging. Although the importance of affect in binge eating has been noted since the earliest accounts (e.g. Fairburn, Cooper & Cooper, 1986), more recently the model has been extended to specify the importance of the role of affect in binge eating and the influence of perfectionism and dichotomous (all-or-nothing) thinking (Fairburn, 1997). The cognitive-behavioural model is shown in Figure 3.1.

In essence, this model proposes that the core cognitive disturbance in bulimia is the tendency to judge the self largely, or even exclusively, in terms of shape and weight. These extreme concerns about shape and weight lead to characteristic extreme and rigid dieting. Such dieting is characterised by rigid rules (e.g. 'I must eat less than 1000 calories'; 'I must not eat any chocolate') which render the dietary restriction brittle and vulnerable to being disrupted. The disruption occurs when dietary rules are violated, for example the person may eat a piece of chocolate. Such rigid dietary rules are particularly vulnerable to violation in

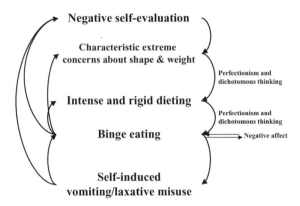

Figure 3.1   Cognitive-Behavioural Model of the Maintenance of Bulimia Nervosa (Fairburn, 1997). Reprinted by permission of Oxford University Press.

the context of an adverse mood state. Since patients have perfectionistic standards (Fairburn et al., 1999) and dichotomous thinking, the violation of the rule is suggested to be interpreted by patients in an all-or-nothing manner so the person may well think 'I've blown it now—if I have had one piece of chocolate I've failed so I may as well eat all of it'.

In this model, such dichotomous thinking, along with the physiological and psychological effects of dietary restraint, is suggested to lead to episodes of objective over-eating accompanied by a sense of loss of control (i.e. an episode of binge eating). Such binge eating tends to moderate negative affect in the short term but also activates and reinforces concerns about shape and weight, and the person attempts to ameliorate the impact of episode of binge eating by purging, commonly by inducing vomiting. Vomiting, in turn, is suggested to reinforce binge eating and, in particular, the size of the binge. This is for two reasons: first, people learn that it is easier to vomit if they have eaten a large amount; second, people discount calories consumed in a binge if they believe that they are 'getting rid' of them by purging.

Wilson (1989) has proposed a similar account and this account includes fear and social factors. A broader model which includes other psychopathological mood states (e.g. depression), distorted body image and cognitive biases has been proposed by Williamson and colleagues (1985, 1990, 1999). A model in which binge eating is suggested to function as an 'escape from awareness' has been proposed (Heatherton & Baumeister, 1991; Waller et al., 1995). This model has been developed further by Waller and colleagues who propose a 'multilevel model of processing where abandonment issues play an early role in the activation of food schemata . . . and hence inducing bulimic behavior as a means of reducing awareness of such cognitions' (Meyer & Waller, 2000, p. 333). Yet another model suggests that there are two pathways to bulimia nervosa, the first concerning dietary restraint and the second relating to affect regulation (Stice, Nemeroff & Shaw, 1996; Stice, Shaw & Nemeroff, 1998; Stice et al., 1996).

Evaluation

Self-Report Questionnaires, Interview and Experimental Data

As with anorexia nervosa, it has been demonstrated that patients with bulimia nervosa have a distinct set of cognitions regarding eating, shape and weight (e.g. Cooper & Fairburn,

1992b; Mizes, 1992; Phelan, 1987) and interview studies also support the importance of the core cognitive disturbance in bulimia nervosa as the over-importance of shape and weight in the judgement of self-worth (Goldfein, Walsh & Midlarsky, 2000). Information-processing studies using a dichotic listening task (Schotte, McNally & Turner, 1990), location of attention (Newman et al., 1993) and, most commonly, the Stroop colour-naming task support the model (see Vitousek, 1996, for a review) although it has correctly been stated that the theoretical implications of the Stroop task are difficult to determine. Other information-processing studies, most notably those conducted by Glenn Waller and colleagues (e.g. McManus, Waller & Chadwick, 1996; Meyer & Waller, 1999; Waller, Quinton & Watson, 1995), provide support for other cognitive-behavioural models that place central emphasis on the role of emotional factors in binge eating rather than shape and weight concerns.

Studies on counter-regulation have also been used to investigate the cognitive-behavioural model and the hypothesis that over-eating is likely to occur in the context of restraint and negative affect. Although such studies are usually conducted on 'restrained eaters' rather than patients with bulimia nervosa, they provide general support for the cognitive-behavioural model (see Polivy & Herman, 2002). A recent review on such laboratory studies supports their use as a means of testing theories of eating disorders (Mitchell et al., 1998). The dual-pathway model has also received empirical support from both cross-sectional and longitudinal studies (e.g., Stice, 2001; Stice & Agras, 1999; Shepherd & Ricciardelli, 1998). Cross-sectional and longitudinal studies have also been used to evaluate Fairburn's (1997) model of bulimia nervosa. In the cross-sectional study using structural equation modelling, many of the main predictions of the theory were supported although the findings regarding binge eating and purging are hard to interpret owing to the methods of assessment (Byrne & McLean, 2002). A well-controlled five-year longitudinal prospective study of the natural course of bulimia also supports the model since it was found that the baseline level of over-evaluation of shape and weight predicted persistence of binge eating over 15 months, and this relationship was partially mediated by dietary restraint (Fairburn et al., in press).

Treatment Outcome Data

The strongest evidence in support of the cognitive account comes from studies of the cognitive-behavioural treatment of the disorder. Indirect support for the account is provided by over 25 randomised-controlled trials (Wilson & Fairburn, 2002). Overall, such trials have demonstrated that cognitive-behavioural therapy for bulimia nervosa based on the above account is a lasting and effective treatment for approximately 40% of cases, and it is superior to comparison treatments that control for non-specific effects (see Wilson & Fairburn, 2002). More direct support is provided from treatment studies that have 'dismantled' the cognitive-behavioural treatment (e.g. by comparing it to behavioural treatment) which have demonstrated that the absence of cognitive procedures greatly influences long-term outcome (Fairburn et al., 1995). Most directly, among patients who have responded to treatment, the residual level of attitudinal disturbance has been shown to predict subsequent outcome (Fairburn et al., 1993). Additional support comes from a study of mediators of response to CBT which found that the treatment's effect on binge eating was mediated by a decrease in dietary restraint (Wilson et al., 2002). It is worth noting that interpersonal psychotherapy has been found in two large studies to be as effective as cognitive-behavioural therapy but takes longer to produce change (Fairburn et al., 1995; Agras et al., 2000).

OBESITY

Behavioural Models

Behavioural treatments of obesity have dominated the field since the 1960s (Ferster, Nurnberger & Levitt, 1962; Stuart, 1967). In essence, behavioural models propose that obesity results from (1) maladaptive eating habits that lead to over-eating that is reinforced, and (2) the absence of exercise which is also reinforced according to the principles of learning theory (Wilson, 1993; Bray, Bouchard & James, 1998). As would be expected, the behavioural treatment deriving from the behavioural models is a set of principles and techniques to help overweight individuals modify inappropriate eating and activity habits (Wadden & Foster, 2000).

Cognitive-Behavioural Models

The limitations of behavioural models have been noted elsewhere (Wooley, Wooley & Dyrenforth, 1979). Criticisms include the assumption of distinctive eating patterns in people with obesity and the failure to incorporate information about the biology of weight regulation. The poor long-term outcome of patients with obesity has also been noted (see Brownell & Fairburn, 2002; Stunkard & Penick, 1979).

With the advent of cognitive theory, an alternative model was proposed in the form of a 'food dependency model' (Goodrick & Foreyt, 1991), which focused on cognitions and emotions related to obesity and to social support (see Wilson, 1993). The need for a combined cognitive-behavioural approach to the understanding and treatment of obesity was highlighted by Wilson (1996) who argued for recognition of combining behavioural treatment with cognitive change, particularly the value of accepting whatever shape and weight changes result from the treatment. However, until recently, cognitive-behavioural treatments of obesity primarily comprised adding cognitive components such as negative thinking or help in decision making to behavioural treatments (Sbrocco et al., 1999). A recent review (Foreyt & Poston, 1998) indicated that most forms of CBT for obesity included five strategies. These were (1) self-monitoring and goal setting, (2) stimulus control for the modification of eating style and activity, (3) cognitive restructuring techniques that focus modifying dysfunctional thinking, (4) stress management, and (5) social support.

Recently, however, a new approach has been taken to cognitive-behavioural accounts of obesity. Recognising that the problem is not one of initial weight loss but rather of the poor long-term outcome of behavioural treatment for obesity (Kramer et al., 1989; Safer, 1991; Wadden et al., 1989), a new approach focuses on factors that account for weight regain after successfully losing weight (Cooper & Fairburn, 2001; in press). According to this new cognitive-behavioural approach, patients with obesity who lose weight fail to maintain their gains for two reasons. First, they do not achieve their weight loss goals, nor the anticipated benefits of achieving them. For example, the patient may anticipate feeling 'more confident' after losing 10 kg but either loses only 5 kg or does not feel any differently about his or her confidence. As a consequence, efforts to lose weight are abandoned (Cooper & Fairburn, 2001). A second, interrelated reason, for failing to maintain weight loss is that when the patient does not achieve his or her goal or its anticipated benefits, the patient neglects the need to acquire skills to maintain the new, lower weight but instead resumes previous eating and exercise habits, and therefore regains the lost weight (Cooper & Fairburn, 2001).

The new cognitive-behavioural therapy based on this theory is delivered on an individual basis and addresses weight loss, the maintenance of weight *lost*, body image, weight goals and, originally, 'primary goals' (Cooper & Fairburn, in press). These 'primary goals' are defined as the objectives which patients hope to achieve as a result of weight loss and include improving self-confidence, increasing one's social life, etc. Equally distinct and original is the emphasis given to the long-term maintenance of weight rather than continuing and indefinite weight loss (Cooper & Fairburn, in press).

Evaluation

Treatment Outcome Studies

The majority of evidence that addresses the cognitive-behavioural models of obesity relate to treatment outcome data which, as previously stated, can only provide indirect support for a theory. Behavioural treatment—with or without the cognitive component—typically incorporates a 1200 kcal/day diet and results in a weight loss of approximately 10% of initial body weight (Wing, 1998; Wadden & Foster, 2000). Therapy is usually conducted in groups in the format of 'lessons' that address self-monitoring of eating, setting of behavioural goals regarding eating and exercise, education about nutrition, problem solving, challenging of cognitions and relapse prevention. Unfortunately, the weight is regained by the majority of patients within the subsequent three years (e.g. Kramer et al., 1989; Safer, 1991; Wadden et al., 1989).

It was these data which led to the development of Cooper and Fairburn's (2001, in press) new cognitive-behavioural treatment of obesity. This treatment is currently being evaluated in a randomised-controlled treatment trial and the format of treatment is deliberately different from existing group interventions for obesity.

In summary, the treatment outcome data are consistent with cognitive-behavioural models of obesity but the long-term outcome of cognitive-behavioural therapy of obesity is poor. It is hoped that a new form of cognitive-behavioural therapy focusing on weight regain will improve treatment outcome as well as testing a new cognitive-behavioural conceptualisation of weight gain following treatment for obesity.

SUMMARY AND CONCLUSIONS

At the beginning of this chapter it was argued that cognitive-behavioural models had two purposes. First, to provide a means of understanding the development or maintenance of the most important cognitive and behavioural aspects of the phenomenology of the disorder and, second, to improve treatments of the disorder. The cognitive-behavioural models of anorexia nervosa have provided a way of understanding the phenomenology of this problem, although they have not yet been demonstrated to lead to any major breakthroughs in the treatment of this disorder and there is little evidence to favour one model over another. On the other hand, the leading cognitive-behavioural model of bulimia nervosa (Fairburn, 1997) has led to the development of a relatively effective treatment for the disorder. It is argued that further theoretical developments are now needed to improve therapies for those patients who do not improve with the existing treatment. Such a development has recently been proposed in the form of a 'transdiagnostic' cognitive behavioural theory and treatment for all forms of clinical eating disorder (Fairburn et al., in press). Finally, the cognitive-behavioural mechanisms in the maintenance of obesity are ill-understood and, at present, the long-term outcome of cognitive-behavioural therapy for this disorder is poor. It is hoped that the new theoretical developments, particularly the focus on mechanisms contributing to weight regain after successful weight loss (Cooper & Fairburn, in press), will improve our understanding of these mechanisms and, consequently, the treatment of obesity.

ACKNOWLEDGEMENTS

RS is supported by a Wellcome Trust Research Career Development Fellowship (063209).

REFERENCES

Agras, W.S., Walsh, T., Fairburn, C.G., Wilson, G.T. & Kraemer, H.C. (2000) A multicenter comparison of cognitive-behavioral therapy and interpersonal psychotherapy for bulimia nervosa. *Archives of General Psychiatry*, **57**, 459–466.
Allyon, T., Haughton, E. & Osmond, H.P. (1964) Chronic anorexia: A behaviour problem. *Canadian Psychiatric Association Journal*, **9**, 147–157.
APA (1994) *Diagnostic and Statistical Manual of Mental Disorders* (4th edition). Washington, D.C.: American Psychiatric Association.
Bachrach, A.J., Erwin, W.J. & Mohr, J.P. (1965) The control of eating behavior in an anorexic by operant conditioning techniques. In L.P. Ullman & L. Krasner (Eds), *Case Studies in Behavior Modification*. New York: Holt, Rinehart & Winston.
Baker, J.D., Williamson, D.A. & Sylve, C. (1995) Body image disturbance, memory bias and body-dysphoria: Effects of negative mood induction. *Behavior Therapy*, **26**, 747–759.
Beck, A.T. (1976) *Cognitive Therapy and the Emotional Disorders*. New York: International Universities Press.
Beck, J.S. (1995). *Cognitive Therapy: Basics and Beyond*. New York: Guilford Press.
Ben-Tovim, D.I., Walker, M.K., Fok, D. & Yap, E. (1989) An adaptation of the Stroop test for measuring shape and food concerns in eating disorders. A quantitative measure of psychopathology? *International Journal of Eating Disorders*, **6**, 681–687.
Beumont, P.J.V., George, G.C.W. & Smart, D.E. (1976) 'Dieters' and 'vomiters and purgers' in anorexia nervosa. *Psychological Medicine*, **6**, 617–622.
Blinder, B.J., Freeman, D.M. & Stunkard, A.J. (1970) Behavior therapy of anorexia nervosa: Effectiveness of activity as a reinforcer of weight gain. *American Journal of Psychiatry*, **126**, 1093–1098.
Braun, D.L., Sunday, S.R. & Halmi, K.A. (1994) Psychiatric comorbidity in patients with eating disorders. *Psychological Medicine*, **24**, 859–867.
Bray, G.A., Bouchard, C. & James, W.P.T. (1998) *Handbook of Obesity*. New York: Marcel Dekker.
Brewin, C. (1988) *Cognitive Foundations of Clinical Psychology*. Hove, UK: Lawrence Erlbaum.
Bruch, H. (1973) *Eating Disorders*. New York: Basic Books.
Bruch, H. (1982) Anorexia nervosa: Therapy and theory. *American Journal of Psychiatry*, **139**, 1531–1538.
Bulik, C.M., Sullivan, P.F., Joyce, P.R. & Carter, F.A. (1995) Tempereament, character and personality disorder in bulimia nervosa. *Journal of Nervous and Mental Diseases*, **183**, 593–598.
Byrne, S.M. & McLean, N.J. (2002) The cognitive-behavioural model of bulimia nervosa: a direct evaluation. *International Journal of Eating Disorders*, **31**, 17–31.
Channon, S., de Silva, P., Hemsley, D. & Perkins, R. (1989) A controlled trial of cognitive-behavioural and behaviour treatment of anorexia nervosa. *Behaviour Research and Therapy*, **27**, 529–535.
Channon, S., Hemsley, D. & de Silva, P. (1988) Selective processing of food words in anorexia nervosa. *British Journal of Clinical Psychology*, **27**, 259–260.
Clark, D.A., Feldman, J. & Channon, S. (1989) Dysfunctional thinking in anorexia and bulimia nervosa. *Cognitive Therapy and Research*, **13**, 377–387

Clark, D.M. (1986) A cognitive approach to panic. *Behaviour Research and Therapy*, **24**, 461–470.

Clark, D.M. (1997) Panic disorder and social phobia. In D.M. Clark & C.G. Fairburn (Eds), *Science and Practice of Cognitive Behaviour Therapy*. Oxford Medical Publications. Oxford: Oxford University Press.

Cooper, M.J. (1997) Cognitive theory in anorexia nervosa and bulimia nervosa: A review. *Behavioural and Cognitive Psychotherapy*, **25**, 113–145.

Cooper, M., Cohen-Tovee, E., Todd, G., Wells, A. & Tovee, M. (1997) The eating disorder belief questionnaire: Preliminary development. *Behaviour Research and Therapy*, **35**, 381–388.

Cooper, M. & Fairburn, C.G. (1992a) Selective processing of eating, weight and shape related words in patients with eating disorders and dieters. *British Journal of Clinical Psychology*, **31**, 363–365.

Cooper, M. & Fairburn, C.G. (1992b) Thoughts about eating, weight and shape in anorexia nervosa and bulimia nervosa. *Behaviour Research and Therapy*, **30**, 501–511.

Cooper, M. & Turner, H. (2000) Underlying assumptions and core beliefs in anorexia nervosa and dieting. *British Journal of Clinical Psychology*, **39**, 215–218

Cooper, Z., & Fairburn, C.G. (2001) A new cognitive behavioural approach to the treatment of obesity. *Behaviour Research and Therapy*, **39**, 499–511.

Cooper, Z. & Fairburn, C.G. (in press) Cognitive behaviour therapy for obesity. In T.A. Wadden & A.J. Stunkard (Eds), *Obesity: Theory and Therapy*. New York: Guilford Press.

Dally, P. & Gomez, J. (1979) *Anorexia Nervosa*. London: Heinemann.

Fairburn, C.G. (1981) A cognitive-behavioural approach to the management of bulimia. *Psychological Medicine*, **11**, 697–706.

Fairburn, C.G. (1985) A cognitive-behavioural treatment of bulimia. In D.M. Garner & P.E. Garfinkel (Eds), *Handbook of Psychotherapy for Anorexia Nervosa and Bulimia*. New York: Guilford Press.

Fairburn, C.G. (1995) Short-Term psychological treatments for bulimia nervosa. In K. Brownell & C.G. Fairburn (Eds), *Eating Disorders and Obesity: A Comprehensive Handbook* (pp. 289–378). New York: Guilford Press.

Fairburn, C.G. (1997) Eating disorders. In D.M. Clark & C.G. Fairburn (Eds), *Science and Practice of Cognitive Behaviour Therapy*. Oxford Medical Publications. Oxford: Oxford University Press.

Fairburn, C.G. & Brownell, K.D. (Eds) (2002) *Eating Disorders and Obesity: A Comprehensive Handbook* (2nd edn). New York: Guilford Press.

Fairburn, C.G., Cooper, Z., Doll, H.A. & Welch, S.L. (1999) Risk factors for anorexia nervosa: Three integrated case control comparisons. *Archives of General Psychiatry*, **56**, 468–476.

Fairburn, C.G., Cooper, Z. & Shafran, R. (in press) Cognitive-behaviour therapy for eating disorders: a 'transdiagnostic' theory and treatment. *Behaviour Research and Therapy*.

Fairburn, C.G., Marcus, M.D. & Wilson, G.T. (1993) Cognitive-behavioral therapy for binge eating and bulimia nervosa: A comprehensive treatment manual. In C.G. Fairburn, G. Christopher & G.T. Wilson (Eds), *Binge Eating: Nature, Assessment, and Treatment*. New York: Guilford Press.

Fairburn, C.G., Norman, P.A., Welch, S.L., O'Connor, M.E., Doll, H.A. & Peveler, R.C. (1995) A prospective study of outcome in bulimia nervosa and the long-term effects of three psychological treatments. *Archives of General Psychiatry*, **52**, 304–312.

Fairburn, C.G., Peveler, R.C., Jones, R., Hope, R. A. & Doll, H.A. (1993) Predictors of 23-month outcome in bulimia nervosa and the influence of attitudes to shape and weight. *Journal of Consulting and Clinical Psychology*, **61**, 696–698.

Fairburn, C.G., Shafran, R. & Cooper, Z. (1999) A cognitive-behavioural theory of anorexia nervosa. *Behaviour Research and Therapy*, **37**, 1–13.

Fairburn, C.G., Stice, E., Cooper, Z., Doll, H.A., Norman, P.A. & O'Connor, M.E. (in press) Understanding persistence in bulimia nervosa: a five-year naturalistic study. *Journal of Consulting and Clinical Psychology*.

Ferster, C.B., Nurenberger, I. & Levitt, E.B. (1962) The control of eating. *Journal of Mathetics*, **1**, 87–109.

Fuller, R.D., Williamson, D.A. & Anderson, T.W. (1995) Selective information processing of body size and food related stimuli in women who are preoccupied with body size. *Advances in Health Care Research*, **14**, 61–66.

Garfinkel, P.E. & Garner, D.M. (1983) *Anorexia Nervosa: A Multi-dimensional Perspective*. New York: Brunner/Mazel.

Garner, D.M. & Garfinkel, P.E. (Eds), *Handbook of Treatment for Eating Disorders* (2nd edn). New York: Guilford Press.

Garner, D.M. & Bemis, K.M. (1982) A cognitive-behavioral approach to anorexia nervosa. *Cognitive Therapy and Research*, **6**, 123–150.

Garner, D.M. & Bemis, K.M. (1985) Cognitive therapy for anorexia nervosa. In D.M. Garner & P.E. Garfinkel (Eds), *Handbook of Psychotherapy for Anorexia Nervosa and Bulimia*. New York: Guilford Press.

Garner, D.M., Vitousek, K.M. & Pike, K.M. (1997) Cognitive-behavioral therapy for anorexia nervosa. In D.M. Garner & P.E. Garfinkel (Eds), *Handbook of Treatment for Eating Disorders* (2nd edn). New York: Guilford Press.

Gelder, M. (1997) The scientific foundations of cognitive behaviour therapy. In D.M. Clark & C.G. Fairburn (Eds), *Science and Practice of Cognitive Behaviour Therapy*. Oxford Medical Publications. Oxford: Oxford University Press.

Gilbert, S. (1986) *Pathology of Eating*. London: Routledge & Kegan Paul.

Goldfein, J.A., Walsh, B.T. & Midlarsky, E. (2000) Influence of shape and weight on self-evaluation in bulimia nervosa. *International Journal of Eating Disorders*, **27**, 435–445.

Goodrick, G.K. & Foreyt, J.P. (1991) Why treatments for obesity don't last. *Journal of American Dietetic Association*, **91**, 1243–1247.

Green, M.W., McKenna, F.P. & deSilva, M.S.L. (1994) Habituation patterns to colour-naming of eating-related stimuli in anorexics and non-clinical controls. *British Journal of Clinical Psychology*, **33**, 499–508.

Guidano, V.F. & Liotti, G. (1983) *Cognitive Processes and Emotional Disorders*. New York: Guilford Press.

Halmi, K.A. (1983) The state of research in anorexia nervosa and bulimia. *Psychiatric Development*, **1**, 247–262.

Halmi, K.A., Agras, S., Crow, S. & Mitchell, J. (2000) *Anorexia Nervosa: Multicentre Treatment Study*. Ninth International Conference on Eating Disorders, Academy for Eating Disorders, 4–7 May 2000, New York.

Heatherton, T.F. & Baumeister, R.F. (1991) Binge eating as escape from self-awareness. *Psychological Bulletin*, **110**, 86–108.

Hermans, D., Pieters, G. & Eelen, P. (1998) Implicit and explicit memory for shape, body weight, and food-related words in patients with anorexia nervosa and nondieting controls. *Journal of Abnormal Psychology*, **107**, 193–202.

Herzog, D.B., Keller, M.B., Strober, M., Yeh, C.J. et al. (1992) The current status of treatment for anorexia nervosa and bulimia nervosa. *International Journal of Eating Disorders*, **12**, 215–220.

Kleifield, E.I., Wagner, S. & Halmi, K.A. (1996) Cognitive-behavioral treatment of anorexia nervosa. *Psychiatric Clinics of North America*, **19**, 715–737.

Kramer, F.M., Jeffery, R.W., Forster, J.L. & Snell, M.K. (1989) Long-term follow-up of behavioral treatment for obesity: Patterns of weight regain among men and women. *International Journal of Obesity*, **13**, 123–136.

Leitenberg, H., Agras, W.S. & Thompson, L.G. (1968) A sequential analysis of the effect of positive reinforcement in modifying anorexia nervosa. *Behaviour Research and Therapy*, **6**, 211–218.

Lilenfeld, L. & Kaye, W.H. (1998) Genetic studies of anorexia and bulimia. In H.W. Hoek, J.L. Treasure & M.A. Katzman (Eds), *Neurobiology in the Treatment of Eating Disorders*. Wiley series on Clinical and Neurobiological Advances in Psychiatry. Chichester: John Wiley & Sons.

Lilenfeld L.R., Kaye, W.H., Greeno, C.G., Merikangas K.R., Plotnicov, K., Pollice, C., Rao, R., Strober, M., Bulik, C.M. & Nagy, L. (1998) A controlled family study of anorexia nervosa and bulimia nervosa: Psychiatric disorders in first degree relatives and effects of proband comorbidity. *Archives of General Psychiatry*, **55**, 603–610.

McManus, F., Waller, G. & Chadwick, P. (1996) Biases in the processing of different forms of threat in bulimic and comparison women. *Journal of Nervous and Mental Disease*, **184**, 547–554.

Meyer, C. & Waller, G. (1999) The impact of emotion upon eating behavior: The role of subliminal visual processing of threat cues. *International Journal of Eating Disorders*, **25**, 319–326.

Mitchell, J.E., Crow, S., Peterson, C.B., Wonderlich, S. & Crosby, R. D. (1998) Feeding laboratory studies in patients with eating disorders: A review. *International Journal of Eating Disorders*, **24**, 115–124.

Mizes, J.D. (1992). Validity of the Mizes Anorectic Cognitions scale: A comparison between anorectics, bulimics, and psychiatric controls. *Addictive Behaviors*, **17**, 283–289.

Mowrer, O.H. (1960) *Learning Theory and Behavior*. New York: John Wiley & Sons.

Newman, J.P., Wallace, J.F., Strauman, T.J., Skolaski, R.L., Oreland, K.M., Mattek, P.W., Elder, K.A. & McNeely, J. (1993) Effects of motivationally significant stimuli on the regulation of dominant responses. *Journal of Personality and Social Psychology*, **65**, 165–175.

Persons, J.B. (1989) *Cognitive Therapy in Practice: A Case Formulation Approach*. New York: W.W. Norton & Co. Inc.

Phelan, P.W. (1987) Cognitive correlates of bulimia: The bulimia Thoughts Questionnaire. *International Journal of Eating Disorders*, **6**, 593–607.

Pike, K.M. (2000) How do we keep patients well? Issues of relapse prevention. *Plenary Session II: New Clinical Trials*. Ninth International Conference on Eating Disorders, Academy for Eating Disorders, 4–7 May 2000, New York.

Pike, K.M., Loeb, K. & Vitousek, K. (1996) Cognitive behavioral therapy for anorexia nervosa and bulimia nervosa. In J. K. Thompson (Ed.), *Body Image, Eating Disorders and Obesity: An Integrated Guide for Assessment and Treatment*. Washington, DC: American Psychological Association.

Polivy, J. & Herman, C.P. (2002) Experimental studies of dieting. In C.G. Fairburn & K.D. Brownell (Eds), *Eating Disorders and Obesity: A Comprehensive Handbook*. (2nd edn) (pp. 84–87). Guilford Press: New York.

Rachman, S. (1984) Anxiety disorders: Some emerging theories. *Journal of Behavioral Assessment*, **6**, 281–299.

Rachman, S. (1997) The evolution of cognitive behaviour therapy. In D.M. Clark & C.G. Fairburn (Eds), *Science and Practice of Cognitive Behaviour Therapy*. Oxford Medical Publications. Oxford: Oxford University Press.

Rosen, J.V. & Leitenberg, E. (1982) Bulimia nervosa: Treatment with exposure and response prevention. *Behaviour Research and Therapy*, **14**, 125–131.

Salkovskis, P.M. (1996) The cognitive approach to anxiety: threat beliefs, safety-seeking behavior, and the special case of health anxiety and obsessions. In P.M. Salkovskis (1996). *Frontiers of Cognitive Therapy*. New York: Guilford Press.

Schotte, D.E., McNally, R.J. & Turner, M.L. (1990) A dichotic listening analysis of body weight concern in bulimia nervosa. *International Journal of Eating Disorders*, **9**, 109–113.

Sebastian, S.B., Williamson, D.A. & Blouin, D.C. (1996) Memory bias for fatness stimuli in the eating disorders. *Cognitive Therapy and Research*, **20**, 275–286.

Shepherd, H. & Ricciardelli, L.A. (1998) Test of Stice's dual pathway model: dietary restraint and negative affect as mediators of bulimic behavior. *Behaviour Research and Therapy*, **36**, 345–352.

Slade, P. (1982) Towards a functional analysis of anorexia nervosa and bulimia nervosa. *British Journal of Clinical Psychology*, **21**, 167–179.

Stice, E. (2001) A prospective test of the dual-pathway model of bulimic pathology: mediating effects of dieting and negative affect. *Journal of Abnormal Psychology*, **110**, 124–135.

Stice, E. & Agras, W.S. (1999) Subtyping bulimic women along dietary restraint and negative affect dimensions. *Journal of Consulting and Clinical Psychology*, **67**, 460–469.

Stice, E., Nemeroff, C. & Shaw, H.E. (1996) Test of the dual pathway model of bulimia nervosa: Evidence for dietary restraint and affect regulation mechanisms. *Journal of Social and Clinical Psychology*, **15**, 340–363.

Stice, E., Shaw, H. & Nemeroff, C. (1998) Dual pathway model of bulimia nervosa: Longitudinal support for dietary restraint and affect-regulation mechanisms. *Journal of Social and Clinical Psychology*, **17**, 129–149.

Stice, E., Ziemba, C., Margolis, J. & Flick, P. (1996) The dual pathway model differentiates bulimics, subclinical bulimics, and controls: Testing the continuity hypothesis. *Behavior Therapy*, **27**, 531–549.

Stroop, J.R. (1935) Studies of interference in serial verbal reactions. *Journal of Experimental Psychology*, **18**, 643–662.

Stuart, R.B. (1967) Behavioural control of overeating. *Behaviour Research and Therapy*, **5**, 357–365.

Stunkard, A.J. & Penick, S.B. (1979) Behavior modification in the treatment of obesity—the problem of maintaining weight loss. *Archives of General Psychiatry*, **36**, 801–806.

Szmukler, G.I. & Tantam, J. (1984) Anorexia nervosa: Starvation dependence. *British Journal of Medical Psychology*, **57**, 303–310.

Treasure, J., Todd, G., Brolly, M., Tiller, J., Nehmed, A. & Denman, F. (1995) A pilot study of a randomised trial of cognitive analytical therapy vs educational behavioral therapy for adult anorexia nervosa. *Behaviour Research and Therapy*, **3**, 363–367.

Vitousek, K.B. & Hollon, S.D. (1990) The investigation of schematic content and processing in eating disorders. *Cognitive Therapy and Research*, **14**, 191–214.

Vitousek, K.B., & Ewald, L.S. (1993) Self-representation in eating disorders: A cognitive perspective. In Z.V. Segal & S.J. Blatt (Eds), *The Self in Emotional Distress: Cognitive and Psychodynamic Perspectives*. New York: Guilford Press.

Vitousek, K.B. Daly, J. & Heiser, C. (1991) Reconstructing the internal world of the eating-disordered individual: Overcoming denial and distortion in self-report. *International Journal of Eating Disorders*, **10**, 647–666.

Vitousek, K.M. (1996) The current status of cognitive-behavioral models of anorexia nervosa and bulimia nervosa. In P.M. Salkovskis (Ed.), *Frontiers of Cognitive Therapy*. New York: Guilford Press.

Vitousek, K. & Manke, F. (1994) Personality variables and disorders in anorexia nervosa and bulimia nervosa. *Journal of Abnormal Psychology*, **103**, 103–147.

Vitousek, K., Watson, S. & Wilson, G.T. (1998) Enhancing motivation for change in treatment-resistant eating disorders. *Clinical Psychology Review*, **18**, 391–420.

Wadden, T.A., Sternberg, J.A., Letizia, K.A., Stunkard, A.J. & Foster, G.D. (1989) Treatment of obesity by very low calorie diet, behavior therapy, and their combination: A five-year perspective. *Journal of Consulting and Clinical Psychology*, **66**, 429–433.

Wadden, T.A., Vogt, R.A., Foster, G.D. & Anderson, D.A. (1998) Exercise and the maintenance of weight loss: 1-year follow-up of a controlled clinical trial *Journal of Consulting and Clinical Psychology*, **66**, 429–433.

Watson, J.B. (1925) *Behaviorism*. New York: North Holland.

Williams, J.M.G., Watts, F.N., MacLeod, C. & Mathews, A. (1988) *Cognitive Psychology and Emotional Disorders*. Chichester: John Wiley & Sons.

Williamson, D.A., Muller, S.L., Reas, D.L. & Thaw, J.M. (1999) Cognitive bias in eating disorders: Implications for theory and treatment. *Behaviour Modification*, **23**, 556–577.

Williamson, D., Kelley, M.L., Davis, C.J., Ruggiero, L. & Vietia, M.C. (1985) The psychophysiology of bulimia. *Advances in Behaviour Research and Therapy*, **7**, 163–172.

Williamson, D.A., Davis, C.J., Duchmann, G.G., McKenzie, S.J. & Watkins, P.C. (1990) *Assessment of Eating Disorders: Obesity, Anorexia and Bulimia Nervosa*. New York: Pergamon.

Wilson, G.T. (1989) The treatment of bulimia nervosa: A cognitive-social learning analysis. In A.J. Stunkard & A. Baum (Eds), *Perspectives in Behavioral Medicine: Eating, Sleeping and Sex*. Hillsdale, NJ: Lawrence Earlbaum.

Wilson, G.T. (1993) Behavioral treatment of obesity: Thirty years and counting. *Advances in Behaviour Research and Therapy*, **16**, 31–75.

Wilson, G.T. (1996) Acceptance and change in the treatment of eating disorders and obesity. *Behaviour Therapy*, **27**, 417–439.

Wilson, G.T. & Fairburn, C.G. (2002) Treatments for eating disorders. In P.E. Nathan & J.M. Gorman, *A guide to treatments that work* (2nd edn) (pp. 559–592). New York: Oxford University Press.

Wilson, G.T., Fairburn, C.G., Agras, W.S., Walsh, B.T. & Kraemer, H. (2002) Cognitive-behavior therapy for bulimia nervosa: time course and mechanisms of change. *Journal of Consulting and Clinical Psychology*, **70**, 267–274.

Wing, R.R. (1998) Behavioral approaches to the treatment of obesity. In G.A. Bray, C. Bouchard & W.P.T. James (Eds), *Handbook of Obesity*. New York: Marcel Dekker.

Wolff, G. & Serpell, L. (1998) A cognitive model and treatment strategies for anorexia nervosa. In H.W. Hoek, J.L. Treasure & M.A. Katzman (Eds), *Neurobiology in the Treatment of Eating Disorders*. Wiley series on Clinical and Neurobiological Advances in Psychiatry. Chichester John Wiley & Sons.

Wolpe, J. (1958) *Psychotherapy by Reciprocal Inhibition*. Stanford: Stanford University Press.

Wolpe, J. (1993) The cognitivist oversell and comments on symposium contributions. *Journal of Behavior Therapy Experimental Psychiatry*, **24**, 141–147.

Wooley, S.C., Wooley, O.W. & Dyrenforth, S.R. (1979) Theoretical, practical and social issues in behavioral treatment of obesity. *Journal of Applied Behavior Analysis*, **12**, 3–25.

CHAPTER 4

Medical Complications

Stephen Zipfel

*Medizinische Universität, Klinik Psychosmatische, Medizin und Psychotherapie,
Tübingen, Germany*

Bernd Löwe

Ruprecht Karls Universität, Medizinische Klinkum, Heidelberg, Germany

and

Wolfgang Herzog

Ruprecht Karls Universität, Medizinische Klinkum, Heidelberg, Germany

SUMMARY

Medical complications play an important role in patients with eating disorders, and this chapter diseases some of the treatments/concerns that should be considered:

- Severe biochemical disturbances should be managed in consultation with a physician.
- Oral intervention is generally preferable to rapid, intravenous treatment.
- A cardiovascular examination and an ECG should be carried out in all patients with anorexia nervosa (AN) and those with bulimia nervosa (BN) who have evidence of electrolyte abnormalities.
- In AN patients, drugs which prolong the QT interval should be avoided, whenever possible.
- AN patients with a chronic course are at high risk for the development of osteoporosis.
- To date the best treatment for osteoporosis is a balanced refeeding diet and the resumption of normal menstruation. AN patients with a very low weight (<70% ABW) may benefit from hormone replacement therapy. Although promising new anti-resorptive drug therapies are currently being developed, most are still in the phase of clinical trails.
- Structural brain changes in AN may have both reversible and irreversible components.
- The most common haematological abnormalities in AN are leucopenia and most likely normocytic anaemia.
- Eating disorder patients with an additional medical comorbidity (e.g. diabetes mellitus) have an increased risk for medical complications and should be managed in consultation with a physician or specialist.

The Essential *Handbook of Eating Disorders*. Edited by J. Treasure, U. Schmidt and E. van Furth.
© 2005 John Wiley & Sons, Ltd.

- Markedly obese patients face a variety of severe medical complications, which could best be treated with an interdisciplinary team.

INTRODUCTION

Although it is well accepted that the aetiology of eating disorders is best understood from a biopsychosocial model, the complex nature of these disorders makes it sometimes difficult to determine which might be the leading aspect in a particular eating-disordered patient—the psyche or the soma. The serious neuropsychological impairments and medical complications which are often associated with eating disorders (Becker et al., 1999; Zipfel et al., 1998) have important implications for clinical practice, particularly for very emaciated anorexic patients.

The first part of this chapter will address the most important acute and chronic medical complications in patients suffering from an eating disorder. In anorexic patients, the consequences of severe malnutrition can be extremely problematic, warranting special consideration during treatment. The clinical picture of bulimia nervosa is influenced by the consequences of purging behaviour, such as self-induced vomiting and the abuse of laxatives and diuretics.

The second part of the chapter will focus on medical complications in individuals with obesity. With nearly every second individual being overweight (BMI $> 25\,\text{kg/m}^2$) and one in three being obese (BMI $> 30\,\text{kg/m}^2$), the rate of obesity has increased by 50% over the past 20 years, reaching epidemic proportions in industrialised countries (Yanovski & Yanovski, 1999). Although psychological aspects do play an important role in most individuals during the course of marked obesity, it should be noted that only a minority of obese people are suffering primarily from a psychiatric disorder, such as an eating or affective disorder. Therefore, we will address the medical risks and complications of this rapidly growing group of individuals.

ACUTE COMPLICATIONS IN ANOREXIA AND BULIMIA NERVOSA

Since patients with eating disorders, particularly those with anorexia nervosa, tend to deny their disorder and the resulting physical damage, acute somatic complications are often the reason they receive medical treatment for the first time. Even though the diagnosis may be obvious to the examiner based on diagnostic criteria set forth by the DSM-IV or ICD-10, an exact recording of physical findings is strongly recommended. A detailed physical assessment of a patient with a history of weight loss or weight cycling is important for making a differential diagnosis between an eating disorder and other somatic diseases, such as malabsorption syndromes, chronic inflammatory intestinal diseases, tumours, tuberculosis, vasculitis, and diabetes mellitus. Since the majority of eating disorder cases are young females, older females and male cases can be easily overlooked by clinicians. Male patients in particular may not present until marked somatic changes have developed (Siegel et al., 1995). Finally, a detailed medical assessment yields important information regarding the altered nutritional status of a patient, as well as any existing complications from bingeing and purging behaviours (see Table 4.1). This information can help to guide decision making with respect to inpatient, day-patient or outpatient treatment.

Table 4.1   Examinations recommended on admission or in the course of refeeding

Obligatory	Optional
• Full medical and psychiatric history	• Body composition measurement (skinfold, BIA, DEXA)
• *Physical assessment* Body mass index Heart rate blood pressure Temperature	• *In severe anaemia*: Reticulocytes, iron, ferritin, transferrin, vitamin B_{12}
	• *In case of elevated creatinine*: Creatinine clearance
• Full blood count, blood sedimentation rate	• *In case of oedema*: Albumin, total protein, protein electrophoresis
• *Biochemical profile* Serum electrolytes: Sodium Potassium Calcium Magnesium Phosphate Creatinine Urea Liver enzyme profile Blood glucose	• *To rule out hyperthyroidism*: Thyroid function test
	• *In case of cardiovascular abnormalities*: Holder ECG, echocardiography
	• *Differential diagnosis*: Chest X-ray, abdominal ultrasound
	• *To rule out an ulcer*: Gastroscopy
	• *In patients with a long-term course*: Osteodensitometry (DEXA scan) and markers of bone turnover
• Electrocardiogram (ECG)	• *In case of seizures or differential diagnosis*: EEG and neuroimaging (CT, MRI)

CARDIOVASCULAR COMPLICATIONS

Cardiovascular complications are common in patients with eating disorders, particularly with anorexia nervosa. Some of these complications are relatively benign (most forms of hypotension and bradycardia) and do not usually require treatment unless a patient is symptomatic (Kreipe et al., 1994). However, cardiovascular complications can cause immediate or premature death in these patients (Beumont et al., 1993). The reasons for these complications are mixed, and may include dehydration and electrolyte disturbances secondary to purging behaviour, or occur as a direct effect of malnutrition. In general, cardiac complications occur mostly in patients with purging behaviour (Sharp & Freeman, 1993), but are not always associated with manifest hypokalemia.

ECG Alterations/Arrhythmias

ECG alterations occur in more than 80% of eating-disordered patients (Alvin et al., 1993). In addition to sinus bradycardia, which is frequently seen, ST-depressions and abnormal U-waves may be found on the ECG. They are often associated with electrolyte imbalances and are considered to be warning signals for arrhythmias. These are responsible for a considerable number of deaths in eating disorders (Schocken et al., 1989). In this context, special emphasis is placed on the extension of the QT interval, which is seen in 15% (Cooke & Chambers, 1995) to 40% (Durakovic et al., 1994) of cases. This QT extension is considered to be a significant predictor of ventricular tachyarrhythmias or of sudden cardiac death.

Kreipe et al. (1994) investigated a possible dysfunction of the autonomic nervous system using the heart rate power spectrum analysis. His results indicate that there is a decrease in sympathetic control of the heart rate. Other recent investigations (for review see Winston & Stafford, 2000) have examined the extent to which additional tests of heart rate variability can provide further diagnostic information when assessing the risk of fatal arrhythmia. Changes in repolarisation, such as an extension of the corrected QT interval in AN patients, showed a significant tendency to revert to normal after refeeding. Only a few studies have focused on cardiovascular disorders in BN. The increased incidence of arrhythmia reported in some studies was usually directly associated with hypokalemia due to frequent vomiting. Consequently, in eating-disordered patients drugs should be avoided which may prolong the QT interval (e.g. tricyclic antidepressants and neuroleptics).

Morphological Changes

Weight loss in AN is associated with a loss in heart muscle mass. Echocardiographic studies of AN patients reported a decreased left ventricular mass and an increased incidence of mitral valve prolapse (MVP) (de Simone et al., 1994). In 62% of the patients, abnormalities of mitral valve motion were found to occur as a result of an imbalance between valve size and ventricle volume, possibly leading to a mitral valve prolapse. The occurrence of MVP in these patients is related to two different factors. First, it is known that MVP is associated with a higher risk of arrhythmia. Second, there is some evidence for an association between MVP and anxiety disorders.

Cardiac failure can also occur as a complication during refeeding (Kahn et al., 1991), especially in cases of simultaneous hypophosphataemia (Schocken et al., 1989). Malnutrition, electrolyte imbalance, and ipecac abuse (Mitchell et al. 1987) can result in a possibly irreversible secondary cardiomyopathy. Male AN patients with an increased heart rate are particularly susceptible to the possibility of congestive heart failure (Siegel et al., 1995). Studies of patients suffering from malnutrition have shown a decrease in heart size and a rotation of the heart's axis into a vertical position during the course of weight loss. These changes were mostly reversible in the refeeding period.

Refeeding Oedema

Peripheral oedema occurs in a substantial proportion of patients undergoing refeeding (Winston, 2000). This may be due to a rapid weight gain of several kilograms and is often alarming for patients and doctors. Why 'rebound oedema' typically develops during the initial weeks of refeeding is unclear, but its effect on body weight should be considered (Bihun et al., 1993). It is very unlikely that this phenomenon is caused by hypoproteinaemia, because this sort of oedema is associated with normal serum albumin levels. It has been suggested that salt and water depletion lead to the development of secondary hyperaldosteronism, which might predispose to the development of oedema when water and salt intake is increased during refeeding. From a clinical point of view this kind of oedema has to be differentiated from cardiac oedema, caused by heart failure, as well as renal and hepatic failure.

GASTROINTESTINAL SYSTEM

Many changes occur in the gastrointestinal physiology in patients suffering from an eating disorder (Robinson, 2000). Some of these changes are particularly important to consider, because they may indicate a chronic course of these disorders.

Hyperamylasemia/Enlargement of the Parotid Gland/Pancreatitis

An increase in serum amylase levels is found in about 50% of patients treated in the hospital. In most cases it is due to vomiting and is not a result of pancreatitis (Mitchell et al., 1983). Correspondingly, this increase is caused by the isoamylase of the parotid gland (Humphries et al., 1987). A distinct enlargement of the parotid gland is often observed, especially in BN. Acute pancreatitis can be assumed if the increase in the serum amylase level is more than three-fold above normal and is associated with abdominal pain. If in doubt, it may be helpful to measure lipase levels. Pancreatitis as a complication of eating disorders is rare; it can, however, develop as a result of refeeding or binge eating.

Impaired Gastric Emptying/Obstipation/Ileus

An impairment of oesophageal motility and gastric emptying is a typical consequence of malnutrition but has also been found variably in patients with bulimia nervosa. After an increase of food intake and stabilisation of weight, this disturbance seems to be fully reversible (Szmukler et al., 1990). It manifests itself as a sensation of fulness after food ingestion, which can make refeeding difficult. Megaduodenum and duodenal immobility are also secondary complications but are reversible (Buchman et al., 1994). Constipation is frequent and is in most cases a result of poor nutrition and hypokalemia due to purging behaviour such as laxative abuse. Abrupt cessation of laxatives could lead to severe water and sodium retention and oedema mainly due to secondary hyperaldosteronism. The possibility of constipation due to antidepressant medication, particularly tricyclic antidepressants, should be considered. Drug treatment with cisapride is not helpful due to cardiovascular side-effects and in many countries, including the UK, this medication has been banned.

Gastric Dilation/Perforation

Gastric dilation typically occurs after binge eating and becomes manifest in spontaneous vomiting and upper abdominal pain. Conservative treatment is usually sufficient; in rare cases, however, circulation disorders of the gastric wall occur, leading to necrosis and gastric perforation (Abdu et al., 1987). In these cases, immediate surgery is required. Five of the 60 cases with spontaneous gastric rupture described since 1960 have been AN patients (Schou et al., 1994). Diagnosis may be difficult since more than 50% of the patients suffer from vomiting, upper abdominal pain, and gastrointestinal disorders.

Gastroduodenal Ulcers/Upper Gastrointestinal Bleeding

Ulcers develop in about one-sixth of the patients (Hall et al., 1989). They can cause bleeding, which may lead to anaemia and circulatory decompensation. However, bleeding can also occur as a result of tears of the oesophagus (Mallory-Weiss Syndrome) due to vomiting.

Hepatitis

Elevated liver function tests are found in about one-third of patients treated in the hospital ('nutritional hepatitis'). Transaminase levels are usually raised and bilirubin can be elevated. If there is no infectious or autoimmune cause, additional treatment is not necessary

(Colombo et al., 1995). If the indirect bilirubin levels are elevated, one should consider the manifestation of Gilbert's syndrom (5% of the total population is affected) in the starving period. Hypercholesterolemia is a result of a reduced bile acid requirement.

HAEMATOLOGICAL AND IMMUNE SYSTEM

Bone Marrow Hypoplasia

A frequent consequence of malnutrition is a reversible, reactive bone marrow hypoplasia (Lambert & Boland, 2000). It leads to anaemia in about 25% of patients, to leukopenia in about 30%, and to thrombopenia in about 10% of cases. Only two of 67 AN patients showed pancytopenia (Devuyst et al., 1993). The bleeding risk is increased if thrombocyte values fall below 30/nl. Anaemia may be accompanied by iron deficiency, rarely by vitamin B12 or folic acid deficiency. In severe anaemia, gastrointestinal bleeding should also be considered. Recently, a significant association between peripheral blood parameters and nutritional parameters has been demonstrated, especially between leucocyte levels and BMI. Blood changes have also prove to be reversible with weight gain. Haematological abnormalities are much less common in patients with BN.

(Bacterial) Infections

Although leukocyte counts and immunoglobulin and other factor levels are often reduced, the immunologic competence is intact in most cases, and serious or opportunistic infections are quite rare. Devuyst et al. (1993), however, reports a 9% rate of serious infections in AN patients, especially occurring in those individuals with neutropenia or very low weight on admission. In any case, infection as a complication of AN has to be taken seriously, since as a result of hypothermia and leukopenia it can take a course without fever or leukocytosis (Tenholder & Pike, 1991). Therefore, weekly controls of the blood sedimentation rate or C-reactive protein are recommended when treating serious cases of anorexia. Zipfel et al. (2000a) demonstrated in a long-term follow-up study, that causes of death in one-third of their patients was directly related to infections (bronchial pneumonia and sepsis).

BIOCHEMICAL ABNORMALITIES

Hypokalemia

($K < 3.5$ mmol/l)   Hypokalemia is found in about one-third of all patients with eating disorders treated in the hospital. The majority of cases are the result of chronic purging, but can also result from an acute case of purgative behaviour. Some of the patients adapt to very low values (<2.0), and symptoms in these patients may be missing (Bonne et al., 1993). Hypokalemia may have fatal consequences, including tachyarrhythmias, paralytic ileus, muscle weakness, cramps, tetany, polyuria or nephropathy. Supplementation should be done slowly and primarily orally. I.V. supplementation with strict heart rate monitoring is rarely necessary.

Hyponatremia

(Na < 135 mmol/l)   In the event of hyponatremia, hydration status as well as urinary sodium and osmolality has to be investigated. It is often due to hypotonic dehydration caused by chronic purging (Challier & Cabrol, 1995). The symptoms are disorientation, myasthenia, and circulatory disorders. In the majority of cases, only oral salt and water replacement is sufficient. In rare cases of fluid overload, a restriction of fluid intake is indicated.

Hypophosphataemia

(Phos < 0.8; severe: <0.3 mmol/l)   A quick decrease in the phosphate levels typically occurs during the refeeding period ('nutritional recovery syndrome', especially in cases of parenteral refeeding) (Fisher et al., 2000; Beumont & Large, 1991), but also as a result of diuretic abuse, renal failure and rapid correction of hypokalaemia. Severe hypophosphatemia can be fatal (Beumont & Large, 1991). It can result in cardiopulmonary decompensation (Cariem et al., 1994), arrhythmia, metabolic acidosis, polyneuropathia, delirium, as well as disorders of the erythrocyte and leukocyte function. As a preventative or supplementary measure, milk powder should be given.

Hypomagnesaemia

(Mg < 0.7 mmol/l)   Severe magnesium deficiency can be caused by diarrhoea, diuretic and alcohol misuse as well as severe malnutrition. It can lead to muscle cramps, intestinal spasms, hypokalaemia, and arrhythmias (Hall et al., 1989).

Hypocalcaemia

(Ca < 2.15 mmol/l)   Hypocalcaemia can be a symptom of calcium deficiency due to chronic malnutrition, but also of alkalosis. It may be associated with ECG changes (Beumont et al., 1993). In the differential diagnosis, possible hypocalcaemic tetany should be distinguished from hyperventilation syndrome.

Glucose Metabolism

In most cases of AN, glucose levels are low and glucose tolerance is reduced (Fukushima et al., 1993). Insulin stimulates glucose oxidation rather than glucose storage. Hypoglycemic coma may develop (Ratcliffe & Bevan, 1985). If the patient is conscious, sugar/glucose drinks should be given. If the patient is unconscious, a 20–50 ml 40% glucose intravenous infusion is recommended.

Metabolic Alkalosis

Generally, metabolic alkalosis occurs in association with the loss of gastric acid due to self-induced vomiting. However, it can also be caused by hypokalaemia, which leads to the loss of renal acid. About one-fourth of BN patients are affected by this disorder (Mitchell et al., 1983). The Pseudo-Bartter Syndrome, which consists of metabolic alkalosis, hypokalaemia, hypochloraemia, polyuria, and dehydration, is a typical result of severe purging behaviour. The Pseudo-Bartter Syndrome should be differentially diagnosed from the syndrome of inadequate ADH secretion (Schwartz–Bartter Syndrome) (Challier & Cabrol, 1995).

Metabolic Acidosis

Metabolic acidosis affects about 8% of BN patients and is a result of enteral bicarbonate loss in cases of laxative abuse (Mitchell et al., 1987). Possible additional causes are a markedly increased endogenous acid formation in AN as well as reduced acid excretion in connection with renal insufficiency.

Water Balance

Dehydration occurs as a result of reduced fluid supply or of chronic purging behaviour and is often associated with circulatory disorders and electrolyte imbalances (hypokalaemia, hypotonic dehydration, see above), which have to be considered in rehydration. Some patients are water loading, sometimes due to weight manipulation or due to additional psychiatric disorders. As a consequence, these patients show a pseudo-anaemia, and a hyponatriemia.

CENTRAL NERVOUS SYSTEM

Imaging methods such as computerised tomography (CT) or magnetic resonance imaging (MRI) play a secondary role in the basic diagnostics of patients with eating disorders. Therefore, the routine use of these methods is not recommended by the guidelines for eating disorders of the American Psychiatric Association (APA, 1994). In individual cases, however, the use of these methods may be indicated. For example, CT or MRI may be useful in excluding the presence of a possible brain tumour, or if a compressive intracerebral process is suspected.

Seizures

About 5% of eating disorder patients are affected by seizures (Patchell et al., 1994). Disturbances in calcium, sodium and glucose metabolism as well as uraemia due to renal failure can be responsible for myoclonic and generalised tonoclonic seizures. Nevertheless, these patients should be examined by an EEG and, if necessary, head CT for differential diagnosis of possible morphological causes.

Morphological and Functional Cerebral Changes

Systematic studies on brain changes in AN patients show dilated and/or enlarged cortical sulci (Golden et al., 1996; Kornreich et al., 1991). Kingston et al. (1996) tested neuropsychological and structural brain changes in AN before and after refeeding. The AN group performed significantly worse than the controls on tasks measuring attention, visuospatial ability, and memory. This group also demonstrated enlarged lateral ventricle sulci on both cortical and cerebellar surfaces. In this study, the correlation between morphological brain changes and cognitive impairment were weak. Lower weight was associated with greater ventricular size on MRI, but not with the duration of illness. However, there are contradictory results as to whether the cognitive deficits occurring in the acute phase were directly connected to the morphological changes (Laessle et al., 1989). In a series of further studies (Schlegel & Kretzschmar, 1997) it was shown that during weight normalisation there was an increase of brain tisssue size of up to 25 vol.% compared to the time of minimum weight.

Interestingly, ventricular enlargements have also been found in patients with BN. Thus, they are not exclusively associated with malnutrition (Krieg, 1991).

Additional Findings

Unspecific EEG changes (i.e. abnormal background activity) are often found in AN as a result of the effect of starvation on cerebral metabolism (Hughes, 1996). Although these atypical EEG findings were seen in a number of studies measuring EEG and sleep-EEG, it has been shown that, compared to other disease groups, these changes were not specific to eating disorders (Rothenberger et al., 1991). Moreover, there were no significant correlations to the body mass index (Delvenne et al., 1996).

Neuromuscular Abnormalities

Nearly 50% of eating-disordered patients are affected by neuromuscular abnormalities. Main symptoms include general muscular weakness, peripheral neuropathy, and headaches (Patchell et al., 1994). Pulmonary function can be severely disturbed due to an impairment of diaphragmatic contractility. A condition which is reversible after malnutrition is treated.

CHRONIC COMPLICATIONS IN ANOREXIA AND BULIMIA NERVOSA

Endocrine System and Reproductive Function

Amenorrhoea

The impairment of the hormonal axes is a main symptom of AN and was included as a diagnostic guideline in the ICD-10 as well as in the DSM-IV. Involvement of the hypothalamo-pituitary-gonadal axis is associated with primary or secondary amenorrhoea, depending on the age of the patient at first manifestation. Although endocrine disorders are not a part of the diagnostic criteria of BN, 20 to 50% of BN patients are found to be amenorrhoic. Menstruation disorders are reported by 40% of BN patients (Fairburn & Cooper, 1984). Studies by Pirke et al. (1989) have shown, however, that self-reports often underestimate the rate of menstrual cycle disorders, especially in BN. For example, he showed by repeatedly measuring plasma oestradiol levels, that the rate of patients with levels of <120 pg/ml was high, making follicle maturation unlikely. Moreover, in 50% of the patients, the progesterone levels measured in the subsequent luteal phase were very low due to an insufficient pulsatile gonadotropin release. In AN, it has also been shown that persistent hypothalamic amenorrhoea does not require permanent inhibition of the GnTH pulse generator (Allouche et al., 1991). At least for some patients in this study, a transient inhibition of pulsatility and qualitative abnormalities of the gonadotropins might be involved in the pathomechanism of amenorrhea. A comparably short fasting period has led to a prepubertal pattern of gonadotropin levels, especially LH levels (Schweiger et al., 1987). Recent studies on the role of leptin in the female cycle (Hebebrand et al., 1997) demonstrated the importance of this protein as a signalling trigger to puberty and link between nutritional status and female cycle (Köpp et al., 1997; Zipfel et al., 1998). In conclusion, the available evidence suggests that disorders of the menstrual cycle are a secondary phenomenon of malnutrition, possibly explaining why amenorrhea often precedes a massive weight loss and may continue even if there is an increase in weight again. Nevertheless, it is still not known whether factors other than malnutrition and weight loss are involved in the development of hormonal disorders.

Eating Disorders and Pregnancy

Hormonal changes also affect fertility. Thus, a reduced fertility and increased spontaneous abortion rate was found due to disturbances of the follicular and luteal phase (Bates et al., 1982). There is evidence that even in successful pregnancy, the infants are clearly underweight. Brinch et al. (1988) carried out a follow-up study on 140 patients with AN after 10–12 years. This study showed that 50 former patients had had children in the interim, 10% had problems with infertility and 20% became pregnant while they continued to be anorectic. In this sample, the rate of premature births was twice as high as in an age-matched population and perinatal mortality was increased by a factor of 6. Willis and Rand (1988) reported a miscarriage rate increased by a factor of 2. There is also evidence that patients with BN have an increased rate of malformations due to laxative and diuretic abuse, as well as due to the increased incidence of alcohol and drug abuse found among these patients (for review see Key et al., 2000).

Non-reproductive Endocrine Abnormalities

In most cases, hormonal changes associated with the eating disorders are directly associated with insufficient energy intake. Beumont (1998) reported an increased basal growth hormone (GH) level in about 50% of patients with AN. The elevated GH level is probably an adaptation to the low energy intake and it is necessary to combat the accompanying hypoglycaemia by mobilising fat tissue. A low T3 syndrome is usually found which helps to conserve energy in the presence of undernutrition. The circulating levels of cortisol are often elevated. Fichter and Pirke (1990) showed that patients with AN have an abnormal

24 hour cortisol secretion, an impaired suppression by dexamethasone, reduced catabolism, and greater hypothalamic effect on cortisol production. In the Munich fasting experiment, five healthy female subjects participated in a starvation experiment. In total they lost about 8 kg in a 3-week phase of complete food abstinence. During this fasting period 24 hours plasma cortisol levels showed a significant increase with blunted dexamethasone suppression tests in half of the subjects. During fasting, basal thyroid-stimulating hormone (TSH) values were lowered and the TSH response to thyrotropin-releasing hormone (TRH) was blunted. The plasma level of growth hormone (GH) over 24 hours was elevated during fasting (Fichter et al., 1986).

OSTEOPOROSIS IN EATING DISORDERS

One of the most serious medical complications in patients suffering from *anorexia nervosa*, is profound osteopenia and osteoporosis of the trabecular and cortical bone compartments (Herzog et al., 1993; Zipfel et al., 2000b). A recent study (Klibanski et al., 1995) demonstrated significantly low bone mineral density (BMD < 2SD) in up to 45% of an anorexic patient sample. In a sample of patients with an average duration of AN of 5.8 years, Rigotti et al. (1991) found a seven-fold increased annual fracture rate in the second and third decade of life compared to an age-matched control. In a long-term follow-up study of anorexic patients, osteoporotic-related fractures were found in 44% of the poor outcome group (Herzog et al., 1993). Such fractures may lead to early invalidism and contribute to the suffering of these patients. Further, a considerable portion of the hospitalisation rate of chronic anorexic patients was due to the consequences of osteoporosis and related fractures. In an intermediate term follow-up study (3.6 years after initial inpatient treatment), Zipfel et al. (in press) showed that non-recovered AN with binge-eating/purging type showed a significantly reduced bone mineral density compared to patients with a restricting type.

Several studies investigating the risk of osteoporosis in patients with bulimia nervosa (BN) have been published over the last 10 years. Unfortunately, these studies have yielded inconsistent findings, making it difficult to reach a consensus regarding the relationship between bone mineral density and bulimia nervosa. One study found no significant differences in bone mineral density levels between BN patients and normal controls (Newman & Halmi, 1989), whereas another demonstrated significantly lower BMD in bulimic patients at the radius and femoral neck than a control group (Joyce et al., 1990). Other findings have further complicated the issue by demonstrating considerable variability in BMD between subgroups of BN patients. A significantly lower BMD of the lumbar spine was found in a subgroup of BN patients with long-lasting secondary amenorrhea (Newton et al., 1993). Additionally, a recent study found differences in BMD between patients classified as sedentary and patients who exercised regularly (Sundgot-Borgen et al., 1998). Specifically, sedentary patients had a lower BMD at the total body, spine, and hip. The authors concluded that weight-bearing exercise prevented or attenuated bone loss in normal weight BN patients. In another recent study, Goebel et al. (1999) demonstrated that a subsample of bulimic patients with a history of low weight had a reduced BMD at the lumbar spine compared to a BN sample without such a low weight history. Zipfel et al. (in press) showed that BN patients without a history of AN had BMD values and markers of bone turnover mostly within the normal range.

Aetiology of Osteoporosis in AN and BN Patients

The precise aetiology of bone demineralisation in patients with AN and BN remains unclear. The development of osteopenia and osteoporosis can be characterised by two major mechanisms that supplement and reinforce each other. Due to the early onset of the eating disorder, often during puberty, the patients fail to reach their peak bone mass, a process which is normally finished at the end of puberty or early adulthood. Second, there is premature and increased bone destruction in patients suffering from these disorders (Ruegsegger et al., 1991). The greatest risk factor for the development of osteoporosis is an oestrogen deficiency, which is reflected by the secondary (sometimes primary) amenorrhea. However, case reports have demonstrated that male anorexic patients can also suffer from osteoporosis, most likely due to testosterone deficiency. In addition, glucocorticoid excess, malnutrition, reduced body mass, and hyperactivity further influence bone turnover in both sexes. Previous studies on recovery from osteoporosis have yielded conflicting results. Some studies conclude that in many cases recovery is possible (Herzog et al., 1993), while others suggest that only partial improvement of BMD can be achieved (Ward et al., 1997).

Essential and Optional Investigations at Assessment and Follow-up

Relatively few clinical risk factors have been identified which can be used to predict or determine affected individuals. Factors associated with an increased risk of osteoporosis include a family history of osteoporosis, low body weight, low calcium intake, immobilisation, and lifestyle factors such as smoking, alcoholism, lack of exercise or excessive exercise. Additionally, it was demonstrated that the duration of the eating disorder is associated with cortical bone mass, whereas the duration of amenorrhea is associated with reduced BMD at the lumbar spine (Herzog et al., 1997a). During assessment, medical problems associated with an increased risk of osteoporosis should be carefully examined. Such medical conditions include: prolonged glucocorticoid therapy, chronic liver and renal disease, proven malabsorptive disorders, and problems associated with thyroxine excess. In addition to a patient history and physical examination, a routine blood test should be conducted to rule out the presence of other medical illnesses which cause bone loss.

Biochemical markers of bone turnover are non-invasive, comparatively inexpensive, and helpful when assessing this process (Seibel et al., 1993). For clinical purposes, markers of bone turnover are classified as either formation markers (e.g. osteocalcin, OC) or bone resorption markers (e.g. desoxypyridinoline, DPD). To ensure the correct interpretation of these markers, it is important to consider other influential factors, such as circadian rhythms, seasonal changes in growth, ageing, diseases, and drugs. The clinical use of biochemical markers in osteoporosis may be especially interesting for the selection of a specific antiresorptive therapy as well as for evaluating treatment outcome. Table 4.1 summarises the routine and additional parameters for the assessment of osteoporotic risk.

Treatment and Prevention Options

The primary goal of preventing or treating osteoporosis in eating-disordered patients should focus on achieving a normal body weight through a calcium-enriched, balanced diet.

Although immense efforts are made by eating disorder researchers to find the optimal treatment for osteoporosis, it is too early to present general guidelines. A selection of bone-specific treatment options are listed below, along with the corresponding research findings.

Serpell and Treasure (1997) are currently involved in a double blind trial to assess the efficacy of calcium and vitamin D supplements in increasing bone density in both current anorexics and those who have recovered from anorexia nervosa. Klibanski et al. (1995) conducted a randomised trial using oestrogen and progesterone replacement therapy (HRT) in anorexic patients. After a mean duration of 1.5 years, the HRT-treated group had no significant change in BMD compared with the control group. However, there was a 4.0% increase in mean BMD in patients with an initial body weight of less than 70% of normal weight who were treated with HRT. Grinspoon et al. (1997) investigated the effect of short-term recombinant human insulin-like growth factor 1 (IGF-1) administration on bone turnover in osteoporotic women with anorexia nervosa. During short-term administration of IGF-1 at a dose of 30 µg/kg, there was a significant increase in markers of bone formation as well as an insignificant increase of bone resorption. At this stage, there are no data on chronic IGF-1 administration. Gordon et al. (1999) studied changes in bone turnover markers and menstrual function after short-term oral dehydroepiandrosterone (DHEA) therapy. Despite the small number of patients ($n = 15$), markers of bone resorption had decreased significantly at 3 months. Resumption of menses in over half of the subjects suggested that DHEA therapy may also lead to oestradiol levels sufficient to stimulate the endometrium. Bisphosphonates have been shown to increase bone mineral density in patients with established osteoporosis as well as those with osteopenia. This group of drugs are safe and effective and are the only agents shown in prospective trails to reduce the risk of hip fractures and other non-vertebral fractures. However to date, they are approved by the US FDA for prevention of bone loss in recently menopausal women, for treatment of postmenopausal osteoporosis, and for management of glucocorticoid-induced bone loss (for review see Watts, 2001). To our knowledge, to date there are no published trials in patients with anorexia nervosa.

Common Problems with Recommended Action

A number of limitations exist in the treatment of osteoporosis in eating-disordered patients, especially those suffering from anorexia nervosa. It is generally accepted that the best treatment option is a balanced refeeding diet with the goal of weight gain, so that the patients resume their normal menstrual cycles. However, the 'weight phobia' characteristic of these disorders often prevents the successful implementation of this physiological, cost-effective and 'side-effect free' treatment option. Although aerobic exercise has been found to prevent bone loss in healthy subjects, anorexic patients should be enrolled in supervised programmes, which could carefully monitor exercise levels, due to the tendency of these patients to over-exercise. Chronic patients who are very low weight (<70% of actual body weight) may benefit from HRT. Due to the resumption of menses, however, a considerable portion of these patients are reluctant to take HRT over a longer period of time. Although promising and new antiresorptive drug therapies are currently being developed, most are still in the phase of clinical trials. Future studies with a broader scope and longer follow-up periods will hopefully improve both treatment recommendations and our understanding of osteoporosis in eating-disordered patients.

Dental defects in patients with eating disorders have increasingly been the focus of attention in the past years. Oral changes are often the first indication that an eating disorder is present. The effect of acid regurgitation on the teeth is well appreciated (Robb et al., 1995), and a history of vomiting may have far-reaching consequences for the condition of the teeth. Apart from deterioration, vomiting increases the need for dental work and increased loss of teeth. A common sign of frequent and long-term vomiting is erosion of the dental enamel (Simmons et al., 1986). Enamel is lost from the lingual and palatal surfaces of the anterior teeth. Touyz et al. (1993) showed that patients with both AN and BN had changes indicative of gingivitis and gingival recession but not of periodontitis.

RENAL SYSTEM

A long-term follow-up study by Herzog et al. (1997b) showed that serum creatinine levels at first admission showed a robust main effect on the likelihood of first recovery which was not confounded by other variables. High serum creatinine (>120 mmol/l) and urea (>6.5 mmol/l) levels were indicators of reduced renal function and may be due to fluid loss. Serum creatinine levels correlated significantly with the frequency of vomiting. In addition, increased creatinine levels were seen in those patients who demonstrated purging behaviour but concealed this information. Finally, an increase in creatinine levels may be a sign of permanent kidney damage after a chronic course of disease and in individual AN patients may even cause death (Deter & Herzog, 1994). Good hydration maximises renal function. However in very dehydrated subjects, a slow rehydration is necessary to avoid fluid overload and electrolyte disturbances. In some patients with a very chronic impaired of renal function, referral to a renal physician becomes necessary, sometime with the need for haemodialysis.

MORTALITY

Neumärker (2000) found a crude mortality rate in eating disorders which ranged from 0 to 20%. A more precise method to analyse and document the mortality rate is the standardised mortality ratio (SMR), which is defined as the relationship between observed and expected deaths, using the subject years method. In his review, MR varied between 1.4 and 17.8. In our own long-term follow-up study (Löwe et al., 2001; Zipfel et al., 2000a), we found a SMR of 9.8, very similar to the SMR (9.6) published by Herzog et al. (2000). This relatively broad range of estimates is mainly due to methodological limitations, such as study design and reporting of missing data. The main causes of death in AN patients are suicide and ventricular tachyarrhythmia. Other important causes of death, however, include disorders of the electrolyte balance (including hypophosphataemia), infections (pneumonia, sepsis), terminal renal failure, shock, ileus and gastric perforation. The mortality in AN patients of the binge-eating/purging type is about twice as high as that of the restricting type (Moller et al., 1996; Norring & Sohlberg, 1993). Mortality rates in BN patients are lower than AN and are mainly due to suicide. This reduced mortality is due to the lack of starvation-related causes, but may also in part be due to the shorter follow-up periods of outcome studies.

OBESITY

More than half of all US adults are classified as overweight (BMI > 25 kg/m^2) and one in three is considered to be obese (BMI > 30 kg/m^2). The rate of obesity has increased by 50% over the past 20 years in the USA (Yanovski & Yanovski, 1999), but a similar increase has been shown world wide. For example, the MONICA study and more recent studies in England (see Seidell & Rissannen, 1998) have demonstrated that the percentage of obesity in Europe has also undergone a sharp increase, making obesity the most common nutritional disease in industrialised countries. Binge eating disorder (BED), which is classified as an 'eating disorder not otherwise specified' in the DSM-IV (APA, 1994), has been described as the most relevant eating disorder for overweight individuals. It has been estimated, that approximately 20–30% of overweight persons seeking help at weight loss programmes are classified as binge eaters (Spitzer et al., 1993). This is one of the reasons why mental health professionals need to know about the highly prevalent condition of obesity (Devlin et al., 2000).

Excess weight increases the risk of other severe illnesses, including hypertension, diabetes, coronary heart disease (CHD) and some forms of cancer. Any treatment approach must recognise that obesity is a chronic, stigmatised, and costly disease. Recently, major advances have been made in identifying the components of the homeostatic system which regulate the control of food intake and body weight (Schwartz et al., 2000). The identification of obesity-related genes and hormones as well as the development of new drugs raises hope for the treatment of this serious epidemic.

HEALTH RISKS ASSOCIATED WITH OBESITY

In clinical practice, body fat is most commonly estimated by using the body-mass index (BMI $=$ kg/m^2). A graded classification of overweight and obesity using BMI values provides valuable information about increasing body fatness. A World Health Organisation (WHO) expert committee has proposed a classification for overweight and obesity based on the BMI with the following cut-off points (Table 4.2). There are a number of recent studies which demonstrated a close relationship between BMI and the incidence of type 2 diabetes, hypertension, coronary heart disease and cholelithiasis (Willett et al., 1999). This

Table 4.2 Cut-off points proposed by the WHO expert committee for the classification of body weight

Body mass index (kg/m^2)	WHO classification	Popular description
<18.5	Underweight	Thin
18.5–24.9	—	Healthy, normal, acceptable
25.0–29.9	Grade 1 overweight	Overweight
30.0–39.9	Grade 2 overweight	Obesity
≥40.0	Grade 3 overweight	Morbid obesity

The data presented in this table reflect knowledge acquired largely from epidemiological studies in developed countries (adapted from Kopelman, 2000).

relationship is approximately linear for a range of BMI less than 29 kg/m^2, but the risks are greatly increased for both genders above this cut-off. In addition, waist circumferences and waist-to-hip ratio provide measures for assessing upper body fat deposition. The waist circumference in particular is associated with the risk of CHD, hypertension, and blood lipid levels. Lean et al. (1995) demonstrated cut-offs for gender-specific waist circumferences associated with increased risk for metabolic complications. An expert panel on overweight has recently suggested that increased risks of metabolic complications exist if waist circumference is greater than 102 cm in men and 89 cm in women (for review, see Willett et al., 1999). Han et al. (1995) found that, in men, a waist circumference of 94 to 102 cm was associated with a relative risk of 2.2 of having one or more cardiovascular risk factors, and in women a circumference of 80 to 88 cm was associated with a relative risk of 1.6.

Metabolic Complications

Obesity is characterised by elevated fasting plasma insulin and exaggerated insulin response to an oral glucose load. Particularly upper body obesity is associated with measures of insulin resistance. The different fat depots vary in their response to hormones that regulate lipolysis, such as noradrenaline and cortisol. As a consequence, the elevated abdominal adipose tissue contributes to an exaggerated release of free fatty acids (FFA). This elevation of FFA leads to an inappropriate maintenance of glucose production and impaired hepatic glucose utilisation responsible for an impaired glucose tolerance. Prospective studies confirm a close relationship between increasing body fat and type 2 diabetes. In women, the risk for diabetes after adjustment for age for those with a BMI of 35 or greater was increased 93-fold, compared with women with a BMI of less than 21 (Colditz et al., 1995). Similar results had been demonstrated for obese men.

Cardivascular Complications

Kopelman (2000) summarises the changes and impairment of cardiovascular function in obesity. Progressive weight gain is accompanied with an increase in blood volume. As a consequence, there is an increase in the heart's pumping capacity and cardiac output. A combination of elevated circulatory preload and after load led to left ventricular (LF) dilatation and hypertrophy. In the long run, the combination of systolic and diastolic dysfunction can lead to clinically significant heart failure. In the Framingham Heart Study, Kim et al. (2000) demonstrated, that body weight was directly related to an increase in the prevalence of coronary heart disease, particularly in men. In addition, the often marked systemic vascular resistance seen in obese individuals results in a marked rise in blood pressure (hypertension) and concentric LV hypertrophy. As a consequence, these factors are responsible for an increased risk of morbidity and mortality from CHD or sudden death, due to ventricular arrhythmia. This may also be due to an increase in sympathetic and decrease in parasympathetic nervous tone (Rosenbaum et al., 1997). Other mediators, such as altered rates of blood flow, altered thrombocyte function, as well as hyperinsulinaemia or sleep apnoea may be important cofactors. Calle et al. (1999) demonstrated the risk of death from cardiovascular diseases throughout the range of moderate to severe obesity for both men and women in all age groups. The risk associated with a high BMI is greater for whites than for blacks. A weight gain of 5–8 kg is associated with an increase for CHD of 25% (Willet et al., 1995)

Additional Complications

In addition to metabolic or cardiovascular impairments, individuals with a significant excess weight show obesity-related changes in respiratory function, particularly during sleep. Besides daytime somnolence, this sleep apnoea syndrome can cause pulmonary hypertension and is associated with an increased risk of myocardial and cerebral infarction.

Studies have shown a positive association between obesity and osteoarthritis of the hand, hip and knee. The Framingham study demonstrated that a decrease in BMI of 2 units or more over 10 years decreased the odds for developing knee osteoarthritis by over 50% (Felson et al., 1992).

There is evidence that obesity is associated with an increased risk for a gall bladder carcinoma in both sexes. In addition, a higher rate of breast carcinomas and endometrium carcinomas was found in female obese individuals.

HEALTH RISKS ASSOCIATED WITH WEIGHT CYCLING

Weight loss in overweight and obese individuals improves the physical, metabolic, endocrinological and psychological complications. Intentional weight loss may also reduce obesity-related mortality. However, recent clinical guidelines, e.g. *Obesity in Scotland* (Scottish Intercollegiate Guidelines Network, 1996) have recommended that there should be a shift away from major weight loss to weight management and risk factor reduction. A modest weight reduction of 5–10 kg is associated with many beneficial health effects, including a fall of 10 mmHg systolic and 20 mmHg diastolic blood pressure, a decrease in fasting glucose levels of up to 50%, and a significant reduction in total cholesterol and LDL cholesterol. Modest weight reductions improve back and joint pain, lung function and reduce the frequency of sleep apnoea. Unbalanced 'crash' diets should be avoided, because of the high risk of weight cycling and protein depletion. Several prospective studies have outlined some disadvantages of weight loss including (a) an increased risk for women who lose 4–10 kg to develop a clinically relevant gallstone disease and (b) a loss of bone mass. These findings provide further support for the shift towards risk factor reduction and weight maintenance, rather than major weight loss.

SUMMARY AND CONCLUSIONS

Medical complications play an important role in patients with eating disorders. In particular the following patient groups are at high risk for medical complications: malnourished anorexic patients, bulimic patients with a severe symptomatology of bingeing and purging, patients with a somatic comorbidity (e.g. diabetes mellitus) as well as those individuals with a marked overweight or weight fluctuations. Therefore it is important to take a full medical history, including current medication. In view of the multiple physical problems which may occur, and their potentially serious consequences, it is advisable that all patients have a thorough physical examination, with a special focus on the cardiovascular system. In addition there is general agreement, that particularly anorexic patients should have a range of screening investigations (e.g. full blood count, biochemical profile). An electrocardiogram (ECG) is mandatory in all patients with anorexia nervosa and for those eating-disordered patients with severe electrolyte disturbances. In anorexic patients with a chronic course or additional risk factors for osteoporosis, it might be advisable to perform an assessment of bone density by dual energy X-ray absorptiometry (DEXA). It is strongly advisable that all cases of medical complications in eating disorders should be managed in consultation with a physician or a specialist (e.g. endocrinologist, cardiologist).

ACKNOWLEDGEMENT

The authors would like to thank Deborah Reas for her assistance with the translation of this chapter.

REFERENCES

Abdu, R.A., Garritano, D. & Culver, O. (1987) Acute gastric necrosis in anorexia nervosa and bulimia. Two case reports. *Arch. Surg.*, **122**, 830–832.

Allouche, J., Bennet, A., Barbe, P., Plantavid, M., Caron, P. & Louvet, J.P. (1991) LH pulsatility and in vitro bioactivity in women with anorexia nervosa-related hypothalamic amenorrhea. *Acta Endocrinol. Copenh.*, **125**, 614–620.

Alvin, P., Zogheib, J., Rey, C. & Losay, J. (1993) Severe complications and mortality in mental eating disorders in adolescence. On 99 hospitalised patients. *Arch. Fr. Pediat.*, **50**, 755–762.

APA (1994) *Diagnostic and Statistical Manual of Mental Disorders* (DSM-IV), Fourth edition. Washington, DC.: American Psychiatric Association.

Bates, G.W., Bates, S.R. & Whitworth, N.S. (1982) Reproductive failure in women who practice weight control. *Fertil. Steril.*, **37**, 373–378.

Becker, A.E., Grinspoon, S.K., Klibanski, A. & Herzog, D.B. (1999) Eating disorders. *N. Engl. J. Med.*, **340**, 1092–1098.

Beumont, P.J. & Large, M. (1991) Hypophosphataemia, delirium and cardiac arrhythmia in anorexia nervosa. *Med. J. Aust.*, **155**, 519–522.

Beumont, P.J.V., Russell, J.D. & Touyz, S.W. (1993) Treatment of anorexia nervosa. *Lancet*, **341**, 1635–1640.

Beumont, P.J.V. (1998) The neurobiology of eating behaviour and weight control. In H.W., Hoeck, J.L., Treasure & M.A., Katzman (Eds), *Neurobiology in the Treatment of Eating Disorders* (pp. 237–253). Chichester: John Wiley & Sons.

Bihun, J.A., McSherry, J. & Marciano, D. (1993) Idiopathic edema and eating disorders: Evidence for an association. *Int. J. Eat. Disord.*, **14**, 197–201.

Bonne, O.B., Bloch, M. & Berry, E.M. (1993) Adaptation to severe chronic hypokalemia in anorexia nervosa: A plea for conservative management. *Int. J. Eat. Disord.*, **13**, 125–128.

Brinch, M., Isager, T. & Tolstrup, K. (1988) Anorexia nervosa and motherhood: Reproduction pattern and mothering behavior of 50 women. *Acta Psychiat. Scand.*, **77**, 611–617.

Buchman, A.L., Ament, M.E., Weiner, M., Kodner, A. & Mayer, E.A. (1994) Reversal of megaduodenum and duodenal dysmotility associated with improvement in nutritional status in primary anorexia nervosa. *Dig. Dis. Sci.*, **39**, 433–440.

Calle, E.E., Thun, M.J., Petrelli, J.M., Rodriguez, C. & Heath-CW, J. (1999) Body-mass index and mortality in a prospective cohort of U.S. adults. *N. Engl. J. Med.*, **341**, 1097–1105.

Cariem, A.K., Lemmer, E.R., Adams, M.G., Winter, T.A. & O'Keefe, S.J. (1994) Severe hypophosphataemia in anorexia nervosa. *Postgrad. Med. J.*, **70**, 825–827.

Challier, P. & Cabrol, S. (1995) Severe hyponatremia associated with anorexia nervosa: role of inappropriate antidiuretic hormone secretion?. *Arch. Pediat.*, **2**, 977–979.

Colditz, G.A., Willett, W.C., Rotnitzky, A. & Manson, J.E. (1995) Weight gain as a risk factor for clincial diabetes mellitus in women. *Ann. Int. Med.*, **122**, 481–486.

Colombo, L., Altomare, S., Castelli, M., Bestetti, A., Stanzani, M., Colombo, N., Picollo, S., Pietrasanta, E.R., Gnocchi, P. & Giavardi, L. (1995) Kinetics of hepatic enzymes in anorexia nervosa. *Recent Prog. Med.*, **86**, 204–207.

Cooke, R.A. and Chambers, J.B. (1995) Anorexia nervosa and the heart. *Br. J. Hosp. Med.*, **54**, 313–317.

De Simone, G., Scalfi, L., Galderisi, M., Celentano, A., Di Biase, G., Tammaro, P., Garofalo, M., Mureddu, G.F., de Divitiis, O. & Contaldo, F. (1994) Cardiac abnormalities in young women with anorexia nervosa. *Br. Heart J.*, **71**, 287–292.

Delvenne, V., Goldman, S., De, M., V, Simon, Y., Luxen, A. & Lotstra, F. (1996) Brain hypometabolism of glucose in anorexia nervosa: normalization after weight gain. *Biol. Psychiat.*, **40**, 761–768.

Deter, H.C. & Herzog, W. (1994) Anorexia nervosa in a long-term perspective: results of the Heidelberg–Mannheim Study. *Psychosom. Med.*, **56**, 20–27.

Devlin, M.J., Yanovski, S.Z., Wilson, G.T. (2000) Obesity: what mental health professionals need to know. *Am. J. Psychiat.*, **157**, 854–866.

Devuyst, O., Lambert, M., Rodhain, J., Lefebvre, C. & Coche, E. (1993) Haematological changes and infectious complications in anorexia nervosa: a case-control study. *Qtly J. Med.*, **86**, 791–799.

Durakovic, Z., Durakovic, A. & Korsic, M. (1994) Changes of the corrected Q-T interval in the electrocardiogram of patients with anorexia nervosa. *Int. J. Cardiol.*, **45**, 115–120.

Fairburn, C.G. & Cooper, P.J. (1984) The clinical features of bulimia nervosa. *Br. J. Psychiat.*, **144**, 238–246.

Felson, D.T., Zhang, Y., Anthony, J.M., Naimark, A. & Anderson, J.J. (1992) Weight loss reduces the risk for symptomatic knee osteoarthritis in women. The Framingham Study. *Ann. Int. Med.*, **116**, 535–539.

Fichter, M.M., Pirke, K.M. & Holsboer, F. (1986) Weight loss causes neuroendocrine disturbances: Experimental study in healthy starving subjects. *Psychiat. Res.*, **17**, 61–72.

Fichter, M.M. & Pirke, K.M. (1990) Endocrine dysfunctions in bulimia nervosa. In M.M., Fichter (Ed.), *Bulimia Nervosa*, Chichester: John Wiley & Sons.

Fisher, M., Simpser, E. & Schneider, M. (2000) Hypophosphatemia secondary to oral refeeding in anorexia nervosa. *Int. J. Eat. Disord.*, **28**, 181–187.

Fukushima, M., Nakai, Y., Taniguchi, A., Imura, H., Nagata, I. & Tokuyama, K. (1993) Insulin sensitivity, insulin secretion, and glucose effectiveness in anorexia nervosa: A minimal model analysis. *Metabolism*, **42**, 1164–1168.

Goebel, G., Schweiger, U., Kruger, R. & Fichter, M.M. (1999) Predictors of bone mineral density in patients with eating disorders. *Int. J. Eat. Disord.*, **25**, 143–150.

Golden, N.H., Ashtari, M., Kohn, M.R., Patel, M., Jacobson, M.S., Fletcher, A. & Shenker, I.R. (1996) Reversibility of cerebral ventricular enlargement in anorexia nervosa, demonstrated by quantitative magnetic resonance imaging. *J. Pediat.*, **128**, 296–301.

Gordon, C., Grace, E., Emans, S., Goodman, E., Crawford, M. & Leboff, M. (1999) Changes in bone turnover markers and menstrual function after short-term oral DHEA in young women with anorexia nervosa. *J. Bone Miner. Res.*, **14**, 136–145.

Grinspoon, S., Herzog, D. & Klibanski, A. (1997) Mechanisms and treatment options for bone loss in anorexia nervosa. *Psychopharmacol. Bull.*, **33**, 399–404.

Hall, R.C., Beresford, T.P. & Hall, A.K. (1989) Hypomagnesemia in eating disorder patients: clinical signs and symptoms. *Psychiat. Med.*, **7**, 193–203.

Hall, R.C. & Beresford, T.P. (1989) Medical complications of anorexia and bulimia. *Psychiat. Med.*, **7**, 165–192.

Han, T.S., van Leer, E.E., Seidell, J.C., Lean, M.E. (1995) Waist circumference action levels in the identification of cardiovascular risk factors: prevalence study in a random sample. *Br. Med. J.*, **311**, 1401–1405.

Hebebrand, J., Blum, W.F., Barth, N., Coners, H., Englaro, P., Juul, A., Ziegler, A., Warnke, A., Rascher, W. & Remschmidt, H. (1997) Leptin levels in patients with anorexia nervosa are reduced in the acute stage and elevated upon short-term weight restoration. *Mol. Psychiat.*, **2**, 330–334.

Herzog, D.B., Greenwood, D.N., Dorer, D.J., Flores, A.T., Ekeblad, E. R., Richards, A., Blais, M.A. & Keller, M.B. (2000) Mortality in eating disorders: a descriptive study. *Int. J. Eat. Disord.*, **28**, 20–26.

Herzog, W., Minne, H., Deter, C., Leidig, G., Schellberg, D., Wuster, C., Gronwald, R., Sarembe, E., Kroger, F., Bergmann, G. et al. (1993) Outcome of bone mineral density in anorexia nervosa patients 11.7 years after first admission. *J. Bone Miner. Res.*, **8**, 597–605.

Herzog, W., Deter, H.C., Fiehn, W. & Petzold, E. (1997a) Medical findings and predictors of long-term physical outcome in anorexia nervosa: a prospective, 12-year follow-up study. *Psychol. Med.*, **27**, 269–279.

Herzog, W., Schellberg, D. & Deter, H.C. (1997b) First recovery in anorexia nervosa patients in the long-term course: a discrete-time survival analysis. *J. Consult. Clin. Psychol.*, **65**, 169–177.

Hughes, J.R. (1996) A review of the usefulness of the standard EEG in psychiatry. *Clin. Electroenceph.*, **27**, 35–39.

Humphries, L.L., Adams, L.J., Eckfeldt, J.H., Levitt, M.D. & McClain, C.J. (1987) Hyperamylasemia in patients with eating disorders. *Ann. Int. Med.*, **106**, 50–52.

Joyce, J.M., Warren, D.L., Humphries, L.L., Smith, A.J. & Coon, J.S. (1990) Osteoporosis in women with eating disorders: comparison of physical parameters, exercise, and menstrual status with SPA and DPA evaluation. *J. Nucl. Med.*, **31**, 325–331.

Kahn, D., Halls, J., Bianco, J.A. & Perlman, S.B. (1991) Radionuclide ventriculography in severely underweight anorexia nervosa patients before and during refeeding therapy. *J. Adolesc. Health.*, **12**, 301–306.

Key, A., Mason, H., Bolton, J. (2000) Reproduction and eating disorders: a fruitless union. *Eur. Eat. Disord. Rev.*, **8**, 98–107.

Kingston, K., Szmukler, G., Andrewes, D., Tress, B. & Desmond, P. (1996) Neuropsychological and structural brain changes in anorexia nervosa before and after refeeding. *Psychol. Med.*, **26**, 15–28.

Kim, K.S., Owen, W.L., Williams, D. & Adams-Campbell, L.L. (2000) A comparison between BMI and conicity index on predicting coronary heart disease: the Framingham Heart Study. *Ann. Epidemiol.*, **10**, 424–431.

Klibanski, A., Biller, B.M., Schoenfeld, D.A., Herzog, D.B. & Saxe, V.C. (1995) The effect of estrogen administration on trabecular bone loss in young women with anorexia nervosa. *J. Clin. Endocrinol. Metab.*, 898–904.

Kopelman, P.G. (2000) Obesity as a medical problem. *Nature*, **404**, 635–643.

Köpp, W., Blum, W.F., Ziegler, A., Lubbert, H., Emons, G., Herzog, W., Herpertz, S., Deter, H.C., Remschmidt, H. & Hebebrand, J. (1997) Low leptin levels predict amenorrhea in underweight and eating disordered females. *Mol. Psychiat.*, **2**, 335–340.

Kornreich, L., Shapira, A., Horev, G., Danziger, Y., Tyano, S. & Mimouni, M. (1991) CT and MR evaluation of the brain in patients with anorexia nervosa. *Am. J. Neuroradiol.*, **12**, 1213–1216.

Kreipe, R.E., Goldstein, B., DeKing, D.E., Tipton, R. & Kempski, M.H. (1994) Heart rate power spectrum analysis of autonomic dysfunction in adolescents with anorexia nervosa. *Int. J. Eat. Disord.*, **16**, 159–165.

Krieg, J.C. (1991) Eating disorders as assessed by cranial computerised tomography (CCT, dSPECT, PET). *Adv. Exp. Med. Biol.*, **291**, 223–229.

Laessle, R.G., Krieg, J.C., Fichter, M.M. & Pirke, K.M. (1989) Cerebral atrophy and vigilance performance in patients with anorexia nervosa and bulimia nervosa. *Neuropsychobiology*, **21**, 187–191.

Lambert, M. and Boland, B. (2000) Haematological complications. *Eur. Eat. Disord. Rev.*, **8**, 158–163.

Lean, M.E., Han, T.S. & Morrison, T.E. (1995) Waist circumference as a measure for indicating need for weight management. *Br. Med. J.*, **331**, 158–161.

Löwe, B., Zipfel, S., Buchholz, C., Dupont, Y., Reas, D.L. & Herzog, W. (2001) Long-term outcome of anorexia nervosa in a prospective 21-year follow-up study. *Psychol. Med.*, **31**, 881–890.

Mitchell, J.E., Pyle, R.L., Eckert, E.D., Hatsukami, D. & Lentz, R. (1983) Electrolyte and other physiological abnormalities in patients with bulimia. *Psychol. Med.*, **13**, 273–278.

Mitchell, J.E., Seim, H.C., Colon, E. & Pomeroy, C. (1987) Medical complications and medical management of bulimia. *Ann. Int. Med.*, **107**, 71–77.

Moller, M.S., Nystrup, J., and Nielsen, S. (1996) Mortality in anorexia nervosa in Denmark during the period 1970–1987. *Acta Psychiat. Scand.*, **94**, 454–459.

Neumärker, K.J. (2000) Mortality rates and causes of death. *Eur. Eat. Disord. Rev.*, **8**, 181–187.

Newman, M.M. & Halmi, K.A. (1989) Relationship of bone density to estradiol and cortisol in anorexia nervosa and bulimia. *Psychiat. Res.*, **29**, 105–112.

Newton, J.R., Freeman, C.P., Hannan, W.J. & Cowen, S. (1993) Osteoporosis and normal weight bulimia nervosa—which patients are at risk? *J. Psychosom. Res.*, **37**, 239–247.

Norring, C.E. and Sohlberg, S.S. (1993) Outcome, recovery, relapse and mortality across six years in patients with clinical eating disorders. *Acta Psychiat. Scand.*, **87**, 437–444.

Patchell, R.A., Fellows, H.A. & Humphries, L.L. (1994) Neurological complications of anorexia nervosa. *Acta Neurol. Scand.*, **89**, 111–116.

Pirke, K.M., Schweiger, U., Strowitzki, T., Tuschl, R.J., Laessle, R.G., Broocks, A., Huber, B. & Middendorf, R. (1989) Dieting causes menstrual irregularities in normal weight young women through impairment of episodic luteinizing hormone secretion. *Fertil. Steril.*, **51**, 263–268.

Ratcliffe, P.J. & Bevan, J.S. (1985) Severe hypoglycaemia and sudden death in anorexia nervosa. *Psychol. Med.*, **15**, 679–681.

Rigotti, N.A., Neer, R.M., Skates, S.J., Herzog, D.B. & Nussbaum, S.R. (1991) The clinical course of osteoporosis in anorexia nervosa. A longitudinal study of cortical bone mass. *JAMA*, **265**, 1133–1138.

Robb, N.B., Smith, B.G. & Geidrys, L.E. (1995) The distribution of erosion on the dentitions of patients with eating disorders. *Br. Dent. J.*, **178**, 171–174.

Robinson, P.H. (2000) The gastrointestinal tract in eating disorders. *Eur. Eat. Disord. Rev.*, **8**, 88–97.

Rosenbaum, M., Leibel, R.L. & Hirsch, J. (1997) Obesity. *N. Engl. J. Med.*, **337**, 396–407.

Rothenberger, A., Blanz, B. & Lehmkuhl, G. (1991) What happens to electrical brain activity when anorectic adolescents gain weight? *Eur. Arch. Psychiat. Clin. Neurosci.*, **240**, 144–147.

Ruegsegger, P., Durand, E.P. & Dambacher, M.A. (1991) Differential effects of ageing and disease on trabecular and compact bone density of the radius. *Bone*, **12**, 99–105.

Schlegel, S. & Kretzschmar, K. (1997) Value of computerised tomography and magnetic resonance tomography in psychiatric diagnosis. *Nervenarzt*, **68**, 1–10.

Schocken, D.D., Holloway, J.D. & Powers, P.S. (1989) Weight loss and the heart. Effects of anorexia nervosa and starvation. *Arch Int. Med.*, **149**, 877–881.

Schou, J.A., Lund, L. & Sandermann, J. (1994) Spontaneous ventricular rupture in adults. *Ugeskr. Laeger*, **156**, 3299–3305.

Schwartz, M.W., Woods, S.C., Porte, D., Seeley, R.J. & Baskin, D.G. (2000) Central nervous system control of food intake. *Nature*, **404**, 661–671.

Schweiger, U., Laessle, R.G., Pfister, H. et al. (1987) Diet induced menstrual irregularities: Effect of age and weight loss. *Fertil. Steril.*, **48**, 746–751.

Scottish Intercollegiate Guidelines Network (1996) *Obesity in Scotland. Integrating Prevention with Weight Management.* http://www.show.scot.nhs.uk/sign/sign8inf.html.

Seibel, M.J., Cosman, F., Shen, V., Gordon, S., Dempster, D.W., Ratcliffe, A. & Lindsay, R. (1993) Urinary hydroxypyridinium crosslinks of collagen as markers of bone resorption and estrogen efficacy in postmenopausal osteoporosis. *J. Bone Miner. Res.*, **8**, 881–889.

Seidell, J.C. & Rissannen, A.M. (1998) Time trends in the world-wide prevalence of obesity. In G.A., Bray, C., Bouchard & W.P.T., James (Eds), *Hanbook of Obesity*, (pp. 79–91). New York: Dekker.

Serpell, L. & Treasure, J. (1997) Osteoporosis: A serious health risk in chronic anorexia nervosa. *Eur. Eat. Disord. Rev.*, **5**, 149–157.

Sharp, C.W. and Freeman, C.P. (1993) The medical complications of anorexia nervosa. *Br. J. Psychiat.*, **162**, 452–462.

Siegel, J.H., Hardoff, D., Golden, N.H. & Shenker, I.R. (1995) Medical complications in male adolescents with anorexia nervosa. *J. Adolesc. Health.*, **16**, 448–453.

Simmons, M.S., Grayden, S.K. & Mitchell, J.E. (1986) The need for psychiatric-dental liaison in the treatment of bulimia. *Am. J. Psychiat.*, **143**, 783–784.

Spitzer, R.L., Yanovski, S., Wadden, T., Wing, R., Markus, M.D. Stunkard, A. (1993) Binge eating disorder: its further validation in a multisite study. *Int. J. Eat. Disord.*, **13**, 137–153.

Sungot-Borgen, J., Bahr, R., Falch, J. A. & Sundgot-Schneider, L. (1998) Normal bone mass in bulimic women. *J. Clin. Endocrinol. Metab.*, 3144–3149.

Szmukler, G.I., Young, G.P., Lichtenstein, M. & Andrews, J.T. (1990) A serial study of gastric emptying in anorexia nervosa and bulimia. *Aust. N.Z. J. Med.*, **20**, 220–225.

Tenholder, M.F. & Pike, J.D. (1991) Effect of anorexia nervosa on pulmonary immunocompetence. *South. Med. J.*, **84**, 1188–1191.

Touyz, S.W., Liew, V.P., Tseng, P. & et al. (1993) Oral and dental complications in dieting disorders. *Int. J. Eat. Disord.*, **14**, 341–347.

Watts, N.B. (2001) Treatment of osteoporosis with bisphosphonates. *Rheum. Dis. Clin. North. Am.*, **27**, 197–214.

Ward, A., Brown, N. & Treasure, J. (1997) Persistent osteopenia after recovery from anorexia nervosa. *Int. J. Eat. Disord.*, **22**, 71–75.

Willett, W.C., Manson, J.E., Stampfer, M.J., Colditz, G.A., Rosner, B. & Speiser, F.E. (1995) Weight, weight change, and coronary heart disease in women. Risk within the normal weight range. *JAMA*, **273**, 461–465.

Willett, W.C., Dietz, W.H. & Colditz, G.A. (1999) Guidelines for healthy weight. *N. Engl. J. Med.*, **341**, 427–434.

Willis, J. & Rand, P. (1988) Pregnancy in bulimic women. *Obstet. Gynecol.*, **71**, 708.

Winston, A.P. & Stafford, P.J. (2000) Cardiovascular effects of anorexia nervosa. *Eur. Eat. Disord. Rev.*, **8**, 117–125.

Yanovski, J.A. & Yanovski, S.Z. (1999) Recent advances in basic obesity research. *JAMA*, **282**, 1504–1506.

Zipfel, S., Specht, T. & Herzog, W. (1998) Medical complications in eating disorders. In H., Hoeck, J., Treasure & M., Katzman (Eds), *The Integration of Neurobiology in the Treatment of Eating Disorders* (pp. 457–484). New York, Toronto: John Wiley & Sons.

Zipfel, S., Specht, T., Blum, W., Englaro, P., Hebebrand, J., Hartmann, M., Wüster, C., Ziegler, R. & Herzog, W. (1998) Leptin—a parameter for body fat measurment in patients with eating disorders. *Eur. Eat. Disord. Rev.*, **6**, 38–47.

Zipfel, S., Lowe, B., Reas, D.L., Deter, H.C. & Herzog, W. (2000a) Long-term prognosis in anorexia nervosa: Lessons from a 21-year follow-up study. *Lancet*, **355**, 721–722.

Zipfel, S., Herzog, W., Beumont, P.J. & Russell, J.D. (2000b) Osteoporosis. *Eur. Eat. Disord. Rev.*, **8**, 108–116.

Zipfel, S., Seibel, M.J., Löwe, B., Beumont, P.J., Kasperk, C., Herzog, W. (in press). Osteoporosis in eating disorders: a follow-up study of patients with anorexia and bulimia nervosa. *J. Clin. Endocrinol. Metab.*

CHAPTER 5

Family, Burden of Care and Social Consequences

Søren Nielsen

*Psychiatric Youth Centre, Storstrøm County Psychiatric Services,
Næstved, Denmark*

and

Núria Bará-Carril

West London Mental Health NHS Trust, Southall, UK

SUMMARY

What do we know?

- High levels of distress—personal and intra-familial
- Burden of care high—familial, psychiatric and somatic
- Loss of productive years—through periods of illness and through premature death
- 'Stunting'—emotional, psychosexual, physical and vocational
- Outcome depends on both patient and treatment factors—'experts' do make a difference

What we need to know more about

- Which patients and families benefit most from which type and dose of treatment
- Outcome if treatment is refused, incomplete or prematurely terminated
- Characteristics of cases untraced or refusing follow-up
- Sibling's roles in the disease process and in the treatment process
- Consumer satisfaction—of patients as well as carers
- Quality of life—with and without eating disorder

INTRODUCTION

The concept 'burden of care' has attracted only limited attention in the field of eating disorders (Treasure et al., 2001). It is clear from outcome studies that there is a lot of suffering in and around persons with eating disorders (Tolstrup et al., 1987; Ratnasuria

The Essential *Handbook of Eating Disorders.* Edited by J. Treasure, U. Schmidt and E. van Furth.
© 2005 John Wiley & Sons, Ltd.

et al., 1991; Crisp et al., 1992; Theander, 1970, 1992, 1996; Keller et al., 1992; Wentz, 2000). Personal reports clearly attest to this (MacDonald, 2000). Our aim is to look at the 'burden' from three perspectives: personal, familial and societal. We will attempt to outline what is known, and what deficits there are in our present knowledge.

PERSONAL BURDEN

Misery

In the acute phase of the illness patients do seem to get some satisfaction from the anorectic way of life. However, later the costs become apparent in terms of loneliness, despair and intense mood swings. The rigid control of all aspects of life tends to kill life as other people know it, and indeed as the patient herself has known it. Despite all efforts, no success seems to be really satisfactory, further goals continue to loom on the horizon. No solutions are in sight, only problems. From an outsider's—e.g. most therapists—perspective the condition is enigmatic. Many autobiographical accounts exist, a few of which can be found in authoritative texts, e.g. Haggiag (2000). Some emphasise the suffering brought about by treatment, rather than the suffering originating from the illness *per se*. This point of view is understandable, given the clinical accounts of some of the more drastic treatment approaches (e.g. Theander, 1970, esp. pp. 115–118; Morgan & Crisp, 2000).

Stunting

Social

The 'hibernation' following from years of existence as a person with an eating disorder, with chronic malnutrition, a limited range of interests and few free choices, can lead to sequelae in many areas of life. The potential for development is seldom fulfilled. Anorexia nervosa can lead to developmental delay, emotionally as well as socially. Ratnasuriya et al. (1991) noted that many in their cohort did not obtain full independence, but stayed with relatives in a dependent relationship, with a limited range of interests, neither completing an education nor holding a job. Tolstrup et al. (1987) found a downward slide in social class in the probands from the initial evaluation to the first follow-up in 1981–1982. The long-term significance of this finding will be fully appreciated only after further follow-up interviews. We have reanalysed some of the published raw data from the interesting follow-up study from Sweden, in particular 'the living situation' given in Wentz (2000) using the program package *StatXact4* (Cytel, 2000). The data set consists of singly ordered R × C tables, and consequently the Kruskall-Wallis test (Siegel & Castellan, 1988) is the relevant analytical tool.

   A smaller proportion of the AN group (study group) shared a flat, and more live alone than in the COMP group (comparison group). Similar numbers in both groups live with parents, and similar numbers are married/cohabitating in each group. At variance with Tolstrup et al. (1987) and Ratnasuriya et al. (1991), Wentz (2000) found no between-group differences in 'occupation' when the cohort was 24 years old, i.e. after 10 years of follow-up.

Table 5.1 Personal contacts and activities at follow-up[a]

	Distribution across categories. Absolute numbers AN group ($N = 51$)	Distribution across categories. Absolute numbers. COMP. group ($N = 51$)	Kruskall–Wallis test. Observed test statistic and 'exact' p-value
Personal contacts at 6 years of follow-up	26 8 11 6	41 5 5 0	11.12; exact p-value 0.0008
Personal contacts at 10 years of follow-up	20 7 20 4	44 1 6 0	23.02; exact p-value 0.0000
Social activities at 6 years of follow-up	27 15 6 3	45 5 1 0	15.81; exact p-value 0.0001
Social activities at 10 years of follow-up	23 14 12 2	42 5 4 0	15.05; exact p-value 0.0001

[a]Reanalysis of published raw data from Wentz (2000), Paper III, Table 4, using the program package *StatXact4* (Cytel, 2000).

On the other hand, a pronounced difference between the AN group and the COMP group is noted in the quantity and quality of the 'personal contacts'. At the 6-year follow-up the AN group has significantly fewer and more superficial friendships than the COMP group, and the situation seems to be even worse at the 10-year follow-up (see Table 5.1). The findings for the dimension 'social activities' are very similar: significantly fewer in the AN group mix well outside the family and more feel solitary or do not take part in activities outside the family. The findings were similar at the 6-year follow-up and at the 10-year follow-up (see Table 5.1 for details).

Sexual

Many former eating-disordered patients have problems with sexuality in general and consequently with procreation (Key et al., 2000). Brinch et al. (1988a) found fertility reduced to one-third of the expected numbers, twice the rate of prematurity in the offspring, and a six-fold increase in perinatal mortality in a cohort of 140 former female anorexia nervosa patients. It is of note that none of the 11 males cases had offspring. A two-fold increase in miscarriage rate was reported for a bulimic population in a controlled study by Willis and Rand (1988). Increased miscarriage rate is also reported by Abraham (1998). In some cases females are helped by gynaecologists who stimulate ovulation with clomiphene. There is controversy about this as it could be argued that unless someone is ready to accept a biologically healthy body weight for themselves they may not be able to meet the demands of intimacy and motherhood. There are several reports of highly problematic interactions between an eating-disordered mother and her baby (i.e. irritability and inability to cope with the child's demands while bingeing) (Smith & Hanson, 1972; Fahy & Treasure, 1989; Stein & Fairburn, 1989; van Wezel-Meijer & Wit, 1989; O'Donoghue et al., 1991; Stein et al., 1999, 2001; Jacobi et al., 2001). In addition, Evans and le Grange (1995) found that at least half the children of the 10 eating-disordered mothers they studied were suffering from emotional difficulties.

A rather unexpected finding from the Gothenburg cohort (see Paper III in Wentz, 2000) is that 10 out of 51 AN probands had become mothers at age 24 (the latest follow-up), against only 4 of 51 in the COMP group (a statistically non-significant difference; $p = 0.15$). The mothers in both groups had on average 1.5 children—a figure almost identical to that reported by Brinch et al. (1988a). Mothering behaviour has not yet been reported in studies from the Gothenburg cohort.

The findings by Wentz (2000) on sexual attitudes and sexual behaviour were that 82% of the AN group and 96% of the COMP group had a positive attitude towards sexual matters (this difference is approaching statistical significance—Fisher statistic 3.883; exact p-value 0.09). Furthermore, pleasurable sexual relationships were reported in 67% of the AN group, and in 84% of the COMP group (this figure is also approaching statistical significance—Fisher statistic 4.241; exact p-value 0.06). However, the AN individuals tended to have fewer and less satisfactory love affairs. The findings on marital status reflect the Scandinavian way of life: in both groups about 10% are married, about 40% are cohabitating (with and without children) and about 50% live alone. There is a statistically significant between-group difference, mainly brought about by 9 in the AN group, as opposed to only 2 in the COMP group, cohabitating with children (Fisher statistic 7.92; exact p-value 0.04).

Intellectual and Vocational Functioning

Several long-term follow-up studies (Tolstrup et al., 1987; Ratnasuria et al., 1991; Crisp et al., 1992; Theander, 1970, 1992, 1996) indicate that a significant number of former eating-disordered patients do not fulfil reasonable expectations, given many probands' apparent resources and family background. More recent studies with a shorter follow-up period cannot be expected to contribute definitive evidence on this issue. A recent Swedish multicentre follow-up study (see Paper I in Wallin, 2000) encompassing five child and adolescent psychiatric treatment centres showed that 3.2 years after the end of treatment 70.3% of 111 female with DSM-III-R anorexia nervosa had a 'good outcome'—they were considered recovered, with a body mass index within the normal range, regular menstruation and normalised eating. Two-thirds of the probands had a global assessment of functioning scale (GAF; APA, 1987) score of 80 or above, indicating good psychological, social and occupational function. No deaths were recorded, but one should keep in mind that the average age at follow-up was 17.3 years. Wentz et al. (2001) report significantly lower mean GAF scores in the AN group ($M = 65$) as opposed to a mean GAF score of 84 in the COMP group. In the AN group there was a significant difference in GAF score between those who had received psychiatric treatment during the period of observation (median GAF score 60) and those who had not (median GAF score 75).

Quality of Life

It follows from the above that a reduced quality can be expectable in many areas of life. Very little eating disorder-specific research has been carried out (e.g. Keilen et al., 1994; Padierna et al., 2000). The latter authors evaluated 196 consecutive patients from an eating disorder outpatient clinic. Compared to 18- to 34-year-old women from the general population, eating-disordered patients were more dysfunctional in all areas measured by the SF-36 (Ware et al., 1993). There were no differences between the diagnostic subgroups. Higher levels of psychopathology (measured by eating attitudes test) were associated with greater impairment on all SF-36 subscales.

Consumer Satisfaction

This is one perspective relevant to quality of life, but it is seldom elucidated. Brinch et al. (1988b) evaluated the child psychiatric probands ($n = 64$) of the Copenhagen Anorexia Nervosa Follow-up Study (Tolstrup et al., 1987) on this dimension. Over 80% were interviewed on average 12.5 years after presentation. One question was: 'When you recall your contact with the department do you think of it as something positive, or negative?' Eleven replies were 'clearly plus somewhat positive', 20 were 'neutral' and 22 'negative'. Outcome status was unrelated to consumer satisfaction, and no difference in consumer satisfaction was detected between inpatients and outpatients. Rosenvinge and Klusmeier (2000) received 321 useful self-report questionnaires out of 600 (54%) that were sent to members of the Norwegian organisations for former and present eating-disordered patients. Combining the response categories 'of some help' and 'extremely helpful' the authors concluded that 57% found treatment helpful. They found no difference in response related to 'expertise', i.e. the satisfaction was similar whether the GP or an 'expert' had provided the treatment. Almost one-third found that family therapy 'made the situation worse'. A remarkable finding is that 57 of 115 persons treated in hospital had been detained against their will, and of these only 34% were satisfied with this legal action in retrospect. The probands suggested the following recommendations for improving eating disorder services: 'improving clinical competence and knowledge of EDs among GPs (17%) and schoolteachers (14%)', 'to provide help to relatives . . .' (12.5%), 'more specialists in eating disorders' (11%), and 'suitable inpatient treatment programmes' (9%). This Norwegian study was a replication of a larger British study (Newton et al., 1993) and the findings are largely similar.

FAMILIAL BURDEN

History: The Family as Cause

Ideas about the role of the family have changed over time, as almost all aspects of our understanding of the eating disorders. A good introduction to this field is found in Part I of Szmukler et al. (1995), and in Tanner and Connan (2003). The seminal works of Selvini-Palazzoli (1974) and Minuchin et al. (1978) stimulated a lot of interest in the role of the family in the aetiology of these disorders. Unfortunately this led to families suffering and experiencing guilt and blame. Some of the concepts of Minuchin et al. (1978) proved elusive (Kog et al., 1987; Dare et al., 1994), whereas other researchers (le Grange et al., 1992b; Papers 2–4 in Wallin, 2000) found some terms (e.g. 'enmeshment', 'adaptability' and 'cohesion') useful.

Present: The Consequences for the Family

As research matured and became less impressionistic the focus shifted towards an under-standing of the suffering of all it involved. More reliable tools for family observation were employed, on "normal" as well as "clinical" families, and researchers became aware of the fact that very few normal family functions remain after living with an eating-disordered person for a year or more. The concept of 'expressed emotion' (Leff & Vaughn, 1985) has found its way into eating disorder research (van Furth, 1991; le Grange et al., 1992a). Expressed emotion is a measure of family interaction originally developed in the schizophrenia field. It assesses the attitudes and behaviours that family members express towards their ill relative. The interaction in families of eating-disordered patients is characterised by low levels of expressed emotion, and particularly of criticism, as compared to those found in families of schizophrenic patients (Dare et al., 1994; Goldstein, 1981; le Grange et al., 1992a; Hodes et al., 1999; Szmukler et al., 1985; van Furth et al., 1996). However criticism is higher in families of bulimic patients than in those of anorexic patients; it has been argued that this could be a result of the greater disruption and lesser acceptability of the bulimic symptoma-tology (Hodes & le Grange, 1993). Higher levels of emotional expression have also been associated to other variables such as older age, laxative use, and presence of comorbidity (van Furth et al., 1996).

The measure of expressed emotion (EE) in relatives is associated with a poor outcome for patients with eating disorders (see Butzlaff & Hooley, 1998). The effect size of the rela-tionship between living with a relative with high EE (critical, hostile or emotionally overin-volved) and poor outcome is 0.51. This is higher than the effect size found for schizophrenia or for mood disorders although this finding must be interpreted with caution as it is based on only one study in anorexia nervosa. One study had some weak evidence which suggested that expressed emotion may be used as a predictor to distinguish differential treatment ef-fectiveness, in that families with high expressed emotion did better with separated rather than conjoint family therapy (Eisler et al., 2000).

Collaborating with the Family

There is an increasing awareness of the necessity of a more positive cooperation with the families. This was brought about in part by the de-institutionalisation movement, and partly by the increased influence of family therapy and family therapy research (Russell et al., 1987; Stierlin & Weber, 1989; Dare et al., 1990; Crisp et al., 1991).

Many treatment centres employ parents' groups as an integral part of the treatment programme (Rose & Garfinkel, 1980; Jeammet & Gorge, 1980; Lewis & MacGuire, 1985). At Rigshospitalet in Copenhagen we noticed a sharp decline in unplanned terminations of treatment after the introduction of group work (a parents' group once a month, and weekly patients' groups—one 'talking group' and one art group) at the department of child psychiatry in 1986 (Tolstrup, 1990).

The principles of psychoeducation for groups of patients (Garner, 1997) and for patients and families (Surgenor et al., 2000) are beginning to be used. Another new development is the introduction of the multi-family group (McFarlane, 1983, 1991) in the treatment of eating disorders (Dare & Eisler, 2000; Scholz & Asen, 2001).

Care

Thus, despite the lack of agreement about the role that the family plays in the aetiology and/or maintenance of eating disorders, it is now widely accepted that the family plays an important role both in the formal and in the informal care of the eating-disordered patient. Caring for a relative with a psychiatric disorder can be a rewarding experience. However, it can also have an adverse effect in a number of areas of family functioning. The household roles and routines may change, and the family relationships, social life, leisure activities, career and finances may also be affected; in addition to these, the subjective distress of the carers can also be considerable, and both their physical and emotional health can suffer (Perring et al., 1990). This is what has often been conceptualised as burden of care (Schene, 1990) or, from a more constructive perspective, caregiving distress (Szmukler, 1996).

The diagnosis of an eating disorder may give rise to a wide variety of feelings and emotions in the family, including surprise, disbelief, relief and, most commonly, shame and guilt. The carers' guilt is often reflected in their immediate desire to find out what they did wrong. They may even believe that they should have noticed the patient's difficulties earlier and should have provided help sooner, or maybe that they had delayed seeking professional help for too long (Perednia & Vandereycken, 1989). In addition, among younger patients the parents' loss of control over their son's or daughter's eating may result in their feeling that they have failed to fulfil a basic parenting task (Walford & McCune, 1991; Wood et al., 1998).

Family daily routines are usually disrupted, with mealtimes becoming a battle that causes distress for the entire family. The family eating pattern is often altered in an attempt to help the patient eat. Carers may end up preparing different foods at different times for different family members and meals are no longer a social event, but a struggle that adds to the carer's distress.

The patient's behavioural changes may disrupt the family life (Morandé, 1999). Thus, in addition to the isolation and secretiveness that often surround eating disorders, bulimic patients may engage in antisocial behaviours such as lying, stealing, or substance misuse. Carers may be confused by the ambivalent message they seem to be getting: while on the one hand patients seem to be struggling to achieve independence, on the other they fail to fulfil their own basic needs and are indeed perceived as special and in need of extraordinary care.

Patients may thus become the focus of attention in the family. Slowly, there is less time devoted to friends and social activities, and more to the ill family member. Families may become isolated and believe that what they are going through is a unique and shameful experience. As Perednia and Vandereycken (1989) pointed out, these feelings may in turn be reinforced by relatives and friends who, in an attempt to help, give advice to the carer on what they should and should not do, which can be seen to imply that there is something the carer is not doing right.

In a recent pilot study, which appears to be the first to specifically examine the experience of caregiving in eating disorders, the General Health Questionnaire (GHQ; Goldberg & Hillier, 1979) and the Experience of Care Giving Inventory (ECI; Szmukler et al., 1996) were used to compare the experiences of carers of anorexic in patients with those of carers of people with a psychotic illness (Treasure et al., 2001). Although no differences were found with regard to the positive aspects of caregiving, carers of the anorexic patients reported more difficulties and higher levels of psychological distress. In addition, carers of the anorexic patients were also asked to write about their particular experience of caring. Among other issues, feelings of guilt, shame and loss were mentioned, as well as difficulties in family functioning and in dealing with the patient's difficult behaviours. Treasure and colleagues (2001) concluded that carers experience many difficulties and high levels of psychological distress, and highlighted the need of further research into carers' distress in the area of eating disorders.

Siblings

Although it is very likely that siblings of eating-disordered patients may also feel the strain of the eating disorder, little is known about the extent of the effect that the eating disorder may have on them. Roberto (1988) and Colahan and Senior (1995) mention that the non-sick sibling(s) get some apparent freedom through a process of de-identification from the sick person. This 'freedom' entails a considerable loss of an appropriate sibling relationship and of parental attention. The existing large body of literature regarding the effects that chronic illnesses may have on the family has shown that, although the incidence of psychiatric disorders is not higher than in the general population, healthy siblings may experience high levels of distress and a wide range of adjustment problems (Sahler et al., 1994). There is a great need of research in order to shed some light into the needs and experiences of siblings, who probably constitute one of the most neglected groups of carers in the eating disorder literature (Moulds et al., 2000).

Parenting

The actual treatment of the eating-disordered patient can also have a deep impact on the family functioning. If the patient's condition is severe enough to require inpatient treatment, this may result in an immediate feeling of relief in the carer; however, the family separation may also add to any existing feelings of guilt, failure, isolation and family fragmenta-tion (Vandereycken, et al., 1989). The recovery from the eating disorder will involve the acquisition of new roles not only for the patient, but also for the remaining family members.

SOCIETAL BURDEN

Burden on Health Care Delivery Systems

The impact of these disorders on the health care delivery systems has been the subject of a few register studies (McKenzie & Joyce, 1992; Nielsen et al., 1996), a single case study (Howlett et al., 1995), and one review (Agras, 2001). Deter and Herzog (1994) found after almost 12 years of follow-up a four-fold increase in the use of both psychiatric and somatic beds. Theander (1970) showed (Table 36, p. 93) that the number of hospital days used by seven cases with 'severe anorexia nervosa at review' ranged from 41 to 1006 (mean 364.4 days; median 295 days). The register study of McKenzie and Joyce (1992) showed a similar variation in length of total inpatient care across all admissions ($n = 190$) for the 112 patients first admitted in 1980 and 1981. Furthermore the admission data showed clear indication of non-Gaussian distribution (range: 1–1380 days; mean 139 days; SD 175 days). First admissions had a mean length of 64 days (SD 46 days; range 1–112 days). Only patients with organic disorders and schizophrenia had a higher cumulative length of inpatient stay over the five years of follow-up. The editorial by Howlett et al. (1995) gives details of a case with a cumulated length of stay of 1161 days over a four-year period—a figure that approaches, but does not exceed, the upper range given in McKenzie and Joyce (1992). The study by Nielsen et al. (1996) investigates data from the Danish nationwide register of psychiatric admissions in the period 1970–1993.

Selected findings from that study are summarised in Figures 5.1, 5.2 and 5.3 below.

In Figure 5.1 please note a highly significant change point (Jones and Dey, 1995) in 1980. See the statistical details in Table 5.2.

In both general psychiatry and adolescent psychiatry the proportion of bed days used by anorexia nervosa patients increased five-fold from 1970 to 1993. The number of available beds in general psychiatry was almost halved in that period. In child psychiatry two highly significant change points (Jones and Dey, 1995) were found in 1981 and 1988. See Figure 5.2 and Table 5.3 below.

We also analysed the proportion of bed days used by anorexia nervosa patients relative to the total number of psychiatric bed days for females under 18 years of age (all psychiatric specialties combined). We found a linear increase from 2% around 1970 to 20% in 1993, a ten-fold increase (see Figure 5.3).

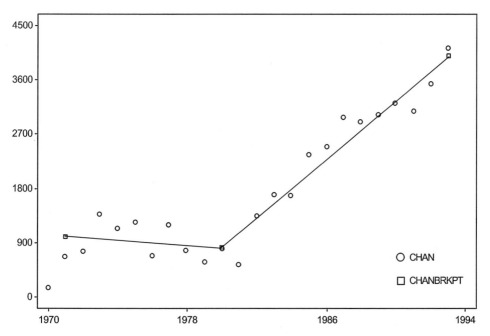

Figure 5.1 Yearly number of child psychiatric bed-days used by AN patients in Denmark 1970–1993. No trend in the period 1971–1980. Note the existence of one significant change point in 1980 where the trend changes into a significant positive value (see text). (*Source*: Nielsen et al., 1996)

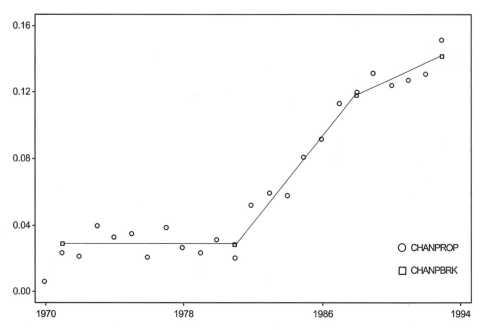

Figure 5.2 Proportion of the the total number of child psychiatric bed-days utilised by AN patients in Denmark 1970–1993. Stable values from 1971 to 1981. Positive trend is evident from 1981 to 1988 where the trend changes into a less positive value. Both change points statistically significant, see Table 5.3. (*Source*: Nielsen et al., 1996)

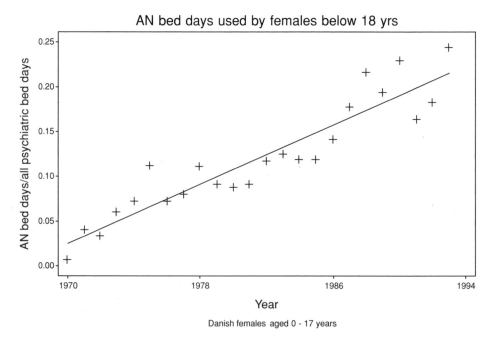

Figure 5.3 Proportion of the total number of psychiatric bed-days utilised by females under 18 years of age, used by AN patients, Denmark 1970–1993. Strong linear trend throughout the period. (*Source*: Nielsen et al., 1996)

Table 5.2 Results of fitting an increasing number of change points to the data in Figure 5.1

| No. of change points | Residual SS | Stepwise *F*-test | Degrees of freedom | | AIC_C |
			Num.	Den.	
0	5.6545×10^6				315.75
1[a]	1.6125×10^6	23.81	2	19	293.16
2	1.1894×10^6	15.95	4	17	294.10
3	1.0656×10^6	10.77	6	15	301.95

[a] Best model: AIC_C attains minimum

The positive trend in Figure 5.3 is highly significant (*t* (df 21) = 10.69; p < 0.00001).

Financial Burden

The cost of the bed days used by Danish anorexia nervosa patients in 1993 was estimated (Nielsen et al., 1996) at ~4.6 million euros. Including all eating disorders, this figure rises to ~6.4 million euros. Current prices for non-residents is set to about 240 euros per day for adult psychiatric inpatients, 295 euros for adolescent psychiatric inpatients and from 740 to 1000 euros for child psychiatric inpatients.

Loss of Productive Years

This dimension of societal burden stem from two sources—the time spent too ill to work or study, whether the person is in actual care or not, and from the increased risk of premature death. The first part has been discussed in depth above, and the second part will be discussed below.

PREMATURE DEATH

Mortality in relation to eating disorders has been reviewed recently (Sullivan, 1995; Nielsen et al., 1998; Nielsen, 2001). Below we shall briefly outline what is presently known about mortality for each eating disorder diagnosis.

Table 5.3 Results of fitting an increasing number of change points to the data in Figure 5.2

| No. of change points | Residual SS | Stepwise *F*-test | Degrees of freedom | | AIC_C |
			Num.	Den.	
0	0.00728377				−155.06
1	0.00188477	27.21	2	19	−179.89
2[a]	0.00102890	25.84	4	17	−185.87
3	0.00098525	15.98	6	15	−176.49

[a] Best model: AIC_C attains minimum

Anorexia Nervosa

Excess mortality is well established (Sullivan, 1995; Møller-Madsen et al., 1996; Nielsen et al., 1998), both in a 10-year perspective and in a longer perspective (Nielsen, 2001). Crude mortality rate is given as 5.9% (178 dead of 3006 AN probands) in Sullivan (1995). Standardised Mortality Ratio (SMR) was 9.6 (95% CI: 7.8 to 11.5) after about 10 years of follow-up and 3.7 (95% CI: 2.8 to 4.7) in four studies with a mean length of follow-up ranging from 20 to 36 years (Nielsen, 2001). Comorbid type 1-diabetes and anorexia nervosa seem to have higher mortality than either disorder alone (Nielsen et al., 2002).

Bulimia Nervosa

A suggested increase in SMR (Nielsen et al., 1998; Nielsen, 2001) seem to be based on a small and highly selected set of studies (Nielsen, 2003). Overviews by Keel and Mitchell (1997) and Nielsen (2001) yielded an overall crude mortality of 0.5% (14 dead of 2692 BN probands). The majority of studies reported no deaths, so selection bias might distort the findings on SMR in BN. Unpublished simulation data by Nielsen (personal communication) indicate that by using information from all 42 available studies instead of just data from the selected studies a highly significant overall aggregate SMR of 7.4 (95% CI: 2.9 to 14.9) changed to a non-significant SMR of 1.56 (95% CI: 0.8 to 2.7). At present the evidence on mortality in bulimia nervosa is inconclusive.

Anorexia Nervosa *and* Bulimia Nervosa

Jørgensen (1992; cited in Nielsen, 2001) report a crude mortality of 20% (5 of 25 probands) after a mean of 12.5 years of follow-up. SMR is 9.9 (95% CI: 3.2 to 23). These findings are almost identical to the overall findings for AN.

Eating Disorder not Otherwise Specified: EDNOS

Jørgensen (1992) found that 4 out of 28 probands (14.3%) had died after 11 years of follow-up. SMR was 2.8 (95% CI: 0.8 to 7.3), a non-significant increase ($p = 0.11$).

CONCLUSION

There seem to be significant differences in mortality from AN to BN (Fisher's exact test $p < 0.0001$). OR for premature death in AN vs BN is 12 (95% CI: 7 to 22.5). More data on BN, EDNOS, BED and atypical and 'subclinical' eating disorders are needed before any firm conclusions can be drawn for these specific eating disorders.

REFERENCES

Abraham, S. (1998) Sexuality and reproduction in bulimia nervosa patients over 10 years. *J. Psychosom. Res.*, **44**, 491–502.

Agras, W.S. (2001) The consequences and costs of the eating disorders. *Psych. Clin. North Am.*, **24**, 371–379.

APA (1987) *Diagnostic and Statistical Manual of Mental Disorders* (3rd edition revised). Wasington, D.C.: American Psychiatric Association.

Brinch, M., Isager, T. & Tolstrup, K. (1988a) Anorexia nervosa and motherhood: reproductional pattern and mothering behavior of 50 women. *Acta Psychiat. Scand.*, **77**, 98–104.

Brinch, M., Isager, T. & Tolstrup, K. (1988b) Patients' evaluation of their former treatment for anorexia nervosa (AN). *Nord. Psykiatr. Tidsskr.*, **42**, 445–448.

Butzlaff, R.L. & Hooley, J.M. (1998) Expressed emotion and psychiatric relapse: a meta-analysis. *Arch. Gen. Psychiat.*, **55**, 547–552.

Colahan, M. & Senior, R. (1995) Family patterns in eating disorders: going round in circles, getting nowhere fasting. In G. Szmukler, C. Dare, & J. Treasure (Eds.), *Handbook of Eating Disorders— Theory, Treatment and Research* (pp. 243–257). Chichester/New York: John Wiley & Sons.

Crisp, A.H., Callendar, J.S., Halek, C. & Hsu, L.K.G. (1992) Long-term mortality in anorexia nervosa. *Br. J. Psychiat.*, **161**, 104–107.

Crisp, A.H., Norton, K. & Gowers, S. (1991) A controlled trial of the effect of therapies aimed at adolescent and family psychopathology in anorexia nervosa. *Br. J. Psychiat.*, **159**, 325–333.

Cytel (2000) *StatXact4.0.1 for Windows. A Statistical Software Program for Exact Nonparametric Inference.* Cambridge MA: CYTEL Software Corporation.

Dare, C., Eisler, I., Russell, G.F.M. & Szmukler, G. (1990) Family therapy for anorexia nervosa: implications from the results of a controlled trial of family and individual therapy. *J. Marital Fam. Ther.*, **16**, 39–57.

Dare, C. & Eisler, I. (2000) A multi-family group day treatment programme for adolescent eating disord. *Eur. Eat. Disord. Rev.*, **8**, 4–18.

Dare, C., le Grange, D., Eisler, I. & Rutherford, J. (1994) Redefining the psychosomatic family: Family process of 26 eating disordered families. *Int. J. Eat. Disord.*, **16**, 211–226.

Deter, H.-C. & Herzog, W. (1994) Anorexia nervosa in a long-term perspective: Results of the Heidelberg-Mannheim study. *Psychosom. Med.*, **56**, 20–27.

Eisler, I., Dare, C., Hodes, M., Russell, G.F.M., Dodge, E. & le Grange, D. (2000) Family therapy for adolescent anorexia nervosa: The results of a controlled comparison of two family interventions. *J. Child Psychol. Psychiat.*, **41**, 727–736.

Evans, J. & le Grange, D. (1995) Body size and parenting in eating disorders: A comparative study of the attitudes of mothers towards their children. *Int. J. Eat. Disord.*, **18**, 39–48.

Fahy, T. & Treasure, J. (1989) Children of mothers with with bulimia nervosa. *Br. Med. J.*, **299**, 1031.

Fernández Aranda, F. & Túron Gil, V. (1998) *Trastornos de la Alimentación. Guia Básica de Tratamiento en Anorexia y Bulimia.* Barcelona: Masson.

Garner, D.M. (1997) Psychoeducational principles in treatment. In Eds *Handbook of Treatment for Eating Disorders* (2nd edition). Garner D.M. & Garfinkel P.E. (Eds), New York: Guilford Press.

Goldberg, D.F. & Hillier, V.F. (1979) A scaled version of the General Health Questionnaire. *Psychol. Med.*, **15**, 139–145.

Goldstein, M.J. (1981) Family factors associated with schizophrenia and anorexia nervosa. *J. Youth Adolesc.*, **10**, 385–405.

Haggiag, T. (2000) The broken jigsaw: A child's perspective. In B. Lask & R. Bryant-Waugh (Eds), *Anorexia Nervosa and Related Eating Disorders in Childhood and adolescence* (2nd edition; pp. 3–10). Hove: Psychology Press.

Hodes, M., Dare, C., Dodge, E. & Eisler, I. (1999) The assessment of expressed emotion in a standardised family interview. *J. Child Psychol. Psychiat.*, **40**, 617–625.

Hodes, M. & le Grange, D. (1993) Expressed emotion in the investigation of eating disorders: a review. *Int. J. Eat. Disord.*, **13**, 279–288.

Howlett, M., McClelland, L. & Crisp, A.H. (1995) The cost of the illness that defies (editorial). *Postgrad. Med. J.*, **71**, 705–706.

Jacobi, C., Agras, W.S. & Hammer, L. (2001) Predicting children's reported eating disturbances at 8 years of age. *J. Am. Acad. Child. Adolesc. Psychiat.*, **40**, 364–372.

Jeammet, P. & Gorge, A. (1980) Une forme de thérapie familiale: Le groupe de parents. *Psychiat. Enfant.*, **23**, 587–636.

Jones, R.H. & Dey, I. (1995) Determining one or more change points. *Chem. Phys. Lipids.*, **76**, 1–6.

Keel, P.K. & Mitchell, J.E. (1997) Outcome in bulimia nervosa. *Am. J. Psychiat.*, **154**, 313–321.

Keilen, M., Treasure, T., Schmidt, U. & Treasure, J. (1994) Quality of life measurements in eating disorders, angina, and transplant candidates: are they comparable?. *J. R. Soc. Med.*, **87**, 441–444.

Keller, M.B., Herzog, D.B., Lavori, P.W. & Bradburn, I.S. (1992) The naturalistic history of bulimia nervosa: Extraordinarily high rates of chronicity, relapse, recurrence, and psychosocial morbidity. *Int. J. Eat. Disord.*, **12**, 1–9.

Key, A., Mason, H. & Bolton, J. (2000) Reproduction and eating disorders: A fruitless union. *Eur. Eat. Disord. Rev.*, **8**, 98–107.

Kog, E., Vertommen, H. & Vandereycken, W. (1987) Minuchin's psychosomatic family model revisited: a concept validation study using a multitrait-multimethod approach. *Fam. Proc.*, **26**, 235–253.

Leff, J. & Vaughn, C.E. (1985) *Expressed Emotion in Families: Its Significance for Mental Illness.* New York: Guilford.

Le Grange, D., Eisler, I., Dare, C. & Hodes, M. (1992a) Family criticism and self starvation: a study of expressed emotion. *J. Fam. Ther.*, **14**, 177–192.

Le Grange, D., Eisler, I., Dare, C. & Russell, G.F.M. (1992b) Evaluation of family treatments in adolescent anorexia nervosa: a pilot study. *Int. J. Eat. Disord.*, **12**, 347–357.

Lewis, H.L. & MacGuire, M.P. (1985) Review of a group for parents of anorexics. *J. Psychiat. Res.*, **19**, 453–458.

MacDonald, M. (2000) Bewildered, blamed and broken-hearted: Parent's views of anorexia nervosa. In B. Lask and R. Bryant-Waugh (Eds), *Anorexia Nervosa and Related Eating Disorders in Childhood and Adolescence* (2nd edition; pp. 11–24). Hove: Psychology Press.

McFarlane, W.R. (1983) Multiple family therapy in schizofrenia. In W.R. McFarlane (Ed.), *Family Therapy in Schizofrenia* (pp. 141–172). New York: Guilford Press.

McFarlane, W.R. (1991) Family psychoeducational treatment. In A.S. Gurman & D.P. Kniskern (Eds), *Handbook of Family Therapy* (Vol. II; pp. 363–395). New York: Brunner/Mazel.

McKenzie, J. & Joyce, P. (1992) Hospitalisation for anorexia nervosa. *Int. J. Eat. Disord.*, **11**, 235–241.

Minuchin, S., Rosman, B.L. & Baker, L. (1978) *Psychosomatic Families: Anorexia Nervosa in Context.* Cambridge, MA: Harvard University Press.

Morandé, G. (1999) *La Anorexia. Cómo Combatir y Prevenir el Miedo a Engordar de las Adolescentes.* Madrid: Colección Vivir Mejor, Ediciones Temas de Hoy.

Morgan, J.F. & Crisp, A.H. (2000) Use of leucotomy for intractable anorexia nervosa: A long-term follow-up study. *Int. J. Eat. Disord.*, **27**, 249–258.

Moulds, M.I., Touyz, S.W., Schotte, D., Beumont, P.J.V., Griffiths, R., Russell, J. & Charles, M. (2000) Perceived expressed emotion in the siblings and parents of hospitalized patients with anorexia nervosa. *Int. J. Eat. Disord.*, **27**, 288–296.

Møller-Madsen, S., Nystrup, J. & Nielsen, S. (1996) Mortality in anorexia nervosa in Denmark during the period 1970–1987. *Acta Psychiatr. Scand.*, **94**, 454–459.

Newton, T., Robinson, P. & Hartley, P. (1993) Treatment for eating disorders in the United Kingdom. Part II. Experiences of treatment: A survey of members of Eating Disorders Association. *Eat. Disord. Rev.*, **1**, 10–21.

Nielsen, S. (2001) Epidemiology and mortality of eating disorders. *Psych. Clin. North Am.*, **24**, 201–214.

Nielsen, S. (2003) Standardized mortality ratio in bulimia nervosa. *Arch. Gen. Psychiatry*, **60**, 851. Erratum in *Arch. Gen. Psychiatry*, **60**, 982.

Nielsen, S., Emborg, C. & Mølbak, A.G. (2002) Mortality in concurrent type 1 diabetes and anorexia nervosa. *Diabetes Care*, **25**, 309–312.

Nielsen, S., Møller-Madsen, S., Nystrup, J. & Emborg, C. (1996) Utilisation of psychiatric beds in the treatment of ICD-8 eating disorders in Denmark 1970–1993. A register study. Paper read at the AEP Conference in London, July 1996.

Nielsen, S., Møller-Madsen, S., Isager, T., Jørgensen, J., Pagsberg, K. & Theander, S. (1998) Standardized mortality in eating disorders—a quantitative summary of previously published and new evidence. *J. Psychosom. Res.*, **44**, 413–434.

O'Donoghue, G., Treasure, J.L. & Russell, G.F.M. (1991) Eating disorders and motherhood. *Signpost* (newsletter for the Eating Disorders Association), **April**, 1–5.

Padierna, A., Quintana, J.M., Arostegui, I., Gonzalez, N. & Horcajo, M.J. (2000) The health-related quality of life in eating disorders. *Quality of Life Research*, **9**, 667–674.

Perednia, C. & Vandereycken, W. (1989) An explorative study on parenting in eating disorder families. In W. Vandereycken, E. Kog & J. Vanderlinden (Eds), *The Family Approach to Eating Disorders* (pp. 119–146). New York: PMA Publishing Corp.

Perring, C., Twigg, J. & Atkin, K. (1990) *Families Caring for People Diagnosed as Mentally Ill: The Literature Re-examined*. London: HMSO Publications.

Ratnasuriya, R.H., Eisler, I., Szmukler, G.I. & Russell, G.F.M. (1991) Anorexia nervosa: Outcome and prognostic factors after 20 years. *Br. J. Psychiat.*, **158**, 495–502.

Roberto, G. (1988) The vortex: siblings in the eating disordered family. In K.G. Lewis & M.D. Kahn (Eds), *Siblings in Therapy*. New York: W.W. Norton.

Rose, J. & Garfinkel, P.E. (1980) A parent's group in the management of anorexia nervosa. *Can. J. Psychiat.*, **25**, 228–232.

Rosenvinge, J.R. & Klusmeier, A.K. (2000) Treatment of eating disorders from a patient satisfaction perspective: A Norwegian replication of a British study. *Eur. Eat. Disord. Rev.*, **8**, 293–300.

Russell, G.F.M., Szmukler, G., Dare, C. & Eisler, I. (1987) An evaluation of family therapy in anorexia nervosa and bulimia nervosa. *Arch. Gen. Psychiat.*, **44**, 1047–1056.

Sahler, O.J.Z., Roghmann, K.J., Carpenter, P.J., Mulhern, R.K., Dolgin, M.J., Sargent, J.R., Barbarin, O.A., Copeland, D.R. & Zelter, L.K. (1994) Sibling adaptation to childhood cancer collaborative study: Prevalence of sibling distress and definition of adaptation levels. *Develop. Behav. Pediat.*, **15**, 353–366.

Schene, A.H. (1990) Objective and subjective dimensions of family burden. Towards an integrative framework for research. *Soc. Psychiat. Psychiat. Epidemiol.*, **25**, 289–297.

Scholz, M. & Asen, E. (2001) Multiple family therapy with eating disordered adolescents: Concepts and preliminary results. *Eur. Eat. Disord. Rev.*, **9**, 33–42.

Smith, S.M. & Hanson, R. (1972) Failure to thrive and anorexia nervosa. *Postgrad. Med. J.*, **48**, 382–384.

Selvini-Palazzoli, M. (1974) *Self-starvation: From the Intrapsychic to the Transpersonal Approach*. London: Chaucer.

Siegel, S. & Castellan, N.J. (1988) *Nonparametric Statistics for the Behavioral Sciences* (2nd edition). New York: McGraw-Hill.

Stein, A. & Fairburn C.G. (1989) Children of mothers with bulimia nervosa. *Br. Med. J.*, **299**, 777–778.

Stein, A., Woolley, H. & McPherson, K. (1999) Conflict between mothers with eating disorders and their infants during mealtimes. *Br. J. Psychiat.*, **175**, 455–461.

Stein, A., Woolley, H., Murray, L., Cooper, P., Noble, F., Affonso, N. & Fairburn, C.G. (2001) Influence of psychiatric disorder on the controlling behaviour of mothers with 1-year-old infants. A study of women with maternal eating disorders, postnatal depression and a healthy comparison group. *Br. J. Psychiat.*, **179**, 157–162.

Stierlin, H. & Weber, G. (1989) Anorexia nervosa: Lessons from a follow-up study. *Fam. Syst. Med.*, **7**, 120–157.

Sullivan, P.F. (1995) Mortality in anorexia nervosa. *Am. J. Psychiat.*, **152**, 1073–1074.

Surgenor, L.J., Rau, J., Snell, D.L. & Fear, J.L. (2000) Educational needs of eating disorders patients and families. *Eur. Eat. Disord. Rev.*, **8**, 59–66.

Szmukler, G. (1996) From family 'burden' to caregiving. *Psychiat. Bull.*, **20**, 449–451.

Szmukler, G., Burgess, P., Herrman, H., Benson, A., Colusa, S. & Bloch, S. (1996) Caring for relatives with serious mental illness: The development of the Experience of Caregiving Inventory. *Soc. Psychiat. Psychiat. Epidemiol.*, **31**, 137–148.

Szmukler, G., Dare, C. & Treasure, J. (Eds) (1995) *Handbook of Eating Disorders—Theory, Treatment and Research*. Chichester/New York: John Wiley & Sons.

Szmukler, G.I., Eisler, I., Russell, G.F.M. & Dare, C. (1985) Anorexia nervosa, parental 'expressed emotion' and dropping out of treatment. *Br. J. Psychiat.*, **147**, 265–271.

Tanner, C. & Connan, F. (2003) Cognitive Analytic Therapy. In J. Treasure, U. Schmidt & E. van Furth (Eds), *Handbook of Eating Disorders* (2nd edn, pp. 279–290). Chichester: Wiley

Theander, S. (1970) Anorexia nervosa: a psychiatric investigation of 94 female patients (MD-thesis). *Acta Psychiat., Scand.*, **214** (suppl.), 1–194.

Theander, S. (1992) Chronicity in anorexia nervosa: Results from the Swedish long-term follow-up study. In W. Herzog, H.-C. Deter & W. Vandereycken (Eds), *The Course of Eating Disorders. Long-term Follow-up Studies of Anorexia Nervosa and Bulimia Nervosa* (pp. 214–227). Berlin: Springer.

Theander, S. (1996) Anorexia nervosa with an early onset: Selection, gender, outcome and results of a long-term follow-up study. *J. Youth Adolesc.*, **25**, 419–429.

Tolstrup, K. (1990) Treatment of anorexia nervosa: Current status. In J.G. Simeon & H. Bruce Ferguson (Eds), *Treatment Strategies in Child and Adolescent Psychiatry* (pp. 115–131). New York: Plenum.

Tolstrup, K., Brinch, M., Isager, T., Nielsen, S., Nystrup, J., Severin, B. & Olesen, N.S. (1987) Long-term outcome of 151 cases of anorexia nervosa. The Copenhagen Anorexia Nervosa Follow-up Study. *Acta Psychiat. Scand.*, **71**, 380–387.

Treasure, J., Murphy, T., Todd, G., Gavan, K., Schmidt, U., James, J. & Szmukler, G. (2001) The experience of care giving for severe mental illness: A comparison between anorexia nervosa and psychosis. *Soc. Psychiat. Psychiat. Epidemiol.*, **36**, 343–347.

Vandereycken, W., Vanderlinden, J. & Van Vreckem, E. (1989) The family, the hospitalized patient and the therapeutic team. In W. Vandereycken, E. Kog & J. Vanderlinden (Eds), *The Family Approach to Eating Disorders* (pp. 239–247). New York: PMA Publishing Corp.

Van Furth, E.F. (1991) *Parental expressed emotion and eating disorders*. PhD thesis, University of Utrecht.

Van Furth, E.F., Van Strien, D.C., Martina, L.M.L., Van Son, M.J.M., Hendrickx, J.J.P. & Van Engeland, H. (1996) Expressed emotion and the prediction of outcome in adolescent eating disorders. *Int. J. Eat. Disord.*, **20**, 19–31.

Van Wezel-Meijer, G. & Wit, J.M. (1989) The offspring of mothers with anorexia nervosa: A high-risk group for under nutrition and stunting? *Eur. J. Pediat.*, **149**, 130–135.

Walford, G. & McCune, N. (1991) Long-term outcome in early-onset anorexia nervosa. *Br. J. Psychiat.*, **159**, 383–389.

Wallin, U. (2000) *Anorexia nervosa in adolescence. Course, treatment and family function* (MD thesis). Lund: KFS AB.

Ware, J.E., Snow, K.K., Kosinski, M. & Gandek, B. (1993) *SF-36 Health Survey: Manual and Interpretation Guide*. Boston, MA: The Health Institute, New England Medical Center.

Wentz, E. (2000) *Ten-year outcome of anorexia nervosa with teenage onset* (MD thesis). Göteborg: Kompendiet.

Wentz, E., Gillberg, C., Gillberg, I.C. & Råstam, M. (2001) Ten-year follow-up of adolescent-onset anorexia nervosa: Psychiatric disorders and overall functioning scales. *J. Child Psychol. Psychiat.*, **42**, 613–622.

WHO (1965) *International Classification of Diseases* (8th edition). Geneva: World Health Organization.

Willis, J. & Rand, P. (1988) Pregnancy in bulimic women. *Obstet. Gynecol.*, **71**, 708.

Wood, D., Flower, P. & Black, D. (1998) Should parents take charge of their child's eating disorder? Some preliminary findings and suggestions for future research. *Int. J. Psych. Clin. Pract.*, **2**, 295–301.

CHAPTER 6

Treatment Overview

Janet Treasure
Department of Psychiatry, Thomas Guy House, London, UK
and
Ulrike Schmidt
Eating Disorders Unit, Institute of Psychiatry, London, UK

When we planned the outline for this book we decided to commission a number of chapters which would describe the major therapeutic approaches which have been evaluated in the management of eating disorders, such as cognitive-behavioural therapy (see Chapter 3), family therapy (see Chapter 11) and interpersonal therapy (see Chapter 9). We also wanted to include some of the newer psychological approaches for which there currently is less evidence available, such as dialectical behaviour therapy (see Chapter 10), as these have recently generated considerable interest as potentially helpful in the treatment of more complex cases. Likewise, we included separate chapters on different service models, such as day care and inpatient treatment (see Chapters 13 and 14). The advantage of this somewhat artificial separation of topics is to allow in-depth descriptions of different models of therapy, service or intervention, explaining the rationale, theoretical underpinning and the evidence supporting them.

The disadvantage is that for clinical decision making or service planning we need to know much more. We need to know how different treatments or service models compare in terms of their efficacy, acceptability and cost. This involves making a judgement on the quality of the available evidence and taking into account potential harms arising from an intervention or model. We also need to know how treatment efficacy translates into effectiveness in clinical settings outside research studies. Moreover, we need to know how best to sequence interventions and/or whether or how to combine them to maximise efficacy. And perhaps the most difficult question of all is what treatment or intervention or service is the most helpful for a given patient (with a given level of severity, chronicity and comorbidity, motivation and coping skills) at a certain point in time (taking into account previous treatment history and current life circumstances). In order to answer these questions we need to integrate the best research evidence with clinical expertise and patient values (Sackett, 2000).

The Essential *Handbook of Eating Disorders.* Edited by J. Treasure, U. Schmidt and E. van Furth.
© 2005 John Wiley & Sons, Ltd.

Table 6.1 Quality of evidence rating system (adapted from National Health and Medical Research Council, 1995)

Level I	Evidence obtained from a review of all relevant randomised-controlled trials
Level II	Evidence obtained from at least one randomised-controlled trial
Level III	Evidence obtained from controlled trials with randomisation
Level IV	Evidence obtained from multiple time series with or without intervention
Level V	Other evidence (such as opinions or policies of respected authorities based on clinical experience, descriptive studies, or reports of expert committees; summary by writers using a variety of written material; expert testimony; reference to the philosophy of a particular practitioner; reference to personal experience).

HOW GOOD IS THE AVAILABLE EVIDENCE?

Anorexia Nervosa

In anorexia nervosa, while there is a detailed, coherent body of research which documents prognostic features, there is very little in the way of good evidence (Level I or II evidence—for details regarding the system of grading see Table 6.1) about the efficacy of treatment. One systematic review of all randomised-controlled trials which have considered the treatment for anorexia nervosa has been conducted (Schmidt & Treasure, 2001). The protocol for a further, similarly comprehensive systematic review has been registered with the Cochrane library (Hay, personal communication). Additionally, there are two systematic reviews (in German) on psychodynamically informed treatments and on psychological treatments of anorexia nervosa (both conducted by the same group (Herzog & Hartmann, 1997). Moreover, there are other systematic reviews (completed or in progress) that have focused on specific aspects of service provision. One of these has specifically attempted to address the question of how inpatient treatment compares with outpatient or day care treatment (Meads, Gold & Burls, 2001). Another, one protocol registered with the Cochrane library, will be reviewing the evidence for treatments in specialist centres compared to non-specialist settings. Lastly, a systematic review has addressed the question of whether early intervention is important in AN (Schoemaker, 1997). Below we outline the conclusions from our own systematic review which gives the most comprehensive assessment of the available evidence (Schmidt & Treasure, 2001):

- One small randomised-controlled trial (RCT) found limited evidence that various psychotherapies (individual focal therapy, cognitive analytical therapy and family therapy) were more effective than treatment as usual. Three small RCTs found no clear differences between various psychotherapies and dietary advice or treatment as usual. Seven small RCTs found no significant differences between different psychotherapies. However, all the RCTs were small and were unlikely to have been powered to detect a difference between treatments.
- Four RCTs found no evidence that the addition of an antidepressant to treatment improved outcomes.
- Three RCTS found no evidence that cyproheptidine increased weight gain compared with placebo.

- Limited evidence from one small RCT found outpatient treatment to be as effective as inpatient treatment in those individuals not so severely ill as to warrant emergency intervention.
- One small RCT found that zinc was of no benefit in the treatment of anorexia nervosa.
- One small trial found no benefit from cisapride in the treatment of anorexia nervosa.
- We found no good evidence of the effect of hormonal treatment on fracture rates. One small RCT found no effect of oestrogen on bone mineral density.
- We found no RCTs to support the use of neuroleptic medication in anorexia nervosa.

The review also identified wide variability in the quality and reporting of studies, in terms of the CONSORT standards (Moher, Jones & Lepage, 2001; Moher, Schulz & Altman, 2001). Many of the RCTs were small and were unlikely to have been powered to detect a difference between treatments.

Bulimia Nervosa

In contrast to anorexia nervosa, the body of treatment research in bulimia nervosa is much larger and of overall better quality. This has been summarised in several systematic reviews which have either focused on psychological treatments (Hay & Bacaltchuk, 2000), drug treatments (Bacaltchuk, Hay & Mari, 2000) or both (Hay & Bacaltchuk, 2002; Whittal, Agras & Gould, 1999) The main conclusions from these reviews can be summarised as follows: cognitive-behavioural treatment (CBT) is the form of psychological treatment that has been best researched to date. There is evidence that this treatment is at least as effective if not more so than other psychological treatments. CBT delivered in a self-help or guided self-help format seems to be nearly as efficacious as full CBT. There is also evidence supporting the use of interpersonal treatment although this is less strong. Medication is less effective compared to psychological treatments, and the combination of medication and psychological treatment seems to be more effective than either treatment on its own, but with greater drop-out rates. Moreover, there is one systematic review addressing the question of the importance of early intervention (Reas et al., 2001), however, with inconclusive results.

INTEGRATING THE BEST AVAILABLE EVIDENCE ON TREATMENT WITH CLINICAL EXPERTISE AND PATIENT VALUES

Anorexia Nervosa

Connecting information about the best evidence to a specific patient's problem is no easy matter. The patient's problems have to be clearly defined and placed within the context of a clinical risk assessment. This needs to include an assessment both of the acute risk and the longer term prognosis, taking into account physical, psychological, psychosocial, developmental and family variables. Elsewhere we discuss the best approach to foster the exchange of necessary information between the person with the eating disorder and the professional.

Assessment of Short-Term Risk

Decisions on short-term risk involve a combined assessment of the medical risk and the person's psychological capacity to consent to treatment, taking into account the possible resources of motivation and psychosocial support.

Medical risk is critically important in guiding the acute management of anorexia nervosa. In Table 6.1 we illustrate a simple guide given to medical practitioners and other members of the multidisciplinary team as a decision aid when evaluating this acute risk in our Unit. A more detailed account of medical risk is given in Chapters 13 and 14 (day patient/inpatient treatment). Body mass index is a better marker than weight alone as a proxy measure of medical risk but a rigid cut-off point is less good for the extremes of height as the relationship is non-linear. Children have smaller fat stores than mature women and so medical complications occur with less weight loss. Bulimic features or refusal to drink also increase the risk. In turn, these medical markers interact with a variety of clinical and psychosocial factors.

High medical risk is often associated with an impairment of capacity for the consent to treatment. The criteria used to assess capacity are detailed below. Individuals are thought to have capacity if they:

- are able to take in and retain the information material to the decision and understand the likely consequences of having and not having the treatment (thus an acute confusional state may seriously impair the person's ability to process the information)
- believe the information (a compulsive disorder, delusion or phobia may stifle the belief in the information)
- weigh up the information as part of a process of arriving at decisions.

A proportion of patients with anorexia nervosa do not have the capacity to make decisions about their own health and safety and in many countries there is a form of Mental Health Law to allow admission to hospital and treatment in case of this contingency. (See Chapter 14 on inpatient treatment for further details.)

The patients' levels of motivation and their psychosocial resources can act as a buffer against some of these risks. Measuring the early response to treatment, such as a change in weight or the ability to show active involvement in treatment, is a good proxy measure of motivation.

Assessment of Longer Term Risk

In addition to its relevance for the acute risk, body mass index is important in terms of the long-term prognosis whether this is defined as mortality or stages of recovery (Nielsen et al., 1998; Steinhausen, 1995; Steinhausen et al., 2000). Another important risk factor is age, which is a proxy measure of duration of illness. Both age and weight correlate with the standardised mortality rate (Nielsen et al., 1998). Many of the randomised-controlled trials on the treatment of anorexia nervosa see (Schmidt & Treasure, 2001) are, in effect, stratified by age and hence duration of illness. Approximately two-thirds of adolescent patients (typically with illness durations of less than 3 years) have remitted from their illness by two years after outpatient treatment, whereas only one-third of adult patients recover with specialised outpatient treatment.

Choosing Treatments

Let us now consider how one might use the available evidence to choose treatment for an individual patient with anorexia nervosa who may present with a high acute medical risk or a poor long-term prognosis and or a combination of the two.

Anorexia Nervosa with High Acute Medical Risk

Cases with a high medical risk and lack of capacity require intensive care such as that offered by a specialised inpatient unit, although it could be argued that day patient care can also give the requisite level of intensity of care (see Chapter 14). However, given the high mortality associated with this subgroup it would be ethically difficult to conduct a randomised-controlled trial in which either of these treatments was compared to no treatment or even outpatient treatment.

The one systematic review which compared inpatient versus outpatient or day patient treatment of the underweight patient (Meads, Gold & Burls, 2001) only identified one published RCT (Crisp et al., 1991; Gowers et al., 1994) and a second unpublished RCT (Freeman, 1992). The review concludes that for the group of people with anorexia nervosa that is ill enough for inpatient care, *but not severe enough for this to be essential*, outpatient treatment is at least as effective (if not more effective) than inpatient treatment. The italics are our own but are essential. The outcome of *severe malnutrition* is known and there is no doubt that the appropriate treatment is food.

There is some Level III evidence from a large prospective, naturalistic outcome study conducted in Germany where inpatient care is the standard treatment for all forms of eating disorder. The study showed that people with severe anorexia nervosa (i.e. long duration and severe weight loss) benefit from longer admission (Kächele (for the study group MZ-ESS.), 1999; Kaechele et al., 2001)

There is Level IV evidence to suggest that decisions on when to admit and for how long are largely dependent on the model of health service provision used in a particular country. For example, current guidelines of the American Psychiatric Association (2000) suggest that intensive 24-hour care should be used when the BMI drops below 16 kg/m^2 or when weight falls by 20%. Admissions in the USA tend to be short. In contrast, in the UK some specialist centres have very high thresholds for intensive care (e.g. BMI $<13 \text{ kg/m}^2$). For example, in Leicester only 20% of adult cases require inpatient care (Palmer et al., 2000). The duration of inpatient admissions in specialist units catering for adults in the UK is typically around 3–4 months, whereas admissions to adolescent units are usually longer.

The type of service, skills mix and treatments, which are included in this form of high-intensity care, are discussed in more detail in the chapters on inpatient care (Chapter 14) and day care (Chapter 13).

Medication as an adjunct to inpatient care does not seem to have any clinical benefit in terms of weight gain (Attia et al., 1998). However, there may be a place for the SSRIs to prevent relapse as one small RCT found a better outcome in the group randomised to fluoexetine (Kaye et al., 2001). There is also some Level III evidence from the naturalistic German study that the group on medication after discharge had a lower risk of relapse (Kächele, 1999) The wider role of pharmacotherapy in the outpatient management of anorexia nervosa is an area worthy of further development.

Anorexia Nervosa with a Good Long-Term Prognosis

As mentioned above, this group mainly consists of adolescents with a short duration of illness. There are several RCTs, which suggest that this group of patients can be managed with outpatient treatment. However, even in this good long-term prognostic (adolescent) group approximately 20% will pose an acute medical risk and may need a higher intensity of care such as inpatient treatment (Eisler et al., 2000; Robin et al., 1994). Involvement of the family is beneficial for younger, early onset cases (Eisler et al., 1997; Russell et al., 1987). However, traditional family therapy is not necessary. Indeed parental counselling may be more effective especially if there is high expressed emotion (Eisler et al., 2000). Recent interest is focused on multiple family meetings in a day care setting (Colahan & Robinson, 2001; Dare & Eisler, 2000; Scholtz & Asen, 2001). (Approaches for this group of patients are discussed in more detail in Chapter 18.)

Anorexia Nervosa with a Poor Long-Term Prognosis

In the poorer long-term prognosis (adult) group there is less certainty about the treatments that work. More care (either in terms of intensity or duration) may be most appropriate. However, even in cases with high long-term risk, a case can be made for giving a trial of outpatient therapy, as this is often the most acceptable form of treatment for these patients. One of the advantages of working with anorexia nervosa is that the outcomes can be determined objectively. Thus treatment can be considered to be having an effect if weight loss can be brought to a halt and there is a reduction in some of the other anorexic behaviours.

In adults, one randomised-controlled trial (RCT) found limited evidence that specialised psychotherapies—family therapy (see Chapter 11), focal psychotherapy (see Dare & Crowther, 1995) and cognitive analytical therapy (see Tanner & Connan (2003))—were more effective than treatment as usual (Dare et al., 2001). However, there is no evidence to suggest that any particular type of specialised psychotherapy produces better outcomes (Treasure et al., 1995; Hall & Crisp 1987). While one small study found no difference in outcome between psychotherapy and dietary management (Hall & Crisp, 1987) another found that standard dietetic management was not accepted by patients as a first-line treatment, with all patients dropping out from this arm of the study (Serfaty, 1999).

Bulimia Nervosa

Bulimia nervosa is an entirely different problem. For the majority of patients the risk to life or limb (for self or others) is not high, the need for admission or even day care is relatively rare and the vast majority of patients can be managed safely as outpatients. There are, however, some particular circumstances in which risk issues need to be identified at assessment and taken into account in planning the patient's care, both in the short and longer term. These concern patients with self-harm and suicidality and other high-risk behaviours; those who are pregnant or have small children; and those with medical comorbidity such as diabetes mellitus. The specific issues involved in planning care for these high-risk groups are discussed later. However, in the absence of major risk issues the main question for clinicians and patients alike is: Is there any evidence that can help us to decide the type of treatment to choose for a particular patient?

Choosing Treatments for the Majority of Patients with Bulimia Nervosa

Although a number of pretreatment prognostic indicators have been identified (Keel & Mitchell, 1997; Vaz, 1998), few of them have been replicated across studies and across different treatments. For example, severity and duration of bulimic symptoms have had an inconsistent link to outcome. There seems to be somewhat more agreement that personality disorder features such as borderline or impulsive features predict a poorer outcome. However, the main conclusion to be drawn with confidence about the literature on pretreatment outcome predictor variables is that none of the ones identified has any major utility in helping us to choose the treatment that is most helpful for a particular patient.

Given the general dearth of information on how to match treatments to patients, it can be argued that the use of a stepped care approach, starting with the least intensive, least costly and least invasive interventions, might generally be best. The obvious candidate for the first step in the treatment of BN is CBT self-help either with or without some therapeutic guidance. However, although there are now a sizeable number of studies on the use of CBT self-help, very little work has been done on the additional treatment needs of these patients thereafter or on the potential harms of such an approach as the first step in treatment (e.g. in terms of drop-out or demoralisation of more severely ill patients who may not do well with this approach). There is also some evidence suggesting that those who are more severely symptomatic may do less well with such an approach. On the face of it, medication might also be a good starting point as a Step I intervention. However, the evidence suggests that drug treatments are less acceptable to patients (high drop-out rates, reduced take up, side-effects) and the longer term effects have not been studied in detail.

The Dose of Treatment

Currently most evidence-based packages for the treatment of BN are brief (less than 20 sessions). A meta-analysis of psychotherapy studies of bulimia nervosa up to 1990 found that 36% of the variance in outcome was explained by the number of treatment sessions in combination with relationship orientation (Hartmann, Herzog & Drinkmann, 1992). If a longer duration of treatment yields potentially better outcomes it would be important to know what dose of treatment is needed to treat what proportion of patients presenting and whether there is a point beyond which offering 'more of the same' is unlikely to improve outcome. The work of Ken Howard and others on the dose–effectiveness relationship in psychotherapy addresses precisely these issues (Lutz et al., 2001). In general, the vast majority of people receiving psychotherapy improve quickly within the first few sessions. Those who have failed to improve at an early stage have much less of a chance of getting well and need vastly more input to get well than those who improve early. And there is a point beyond which very few patients get better, if the same sort of treatment is continued. However, the exact shape of this curve of the pattern of improvement varies according to diagnosis, type of symptoms, the presence of interpersonal problems and comorbidity (Lueger, Lutz & Howard, 2000). Unfortunately, at present we don't really know what the shape of this curve looks like for different treatments of bulimia nervosa. What we do know from Level II evidence is that, in CBT treatment, early response within 4 to 6 weeks is an excellent predictor of longer term outcome (Agras et al., 2000) In other words, if someone has failed to show any symptomatic improvement with CBT at an early stage, one seriously needs to consider the reasons for this and think about altering the plan of treatment. However, findings from the German multi-centre TREAT study showed that the response to early intensive treatment (mostly inpatient care) in bulimia nervosa did not predict outcome at 2.5 years and that, in some settings, giving prolonged treatment leads to increasing benefits (Kordy, personal communication).

Intensity of Treatment

Many outpatient treatments for bulimia nervosa offer sessions on a once-weekly basis, but there is evidence that a more intensive outpatient approach is more effective in inducing remission in patients with bulimia nervosa compared with a weekly psychotherapy that uses the same manual-based CBT approach (Mitchell et al., 1993).

SPECIAL CONSIDERATIONS FOR HIGH-RISK GROUPS

Self-harm, Suicidality and Other High-Risk Behaviours

The most commonly identified issues of risk in bulimia nervosa are around repeated self-harm and suicidality. It is rare for bulimic patients to present as acutely suicidal, and indeed the risk of death through suicide in bulimia nervosa patients is low (Keel & Mitchell, 1997; Keel et al., 2000). In those who do present as acutely depressed and suicidal a standard suicide risk assessment should be conducted. Having said that, repeated self-harm through cutting, burning and overdosing is common and occurs in approximately 15–25% of clinic samples (Favaro & Santonastaso, 1997). This is often associated with other high-risk behaviours such as alcohol or substance abuse, unprotected casual sex or repeated shop-lifting. These impulsive features have been found to predict poorer outcome for review (see Vaz, 1998). Therapeutic approaches for the management of these complex cases have been developed (DBT, CAT), and Level II evidence suggests that DBT is promising in those with repeated self-harm (for review see Hawton et al., 2001).

Pregnancy and Motherhood

Sometimes there is also a risk involving the safety of others, especially in cases where the person with bulimia presents during pregnancy or has small children. In the majority of cases bulimic symptoms will improve during pregnancy and for a period of time after the birth, as the woman is aware of needing to eat healthily for the good of the baby (Blais et al., 2000). Nonetheless women with bulimia nervosa are at risk of having small babies, and have higher rates of Caesarian sections and perinatal problems. The risk of postnatal depression is also raised. (Abraham, 1998; Franko et al., 2001). The management of the patient with unremitting bulimic symptoms during pregnancy is difficult. Health professionals can become frustrated, angry and anxious. In this context it is important to remember the principles of motivational interviewing and to try to understand the nature of the woman's inability to ensure the safety of her unborn baby.

Bulimic mothers have been shown to affect the well-being of their young children subtly through a negative emotional atmosphere and being more intrusive and controlling of their children both at meal and at play times (Stein & Fairburn, 1989; Stein et al., 2001). Thus the risk to the health and safety of the child needs to be thought about, especially if the mother is severely bulimic and/or has severe impulsive features and/or is currently in an abusive relationship.

Comorbid diabetes mellitus

Type I diabetes is associated with an increased risk of developing bulimia nervosa. Typically the development of the diabetes precedes the onset of the bulimia nervosa, which in turn usually arises in the context of other psychiatric disturbance. The risk of severe diabetic complications is raised in diabetics with eating disorders. Standard CBT for bulimia nervosa is not unproblematic for these patients as many of the psycho-educational recommendations of CBT for bulimia nervosa aim to relax control over eating and may conflict with the nutritional advice given to diabetics (Peveler et al., 1993). However, so far no evidence base for treatments for this difficult subgroup exists.

CONCLUSION

Common sense (rather than documented evidence) dictates that patients who present with major risk issues as outlined above are likely to need more intensive and perhaps longer treatments than those without, and of course ongoing risk monitoring and management.

REFERENCES

Abraham, S. (1998) Sexuality and reproduction in bulimia nervosa patients over 10 years. *J. Psychosom. Res.*, **44**, 491–502.

Agras, W.S., Crow, S.J., Halmi, K.A. et al. (2000) Outcome predictors for the cognitive behavior treatment of bulimia nervosa: Data from a multisite study. *Am. J. Psychiat.*, **157**, 1302–1308.

American Psychiatric Association (2000) Practice guideline for the treatment of patients with eating disorders (revision). American Psychiatric Association Work Group on Eating Disorders. *Am. J. Psychiat.*, **157**, 1–39.

Attia, E., Haiman, C., Walsh, B.T. et al. (1998) Does fluoxetine augment the inpatient treatment of anorexia nervosa? *Am. J. Psychiat.*, **155**, 548–551.

Bacaltchuk, J., Hay, P. & Mari, J.J. (2000) Antidepressants versus placebo for the treatment of bulimia nervosa: A systematic review. *Aust. N. Z. J. Psychiat.*, **34**, 310–317.

Blais, M.A., Becker, A.E., Burwell, R.A. et al. (2000) Pregnancy: Outcome and impact on symptomatology in a cohort of eating- disordered women. *Int. J. Eat. Disord.*, **27**, 140–149.

Colahan, M. & Robinson, P. (2001) Multifamily groups in the treatment of young eating disorder adults. *J. Fam. Ther.*

Crisp, A.H., Norton, K., Gowers, S. et al. (1991) A controlled study of the effect of therapies aimed at adolescent and family psychopathology in anorexia nervosa. *Br. J. Psychiat.*, **159**, 325–333.

Dare, C. & Crowther, C. (1995) Psychodynamic models of eating disorders. In G. Szmukler, C. Dare & J. Treasure (Eds), *Handbook of Eating Disorders: Theory, Treatment and Research* (pp. 125–141). Chichester: John Wiley & Sons.

Dare, C. & Eisler, I. (2000) A multi-family group day treatment for adolescent eating disorder. *Eur. Eat. Disord. Rev.*, **8**, 4–18.

Dare, C., Eisler, I., Russell, G. et al. (2001) Psychological therapies for adults with anorexia nervosa: randomised controlled trial of out-patient treatments. *Br. J. Psychiat.*, **178**, 216–221.

Eisler, I., Dare, C., Hodes, M. et al. (2000) Family therapy for adolescent anorexia nervosa: the results of a controlled comparison of two family interventions [In Process Citation]. *J. Child Psychol. Psychiat.*, **41**, 727–736.

Eisler, I., Dare, C., Russell, G.F. et al. (1997) Family and individual therapy in anorexia nervosa. A 5-year follow-up. *Arch. Gen. Psychiat.*, **54**, 1025–1030.

Favaro, A. and Santonastaso, P. (1997) Suicidality in eating disorders: Clinical and psychological correlates. *Acta Psychiat. Scand.*, **95**, 508–514.

Franko, D.L., Blais, M.A., Becker, A.E. et al. (2001) Pregnancy complications and neonatal outcomes in women with eating disorders. *Am. J. Psychiat.*, **158**, 1461–1466.

Freeman, C. (1992) Day patient treatment for anorexia nervosa 6,1:3–8. *Br. Rev. Bulimia Anorexia Nervosa*, **6**, 3–8.

Gowers, S., Norton, K., Halek, C. et al. (1994) Outcome of outpatient psychotherapy in a random allocation treatment study of anorexia nervosa. *Int. J. Eat. Disord.*, **15**, 165–177.

Hall, A. & Crisp, A.H. (1987) Brief psychotherapy in the treatment of anorexia nervosa. Outcome at one year. *Br. J. Psychiat.*, **151**, 185–191.

Hartmann, A., Herzog, T. & Drinkmann, A. (1992) Psychotherapy of bulimia nervosa: What is effective? A meta-analysis. *J. Psychosom. Res.*, **36**, 159–167.

Hawton, K., Townsend, E., Arensma, E., Gunnell, D., Hazell, P., House, A. & van Heeringen, K. (2001) Psychosocial and pharmacological treatments for deliberate selfharm. *Cochrane Rev.*

Hay, P. & Bacaltchuk, J. (2000) Psychotherapy for bulimia nervosa and binging (Cochrane Review). *Cochrane. Database. Syst. Rev.*, **4**, CD000562.

Hay, P. & Bacaltchuk, J. (2002) Bulimia nervosa. *Clinical Evidence*, 642–651.

Herzog, T. & Hartmann, A. (1997) Psychoanalytically oriented treatment of anorexia nervosa. Methodology-related critical review of the literature using meta-analysis methods. *Psychother. Psychosom. Med. Psychol.*, **47**, 299–315.

Kaechele, H., Kordy, H., Richard, M. et al. (2001) Therapy amount and outcome of inpatient psychodynamic treatment of eating disorders in Germany. Data from a multicentre study. *Psychother. Res.*, **11**, 239.

Kaye, W.H., Nagata, T., Weltzin, T.E. et al. (2001) Double-blind placebo-controlled administration of fluoxetine in restricting- and restricting-purging-type anorexia nervosa. *Biol. Psychiat.*, **49**, 644–652.

Kächele, H. (for the study group MZ-ESS) (1999) Eine multizentrische Studie zu Aufwand und Erfolg bei psychodynamischer Therapie von Eßstörungen. *Psychother. med. Psychol.*, **49**, 100–108.

Keel, P.K. & Mitchell, J.E. (1997) Outcome in bulimia nervosa. *Am. J. Psychiat.*, **154**, 313–321.

Keel, P.K., Mitchell, J.E., Miller, K.B. et al. (2000) Social adjustment over 10 years following diagnosis with bulimia nervosa. *Int. J. Eat. Disord.*, **27**, 21–28.

Lueger, R.J., Lutz, W. & Howard, K.I. (2000) The predicted and observed course of psychotherapy for anxiety and mood disorders. *J. Nerv. Ment. Dis.*, **188**, 127–134.

Lutz, W., Lowry, J., Kopta, S.M. et al. (2001) Prediction of dose-response relations based on patient characteristics. *J. Clin. Psychol.*, **57**, 889–900.

Meads, C., Gold, L. & Burls, A. (2001) How effective is outpatient care compared to inpatient care for the treatment of anorexia nervosa? A Systematic review. *Eur. Eat. Disord. Rev.*, **9**, 229–241.

Mitchell, J.E., Pyle, R.L., Pomeroy, C. et al. (1993) Cognitive-behavioral group psychotherapy of bulimia nervosa: Importance of logistical variables. *Int. J. Eat. Disord.*, **14**, 277–287.

Moher, D., Jones, A. & Lepage, L. (2001) Use of the CONSORT statement and quality of reports of randomized trials: A comparative before-and-after evaluation. *JAMA*, **285**, 1992–1995.

Moher, D., Schulz, K.F. & Altman, D.G. (2001) The CONSORT statement: Revised recommendations for improving the quality of reports of parallel group randomized trials. *Med. Res. Methodol.*, **1**, 2.

Nielsen, S., Moller-Madsen, S., Isager, T. (1998) Standardized mortality in eating disorders—a quantitative summary of previously published and new evidence. *J. Psychosom. Res.*, **44**, 413–434.

Palmer, R.L., Gatwood, N., Black, S. & Park S. (2000) Anorexia nervosa: Service consumption and outcome of local patients. *Psychiat. Bull.* **24**, 298–300.

Peveler, R.C., Davies, B.A., Mayou, R.A. et al. (1993) Self-care behaviour and blood glucose control in young adults with type 1 diabetes mellitus. *Diabet. Med.*, **10**, 74–80.

Reas, D.L., Schoemaker, C., Zipfel, S. et al. (2001) Prognostic value of duration of illness and early intervention in bulimia nervosa: A systematic review of the outcome literature. *Int. J. Eat. Disord.*, **30**, 1–10.

Robin, A.L., Siegel, P.T., Koepke, T. et al. (1994) Family therapy versus individual therapy for adolescent females with anorexia nervosa. *J. Dev. Behav. Pediatr.*, **15**, 111–116.

Russell, G.F., Szmukler, G.I., Dare, C. et al. (1987) An evaluation of family therapy in anorexia nervosa and bulimia nervosa. *Arch. Gen. Psychiat.*, **44**, 1047–1056.

Sackett, D.L. (2000) The fall of 'clinical research' and the rise of 'clinical-practice research'. *Clin. Invest. Med.*, **23**, 331–333.

Schmidt, U.H. & Treasure, J.L. (2001) A systematic review of treatments for anorexia nervosa. pp 0–5.

Schoemaker, C. (1997) Does early intervention improve the prognosis in anorexia nervosa? A systematic review of the treatment outcome literature. *Int. J. eat. Disord.*, **21**, 1–15.

Scholtz, M. & Asen, E. (2001) Multiple family therapy with eating disordered adolescents. *Eur. Eat. Disord. Rev.*, **9**, 33–42.

Serfaty, M.A. (1999) Cognitive therapy versus dietary counselling in the outpatient treatment of anorexia nervosa: Effects of the treatment phase. *Eur. Eat. Disord. Rev.*, **7**, 334–350.

Stein, A. & Fairburn, C.G. (1989) Children of mothers with bulimia nervosa [see comments]. *Br. Med. J.*, **299**, 777–778.

Stein, A., Woolley, H., Murray, L. et al. (2001) Influence of psychiatric disorder on the controlling behaviour of mothers with 1-year-old infants. A study of women with maternal eating disorder, postnatal depression and a healthy comparison group. *Br. J. Psychiat.*, **179**, 157–162.

Steinhausen, H.-C. (1995) The course and outcome of anorexia nervosa. In K. Brownell & C.G. Fairburn (Eds), *Eating Disorders and obesity: A Comprehensive Handbook*. (pp. 234–237). New York: Guilford Press.

Steinhausen, H.C., Boyadjieva, S., Grigoroiu-Serbanescu, M. et al. (2000) A transcultural outcome study of adolescent eating disorders. *Acta Psychiat. Scand.*, **101**, 60–66.

Tanner, C. & Connan, F. (2003) Cognitive Analytic Therapy. In J. Treasure, U. Schmidt & E. van Furth (Eds) *Handbook of Eating Disorders* (2nd edn, pp. 279–290). Chichester: Wiley.

Treasure, J., Todd, G., Brolly, M. et al. (1995) A pilot study of a randomised trial of cognitive analytical therapy vs educational behavioral therapy for adult anorexia nervosa. *Behav. Res. Ther.*, **33**, 363–367.

Turnbull, S.J., Schmidt, U., Troop, N.A. et al. (1997) Predictors of outcome for two treatments for bulimia nervosa: Short and long-term. *Int. J. Eat. Disord.*, **21**, 17–22.

Vaz, F.J. (1998) Outcome of bulimia nervosa: Prognostic indicators. *J. Psychosom. Res.*, **45**, 391–400.

Whittal, M.L., Agras, W.S. & Gould, R.A. (1999) Bulimia nervosa: A meta analysis of psychosocial and pharmacological treatments. *Behav. Ther.*, **30**, 117–135.

CHAPTER 7

Assessment and Motivation

Janet Treasure

Department of Psychiatry, Thomas Guy House, London, UK

and

Beatrice Bauer

Università Luigi Bocconi, Milan, Italy

SUMMARY

This chapter discusses the treatment of anorexia nervosa and bulimia nervosa under the following headings:

- Why do we need to consider readiness to change?
- Models of behaviour change
- Tailoring treatment
- How to measure readiness, importance and confidence
- Benefits of motivational strategies
- Limitations of motivational strategies
- The use of information to enhance motivation
- Implementing motivational strategies for patients with eating disorders

WHY DO WE NEED TO CONSIDER READINESS TO CHANGE?

Several assumptions underlie the agenda of the assessment interview. The first is that the client has decided that he or she wants something, a diagnosis or treatment. The health provider works on the usual premise that he or she needs to give information or practical help. To a degree these assumptions are true but there may be disparities between the perceived goals of the two partners. For example, when a women with anorexia nervosa walks into the room she may not want a diagnosis and/or treatment; instead she may be coming to stop her parents or her school nagging her to attend. A woman with bulimia nervosa may want help to stop her bingeing but she may not be prepared to do anything that may jeopardise the solutions for weight control that she has hit upon. An obese person may

---

The Essential *Handbook of Eating Disorders.* Edited by J. Treasure, U. Schmidt and E. van Furth.
© 2005 John Wiley & Sons, Ltd.

show a very high motivation to lose weight in order to avoid orthopaedic surgery or social stigmatisation. The health provider needs to find the balance between what may be wanted and what his expertise indicates may be needed and realistic. The concept of readiness to change can be a helpful structure to frame this intervention.

MODELS OF BEHAVIOUR CHANGE

The transtheoretical model of change of Prochaska and DiClemente (1984; Velicer, et al., 1996; Prochaska & Velicer, 1997a), is one model that recognises that people do not make a simple black or white decision to change their behaviour. Rather it assumes that there is a gradual process, divided into phases. The transtheoretical model (TTM) posits that health behaviour change involves progress through six stages of change: precontemplation, contemplation, preparation, action, maintenance and termination. In addition this transtheoretical model conceptualises psychotherapeutic change in three dimensions: firstly, the 'stages of change', or the *when* of change, and readiness to work towards a goal; secondly, the 'processes' of change, the *how* of change, and activities brought into play to modify thinking, behaviour or affect in relation to a problem; thirdly, the 'level' of change, the *what* of change, or domain in which change will occur. The other elements of the model comprise decisional balance (the balance of pros and cons (Prochaska & Norcross, 1994; O'Connell & Velicer, 1988), self-efficacy (Temoshok et al., 1985) and temptations. There is some evidence that these factors predict movement through the stages (Prochaska & Velicer, 1997b; Schwab et al., 2000). An analysis of the probability of movement among the stages revealed three findings in support of TTM: the probability of forward movement was greater than that of backward movement; the probability of moving to adjacent stages was greater than the probability of two-stage progression (Martin Velicer & Fava, 1996); and movement through the stages is not always linear. However, the concept of circularity or perhaps a spiral may be a better analogy to describe the movement; that is, people can progress from one stage to another or drop back to an earlier stage before stable change occurs. In the case of smoking, on average people enter the change cycle three times. Basic research has generated a rule of thumb for at-risk populations: 40% in precontemplation, 40% in contemplation, and 20% in preparation (Prochaska & Velicer, 1997a).

This model, however, has had its critics (Davidson, 1998): some argue for a continuum rather a series of stages; others question the processes that have been defined.

TAILORING TREATMENTS

The transtheoretical model has been used to tailor interventions. A computer program—an expert system (Velicer et al., 1993—measures the key elements of the TTM using validated questionnaires (Prochaska et al., 1988; Prochaska & Norcross, 1994; Velicer et al., 1990). From the results of this, an individual's stage, process use, decisional balance, self-efficacy and temptation scores are integrated to predict movement to the next stage (Velicer & Plummer, 1998). This is then given as feedback to the individual along with information about possible strategies, which may facilitate change. Such a system was found to be more effective in smoking cessation in adults than a stage-based manual alone (Velicer et al., 1999). This system has also been tested in adolescents where the results are less conclusive (Pallonen et al., 1998).

The transtheoretical model has been successfully applied to a variety of health behaviours (Prochaska et al., 1994; Nigg et al., 1999), including smoking cessation (Prochaska et al., 1993), weight control (Rossi et al., 1995; Jeffery et al., 1999), fat intake (Greene et al., 1999; Hargreaves et al., 1999), quitting cocaine (Prochaska et al., 1994), exercise acquisition (Marcus et al., 1992; Biddle & Fox, 1998) and the take-up of screening for mammography (Prochaska et al., 1994; Rakowski & Clark, 1998). An adaptation of TTM was proposed to predict engagement in outpatient psychotherapy (Derisley & Reynolds, 2000).

The distribution of individuals across the stages of change can provide a valuable tool for designing health intervention (Laforge et al., 1999; Jeffery et al., 1999; Abrams et al., 2000). Five independent studies from the USA and Australia examined the pattern of distribution across the stages of change for five behavioural risk factors (smoking, low fat diet, regular exercise, reducing stress, and losing weight). These studies showed that the single-item survey measures of the stage of change are readily applicable to population studies and appear to provide important information about the population characteristics linked to readiness to modify behavioural risk factors (Laforge et al., 1999).

We have examined whether the transtheoretical model can be applied to patients with eating disorders (Ward et al., 1996; Blake et al., 1997) as some preliminary work suggested that it could be applied to women with bulimia nervosa (Stanton et al., 1986). We adapted the measurement instruments devised by Prochaska's Rhode Island group to measure stage of change, processes of change and decisional balance (Rossi et al., 1995). We gave these instruments to patients with anorexia nervosa before their first assessment at our eating disorder clinic. Their primary care physicians referred most of the cases although many had had treatment before. We found that less than 50% of patients with anorexia nervosa were in action; 20% were in precontemplationi; and 30% in contemplation (Blake et al., 1997). We also found that the majority of patients with anorexia nervosa in our inpatient unit were in precontemplation or contemplation (Ward et al., 1996). We also examined the processes of change that our patients were currently using. As would be predicted from the model, those in precontemplation used very few processes of change. On the decisional balance questionnaire the precontemplation group endorsed few positive reasons for change and had a greater number of negative expectations from change. In contrast the group who were in action were using strategies such as self- liberation, self re-evaluation and dramatic relief significantly more. The group in action had a greater number of positive reasons for change and a small decrease in the reasons not to change. Patients undergoing treatment on our inpatient unit showed a similar profile (Ward et al., 1996).

We concluded from this research that the transtheoretical approach did seem to be applicable to patients with eating disorders, and studies from other authors support our findings (e.g. Vitousek et al., 1998).

We have also used this model in examining the treatment of obese patients. Fifty-six obese treatment-seekers (41 female and 15 male, age 44 ± 6.7 yr, BMI kg/m^2 37 ± 6.2, $M \pm SD$) were randomly assigned to two treatment groups after clinical assessment. The first group was assigned to an individualised six-month weight loss treatment integrated by the use of a manual. The second group started with a self-help manual for motivation enhancement (four weeks), according to the key construct of the TTM, before beginning the weight loss treatment offered to Group 1.

The reasons for seeking weight loss treatment were similar in the two groups: high pressure from family physicians to improve health (65%), family pressure (22%), difficulties in becoming pregnant (4%) and recent onset of diabetes mellitus and/or hypertension (9%).

All the participants had experienced repeated weight loss treatments during the last 10 years (very low calorie diet, drugs, etc.), while failing to maintain results.

At assessment, no statistically significant differences between the two groups were found in the distribution of individuals among the six stages of change: 17% in precontemplation, 60% in contemplation, 21% in determination and 2% in action. After the end of the first month we observed a large difference between the two groups in the distribution of patients among the six stages of change: in Group 1, at the end of one month of treatment, 15% of patients were in precontemplation, 64% in contemplation, and 21% in action; in Group 2, at the end of the motivation enhancement self-help manual, no patient was in precontemplation, 40% were in contemplation, 52% in determination and 8% in action. At the end of the second month, the difference in drop-out rate was statistically significant between Group 1 (17%) and Group 2 (0%) and these results were confirmed at the end of the treatment programme (Group 1, 27%; Group 2, 3%). Our preliminary findings (not yet published) at follow-up after three and six months have shown a statistically significant ($p < 0.001$) difference in weight loss achieved, between Group 1 (M $\pm$ SD respectively 3.7 $\pm$ 1.2% and 4.8 $\pm$ 3.1% of initial weight) and Group 2 (M $\pm$ SD respectively 6.3 $\pm$ 1.7% and 8.3.1 $\pm$ 3.6%).

The transtheoretical approach seems to offer promising results in the assessment and treatment of obesity, but our data also show that motivation needs to be monitored and enhanced repeatedly; to be successful the process needs time, so to increase motivation means to procrastinate action, even in severe cases of obesity, in favour of more realistic expectations and goals and better compliance with treatment at a later stage. In contrast, pushing patients towards action splits the patient groups into patients who still resist and those more prone to change, and seems to favour a much greater drop-out rate.

Several other models include stages in behaviour change. For example, Weinstein (1988) distinguished five stages in the precaution adoption process; De Vreis and Backbier (1994) describe change in attitudes, social influence and self-efficacy through motivational stages in their Attitude, Social Influence, and Efficacy (ASE) model. Most models of health behaviour change include the idea that there are two components to readiness to change. These are importance/conviction and confidence/self efficacy (Keller & Kemp White 1997; Rollnick 1998; Rollnick et al., 1999) encapsulated in the adage 'ready, willing and able'. *Importance* relates to why change is needed, and this concept includes the personal values and expectations that will accrue from change; confidence relates to a person's belief that he or she has the ability to master behaviour change.

For example, someone with anorexia nervosa may see no reason why she should change. She may not want to eat. However, she may be confident that if she decided to change she could do it. She is sceptical about change. This contrasts with an obese person, who may be very ready to change but may have no confidence that she can instigate or maintain the steps that are necessary, which causes frustration.

READINESS, IMPORTANCE AND CONFIDENCE

Several methods have been used to measure readiness to change.

In 1990 Brownell developed the Diet Readiness Test (DRT) widely used in the obese population as a means of measuring a person's readiness to begin a weight loss programme (Brownell, 1990). This test has had his critics (Carlson et al., 1994; Pendleton et al., 1998; Fontaine & Wiersema, 1999), who found no relationship between the DRT total score and weight loss, suggesting that DRT has no factorial or predictive validity in a clinical population.

There is a 32-item self-report measure called the URICA (University of Rhode Island Change Assessment) which can be used as a continuous change assessment scale (McConnaughty et al., 1989). We used this instrument in our pilot work with eating-disordered patients (Treasure & Ward, 1997). This measure is not designed to allocate individuals to different stages; algorithms have been designed to do this job, and in our preliminary work we adapted algorithms used for other behaviours (Blake et al., 1997). We have developed this approach further and have evaluated a variety of different algorithms for use in anorexia nervosa (Jordan et al., 2002). The most useful algorithm was one which assessed the readiness to stop restricting/bingeing and purging. However, Davidson (1998) has criticised the methodology used for stage allocation. In particular he notes that the chronological cut-offs are arbitrary.

Several groups have also developed different measures specifically for people with eating disorders. Rieger and colleagues have developed a self-report measure (Rieger et al., 2000), and Geller (2002) has introduced an interview measure based on the eating disorder examination (see also Geller et al., 2001).

We would caution against the use of sophisticated measures of motivation to change symptomatic behaviours that clinicians have used for diagnostic purposes as these may bear no relevance for the client herself. Readiness to change is a dynamic concept that can vary within and between sessions, therefore it is not reasonable to spend a great deal of effort measuring readiness accurately at one point in time. One reason driving this interest in measurement was the idea that it might be useful to match treatment to the readiness to change. It can be argued that every clinician should be able to rapidly evaluate these concepts within the session whatever the agenda of the moment. Linear visual analogue scales, which measure readiness and the dimensions of importance and confidence on a continuum, are useful tools (Keller & Kemp White, 1997; Rollnick et al., 1999). The issues of importance and confidence can then be addressed in more detail.

We have also found that it is useful to have an additional scale that measures how eager others (i.e. those who are close to the respondent) are to see change. This highlights the social context and its impact upon change. For example, if there is a great disparity between the readiness of family members for change and the individual's readiness to change, this can cause conflict. In the case of anorexia nervosa the family may be insistent upon change and this may lead to an 'anti-motivational' environment in which there is confrontation and high negative expressed emotion. In obesity family members may be *more* or *less* motivated

Table 7.1 Questions to explore 'Importance'

What would have to happen for it to become more important for you to change?
You have given yourself x on the scale. What would need to happen before your score to move from x to 10?
What stops you moving from x to 10?
What are the things that you take into account which make you give yourself as high a score as you do?
What are the good things about x behaviour? What are some of the less good things about x behaviour?
What concerns do you have about x behaviour?
If you were to change, what would it be like?

Table 7.2   Questions to explore 'Confidence'

What would make you more confident about making these changes?
Why have you given yourself as high a score as you have on 'confidence'?
How could you go up higher so that your score goes from x to y?
How can I or anybody else help you to succeed?
Is there anything that you found helpful in any previous attempts to change?
What have you learned from the way things went wrong last time you tried?
If you decided to change, what might your options be? Do you know of any ways that have
    worked for other people?
What are the practical things you would need to do to achieve this goal? Are they achievable?
Is there anything you can think of that would make you feel more confident?

for change than the individual concerned. In a group of 111 obese patients seeking weight loss treatment, 54% admitted to registering for treatment because of strong family pressure, but considered themselves unable to carry out the programme (Caputo et al., 1993). We can also find obese patients who get highly involved in changing their lifestyle but with their family members *resenting* the time they spend away from home in the gym doing exercise and *opposed* to sharing healthier but less palatable food during meals. A husband may suspect that his wife may become more attractive to other men and be tempted to infidelity. This emphasises the need for a broad exploration of the psychosocial environment.

BENEFITS OF MOTIVATIONAL STRATEGIES TO FACILITATE CHANGE

As we discussed above, the transtheoretical model can be used to tailor self-help interventions (DiClemente & Prochaska 1998; Butler et al., 1999). It may also help to guide the therapist as to how to make the content of sessions congruent with the client's readiness to change. Motivational interviewing is a useful technique which can help to move an individual closer to the position where he or she is ready to change (Miller & Rollnick, 1991) and was used in conjunction with the TTM to examine the concept of psychotherapy matching. The results were somewhat disappointing (Project MATCH Research Group, 1997) in that the motivational enhancement therapy only improved the 15-month outcome in the less-motivated group whereas cognitive-behavioural therapy did relatively better in the short term. There was a large difference in the dose effect where motivational treatment was given in 4 sessions contrasting with 12 sessions of CBT. In a study of bulimia nervosa, comparing 4 sessions of MET with 4 sessions of CBT, there was no difference in the short-term outcome (Treasure et al., 1999).

Thus there is little evidence to support the simple model that patients in the precontemplation and contemplation stages should be given motivational treatment and that those in the action stage should have a skill-based intervention. On the other hand, there is increasing evidence that motivational interviewing is a cost-effective technique to facilitate change. Miller and his group at Albuquerque found that the style of the therapist's interaction was a critical component in facilitating change (for a review of this literature, see Miller, 1995, 1998) as the therapist's expectancies for patient change can influence the patient's compliance and outcomes. Therapists also differ markedly in their retention rates. When patients are randomly assigned to therapists, their outcomes differ substantially depending upon the therapist to whom they are assigned. By changing their therapeutic style between confrontation and client centred, therapists can drive client resistance rates up and down. This non-confrontational style contrasts with the model suggesting that people with alcohol abuse and dependence are resistant because of personality factors that must be broken down. Miller developed a short intervention ('the drinker's check-up') which operationalised some of the factors found to be useful to increase motivation. This check-up with motivational feedback was compared with standard confrontation. The outcome, in terms of drinking one year later, was worse in the group of patients who were given feedback from the drinker's check-up in a confrontational manner (Miller et al., 1993). In a further study it was found that if the motivational feedback of the drinker's check-up was given as an initial intervention prior to entry into an inpatient clinic, patients were found to have a better outcome. The therapists for this group reported that their patients had participated more fully in treatment and appeared to be more motivated (Brown & Miller, 1993; Bien et al., 1993).

Motivational interviewing has been found to be effective in several forms of behaviour change. The effectiveness has been demonstrated in randomised-controlled trials for alcohol abuse (Project Match Research Group, 1997; Heather, 1996; Gentilello et al., 1999; Handmaker et al., 1999; Senft, 1997), smoking (Butler et al., 1999; Colby, 1998), exercise acquisition (Harland et al., 1999), weight loss (Smith et al., 1997), and fat intake (Mhurchu et al., 1998).

Motivational interviewing is a directive, client-centred counselling style that aims to help patients to explore and resolve their ambivalence about behaviour change. It combines elements of style (warmth and empathy) with technique (e.g. key questions and focused reflective listening). One of the principles of this approach is that head to head conflict is unhelpful. What is more helpful is a collaborative, shoulder to shoulder relationship in which therapist and patient tackle the problem together. The patient's motivation to change is enhanced if there is a gentle process of negotiation in which the patient, not the practitioner, articulates the benefits and costs involved.

Rollnick and Miller (1995) were able to define specific and trainable therapist behaviours that they felt led to a better therapeutic alliance and better outcome (Rollnick & Miller, 1995) A good motivational therapist was able to:

(1) understand the other person's frame of reference
(2) express acceptance and affirmation
(3) filter the patient's thoughts so that motivational statements are amplified and non-motivational statements are dampened
(4) elicit self-motivational statements from the client: expressions of problem recognition, concern, desire, intention to change and ability to change
(5) match processes to the stage of change, and ensure that they do not jump ahead of the client
(6) affirm the client's freedom of choice and self-direction.

(1), (3), (4) and (5) cover issues relating to the transtheoretical model of change. They explore the reasons that sustain the behaviour and aim to help the client to shift the decisional balance of pros and cons into the direction of change. Items (2) and (6) cover the interpersonal aspects of the relationship. The therapist needs to provide a warm, optimistic setting and take a subordinate, non-powerful position by emphasising the client's autonomy and right to choose.

The fable about the sun and the wind is a rather nice metaphor about the spirit of motivational interviewing.

> The Sun and the Wind were having a dispute as to who was the most powerful. They saw a man walking along and they challenged each other about which of them would be most successful at getting the man to remove his coat. The Wind started first and blew up a huge gale, the coat flapped but the man only closed all his buttons and tightened up his belt. The Sun tried next and shone brightly making the man sweat. He proceeded to take off his coat.

Therapists need to model themselves on the Sun! Motivational interviewing seems to work by reducing negativity. A low level of resistance predicted change (Miller et al., 1993) and appeared to have a more powerful effect than increasing the number of positive statements about change. Resistance often occurs in the presence of confrontation. Confrontation occurs with low frequency in 5–15% of therapy sessions and unless this behaviour is reduced there is little change in client outcome. In some settings, such as probation/legal services, it is difficult to train workers to reduce the amount of confrontation.

LIMITATIONS OF MOTIVATIONAL STRATEGIES

There are some problems in using the standard techniques of motivational interviewing for patients with eating disorders. The style involves an equal balance of power between client and therapist. Patients with anorexia nervosa are often young adolescents and they may find this approach novel and somewhat alien and threatening. They tend to be wary and suspicious and are sensitised to being misunderstood. In this context the therapist may need to give more structure to the session and not use too many open questions, especially at the beginning. The therapist will be judged during the information exchange process as to whether he or she understands the problem.

One of the tenets of motivational interviewing is that the client is able to choose whether he or she will decide to change. In the case of anorexia nervosa there has to be a limit to this freedom because it is physiologically impossible to make the choice not to eat for longer than 2–3 months, and in most countries there is mental heath legislation limiting the individuals freedom to make such a choice. One way to use this within a motivational framework is for the therapist to bring in the concept of a higher power or authority, which constrains the action of both therapist and patients. This means that the therapist does not have to use confrontation or coercion directly but indirectly through society's rules. For example:

> The rules of good medical practice for the management of anorexia nervosa are to weigh the patient at every session. You can see [from this chart] that your weight is now in the range in which we have to recommend inpatient treatment.

The other problem is that families are intimately involved in the management of anorexia nervosa and they may be much more ready to see change than is your patient. It can be difficult to balance these different agendas. Families are well into action and the danger is that this can merely lead to high levels of confrontation at home which counteracts the non-confrontational approach of the clinic. We have therefore developed an intervention which involves teaching the family the basic principles of motivational interviewing. This approach overlaps with the techniques used to reduce expressed emotion in families. In addition to developing communication skills the family are also taught how to reinforce non eating disorder behaviour and to remove attention from eating disorder behaviour. These techniques are based upon Community Reinforcement Approach — CRAFT (Meyers & Smith, 1995; Meyers et al., 1998).

THE USE OF INFORMATION TO ENHANCE MOTIVATION

Most patients consider themselves well informed about how to solve eating and weight problems. They mainly gather their information from the media (American talk ..., 1997), but such information can be either wrong, exaggerated or tendentious (Johnson, 1998). Correct information can make a difference in motivation, but this mostly depends on how data and knowledge are offered to patients. The information may lead to new ways of thinking, feeling or acting but may also deaden or destroy whatever curiosity or motivation already exists.

To increase motivation and at the same time reduce treatment costs, most institutions use written material, tapes or lectures for patients, organised in sessions of psychoeducation. These sessions, usually in a group format or in the form of written material or manuals, are mostly standardised, making it easy for less skilled therapists to inform patients about health, eating and weight problems, etc. The importance of delivering this information in the change process has been largely overvalued, and the belief in its intrinsic power to change behaviour has fostered a massive use of it. Often the term psychoeducation is misleading in terms of its pedagogical content.

Lecturing patients gives a sense of control and efficient time management, but inevitably means that the patients' participation will be low—they will be mostly passive. The strength of a lecture is in presenting an example and first of all in generating a stimulus, not in shaping a response. It solicits further work, but does not in itself demand it (Wilkinson, 1984). The therapist in most cases must try to awaken a curiosity that is dormant as a consequence of long periods of strenuously defending one's position in precontemplation and contemplation from excessive stigmatisation. The insights that come from a lecture or an unsupervised reading, however intense, are often random experiences; they cannot duplicate the careful sequence and sustained growth of ideas fostered by a dialogue. In a motivation enhancement session the patient is not only required to absorb notions but is also asked to develop critical thinking skills while answering questions, discussing different positions or searching for solutions. Such probing often reveals fundamental gaps in knowledge and information or misconceptions that must be pointed out before they can be corrected. Once acquired, the new information and conceptual categories need to be related to an untidy reality. The patient must create a link between a well-organised number of facts and a less-structured personal experience. Only by encouraging critical thinking and experimenting can a patient be helped to fully grasp the complexity of a notion and to understand what that notion means when adapted to his or her specific problem (Ventura & Bauer, 1999). This is in contrast to the temptation to reduce the complexity of any human condition and change process to simplistic categories of good and bad, black and white (so typical of mass media information about eating and weight) that may encourage a false confidence and hinder real change.

The discussion during a group treatment, and the white space in a manual where patients are asked to register observations, allow therapists to follow the growth in this direction and monitor the change process through the different stages. The therapist can then orient the treatment according to the information that seems to be needed.

When asking an eating-disordered patient to consider entering a treatment programme, it may be of great importance to explain the why and how of treatment and offer information about the way we want her or him to eat. If we ask the patient to simply increase the amount of daily calories and to trust the therapist that a certain amount of calories are needed for recovery, or if we force the patient to eat whatever food is presented with the explanation that he or she is for the moment unable to decide autonomously, we may be reducing the complexity of this difficult task too much. Furthermore, such a therapeutic attitude may also be inconsistent with the empowerment principle of motivational interviewing. Asking an obese patient to reconsider losing weight after many failures by simply presenting another diet may not increase the confidence level. Introducing new information, like the satiating effect of food, or the psychobiological background of our eating behaviour and the way to control it, may be more inspiring and stimulate enough interest to try a new solution (Ventura & Bauer, 1999).

We should always consider whether the explanation we offer for the causes of past failures or future success stimulates passive compliance or an increase in patient autonomy. The General Causality Orientation Scale was used to test the autonomy orientation in 128 patients in a six-month long (very low calorie) weight-loss program with a 23-month follow-up. Analyses confirmed that participants whose motivation for weight loss was more autonomous would attend the programme more regularly, lose more weight during the programme, and maintain their lower weight after, as measured at follow-up (William et al., 1996). In a smoking cessation programme the movement through the different stages of motivation was influenced favourably by an experientially oriented process, and less favourably when the process was more oriented toward environmental events, such as dramatic relief and social liberation (Prochaska et al., 1985).

The level of involvement offered by a therapist and accepted by a patient may also vary because of cultural factors (Bauer et al., 1999). Even if treatment programmes of different countries share the same treatment principles, some aspects of therapy such as as power differentials, distance and participation are strongly culture-specific and need to be considered when defining the level of involvement and collaboration we initially expect from a patient. In treatment, it may, therefore, be easier to ask Scandinavian participants to express their point of view or their ambivalence in front of the group than in a Mediterranean or Latin American culture, and it may take more time in some cultures to ask patients to do homework than in others. These difficulties, however, should not be an excuse to think that patients don't need to be involved in a decision process.

REFERENCES

Abrams, D.B., Herzog, T.A., Emmons, K.M. & Linnan, L. (2000) Stages of change versus addiction: a replication and extension. *Nicotine Tob. Res.*, **2** (3), 223–229.
American talk about science and medical news: The National Health Report. (1997) New York: Roper Starch Worldwide.
Bauer, B., Katzman, M. & Ventura, M. (1999) Recognizing and working with cultural differences in patient support program. *Int. J. Obes.*, **23** (Suppl. 5), S58.
Biddle, S.J. & Fox, K.R. (1998) Motivation for physical activity and weight management. *Int. J. Obes. Relat. Metab. Disord.*, **22** (Suppl. 2), S39–S47.
Bien, T.H., Miller, W.R. & Tonigan, J.S. (1993) Brief interventions for alcohol problems: A review. *Addiction*, **88**, 315–335.
Blake, W., Turnbull, S. & Treasure, J. (1997) Stages and processes of change in eating disorders. Implications for therapy. *Clin. Psychol. Psychother.*, **4**, 186–191.
Brown, K.L. & Miller, W. (1993) Impact of motivational interviewing on participation and outcome in residential alcoholism treatment. *Psychology of Addictive Behaviours*, **7**, 238–245.

Brownell, K. (1990) Dieting readiness. *Weight Control Digest*, **1**, 5–10.

Butler, C.C., Rollnick, S., Cohen, D., Russell, I., Bachmann, M. & Stott, N. (1999) Motivational counselling versus brief advice for smokers in general practice: A randomised trial. *Br. J. Gen. Prac.*, **49**, 611–616.

Caputo, G., Arovini, C., Cuzzolaro, M. (1993) Restriction and disinhibition in obesity: Biological, behavioural or psychiatric symptoms? In M. Cuzzolaro, G. Caputo, V. Guidetti, G. Ripa di Meana (Eds), *Proceedings of the 2nd International Rome Symposium on Eating Disorders*, pp. 316–322.

Carlson, S., Sonnenberg, L.M. & Cummings, S. (1994) Dieting readiness test predicts completion in a short-term weight loss program. *J. Am. Diet. Assoc.*, **94**, 552–554.

Colby, S.M., Monti, P.M., Barnett, N.P., Rohsenow, D.J., Weissman, K., Spirito, A., Woolard, R.H. & Lewander, W.J. (1998) Brief motivational interviewing in a hospital setting for adolescent smoking: A preliminary study. *J. Consult. Clin. Psychol.*, **66**, 574–578.

Davidson, R. (1998) The transtheoretical model. A critical overview. In W. Miller & N. Heather (Eds), *Treating Addictive Behaviours* (2nd edn; pp. 25–38). New York: Plenum Press.

Derisley, J. & Reynolds, S. (2000) The transtheoretical stages of change as a predictor of premature termination, attendance and alliance in psychotherapy. *Br. J. Clin. Psychol.*, **39** (Pt 4), 371–382.

De Vries, H. & Backbier, E. (1994) Self-efficacy as an important determinant of quitting among pregnant women who smoke the Ø pattern. *Preventive Medicine*, **23**, 167–174.

DiClemente, C. & Prochaska, J.O. (1998) Towards a comprehensive, transtheoretical model of change. In W. Miller & N. Heather (Eds), *Treating Addictive Behaviours* (pp. 3–24) New York: Plenum Press.

Fontaine, K.R. & Wiersema, L. (1999) Dieting readiness test fails to predict enrollment in a weight loss program. *J. Am. Diet. Assoc.*, **99**, 664.

Geller, J. (2002) Estimating readiness for change in anorexia nervosa: Comparing clients, clinicians, and research assessors. *Int. J. Eat. Disord.*, **31**, 251–260.

Geller, J., Cockell, S.J. & Drab, D.L. (2001) Assessing readiness for change in the eating disorders: The psychometric properties of the readiness and motivation interview. *Psychol. Assess.*, **13**, 189–198.

Gentilello, L.M., Rivara, F.P., Donovan, D.M., Jurkovich, G.J., Daranciang, E., Dunn, C.W., Villaveces, A., Copass, M. & Ries, R.R. (1999) Alcohol interventions in a trauma center as a means of reducing the risk of injury recurrence. *Ann. & Surg.*, **230**, 473–480.

Greene, G.W., Rossi, S.R., Rossi, J.S., Velicer, W.F., Fava, J.L. & Prochaska, J.O. (1999) Dietary applications of the stages of change model. *J. Am. Diet. Assoc.*, **99**, 673–678.

Handmaker, N.S., Miller, W.R. & Manicke, M. (1999) Findings of a pilot study of motivational interviewing with pregnant drinkers. *J. Stud. Alcohol.*, **60**, 285–287.

Hargreaves, M.K., Schlundt, D.G., Buchowski, M.S., Hardy, R.E., Rossi, S.R. & Rossi, J.S. (1999) Stages of change and the intake of dietary fat in African-American women: Improving stage assignment using the Eating Styles Questionnaire. *J. Am. Diet. Assoc.*, **99**, 1392–1399.

Harland, J., White, M., Drinkwater, C., Chinn, D., Farr, L. & Howel, D. (1999) The Newcastle exercise project: A randomised controlled trial of methods to promote physical activity in primary care. *Br. Med. J.*, **319**, 828–832.

Heather, N. (1996) The public health and brief interventions for excessive alcohol consumption: The British experience. *Addict. Behav.*, **21**, 857–868.

Jeffery, R.W. & French, S.A. (1999) Preventing weight gain in adults: The pound of prevention study. *Am. J. Public Health*, **89**, 747–751.

Johnson, T. (1998) Shattuck lecture — medicine and the media *N. Engl. J. Med.*, **339**, 87–92.

Jordan, T. (in press) Measurement. *Int. J. Eat. Disord.*

Keller, V.F. & Kemp-White, M. (1997) Choices and changes: A new model for influencing patient health behavior. *J. Clin. Outcome Management*, **4**, 33–36.

Laforge, R.G., Rossi, J.S., Prochaska, J.O., Velicer, W.F., Levesque, D.A. & McHorney, C.A. (1999) Stage of regular exercise and health-related quality of life. *Prev. Med.*, **28**, 349–360.

Marcus, B.H., Banspach, S.W., Lefebvre, R.C., Rossi, J.S., Carleton, R.A. & Abrams, D.B. (1992) Using the stages of change model to increase the adoption of physical activity among community participants. *Am. J. Health Promot.*, **6**, 424–429.

Martin, R.A., Velicer, W.F. & Fava, J.L. (1996) Latent transition analysis to the stages of change for smoking cessation. *Addict. Behav.*, **21**, 67–80.

McConnaughy, E., DiClemente, C.C., Prochaska, J.O. & Velicer, W.F. (1989) Stages of change in psychotherapy. *Psychotherapy*, **26**, 494–503.

Meyers, R.J. & Smith, J.E. (1995) *Clinical Guide to Alcohol Treatment: The Community Reinforcement Approach*. New York: Guilford Press.

Meyers, R.J., Smith, J.E. & Miller, E.J. (1998) Working through the concerned significant other. In W.R. Miller & N. Heather (Eds), *Treating Addictive Behaviours* (2nd edn; pp. 149–161). New York: Plenum Press.

Mhurchu, C.N., Margetts, B.M. & Speller, V. (1998) Randomized clinical trial comparing the effectiveness of two dietary interventions for patients with hyperlipidaemia. *Clin. Sci. (Lond.)*, **95**, 479–487.

Miller, W.R., Benefield, R.G. & Tonigan, J.S. (1993) Enhancing motivation for change in problem drinking: A controlled comparison of two therapist styles. *J. Consult. Clin. Psychol.*, **61**, 455–461.

Miller, W. (1995) Increasing Motivation for change. In M. Hetherington & W. Miller (Eds), *Handbook of Alcoholism Treatment Approaches* (2nd edn). Needham Heights. MA: Allyn & Bacon.

Miller, W.R. (1998) Enhancing motivation to change. In W.R. Miller & N. Heather (Eds), *Treating Addictive Behaviours: Processes of change* (2nd edn; pp. 121–132). New York: Plenum Press.

Miller, W. & Rollnick, S. (1991) *Motivational Interviewing: Preparing People to Change Addictive Behaviour*. New York: Guilford.

Nigg, C.R., Burbank, P.M., Padula, C., Dufresne, R., Rossi, J.S., Velicer, W.F., Laforge, R.G. & Prochaska, J.O. (1999) Stages of change across ten health risk behaviors for older adults. *Gerontologist*, **39**, 473–482.

O'Connell, D. & Velicer, W.F. (1988) A decisional balance measure and the stages of change model for weight loss. *Int. J. Addict.*, **23**, 729–750.

Pallonen, U.E., Prochaska, J.O., Velicer, W.F., Prokhorov, A.V. & Smith, N.F. (1998) Stages of acquisition and cessation for adolescent smoking: an empirical integration. *Addict. Behav.*, **23**, 303–324.

Pendleton, V.R., Poston, W.S., Goodrick, G.K., Willems, E.P., Swank, P.R., Kimball, K.T. & Foreyt, J.P. (1998) The predictive validity of the Diet Readiness Test in a clinical population. *Int. J. Eat. Disord.*, **24**, 363–369.

Prochaska, J.O. & Norcross, J. (1994) *Systems of Psychotherapy: A Transtheoretical Analysis* (3rd edn). Pacific Grove California: Brooks /Cole Publishing Company.

Prochaska, J.O., DiClemente, C.C., Velicer, W.F., Ginpil, S. & Norcross, J.C. (1985) Predicting change in smoking status for self-changers. *Addict. Behav.*, **10**, 395–406.

Prochaska, J.O., Diclemente, C.C., Velicer, W.F. & Rossi, J.S. (1993). Standardized, individualized, interactive, and personalized self-help programs for smoking cessation. *Health Psychol.*, **12**, 399–405.

Prochaska, J.O. & Velicer, W.F. (1997a) Misinterpretations and misapplications of the transtheoretical model. *Am. J. Health Promot.*, **12**, 11–12.

Prochaska, J.O. & Velicer, W.F. (1997b) The transtheoretical model of health behavior change. *Am. J. Health Promot.*, **12**, 38–48.

Prochaska, J.O., Velicer, W.F., DiClemente, C.C. & Fava, J. (1988) Measuring processes of change: applications to the cessation of smoking. *J. Consult. Clin. Psychol.*, **56**, 520–528.

Prochaska, J. & DiClemente, C. (1984) *The Transtheoretical Approach: Crossing the Traditional Boundaries of Therapy*. Homewood, IL: Dow Jones Irwen.

Project MATCH Research Group (1997) Matching alcoholism treatments to client heterogeneity: Project MATCH posttreatment drinking outcomes. *J. Stud. Alcohol.*, **58**, 7–29.

Rakowski, W. & Clark, M.A. (1998) Do groups of women aged 50 to 75 match the national average mammography rate? *Am. J. Prev. Med.*, **15**, 187–197.

Rieger, E., Touyz, S., Schotte, D., Beumont, P., Russell, J., Clarke, S., Kohn, M. & Griffiths, R. (2000) Development of an instrument to assess readiness to recover in anorexia nervosa [In Process Citation]. *Int. J. Eat. Disord.*, **28**, 387–396.

Rollnick, S. (1998) Readiness, importance and confidence: Critical conditions of change in treatment. In W.R. Miller & N. Heather (Eds), *Treating Addictive Behaviours* (2nd edn; pp. 49–60). New York: Plenum Press.

Rollnick, S., Mason, P. & Butler, C. (1999) *Health Behaviour Change*. Edinburgh: Churchill Livingstone.

Rollnick, S. & Miller, W.R. (1995) What is motivational interviewing? *Behav. Cognit. Psychother.*, **23**, 325–335.

Rossi, J., Rossi, S., Velicer, W. & Prochaska, J. (1995) Motivational readiness to control weight. In D. Allison (Ed.), *Handbook of Assessment Methods for Eating Behaviours and Weight Related Problems* (pp. 387–430). London: Sage Publications.

Schwab, M., Schmidt, K., Witte, H. & Abrams, M. (2000) Investigation of nonlinear ECG changes during spontaneous sleep state changes and cortical arousal in fetal sheep. *Cereb. Cortex*, **10**, 142–148.

Senft, R.A., Polen, M.R., Freeborn, D.K. & Hollis, J.F. (1997) Brief intervention in a primary care setting for hazardous drinkers. *Am. J. Prev. Med.*, **13**, 464–470.

Smith, K.A., Fairburn, C.G. & Cowen, P.J. (1997) Relapse of depression after rapid depletion of tryptophan [see comments]. *Lancet*, **349**, 915–919.

Stanton, A.L., Rebert, W.M. & Zinn, L.M. (1986) Self change in bulimia: A preliminary study. *Int. J. Eat. Disord.*, **5**, 917–924.

Temoshok, L., Heller, B.W., Sagebiel, R.W., Blois, M.S., Sweet, D.M., DiClemente, R.J. & Gold, M.L. (1985) The relationship of psychosocial factors to prognostic indicators in cutaneous malignant melanoma. *J. Psychosom. Res.*, **29**, 139–153.

Treasure, J.L. & Ward, A. (1997) A practical guide to the use of motivational interviewing in anorexia nervosa. *Eur. Eat. Disord. Rev.*, **5**, 102–114.

Treasure, J.L., Katzman, M., Schmidt, U., Troop, N., Todd, G. & de Silva, P. (1999) Engagement and outcome in the treatment of bulimia nervosa: First phase of a sequential design comparing motivation enhancement therapy and cognitive behavioural therapy. *Behav. Res. Ther.*, **37**, 405–418.

Velicer, W.F., DiClemente, C.C., Rossi, J.S. & Prochaska, J.O. (1990) Relapse situations and self-efficacy: An integrative model. *Addict. Behav.*, **15**, 271–283.

Velicer, W.F. & Plummer, B.A. (1998) Time series analysis in historiometry: A comment on Simonton. *J. Pers.*, **66**, 477–486.

Velicer, W.F., Prochaska, J.O., Bellis, J.M., DiClemente, C.C., Rossi, J.S., Fava, J.L. & Steiger, J.H. (1993) An expert system intervention for smoking cessation. *Addict. Behav.*, **18**, 269–290.

Velicer, W.F., Prochaska, J.O., Fava, J.L., Laforge, R.G. & Rossi, J.S. (1999) Interactive versus noninteractive interventions and dose-response relationships for stage-matched smoking cessation programs in a managed care setting. *Health Psychol.*, **18**, 21–28.

Velicer, W.F., Rossi, J.S., DiClemente, C.C. & Prochaska, J.O. (1996) A criterion measurement model for health behavior change. *Addict. Behav.*, **21**, 555–584.

Ventura, M. & Bauer, B. (1999) Empowerment of women with purging-type bulimia nervosa through nutritional rehabilitation. *Eat. Weight Disord.*, **4**, 55–62.

Vitousek, K., Watson, S. & Wilson, G.T. (1998) Enhancing motivation for change in treatment-resistant eating disorders. *Clin. Psychol. Rev.*, **18**, 391–420.

Ward, A., Ward, A., Troop, N., Todd, G. & Treasure, J. (1996) To change or not to change—'how' is the question? *Br. J. Med. Psychol.*, **69** (Pt 2), 139–146.

Weinstein, N.D., Rothman, A.J. & Sutton, S.R. (1998) Stage theories of health behavior: Conceptual and methodological issues. *Health Psychol.*, **17**, 290–299.

Wilkinson, J. (1984) *The Art and Craft of Teaching*. Cambridge, MA: Harvard Press.

Williams, G.C., Grow, V.M., Freedman, Z.R., Ryan, R.M. & Deci, E.L. (1996) Motivational predictors of weight loss and weight-loss maintenance. *J. Pers. Soc. Psychol.*, **70**, 115–126.

CHAPTER 8

Cognitive-Behavioural Treatments

Glenn Waller

Department of Psychiatry, St. George's Hospital Medical School,
University of London, London, UK
and

Helen Kennerley

Department of Clinical Psychology, Warneford Hospital, Oxford, UK

Cognitive-behaviour therapy (CBT) has been the most exhaustively researched form of treatment for the eating disorders. The focus in this literature has largely been on work with bulimia nervosa and binge eating disorder, and there is substantially less evidence regarding its long-term efficacy with anorexia nervosa or obesity. In polls of specialist clinicians' preferred mode of practice (e.g. Mussell et al., 2000), many report that their therapeutic work with the eating disorders involves some elements of CBT. However, it is clear that many clinicians who describe their work as CBT are not actually practising within a recognisable CBT framework—either using protocol-driven therapies in the appropriate manner or using cognitive-behavioural theory to drive individualised assessment, formulation and treatment. Therefore, we think that it is important that we should start by defining our central terms.

WHAT IS COGNITIVE-BEHAVIOURAL THERAPY?

Any cognitive therapy recognises the reciprocal role of cognitions (mental representations in the form of thoughts or images), affect and behaviour. The way we think affects the way we feel and behave, which then affect the way we think. Simply put, if our cognitions or interpretations are valid, we feel and react appropriately: if our interpretations are skewed or distorted, we feel and behave in ways that do not reflect reality and can cause difficulties.

Cognitive-behavioural therapy was developed by A.T. Beck throughout the 1960s and 1970s, and is one of several cognitive therapies that emerged at this time. Beck's cognitive therapy emphasises the understanding of the cognitive element of a problem, and stresses

The Essential *Handbook of Eating Disorders.* Edited by J. Treasure, U. Schmidt and E. van Furth.
© 2005 John Wiley & Sons, Ltd.

the powerful role of behaviour in maintaining and changing the way that we think and feel. In his original description of emotional problems, Beck recognised that biology and external environment impact on our well-being. He noted that readily accessible cognitions and observable behaviours were underpinned by fundamental belief systems (or schemata). However, 'classic' CBT was evolved to exploit the fact that much radical change (impacting on deeper structures) can be effected through active work at the level of current cognitions and behaviours.

The aim of CBT is first to help the client to identify the cognitions that underpin problem behaviours and/or emotional states, and then to help that person to reappraise these cognitions. Insights that are evolved in this way are then 'tested', in that the client is encouraged to check out the veracity of the new belief. Insights are developed using guided discovery (or 'Socratic questioning'), often combined with self-monitoring in the form of 'daily thought records'. Clients are taught the technique of appraising automatic thoughts and images, identifying cognitive distortions and substituting statements (or images) that carry greater validity and which do not promote the problem affect/behaviour. Clients are also encouraged to use structured data collection and behavioural tests to evaluate all new perspectives.

Although clearly structured, CBT has always been more than a protocol-driven therapy that can be applied to particular psychological problems. Beck et al. (1979) emphasise the importance of developing and using the therapeutic relationship (p. 27) and stress the need to tailor the therapy to meet the needs of the individual (p. 45). Beck also warns the therapist against being overly didactic or interpretative, encouraging genuine 'collaborative empiricism' instead (p. 6).

The model underpinning this form of psychological therapy provides such a general heuristic for understanding human learning, behaviour, emotion and information processing that it is almost impossible to encounter a client who does not 'fit' the model. However, this does not mean that every patient can benefit from CBT. Safran and Segal (1990) have identified certain client characteristics as being necessary if CBT is to match the style and needs of the client. Those characteristics include: an ability to access relevant cognitions; an awareness of and ability to differentiate emotional states; acceptance of the cognitive rationale for treatment; acceptance of personal responsibility for change; and the ability to form a real 'working alliance' with the therapist. This means that there will be clients who are better suited to other forms of psychotherapy (such as analytical, systemic, social and pharmacological approaches), and it is the task of the assessing therapist to consider the most appropriate intervention.

How is CBT Relevant to the Eating Disorders?

Anyone who works with clients with eating disorders will appreciate the interacting role of cognitions, feelings and behaviours in the maintenance of the problem, whatever the presentation. Figure 8.1 shows examples of some of the ways in which cognition and affect are related to the behavioural manifestations of the eating disorders. In principle, given this interaction of cognition, emotion and behaviour, CBT should be an appropriate intervention for a range of eating disorders, enabling the client to identify prominent maintaining cycles in their problem and, ultimately, to break these cycles through cognitive and behavioural

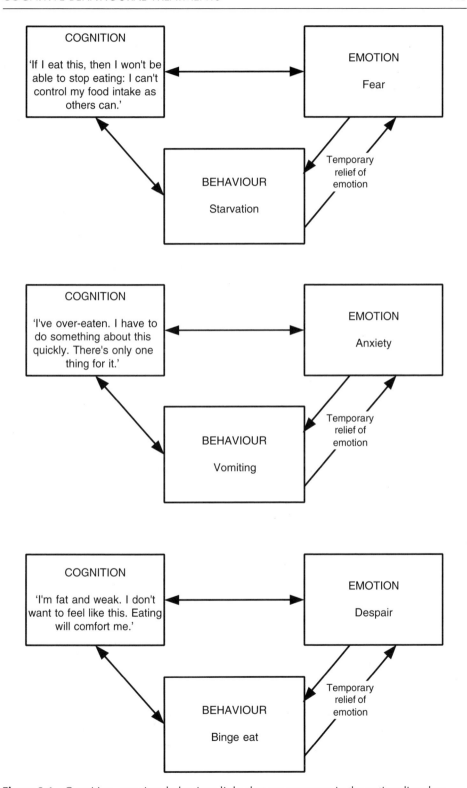

Figure 8.1 Cognition–emotion–behaviour links that are common in the eating disorders

methods. As outlined above, the practical utility of CBT is such cases will be limited if the client is not able to identify with the model and collaborate with the methods. Given the nature of some aspects of eating pathology (outlined below), it will be important to consider ways of helping some clients to overcome their difficulties with CBT (e.g. recognition of emotion, or coping with abandonment fears and control issues for long enough to develop a working relationship).

Cognitive-behavioural theory has been used as the basis for treatment programmes for eating disorders since the early 1980s. Garner and Bemis (1982) suggested a CBT approach to the management of anorexia nervosa, while Fairburn (1981; Fairburn & Cooper, 1989) developed a similar programme for bulimia nervosa. More recently, various clinicians and researchers have extended this work to address binge eating disorder, and others (e.g. Agras et al., 1997) have discussed the application of CBT methods as part of the broad-based approach that is most likely to be effective in working with obesity. However, CBT is still relatively underdeveloped in work with children and adolescents with eating disorders. In addition, CBT in this field has been limited by a focus on diagnosable cases, with inevitable difficulties of generalisability to the many atypical cases. Nevertheless, understanding the principles of CBT should enable us to develop a focus for understanding, and perhaps managing, problem eating behaviours.

THE DEVELOPMENT AND NATURE OF EXISTING FORMS OF CBT IN THE EATING DISORDERS

CBT for eating disorders has been developed over the past two decades, and is the most extensively researched and validated psychological therapy used with the eating disorders. Its scientific base means that such research has employed strong designs and allows for clear conclusions. However, that same scientific approach means that we need to be critical of our models and the treatments that have been developed from them. Therefore, the review that follows will consider the strengths and weaknesses of CBT as it stands. In order to understand the added value of introducing the cognitive element, we will begin by considering the earlier literature regarding the impact of treatments based solely on behavioural principles.

Behavioural Treatments

There is a long tradition of using behavioural methods in working with *anorexia nervosa*, particularly to reinforce weight gain or address weight 'phobias'. In the short term, such methods are relatively effective in ensuring weight gain, and have a clear role in stabilising physiological and physical health status. However, the long-term benefit of these methods is dubious, since there is often marked weight loss after treatment. Clinical experience would suggest that this is often due to the behavioural programmes addressing the wrong behaviour. For example, the clinician may intend to reinforce 'positive' behaviour (eating), while the patient may see eating as a means to a completely different contingency (e.g. getting out of hospital, and being able to re-establish personal control). While the initial effect on the overt behaviour will be identical (eating more), the impact on eating attitudes and ultimate weight gain might be minimal. In short, the perceived success of behavioural methods in this group (as with all others) depends on an emphasis on behavioural analysis, rather than an understanding of the contingencies involved.

In *bulimia nervosa*, behaviour therapy has been examined both in isolation and as an adjunct to cognitive work. In isolation, it has produced disappointing results, yielding much lower remission rates than either CBT or interpersonal psychotherapy (IPT; Fairburn et al., 1995). By analogy with the addiction literature, it has been argued that a key behavioural technique in working with bulimia will be exposure with response prevention. For example, a person might be dissuaded from purging after a binge. In theory, this would promote extinction or habituation of the anxiety that follows a binge. However, a number of researchers (e.g. Bulik et al., 1998) have concluded that exposure and response prevention adds nothing to the therapeutic benefits of CBT, thus calling into doubt the usefulness of a behavioural approach and of the addiction link.

Until relatively recently, psychological treatment for *obesity* and *binge eating disorder* (BED) has been based largely upon a mixture of behavioural and dietary methods. Results in the published literature (i.e. a research base that is likely to be biased in favour of positive findings) indicate that weight loss and its maintenance are generally poor (e.g. Wooley & Garner, 1991). The best impact is on the frequency of binge eating, rather than weight loss. Although normalisation of eating patterns is a major achievement, weight loss is not achieved reliably in the obese. Several authors (e.g. Levine, Marcus & Moulton, 1996) have demonstrated that introducing an exercise component to a treatment programme for obese women with BED can have positive benefits in terms of abstinence from bingeing but, again, there is no comparable impact on weight loss. Overall, we have a very limited understanding of individual prognosis and suitability for a behavioural treatment of obesity and BED. While there is generally a modest amount of weight reduction during treatment (e.g. Wooley & Garner, 1991), this gain is usually poorly maintained at follow-up. While some individuals are able to sustain and improve upon the therapeutic gain, we lack a clear picture of what is different about the psychology of those successful individuals. Our understanding is further confused because researchers tend not to differentiate obese patients from obese binge eaters. In addition, treatment programmes for these complex disorders lack diversity. Wilson (1996) suggests that part of the failure of behaviour therapy to produce change in weight levels among obese patients is that this approach fails to address the concept of self-acceptance, in the way that CBT does. In other words, if the clinician's target is for the patient to achieve a modest but stable level of weight loss over an extended time period, that may conflict with the patient's own goal (often substantial and rapid weight loss). If behaviour therapy fails to address the utility of their goals, then it is not surprising that patients will come to see the therapy as unhelpful.

Summary

The failure of behaviour therapy in the eating disorders has indicated a need to develop cognitive-behavioural approaches to the eating disorders, with a greater stress on modifying the belief structures of these patients. As will be seen in the next section, these formulations and the resulting treatments have yielded a very mixed pattern of utility, ranging from poor to relatively successful.

The Conceptual Base of Existing Cognitive-Behavioural Treatments

To date, CBT with the eating disorders has been based on models where the central pathology involves cognitions and behaviours that are highly focused on food, weight and body shape (e.g. Fairburn, 1981; Garner & Bemis, 1982). The aims of treatment within these models have been clearly described elsewhere (e.g. Fairburn & Cooper, 1989), but centre on the modification of behaviours and cognitions that maintain the existing behaviour. In CBT terms, the main foci are the modification of negative automatic thoughts and dysfunctional assumptions relating to food, weight and shape, and the breaking of behavioural and physiological chains that maintain the unhealthy eating behaviours and cognitions. This model has been used to develop clearly operationalised treatments, although it would be a mistake to conclude that these manualised protocol-driven treatments lack an individualised component (see above). Nor are these models static, as evidenced by the recent modifications to Fairburn's model of bulimia nervosa (Fairburn, 1997). From a clinical and scientific perspective, the benefit of the clear operationalisation of these (or any other) treatments is that one can be more conclusive about their effectiveness and limitations.

The Effectiveness of Existing CBT with Different Eating Disorders

There is only a relatively limited evidence base for the efficacy of CBT with *anorexia nervosa*, possibly due to the inadequacy of most cognitive and behavioural models of restrictive behaviours. It is also important to note that some studies are based on work with restrictive anorexics only, while others involve mixed groups of restrictive and bulimic anorexics. The little evidence that has been generated by controlled trials tends to suggest that individual CBT is moderately effective for anorexia nervosa, but no more effective than less focused psychotherapies (Channon et al., 1989). At the symptomatic level, however, there is some strong evidence that CBT can be effective in producing change in specific aspects of anorexia nervosa. For example, body image disturbance has been shown to respond to exposure and cognitive challenge (e.g. Norris, 1984). Although group work has been advocated for anorexia nervosa, the evidence regarding group CBT with anorexics shows that has very poor therapeutic efficacy (Leung, Waller & Thomas, 1999a), and it cannot be recommended at present.

In contrast, the evidence base for conventional CBT with *bulimia nervosa* is very strong, particularly given its basis in well-controlled studies with long follow-up times (e.g. Fairburn et al., 1995). At the syndromal level, individual CBT induces remission in approximately 40–50% of cases, and an overall level of symptom reduction of approximately 60–70% (e.g. Vitousek, 1996; Wilson, 1999). This level of symptom reduction is only marginally lower when CBT is presented in a group format (Leung, Waller & Thomas, 2000). Indeed, there is evidence that a proportion of bulimics can benefit substantially from the use of self-help manuals (e.g. Cooper, Coker & Fleming, 1996). In controlled trials, existing CBT methods have been established to be superior to most other therapies in terms of either the magnitude or the immediacy of effect. They also have a clear superiority over the impact of antidepressant medication (e.g. Johnson, Tsoh & Varnado, 1996). While the most widely validated forms of CBT for bulimia tend to require between 16 and 20 sessions, Bulik et al. (1998) have reported equivalent results from an eight-session programme (although there are no long-term follow-up data on this variant).

The picture is somewhat less well developed in the case of *binge eating disorder* and *obesity*, partly due to the tendency to confound the two disorders. However, the conclusion is relatively similar to that with behaviour therapy—CBT is effective in reducing binge frequency, but not in reducing weight substantially in the long term. Long-term weight reduction (albeit modest) is more dependent on achieving abstinence from binge eating during the CBT (Agras et al., 1997). In the case of the non-binge-eating obese, a multifactorial approach to therapy (e.g. CBT plus exercise plus diet) appears to promote the most sustained weight loss (e.g. Leermakers et al., 1999), although the amount of weight lost is still only moderate in most cases. In the case of failure to benefit from the standard course of CBT, it is worth extending the treatment for binge eating disorder patients, since this helps a substantial number of individuals to achieve abstinence from binge eating (Eldredge et al., 1997).

Summary: Strengths and Limitations of Existing CBT for the Eating Disorders

Existing forms of CBT have been researched well enough that we can conclude that they have a number of strengths and limitations (Wilson, 1999). First, they are effective in reducing the presence of bulimic behaviours, cognitions and syndromes (Vitousek, 1996), and show clear advantages in the magnitude of change, the rapidity of change, or both. There is clearly a need to understand why CBT does not induce remission or symptom reduction in a large number of bulimics, and this may require consideration of the sufficiency of existing cognitive-behaviour models that have been applied to bulimia (Hollon & Beck, 1994). Second, CBT is no more effective than other approaches in some domains, particularly in the treatment of restrictive disorders and in the long-term reduction of obesity. Third, as is the case with other therapies, there is some evidence that CBT is less effective in working with complex cases, such as those bulimics with a history of trauma, high levels of dissociation or comorbid personality disorders (e.g. Sansone & Fine, 1992; Waller, 1997). Finally, since the basis of these forms of CBT was laid down (in the early 1980s), there have been substantial developments in the cognitive psychology of the eating disorders (see Shafran & de Silva, this volume) and in the conceptual base of CBT itself.

CBT remains demonstrably as or more effective than other forms of therapy for the eating disorders. However, given these strengths and limitations, it is clear that we should treat existing forms of CBT as necessary but not sufficient in this field. Therefore, it is timely to consider how to integrate the literature on the cognitive psychology of the eating disorders with the existing forms of CBT, in order to develop therapies that might be more effective. It will also be valuable to consider whether this elaboration of the cognitive structure of the eating disorders might explain the benefits found with some other (non-CBT) therapies. Rather than leaping in with suggestions about more advanced forms of CBT that might be considered when working with the eating disorders, it is important to consider the advances in our understanding of the eating disorders over recent years. Such an approach should have the benefit of allowing us to suggest more appropriate, theory-based formulations of eating psychopathology, which in turn should inform the development of CBT.

RECENT DEVELOPMENTS IN COGNITIVE-BEHAVIOURAL FORMULATIONS OF THE EATING DISORDERS

Whether in the eating disorders or elsewhere, the progressive development of models of psychopathology should be seen as an inherent part of clinical and research work. Such development needs to be both 'top–down' (driven by theories of psychological function) and 'bottom–up' (driven by the data that emerge from clinical practice and research). There is bound to be some lag time, as existing models are properly tested. However, it is clear that progress in the field of the eating disorders has been relatively slow, with a failure to absorb the lessons that have been present for some time both in our conceptualisation of CBT (Hollon & Beck, 1994) and in the evidence base (e.g. Meyer, Waller & Waters, 1998). Clearly, the most pressing issue is the failure of CBT (and other therapies) to have any substantial impact in two areas—the level of restriction in anorexia, and weight loss in conditions that include obesity. However, it is also necessary to consider how we can build on the strong start that has been made in the field of reducing bulimic behaviours. While pioneering work in this field (e.g. Bulik et al., 1998; Fairburn et al., 1995) shows that CBT for bulimia nervosa has impressive results (Vitousek, 1996), there are still many with bulimia who do not benefit from it (e.g. Wilson, 1996, 1999).

The Role of Individual Formulations

At the heart of any form of CBT, there must lie two things. The first is a broad assessment, driven both by the existing evidence base and by the material that the patient brings to the session. The second is an individualised formulation, which takes into account both the aetiology and the maintenance of the relevant cognitions, behaviours and emotions (e.g. Persons, 1989). Such a formulation needs to be based both on the broad psychology and physiology of eating problems and on the individual's circumstances. This formulation will act as the key in illustrating the cognitive and behavioural factors that need to be addressed in therapy.

There are two errors commonly made in constructing such formulations. The first is ignoring the individual's idiosyncratic situation and experience, instead falling back on generalised formulations of the disorder (e.g. Fairburn & Cooper, 1989; Lacey, 1986; Slade, 1982). This ignores the fact that these broad formulations are better used as templates, using existing theory and evidence to assist in deciding what elements are relevant to the individual case. The second error is forgetting that an individual formulation is a working hypothesis rather than a proven fact—an error that often leads us to assume that we understand the individual, thereby blinding us to evidence that we are wrong. A formulation is never anything more than the best model that we can achieve at the time, and we should always be ready to find that we have to reformulate to accommodate the unexpected (e.g. when treatment is failing, or when the patient tells us that we are wrong). Within CBT, both assessment and formulation have a strong evidence base to draw upon, meaning that our templates of the general case are likely to have some relevance to the individual patient. However, there is still plenty of room for improvement in our models (and always will be, however well developed they might become).

Emerging Themes in the Formulation of the Eating Disorders

As outlined above, CBT models of the eating disorders have been very much driven by a focus on cognitions and behaviours regarding food, shape and weight (Fairburn, 1981; Fairburn & Cooper, 1989; Garner & Bemis, 1982). While the evidence to date shows that understanding these negative automatic thoughts and dysfunctional assumptions is necessary to understand the eating disorders (e.g. Channon, Hemsley & de Silva, 1989; Cooper, 1997), these cognitions are clearly not sufficient explanatory constructs. Both research and clinical reports have suggested that comprehensive cognitive-behavioural models of eating disorders will need to include the following (often overlapping) factors.

Social and Interpersonal Issues

The impact of interpersonal psychotherapy on bulimic psychopathology (Fairburn et al., 1995) gives us the strongest clue that there are important interpersonal and social issues that contribute to eating pathology. Those issues include abandonment fears (e.g. Patton, 1992; Meyer & Waller, 1999), fear of negative social evaluation (e.g. Steiger et al., 1999), and the socially-marked experience of shame (e.g. Murray, Waller & Legg, 2000; Striegel-Moore, Silberstein & Rodin, 1993). However, this research is in its early stages, and needs considerable extension to determine the role of social factors across the eating disorders.

Control Issues

It has often been noted that control is a particularly powerful factor in the aetiology and maintenance of restrictive disorders. Slade (1982) incorporated a need for control into his early formulation of anorexia nervosa. However, the construct was largely overlooked within the more predominant early models (e.g. Fairburn, 1981; Garner & Bemis, 1982). It is only recently that Fairburn, Shafran and Cooper (1999) have revisited the issue of control, elaborating on Slade's work in order to develop a more refined cognitive-behavioural model of restrictive pathology. Where there has been research into the construct (e.g. King, 1989), it has largely focused on the role of perceived control over life and events. However, Slade's model really addresses the discrepancy between *perceived* and *desired* control. While control has generally been considered in relation to the restrictive aspects of anorexia, it is also possible to see a critical role for control in bulimia. In particular, bulimic symptoms often serve an emotion regulation function (Lacey, 1986; Root & Fallon, 1989). There is a clear, long-standing gap in our understanding of the impact of control discrepancies, and this gap needs to be closed in order to refine our understanding of this factor in CBT. Such research would benefit from distinguishing between discrepancies in control over life and discrepancies in control over affective states, to determine whether these patterns distinguish different forms of eating psychopathology.

Motivation

Given the ego-syntonic nature of some eating pathology (e.g. Serpell et al., 1999), it has been suggested that there is a need to enhance motivation in eating-disordered patients

before treatment can have its maximal effect. This principle would apply as much to CBT
as to any other disorder (if not more, given the importance of the working alliance in CBT).
However, it seems to be too early to be optimistic. While it is clear that women with eating
disorders often have very low levels of motivation to change (e.g. Serpell et al., 1999), it is
far from evident that adding a motivational element to CBT for the eating disorders actually
produces any improvement in therapeutic outcome (Treasure et al., 1999). It appears either
that we lack a good motivational enhancement method in such cases at present, or that the
motivational enhancement model used is inappropriate to the eating disorders.

Cognitive Content and Process

Perhaps the most critical issue in existing CBT for the eating disorders is that it is based on
cognitive-behavioural formulations that fail to reflect contemporary knowledge about the
cognitive psychology of the eating disorders. This point has been identified in restrictive
anorexia by Fairburn, Shafran and Cooper (1999), although their control-based model is still
in the early days of testing. Recent conceptualisations of psychopathology (e.g. Wells &
Matthews, 1994; Williams et al., 1997) have stressed the importance of understanding
both cognitive content (beliefs and emotions) and cognitive process (attentional processes,
cognitive avoidance, dissociation, etc.). Both of these aspects have begun to be addressed
in contemporary research into the eating disorders.

As has been mentioned above, cognitive-behavioural formulations have stressed the role
of two levels of *cognitive representation*—negative automatic thoughts (which are largely
immediate, conscious cognitions) and underlying assumptions (conditional rules, such as:
'Gaining one pound will mean that I put on a hundred pounds'). These can be characterised
as 'superficial' levels of cognition, and each primarily involves beliefs that are focused
on weight, shape and eating. However, it has been suggested that this superficial level of
analysis is responsible for the failure of much contemporary CBT for the eating disorders
(Hollon & Beck, 1994). Recent research has supported Kennerley's (1997) and Cooper's
(1997) arguments that we need to understand the role of 'deeper' schema-level representations in the eating disorders. Eating psychopathology (at the diagnostic and the behavioural
levels) appears to be directly related to unconditional core beliefs that are unrelated to eating, weight and shape, such as defectiveness/shame and emotional inhibition beliefs (e.g.
Leung, Waller & Thomas, 1999b; Waller et al., 2000). In addition, the presence of unhelpful core beliefs has a negative impact on the outcome of 'conventional' CBT for bulimia
nervosa (Leung, Waller & Thomas, 2000), thus suggesting that the failure of some CBT
cases is a product of pathological schema-level representations.

Reflecting this core belief literature, there is now substantial evidence that bulimics
process *threat cognitions* preferentially, being influenced by threats that are not directly
relevant to food, shape and weight. For example, bulimic psychopathology is associated
with a strong attentional bias towards self-esteem threats, with a lower level of bias towards
physical threats (Heatherton & Baumeister, 1991; Heatherton, Herman & Polivy, 1991;
McManus, Waller & Chadwick, 1996; Schotte, 1992). In addition, bulimic women have been
shown to avoid processing self-esteem threats, where the task involves strategic processing
(Meyer et al., under consideration). Finally, a number of studies have used subliminal visual
presentation of cues to show that non-clinical women with disturbed eating attitudes are
influenced by preconscious processing of information that they are not even aware of. Such

women eat more after being exposed to subliminal abandonment threat cues, but not by subliminal appetitive cues (Meyer & Waller, 1999). Overall, these findings show that eating psychopathology is strongly associated with threat cognitions that are unrelated to the overt pathology of the disorders.

Affect

Finally, there is now substantial evidence for the role of emotionally driven eating behaviours (e.g. Agras & Telch, 1998; Meyer, Waller & Waters, 1998; Waters, Hill & Waller, 2001). This element has now been added to (although not incorporated into) Fairburn's model of bulimia nervosa (Fairburn, 1997), but has not been widely investigated. Any clinically useful formulation of the eating disorders needs to take full account of phenomena such as emotional eating in bulimic and restrictive pathologies (e.g. Arnow, Kenardy & Agras, 1992, 1995; Herman & Polivy, 1980).

Summary

We have briefly reviewed the current state of the cognitive-behavioural models that underpin CBT for the eating disorders, and have identified a number of psychological and interpersonal domains that existing cognitive-behavioural formulations and treatments fail to take into account adequately. In keeping with the spirit of scientific enquiry that drives CBT, these deficits should be seen as giving directions to the future content and format of CBT for the eating disorders. At one level, one could suggest adding these to the targets of existing forms of CBT (e.g. adding treatment components that address social and emotional issues). However, this would be a radical revision, given the limited focus of existing CBT and the models that have underpinned it (Fairburn, 1981; Garner & Bemis, 1982).

Before adopting a 'bottom–up' approach (changing CBT in line with data alone), we should revisit broader cognitive-behavioural models, to see whether there is a case for 'top–down', conceptually driven change in our understanding and treatment of the eating disorders. Cognitive-behavioural models and treatments in other areas of psychopathology have moved on in the 20 years since the bases of our current cognitive-behavioural models of the eating disorders were first formulated (e.g. Garner & Bemis, 1982). Therefore, in the next section, we will consider recent developments in cognitive-behavioural and related therapies, in order to determine whether those developments have therapeutic potential, given the developments in cognitive-behavioural formulations outlined in this section. We will then outline some of the key principles of the cognitive-behavioural model and therapy that we argue best compensates for the shortfall in our therapeutic efficacy and effectiveness—schema-focused CBT.

NEW DEVELOPMENTS IN CBT: POTENTIAL APPLICATION TO THE EATING DISORDERS

We have suggested that there is a need to return to the principles of cognitive-behavioural theory in order to understand the eating disorders better. Using these principles, models can be developed that incorporate the wide range of empirical and clinical findings that have been generated since our existing CBT models of the eating disorders were first proposed. There have been a number of developments in cognitive-behavioural models and therapies in recent years, and we will briefly consider some of the more important of them. Each will be considered in terms of its capacity to address the elements of the cognition–emotion–behaviour matrix that have been shown to be most relevant to eating psychopathology (see above). This explanatory power also needs to take account of cognition, emotion and behaviour in their social/interpersonal context.

A number of clinicians (e.g. Wiser & Telch, 1999) have considered the clinical utility of *dialectical behaviour therapy* (DBT; Linehan, 1993) with the eating disorders. Telch (1997) has published a case suggesting that DBT is potentially useful with binge eating disorder. However, it should be stressed that this case study appears to show some substantial deviations from the protocol that Linehan suggests (using individual skills training only; re-ordering skills modules). Nor is it clear whether DBT per se was necessary, or whether individual skills were the effective elements of successful treatment. Finally, there is no clear rationale for using DBT with restrictive behaviours, and there is no evidence that it will be effective in treating purging behaviours.

It has been suggested that *cognitive analytic therapy* (CAT; Ryle, 1997) is appropriate for complex cases where eating disturbance is present (Bell, 1996). However, while there is now some preliminary evidence of effectiveness with borderline personality disorder (e.g. Wildgoose, Clarke & Waller, 2001), CAT has been developed largely with personality pathology features in mind, and it is not clear how appropriate it is for understanding and treating the specific features of eating pathology. Given its foci, it might be expected to share some of the beneficial characteristics of *interpersonal psychotherapy* (Fairburn et al., 1995), but there is no empirical base to support this as yet.

SCHEMA-FOCUSED COGNITIVE-BEHAVIOUR THERAPY

We argue that schema-focused cognitive-behaviour therapy (SFCBT) is likely to be beneficial in complex eating cases, both on the basis of our clinical experience (Kennerley, 1997; Ohanian & Waller, 1999) and on theoretical grounds. The schema-focused approach is the development of CBT that most comprehensively addresses all of the elements of eating psychopathology that we have described as important (above). The conceptual basis for SFCBT accommodates the possibility of working with cognitions (at a range of levels), emotions, behaviours and interpersonal function. There is also a growing empirical base that stresses the need to consider schemata in our understanding of eating psychopathology (see below). However, we would also acknowledge that the empirical base for therapeutic outcome is small and is, to date, dependent on case studies (e.g. Kennerley, 1997; Ohanian & Waller, 1999). In order to explain the potential utility of SFCBT in the eating disorders, it is first necessary to expand on its general principles and practice.

The obvious first question is: What is a schema? Generally, this is defined as a mental structure that: 'consists of a stored domain of knowledge which interacts with the processing of new information' (Williams et al., 1997). It is a mental 'filter', shaped by our previous experiences and which colours subsequent interpretations. Recently, several theoretical models have been advanced to refine this definition of the schema (e.g. Beck, 1996; Layden et al., 1993; Power, 1997; Teasdale, 1996), and these definitions have several common features. First, schemata are seen as multi-modal structures—a schema is rich in meaning,

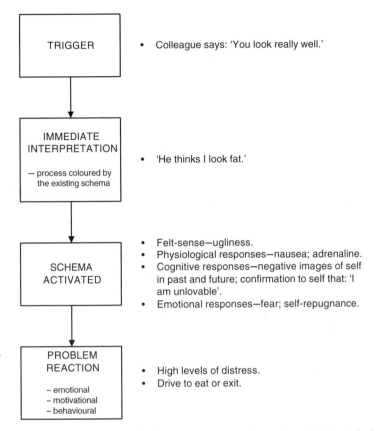

Figure 8.2 Anna: Typical pattern of schema activation and emotional–behavioural responses

and represents much more than a single belief. They comprise 'meaning' held in physical, emotional, verbal, visual, acoustic, kinetic, olfactory, tactile and kinaesthetic form. These aspects of meaning interact to convey the powerful 'sense' that is carried by the schema. The following example (see Figure 8.2) illustrates the complexity of schemata, explaining their resilience to 'classic' challenging:

> Anna had a schema that was best represented by the simple label: 'I am unlovable'. It was this that made sense of her low self-esteem, her difficulty maintaining her relationships, and her comfort-eating. When a colleague said: 'You look well', her interpretation (coloured by her belief system) was: 'He thinks that I look fat.' This activated her schemata, which triggered a powerful 'felt sense' of ugliness, fatness and self-revulsion, resulting in a physiological reaction of nausea and a flood of adrenaline. She also had an uneasy sense of *déjà vu* and a negative projection into the future, accompanied by a fleeting image of being rejected—which was actually a restimulation of a past experience. This promoted a drive to protect herself through escape (e.g. eating to dissociate, exiting the situation). For Anna, in an instant, she had experienced something powerfully awful that she could not easily put into words but which was best represented by the component core belief: 'I am unlovable.' Sometimes this phrase echoed in her mind.

Schema-focused cognitive-behavioural therapy addresses the schemata directly. It is an extension or elaboration of CBT, rather than being distinct from CBT. 'Classic' CBT, though effective with a range of psychological problems, has de-emphasised the role of schemata and often fails to generate sufficient understanding of complex, chronic and characterological problems. Fortunately, by the late 1980s, the aetiological factors in the development of persistent dysfunctional beliefs and schemata were made more explicit by cognitive therapists, and the role of those factors in the maintenance of problems was refined (Beck et al., 1990; Young, 1994). This development has helped us to understand the persistence and complexity of certain psychological problems.

Schema Identification

In order to develop a schema-based conceptualisation, key schemata need to be identified. This is often achieved using guided discovery, as in 'classic' CBT, although the use of phrases like 'How does that feel?' and 'What's happening in your body?' might commonly supplement 'What images or thoughts run through your mind?'. The process of 'unpacking' meaning can be lengthy and should take into account a client's difficulty in accessing and/or acknowledging painful core belief systems. Assessment might be supplemented by questionnaires devised to aid schema identification (e.g. Cooper et al., 1997; Young, 1994), although care should be taken not to lose idiosyncratic meanings, which might not be reflected in such measures.

Strategies to Effect Change

Clearly, schemata may shift as a direct result of a 'classic' CBT intervention creating sustainable changes that impact on these fundamental structures. However, some schemata are resilient and require interventions that address them directly. SFCBT has evolved to meet this need.

Beck and colleagues (1990), Padesky (1994) and Young (1994) all provide useful descriptions of schema change strategies. Schema-focused strategies in cognitive therapy often require relatively simple modification of standard techniques. Commonly used schema change approaches include scaling, positive data logs, historical review and visual restructuring. *Scaling/continuum techniques* are an elaboration of the exploration and balancing of a dichotomous thinking style that is commonly used in CBT. *Positive data logs* (Padesky, 1994) require focused, systematic collection of evidence supporting the development of an adaptive core belief. As such, the technique has its roots in the data collection exercises typical of traditional CBT. *Historical reviews* (Young, 1994) represent an elaboration of the familiar 'daily thought records', but the identification and challenging of key cognitions becomes a retrospective exercise to re-evaluate schema-relevant experiences and beliefs. Also, much *visual restructuring* (Layden et al., 1993), which aims to transform the meanings held by memories and images, has built on the imagery exercises that have been a component of CBT since the 1970s. *Imagery rescripting* has also been developed to allow individuals to modify schemata that are not encoded verbally (Ohanian, 2002; Smucker et al., 1995). More recently, there have been clinical developments in helping clients to combat unhelpful 'felt-sense' (Kennerley, 1996; Mills & Williams, 1997; Rosen, 1997), using *guided discovery and challenging*. Thus, schema-change strategies can target meanings that are held in verbally, visually and somatically accessible modalities, each of which interacts with affect and motivation. Finally, Safran and Segal (1990) have established a further branch of

SFCBT that targets *interpersonal schemata*, using the interpersonal domain as a medium for change.

Can SFCBT Contribute to our Work with the Eating Disorders?

We are developing a much better understanding of the 'inner world' of people with eating disorders, well beyond their concerns about weight, shape and food. For example, Waller et al. (2000) have used Young's Schema Questionnaire (1994) to show that the prominent belief systems of women suffering from bulimic disorders include core beliefs regarding defectiveness and shame, poor self-control, emotional inhibition, and vulnerability to harm. Similarly, Serpell et al. (1999) have shown that a fundamental sense of worthlessness, badness and powerlessness are central to eating pathology in anorexia nervosa, and Cooper and Hunt (1998) have demonstrated the prominence of such beliefs in bulimia nervosa. Although some of these fundamental beliefs can shift as a direct result of challenging the underlying assumptions concerning weight, shape and food, some will require a more direct approach, such as is offered by SFCBT.

In addition, it is pertinent that SFCBT was developed for use with clients with characterological difficulties, as most of us will have met eating-disordered clients with complex social and interpersonal problems, who relapse frequently and who seem ambivalent about therapy. In fact, Baker and Sansone (1997) suggest that the majority of non-responders to eating disorder programmes may be individuals with axis II pathology. Thus, SFCBT might well contribute to our work with this client group.

Finally, schema theory and SFCBT recognise the relevance of somatic or kinetic meaning, which can contribute to the persistence of eating disorders—how often does the therapist hear: '. . . but I just *feel* fat'? We all have mental representations of our body size, state and position (i.e. 'body schemata'; Berlucchi & Aglioti, 1997). These internal representations of body state can be distorted, even to the extent that a person can experience 'phantom' limbs (Ramachandran, 1998). It has long been recognised that abnormality of body image frequently plays a part in the maintenance of eating disorders, and this remains one of the diagnostic criteria for both anorexia nervosa and bulimia nervosa (APA, 1994). In fact, Rosen (1997) concludes that: 'Of all psychological factors that are believed to cause eating disorders, body image dissatisfaction is the most relevant and immediate antecedent.' Again, within the field of schema-focused work, there is scope for helping clients to recognise and restructure distorted body image (or 'felt-sense'), as well as tackling the complex belief systems and the interpersonal difficulties that can contribute to the chronicity and complexity of some disorders.

Who will Benefit?

Just as we cannot assume that a person will benefit from CBT because she or he can identify key cognitions, we cannot assume that someone will benefit from SFCBT simply because the problem is schema-driven. Although SFCBT particularly targets the client who presents with diffuse problems, interpersonal difficulties, rigid and inflexible traits, and avoidance of cognition and affect (McGinn & Young, 1996), this form of therapy (like 'classic' CBT) requires that the client is able to establish a collaborative alliance and has an ability to relate to psychological models. Some clients will not be at the stage of engagement that would allow them to use SFCBT, and might possibly benefit from preliminary motivational counselling. Such work would aim particularly to reduce the perceived positive benefits of the eating problem, which appear to be the best predictors of the severity of eating pathology (Serpell et al., 1999). Others might experience such pronounced interpersonal difficulties that an analytic intervention would best meet their needs. Finally, some patients will have ongoing environmental stresses that need to be addressed (through social or systemic intervention) before they can engage in any cognitive therapy. Again, we are reminded of the importance of a rigorous assessment of our clients.

WHERE TO NEXT? THE NEED FOR FURTHER INQUIRY

Cognitive-behavioural models and therapy have made the greatest contribution to date to our understanding and treatment of bulimic disorders. However, they do not appear to explain all cases of bulimia, and have very poor therapeutic power in explaining and treating restrictive pathology and obesity. There is a clear need to address these deficits, drawing on developments in the broader fields of cognitive-behavioural theory, principles and therapy. Current developments (e.g. Cooper, 1997; Fairburn, Shafran & Cooper, 1999; Kennerley, 1997) suggest that there is now a movement towards returning to the combination of flexibility, innovation and empiricism that characterises CBT. This gives us some hope that it will be possible to add to the existing therapeutic benefits of CBT, applying it to a much broader range of those cases that have so far defeated this form of therapy.

REFERENCES

Agras, W.S., Telch, C.F., Arnow, B., Eldredge, K. & Marnell, M. (1997) One-year follow-up of cognitive-behavioral therapy for obese individuals with binge eating disorder. *Journal of Consulting and Clinical Psychology*, **65**, 343–347.

Agras, W.S. & Telch, C.F. (1998) The effects of caloric deprivation and negative affect on binge eating in obese binge eating disordered women. *Behaviour Therapy*, **29**, 491–503.

APA (1994) *Diagnostic and Statistical Manual of Mental Disorders* (4th edition). Washington, D.C.: American Psychiatric Association.

Arnow, B., Kenardy J. & Agras, W.S. (1992) Binge eating among the obese: a descriptive study. *Journal of Behavioral Medicine*, **15**, 155–170.

Arnow, B., Kenardy, J. & Agras, W.S. (1995) The Emotional Eating Scale: The development of a measure to assess coping with negative affect by eating. *International Journal of Eating Disorders*, **18** 79–90.

Baker, D.A. & Sansone, R.A. (1997) Treatment of patients with personality disorders. In D. Garner & P.E. Garfinkel (Eds), *Handbook of Treatments for Eating Disorders*. New York: Guilford Press.

Beck, A.T. (1996) Beyond belief: A theory of modes, personality and psychopathology. In P.M. Salkovskis (Ed.), *Frontiers of Cognitive Therapy*. New York: Guilford Press.

Beck, A.T., Rush, A.J., Shaw, B.F. & Emery, G. (1979) *Cognitive Therapy of Depression*. New York: Guilford Press.

Beck, A.T. and *co-workers* (1990) *Cognitive Therapy of Personality Disorders.* New York: Guilford Press.

Bell, L. (1996) Cognitive analytic therapy: Its value in the treatment of people with eating disorders. *Clinical Psychology Forum*, **92**, 5–10.

Berlucchi, G. & Aglioti, S. (1997) The body in the brain: neural bases of corporeal awareness. *Trends in Neuroscience*, **20**, 560–564.

Bulik, C.M., Sullivan, P.F., Carter, F.A., McIntosh, V.V. & Joyce, P.R. (1998) The role of exposure with response prevention in the cognitive-behavioural therapy for bulimia nervosa. *Psychological Medicine*, **28**, 611–623.

Channon, S., de Silva, P., Hemsley, D. & Perkins, R. (1989) A controlled trial of cognitive-behavioural and behavioural treatment of anorexia nervosa. *Behaviour Research and Therapy*, **27**, 529–35.

Cooper, P.J., Coker, S. & Fleming, C. (1996) An evaluation of the efficacy of supervised cognitive behavioral self-help bulimia nervosa. *Journal of Psychosomatic Research*, **40**, 281–287.

Cooper, M. (1997) Cognitive theory in anorexia nervosa and bulimia nervosa: A review. *Behavioural and Cognitive Psychotherapy*, **25**, 113–145.

Cooper, M., Cohen-Tovée, E., Todd, G., Wells, A. & Tovée, M. (1997) The Eating Disorder Belief Questionnaire: Preliminary development. *Behaviour Research and Therapy*, **35**, 381–388.

Cooper, M. & Hunt, J. (1998) Core beliefs and underlying assumptions in bulimia nervosa and depression. *Behaviour Research and Therapy*, **36**, 895–898.

Eldredge, K.L., Agras, W.S., Arnow, B., Telch, C.F., Bell, S. & Castonguay, L. (1997) The effects of extending cognitive-behavioral therapy for binge eating disorder among initial treatment nonresponders. *International Journal of Eating Disorders*, **21**, 347–352.

Fairburn, C.G. (1981) A cognitive behavioural approach to the treatment of bulimia. *Psychological Medicine*, **11**, 707–711.

Fairburn, C.G. (1997) Eating disorders. In D.M. Clark & C.G. Fairburn (Eds), *Science and Practice of Cognitive Behaviour Therapy*. Oxford: Oxford University Press.

Fairburn, C.G. & Cooper, P. (1989) Eating disorders. In K. Hawton, P.M. Salkovskis, J. Kirk. & D.M. Clark (Eds), *Cognitive Behaviour Therapy for Psychiatric Problems*. New York: Oxford University Press.

Fairburn, C.G., Norman, P.A., Welch, S.L., O'Connor, M.E., Doll, H.A. & Peveler, R.C. (1995) A prospective study of outcome in bulimia nervosa and the long-term effects of three psychological treatments. *Archives of General Psychiatry*, **52**, 304–312.

Fairburn, C.G., Shafran, R. & Cooper, Z. (1999) A cognitive-behavioural theory of anorexia nervosa. *Behaviour Research and Therapy*, **37**, 1–13.

Garner, D. & Bemis, K.M. (1982) A cognitive-behavioural approach to anorexia nervosa. *Cognitive Therapy and Research*, **6**, 123–150.

Heatherton, T.F., Herman, C.P. & Polivy, J. (1991) Effects of physical threat and ego threat on eating behaviour. *Journal of Personality and Social Psychology*, **60**, 138–143.

Heatherton, T.F. & Baumeister, R.F. (1991) Binge-eating as an escape from self-awareness. *Psychological Bulletin*, **110**, 86–108.

Herman, C.P. & Polivy, J. (1980) Restrained eating. In A.J. Stunkard (Ed.), *Obesity* (pp. 208–225) Philadelphia: Saunders.

Hollon, S.D. & Beck, A.T. (1994) Cognitive and cognitive-behavioural therapies. In A.E. Bergin & S.L. Garfield (Eds), *Handbook of Psychotherapy and Behavioural Change* (pp. 428–466) Chichester: John Wiley & Sons.

Johnson, W.G., Tsoh, J.Y. & Varnado, P.J. (1996) Eating disorders: Efficacy of pharmacological and psychological interventions. *Clinical Psychology Review*, **16**, 457–478.

Kennerley, H. (1996) Cognitive therapy of dissociative symptoms associated with trauma. *British Journal of Clinical Psychology*, **35**, 325–340.

Kennerley, H. (1997, July) Managing complex eating disorders using schema-based cognitive therapy. Paper presented at the British Association of Behavioural and Cognitive Psychotherapy conference, Canterbury, UK.

King, M. (1989) Locus of control in women with eating pathology. *Psychological Medicine*, **19**, 183–187.

Lacey, J.H. (1986) Pathogenesis. In L.J. Downey & J.C. Malkin (Eds), *Current Approaches: Bulimia Nervosa*. Southampton: Duphar.

Layden, M.A., Newman, C.F., Freeman, A. & Morse, S.B. (1993) *Cognitive Therapy of Borderline Personality Disorder*. Boston: Allyn & Bacon.

Leermakers, E.A., Perri, M.G., Shigaki, C.L. & Fuller, P.R. (1999) Effects of exercise-focused versus weight-focused maintenance programs on the management of obesity. *Addictive Behaviors*, **24**, 219–227.

Leung, N., Waller, G. & Thomas, G.V. (1999a) Group cognitive-behavioural therapy for anorexia nervosa: A case for treatment? *European Eating Disorders Review*, **7**, 351–361.

Leung, N., Waller, G. & Thomas, G.V. (1999b) Core beliefs in anorexic and bulimic women. *Journal of Nervous and Mental Disease*, **187**, 736–741.

Leung N., Waller G. & Thomas G.V. (2000) Outcome of group cognitive-behavior therapy for bulimia nervosa: The role of core beliefs. *Behaviour Research and Therapy*, **38**, 145–156.

Leung, N., Thomas, G.V. & Waller, G. (2000) The relationship between parental bonding and core beliefs in anorexic and bulimic women. *British Journal of Clinical Psychology*, **39**, 203–213.

Levine, M.D., Marcus, M.D. & Moulton, P. (1996) Exercise in the treatment of binge eating disorder. *International Journal of Eating Disorders*, **19**, 171–177.

Linehan, M.M. (1993) *Cognitive-Behavioural Treatment for Borderline Personality Disorder: The Dialectics of Effective Treatment*. New York: Guildford Press.

McGinn, L.K. & Young, J. (1996) Schema-focused Therapy. In P.M. Salkovskis (Ed.), *Frontiers of Cognitive Therapy*. New York: Guilford Press.

McManus, F., Waller, G. & Chadwick, P. (1996) Biases in the processing of different forms of threat in bulimic and comparison women. *Journal of Nervous and Mental Disease*, **184**, 547–554.

Meyer, C., Serpell, L., Waller, G., Murphy, F., Treasure, J. & Leung, N. (under consideration) Schema avoidance in the strategic processing of ego threats: Evidence from eating—disordered patients. *British Journal of Clinical Psychology*.

Meyer, C., Waller, G. & Waters, A. (1998) Emotional states and bulimic psychopathology. In H. Hoek, M. Katzman & J. Treasure (Eds), *The Neurobiological Basis of Eating Disorders*. Chichester: John Wiley & Sons.

Meyer, C. & Waller, G. (1999) The impact of emotion upon eating behaviour: The role of subliminal visual processing of threat cues. *International Journal of Eating Disorders*, **25**, 319–26.

Mills, N. & Williams, R. (1997) Cognitions are never enough: The use of 'body metaphor' in therapy with reference to Barnard and Teesdale's ICS model. *Clinical Psychology Forum*, **110**, 9–13.

Murray, C., Waller, G. & Legg, C. (2000) Family dysfunction and bulimic psychopathology: The mediating role of shame. *International Journal of Eating Disorders*, **28**, 84–89.

Mussell, M.P., Crosby, R.D., Crow, S.J., Knopke, A.J., Peterson, C.B., Wonderlich, S.A. & Mitchell, J.E. (2000) Utilization of empirically supported psychotherapy treatments for individuals with eating disorders: A survey of psychologists. *International Journal of Eating Disorders*, **27**, 230–237.

Norris, D.L. (1984) The effects of mirror confrontation on self-estimation of body dimensions in anorexia nervosa, bulimia and two control groups. *Psychological Medicine*, *14*, 835–842.

Ohanian, V. (2002) Imagery rescripting within cognitive behaviour therapy for bulimia nervosa: An illustrative case report. *International Journal of Eating Disorders*, **31**, 352–357.

Ohanian, V. & Waller, G. (1999, April) Cognitive behavioural treatment of complex cases of bulimia: Use of schema-focused therapy and imagery rescripting. Conference paper presented at *Eating Disorders'99*, London.

Padesky, C. (1994) Schema change processes in cognitive therapy. *Clinical Psychology and Psychotherapy*, **1**, 267–278.

Patton, C.J. (1992) Fear of abandonment and binge eating: A subliminal psychodynamic activation investigation. *Journal of Nervous and Mental Disease*, **180**, 484–490.

Persons, J. (1989) *Cognitive Therapy in Practice: A Case Formulation Approach*. New York: Norton.

Power, M. (1997) Conscious and unconscious representations of meaning. In M. Power & C. Brewin (Eds), *The Transformation of Meaning in Psychological Therapies*. Chichester: John Wiley & Sons.

Ramachandran, V.S. (1998) Consciousness and body image: lessons from phantom limbs, Capgrass syndrome and pain asymbolia. *Philosophical Transactions of the Royal Society of London: Brain and Biological Sciences*, **353**, 1851–1859.

Root, M.P.P. & Fallon, P. (1989) Treating the victimized bulimic. *Journal of Interpersonal Violence*, **4**, 90–100.

Rosen, J. (1997) Cognitive behavioural body image therapy. In D. Garner & P. Garfinkel (Eds), *Handbook of Treatments for Eating Disorders*. New York: Guilford Press.

Ryle, A. (1997) The structure and development of borderline personality disorder: A proposed model. *British Journal of Psychiatry*, **170**, 82–87.

Safran, J.D. & Segal, Z.V. (1990) Interpersonal process. In *Cognitive Therapy.* New York: Basic Books.

Sansone, R.A. & Fine, M.A. (1992) Borderline personality disorder as a predictor of outcome in women with eating disorders. *Journal of Personality Disorders*, **6**, 176–186.

Schotte, D.E. (1992) On the special status of 'ego threats'. *Journal of Personality and Social Psychology*, **62**, 798–800.

Serpell, L., Treasure, J., Teasdale, J. & Sullivan V. (1999) Anorexia nervosa: Friend or foe? *International Journal of Eating Disorders*, **25**, 177–186.

Slade, P. (1982) Towards a functional analysis of anorexia nervosa and bulimia nervosa. *British Journal of Clinical Psychology*, **21**, 167–179.

Smucker, M.R., Dancu, C., Foa, E.B. & Niederee, J.L. (1995) Imagery rescripting: A new treatment for survivors of childhood sexual abuse suffering from posttraumatic stress. *Journal of Cognitive Psychotherapy: An International Quarterly*, **9**, 3–17.

Steiger, H., Gauvin, L., Jabalpurwala, S., Seguin, J.R. & Stotland, S. (1999) Hypersensitivity to social interactions in bulimic syndromes: Relationship to binge eating. *Journal of Consulting and Clinical Psychology*, **67**, 765–775.

Striegel-Moore, R.H., Silberstein, L.R. & Rodin, J. (1993) The social self in bulimia nervosa: Public self-consciousness, social anxiety, and perceived fraudulence. *Journal of Abnormal Psychology*, **102**, 297–303.

Teasdale, J.D. (1996) Clinically relevant theory: Integrating clinical insight with cognitive science. In P.M. Salkovskis (Ed.), *Frontiers of Cognitive Therapy.* New York: Guilford Press.

Telch, C.F. (1997) Skills training treatment for adaptive affect regulation in a woman with binge-eating disorder. *International Journal of Eating Disorders*, **22**, 77–81.

Treasure, J.L., Katzman, M., Schmidt, U., Troop, N., Todd, G. & de Silva, P. (1999) Engagement and outcome in the treatment of bulimia nervosa: First phase of a sequential design comparing motivation enhancement therapy and cognitive behavioural therapy. *Behaviour Research and Therapy*, **37**, 405–418.

Vitousek, K.B. (1996) The current status of cognitive behavioural models of anorexia nervosa and bulimia nervosa. In P.M. Salkovskis (Ed.), *Frontiers of Cognitive Therapy* (pp. 383–418) New York: Guilford Press.

Waller, G. (1997) Drop-out and failure to engage in individual outpatient cognitive-behaviour therapy for bulimic disorders. *International Journal of Eating Disorders*, **22**, 35–41.

Waller, G., Ohanian, V., Meyer, C. & Osman, S. (2000) Cognitive content among bulimic women: The role of core beliefs. *International Journal of Eating Disorders*, **28**, 235–241.

Waters, A., Hill, A. & Waller, G. (2001) Bulimics' responses to food cravings: Is binge-eating a product of hunger or emotional state? *Behaviour Research and Therapy*, **39**, 877–886.

Wells, A. & Matthews, G. (1994) *Attention and Emotion: A Clinical Perspective.* Hillsdale, NJ: Lawrence Erlbaum Associates.

Wildgoose, A., Clarke, S. & Waller, G. (2001) Treating personality fragmentation and dissociation in borderline personality disorder: A pilot study of the impact of cognitive analytic therapy. *British Journal of Medical Psychology*, **74**, 47–55.

Williams, J.M.G., Watts, F.N., MacLeod, C. & Mathews, A. (1997) *Cognitive Psychology and Emotional Disorders* (2nd edition). New York: John Wiley & Sons.

Wilson, G.T. (1996) Treatment of bulimia nervosa: When CBT fails. *Behaviour Research and Therapy*, **34**, 197–212.

Wilson, G.T. (1999) Cognitive behavior therapy for eating disorders: Progress and problems. *Behaviour Research and Therapy*, **37**, S79–S95.

Wiser, S. & Telch, C.F. (1999) Dialectical behavior therapy for binge-eating disorder. *Journal of Clinical Psychology*, **55**, 755–768.

Wooley, S.C. & Garner, D.M. (1991) Obesity treatment: The high cost of false hope. *Journal of the American Dietetic Association*, **91**, 1248–1251.

Young, J.E. (1994) *Cognitive Therapy for Personality Disorders: A Schema-Focused Approach* (2nd edition). Sarasota, FL: Professional Resource Exchange.

CHAPTER 9

Interpersonal Psychotherapy

Denise Wilfley

Department of Psychiatry, Washington University in St. Louis School of Medicine,
USA

Rick Stein

Department of Psychiatry, Washington University in St. Louis School of Medicine,
USA

and

Robinson Welch

Department of Psychiatry, Washington University in St. Louis School of Medicine,
USA

SUMMARY

- IPT is a focused, goal-driven treatment which targets interpersonal problem(s) associated with the onset and/or maintenance of the eating disorder.
- IPT is supported by substantial empirical evidence documenting the role of interpersonal factors in the onset and maintenance of eating disorders.
- IPT is a viable alternative to CBT for the treatment of BN and BED and is under investigation for the treatment of AN.
- Future research directions include the identification of mechanisms and predictors of IPT, the dissemination of IPT in applied settings, and the examination of IPT with specific subgroups of eating-disordered patients.

INTRODUCTION

Interpersonal psychotherapy (IPT), initially developed as a short-term, outpatient psychological treatment for major depression (Klerman et al., 1984), has been successfully adapted to treat other types of mood and several non-mood disorders including bulimia nervosa (BN) and binge eating disorder (BED) (for a review see Weissman et al., 2000). Although cognitive-behavioral therapy (CBT) for BN produces more rapid changes in the short-term, IPT for BN has consistently demonstrated equal efficacy in the long-term (Agras et al., 2000; Fairburn et al., 1991, 1993, 1995). In treating BED, IPT has demonstrated similar efficacy to CBT in both the short and long term (Wilfley et al., 1993, 2002). At this time,

The Essential *Handbook of Eating Disorders*. Edited by J. Treasure, U. Schmidt and E. van Furth.
© 2005 John Wiley & Sons, Ltd.

there are no empirical data on the use of IPT for AN, but a psychotherapy trial is currently underway to evaluate its effectiveness (McIntosh et al., 2000).

IPT is derived from theories in which interpersonal function is recognized to be a critical component of psychological adjustment and well-being. It is also based on empirical research which has linked change in the social environment to the onset and maintenance of depression. As applied to eating disorders, IPT assumes that the development of eating disorders occurs in a social and interpersonal context. Both the maintenance of the disorder and response to treatment are presumed to be influenced by the interpersonal relationships between the eating-disordered patient and significant others. Consequently, IPT for eating disorders focuses on identifying and altering the interpersonal context in which the eating problem has been developed and maintained. This chapter provides the empirical basis of IPT for eating disorders and describes its application to eating disorders. Emphasis is placed on the use of IPT with BN and BED, given that the status of IPT as an effective treatment for AN still remains unknown. Case examples are provided to illustrate IPT methods, strategies and techniques. Areas in need of further investigation are also delineated.

EMPIRICAL BASIS FOR AN INTERPERSONAL APPROACH TO EATING DISORDERS

There is compelling evidence that interpersonal factors play a significant role in the etiology and maintenance of eating disorders. As basic examples, many AN and BN patients report having experienced serious stressors related to relationships with family or friends prior to the onset of the disorder (Schmidt et al., 1997). With BN and BED, a history of exposure to negative interpersonal factors (e.g. critical comments from family about shape, weight, or eating; low parental contact) are among the specific retrospective correlates (Fairburn et al., 1997, 1998). Identification of such interpersonal factors fills a gap in other etiological theories. For example, restraint theory, a widely embraced theory emphasizing the role of dieting in the etiology of binge-eating problems does not seem satisfactory to account for the development of BED, particularly since only about half of BED patients dieted before the onset of their eating disorder (Spurrell et al., 1997). According to interpersonal vulnerability models of eating disorders (e.g. Wilfley et al., 1997), some of the missing factors in the restraint model include interpersonal functioning, mood, and self-esteem, all of which are empirically supported as related to the onset/maintenance of eating disorder symptoms.

First, there is a great deal of evidence that interpersonal problems and deficits play a significant role in all three eating disorders. Individuals with eating disorders are more lonely (O'Mahony & Hollwey, 1995) and perceive lower social support than do non-eating-disordered individuals. They have fewer support figures, less emotional and practical support, and are less likely to seek out support as a way to cope with problems (Ghaderi & Scott, 1999; Rorty et al., 1999; Tiller et al., 1997; Troop et al., 1994). Eating disorders are associated with difficulty in various areas of social adjustment including work, social/leisure, extended family, and global functioning (Herzog et al., 1987). Eating disordered women also report and demonstrate lower competence, relative to subclinical and normal control women, in coping with social stress and social problem situations, including independence from family, family conflict, female peer conflict, and male rejection (Grissett & Norvell, 1992; McFall et al., 1999). This lack of competence is especially relevant because serious life stresses that involve the patients relationships with family or friends tend to precede

AN and BN (Schmidt et al., 1997). Interpersonal stress may create more disinhibited eating among restrained eaters (Tanofsky-Kraff et al., 2000) and bulimics (Tuschen-Caffier & Vögele, 1999) than do other types of stressors. In addition, obese women with BED experience significantly higher levels of interpersonal problems than those without BED (Telch & Agras, 1994). This set of findings indicates that some eating-disordered individuals may lack the social skills necessary to establish and/or sustain supportive relationships and to cope with problem social situations, and these problems may be directly linked with the onset and maintenance of eating disorder symptomatology.

Some research has focused on difficulties that eating-disordered women may have in their relationships with men. For example, level of bulimic symptomatology among female college students is significantly correlated with dissatisfaction in relationships with men, as well as reported level of difficulty forming and maintaining friendships and romantic relationships with men (Thelen et al., 1990, 1993). Other data indicate that eating disorder symptomatology is correlated with lower ratings of closeness in romantic relationships (O'Mahony & Hollwey, 1995), and that eating-disordered women may even avoid sexual activity within their romantic relationships (see, e.g., McIntosh et al., 2000; Segrin, in press, for reviews; see also Woodside et al., 1993). Indeed, married women seeking treatment for an eating disorder had levels of marital distress comparable to couples seeking marital therapy (Van Buren & Williamson, 1988). This set of findings suggests that eating-disordered women may have difficulty negotiating their roles within their platonic and romantic relationships with men.

A considerable amount of research has focused on the family-of-origin history prior to the onset of the disorder. Eating disorders are associated with low perceived family cohesion (see Segrin, in press). Eating-disordered individuals are more likely to receive critical comments from their families about shape, weight, or eating, and experience low parental contact (Fairburn et al., 1997, 1998). They may also experience parental pressure that is inappropriate for their age, gender, or abilities (Horesh et al., 1996). In addition, several aspects of family dynamics—warmth, communication, affective expression, and control—have been identified as problematic for some eating-disordered patients (see Segrin, in press, for a review). These kinds of problems in family relationships and family environment have been prospective predictors of the later development of eating disorders (e.g. Calam & Waller, 1998). Finally, women with BN and BED report more sexual and physical abuse experiences than non-eating-disordered women, but similar levels as individuals with other psychiatric disorders (e.g. Striegel-Moore et al., 2001; Welch & Fairburn, 1994).

In addition, many studies have supported the notion that interpersonal problems may be linked to eating disorder symptomatology through lowered self-esteem and negative affect. Low self-esteem often predates AN and may be a core aspect of problematic thinking patterns in AN (Garner et al., 1997). Similarly, retrospective risk factor research indicates that negative self-evaluation predates the eating disorder and distinguishes BN patients from both normal and general psychiatric controls (Fairburn et al., 1997); it may also be associated with a desire to binge in the face of stress (Cattanach et al., 1988). Eating-disordered women may experience self-esteem problems specifically in the social domain, for example, they have elevated concern with how others view them, and have a high need for social approval, relative to non-eating-disordered individuals (see Wilfley et al., 1997).

In terms of mood, evidence supports that affective restraint is a common distinguishing personality trait of premorbid AN patients (Wonderlich, 1995), and that negative affect strengthened the relation between dietary restraint and binge eating among a community sample of adolescents (Stice et al., 2000). For eating-disordered individuals, data indicates that negative affect often precipitates a binge-eating episode (e.g. Greeno et al., 2000; Kenardy et al., 2001; Steiger et al., 1999; Telch & Agras, 1996). Purging among bulimics may partly serve to manage negative affect (e.g. Powell & Thelen, 1996; Schupak-Neuberg & Nemeroff, 1993). Even more specifically relevant for IPT, a recent experience-sampling study among bulimics found that negative social interactions are associated with increased self-criticism and lowered mood (Steiger et al., 1999). In this study, negative social interactions, self-criticism, and lowered mood all tended to precede binge episodes. After bingeing, participants experienced further deteriorations in self-esteem and mood, as well as more negative perceptions of social experiences. These findings underscore the theoretical link among eating disorder symptomatology and these three factors—interpersonal functioning, self-esteem, and mood, all of which are targeted by IPT (see also reviews by Heatherton & Baumeister, 1991; McManus & Waller, 1995; Wilfley et al., 1997).

Overall, it appears that eating-disordered individuals have a history of more frequent difficult social experiences, including problematic family histories and specific interpersonal stressors, than non-eating-disordered individuals. They also experience a wide range of social problems such as loneliness, lack of perceived social support, low social adjustment, and poor social problem-solving skills, possibly leaving them with inadequate resources and social competence to cope with interpersonal stressors. Finally, interpersonal difficulties, low self-esteem, and negative affect may all be interconnected and related to eating disorder problems. These factors may thus create a vicious cycle of exacerbating each other and combine to precipitate and/or maintain symptoms among eating-disordered individuals. IPT aims to improve interpersonal functioning, self-esteem, and negative affect, as they relate to each other and to eating disorder symptoms. The specific areas of interpersonal functioning that are identified and targeted by IPT are consistent with the pattern of problems described above.

IMPLEMENTATION OF THE TREATMENT

Timeline for Therapy

The typical course of IPT for eating disorders lasts 15–20 sessions over a four-to five-month time period (Fairburn et al., 1998; Wilfley et al., 1998). Treatment progresses through three distinct phases: the initial phase of identifying the problem area in significant relationships, the middle phase of working on the target problem area(s), and the late phase of consolidating work and preparing patients for future work on their own.

Interpersonal Problem Areas

IPT focuses on the resolution of problems within four social domains that are associated with the onset and/or maintenance of the disorder namely: grief, interpersonal deficits, interpersonal role disputes, and role transitions. Grief is identified as the problem area when the onset of the patients symptoms are associated with the loss of a person or a relationship, either recent or past. Interpersonal deficits apply to those patients who are socially isolated or who are in chronically unfulfilling relationships. Interpersonal role disputes are conflicts with a significant other (e.g. a partner, other family member, coworker, or close friend) which emerge from differences in expectations about the relationship. Role transition includes any difficulties resulting from a change in life status (e.g. leaving a job or one's home, going away to school, divorce, other economic, health, or family changes). See Table 9.1 for a fuller description of the interpersonal problem areas, as well as treatment goals and therapeutic strategies.

Generally, one of the four IPT problem areas can be readily applied to eating-disordered patients. For example, in Table 9.2, the distribution of primary problem areas are presented across the three disorders. The percentages of problem areas were obtained from psychotherapy studies for BN and BED (Fairburn et al., 1993; Wilfley et al., 2002), and from an interview-based study for AN (McIntosh et al., 2000). For all three disorders, grief was uncommon whereas role disputes were fairly common. The notable differences among the disorders were that interpersonal deficits were more likely to be found among BED and AN patients, and role transitions were more common among BN patients.

TREATMENT PHASES, GOALS AND STRATEGIES

The *initial phase*, ordinarily four to five sessions, includes diagnostic assessment and psychiatric history and establishes the context for the treatment. After a standardized diagnostic symptom review is conducted, the patient is diagnosed as having an eating disorder and assigned a sick role. The sick role identifies patients as in need of help, exempts them from additional social pressures and elicits their cooperation in the process of recovery. Because many eating-disordered individuals camouflage their own social difficulties by meeting others' needs rather than their own, the sick role is assigned to relieve them of excessive caretaking tendencies. It is explained to them that only by confronting their need to please others and redirecting some of this energy toward themselves, will they be able to recover from their eating problems. The therapist and patient then discuss the diagnosis and what the patient might expect from treatment. Symptom relief starts with helping the patient to understand that the eating disorder symptoms (e.g. recurrent pattern of binge eating, extreme dietary restriction, and dysfunctional attitudes about shape and weight) are part of a known syndrome, which responds to several treatments and has a good prognosis. Patients are informed that IPT focuses on altering current interpersonal patterns and life situations in order to eliminate their eating disorder.

The therapist conducts an interpersonal inventory which includes a review of the patient's past/current social functioning and close relationships. For each person who is important in the patient's life the following information is assessed: frequency of contact, activities shared, satisfactory and unsatisfactory aspects of the relationship, and ways that the patient would like to change the relationship. The interpersonal inventory provides a structure for elucidating the social and interpersonal context of the onset and maintenance of eating disorder symptoms and delineates the focus of treatment. Of particular importance are changes in relationships proximal to the onset of symptoms (e.g. the death of a significant other, changing to a new job, increasing marital discord, or disconnection from a friend). The therapist obtains a chronological history of significant life events, fluctuations in mood and self-esteem, interpersonal relationships, and eating disorder symptoms. From this review, the therapist can make a connection between certain life experiences and eating disorder symptoms. As this interrelationship is delineated, patients understand more clearly the rationale of IPT.

Table 9.1 Interpersonal problem areas: description, goals, and strategies (Klerman et al., 1984; Weissman et al., 2000)

Interpersonal problem area	Description	Goals	Strategies
Grief	Complicated bereavement following the death of a loved one	• Facilitate the mourning process • Help patient re-establish interest in new activities and relationships to substitute for what has been lost	• Reconstruct the patient's relationship with the deceased • Explore associated feelings (negative and positive) • Consider ways of becoming re-involved with others
Interpersonal deficits	A history of social impoverishment, inadequate, or unsustaining interpersonal relationships	• Reduce patient's social isolation • Enhance quality of any existing relationships • Encourage the formation of new relationships	• Review past significant relationships including negative and positive aspects • Explore repetitive patterns in relationships • Note problematic interpersonal patterns in the session and relate them to similar patterns in the patient's life
Interpersonal role disputes	Conflicts with a significant other: a partner, other family member, coworker, or close friend	• Identify the nature of the dispute • Explore options to resolve the dispute • Modify expectations and faulty communication to bring about a satisfactory resolution • If modification is unworkable, encourage patient to reassess the expectations for the relationship and to generate options to either resolve it or to dissolve it and mourn its loss	• Determine the stage of the dispute: renegotiation (calm down participants to facilitate resolution); impasse (increase disharmony in order to reopen negotiation); dissolution (assist mourning and adaptation) • Understand how non-reciprocal role expectations relate to the dispute • Identify available resources to bring about change in the relationship
Role transitions	Economic or family change: the beginning or end of a relationship or career, a move, promotion, retirement, graduation, diagnosis of a medical illness	• Mourn and accept the loss of the old role • Recognize the positive and negative aspects of the new role, and assets and liabilities of the old role • Restore self-esteem by developing a sense of mastery regarding the demands of the new role	• Review positive and negative aspects of old and new roles • Explore feelings about what is lost • Encourage development of social support system and new skills called for in new role

Table 9.2 Distribution of problem areas

Problem areas	Anorexia nervosa[a]	Bulimia nervosa[b]	Binge eating disorder[c]
Grief	6%	12%	6%
Interpersonal disputes	33%	16%	60%
Role disputes	33%	64%	30%
Role transitions	17%	36%	4%
Other	11%	N/A	N/A

[a] It is important to note that the percentages of problem areas for AN were taken as patient report during a 10-year follow-up by Sullivan et al. Patients were asked in an open-ended fashion what they believed contributed to their eating disorder. Their answers were then coded into one of the four problem areas. Patient answers that could not be coded into one of the four problem areas were placed in other. (*Source*: McIntosh et al., 2000.)

[b] The percentages total over 100% because some patients were identified as having more than a single problem area. (*Source*: Fairburn, 1997.)

[c] The percentages total 100% as they reflect each patient's primary problem area. (*Source*: Wilfley et al., 2000a.)

The therapist then links the eating disorder syndrome to one of the four interpersonal problem areas: grief, interpersonal deficits, interpersonal role disputes, or role transitions. Although the therapist explicitly assigns a problem area (i.e. the interpersonal formulation), the patient needs to concur with the salience of the problem area proposed and agree to work on it in treatment. Because the four problem areas are relatively inclusive, it is typically quite easy for the therapist to provide an individualized formulation. While patients may fit into several problem areas, the time-limited nature of treatment dictates limiting the choice to one, or at most two, problem areas, in order to clearly define a treatment focus. Once the problem area(s) is agreed upon, a treatment plan with specified goals to work on is formulated. These goals guide day-to-day work and are referenced at each meeting in order to maintain the focus of treatment. If more than one problem area is identified, the patient may elect to work on both simultaneously or to address first the problem that seems to be most responsive to treatment.

During the *intermediate phase* of treatment, typically eight to ten sessions, the therapist implements treatment strategies that are specific to the identified problem area as specified by Klerman and colleagues (1984). For grief, the goals include facilitating mourning and helping the patient find new activities and relationships to substitute for the loss. For role transition, the therapist helps the patient to manage the change by recognizing positive and negative aspects of the new role he or she is assuming, as well as the pros and cons of the old role this replaces. For interpersonal role disputes, the therapist assists the patient in identifying the nature of the dispute and generates options to resolve it. If the patient and therapist conclude that resolution is impossible, the therapist assists the patient in dissolving the relationship and in mourning its loss. For interpersonal deficits, the goal is to improve the patient's social skills and to reduce the patient's social isolation by helping to enhance the quality of existing relationships and encourage the formation of new relationships.

In the *termination phase* of treatment, usually four to five sessions, patients are encouraged to describe specific changes in their eating behaviors, especially as they relate to improvements in the identified problem area(s). The therapist assists the patient in evaluating and consolidating gains, acknowledging the feelings associated with termination, detailing plans for maintaining improvements in the identified interpersonal problem area(s), and outlining remaining work for the patient to continue on his or her own. Patients are also encouraged to identify early warning signs of symptom recurrence (e.g. dietary restriction) and to identify plans of action.

Throughout the three phases, focus stays on the interpersonal context of a patient's life. Thus, in the case of a patient with eating disorder symptoms, the therapist will focus on relationship difficulties that exacerbate the symptoms rather than review cognitions or inner conflict associated with the eating disorder. Once the treatment goals have been established, the therapist refers to them in each session. Descriptive phrases such as moving forward on your goals, and making important changes are used to encourage patients to be responsible for their treatment while reminding them that altering interpersonal patterns requires attention and persistence. Indeed, research on IPT maintenance treatment for recurrent depression has demonstrated that the therapist's ability to maintain focus on interpersonal themes is associated with better outcomes (Frank et al., 1991). In session, unfocused discussions are redirected to the key interpersonal issues, and abstract or general discussions are minimized in order to preserve focus. Therapists refrain from making inquiries that evoke vague or passive responses, such as general questions about the patient's week. Rather, sessions begin with questions such as what would you like to work on today? Or how have you worked on your goals since we last met? These questions provide more direction for the patient and focus them on the present. The therapist assists the patient in drawing connections between interpersonal events and eating problems. Patients are asked to pay careful attention to what triggers binge eating, as these episodes are often precipitated by interpersonal stressors and negative mood. Consequently, patients begin to recognize that problematic eating is often an important indicator of interpersonal problems that might otherwise go unnoticed (Fairburn, 1997).[1]

THERAPEUTIC STANCE AND TECHNIQUES

Similar to many other therapies, in IPT, the focus is on establishing a positive therapeutic alliance. Specifically, the IPT therapeutic stance is one of warmth, support, and empathy. The therapist is active and serves as patient advocate. The therapist helps the patient feel comfortable by phrasing comments positively in order to foster a safe and supportive working environment. In addition, the therapist conveys a hopeful stance and optimistic attitude about the patient's ability to recover. Confrontations and clarifications are offered in a gentle and timely manner and the therapist is careful to encourage the patient's positive expectations of the therapeutic relationship.

Techniques include exploratory questions, encouragement of affect, clarification, communication analysis, use of therapeutic relationship, behavior change techniques, and adjunctive techniques (for a description of these techniques, see Klerman et al., 1984). IPT's focus on affect evocation and exploration is especially relevant for eating-disordered patients, given that problematic eating often functions as a way to regulate negative affect. Specifically, the IPT therapist helps patients: (1) acknowledge and accept painful affects, (2) use affective experiences to bring about desired interpersonal changes, and (3) experience suppressed affects.

---

[1] To minimize procedural overlap with CBT, research applications of IPT have not included a symptom focus during the second and third phases of treatment.

CASE EXAMPLES

The first case example illustrates the therapist's presentation to the patient of the interpersonal formulation that links the onset of the eating disorder to one of the four interpersonal problem areas. The therapist's ability to rapidly discern patterns in interpersonal relationships, connect events with the onset and maintenance of the disorder, and formulate goals are crucial to the time-limited nature of IPT. In addition, the case vignettes illustrate the strategies and techniques used with each of the four problem areas (i.e., role transitions, role disputes, interpersonal deficits, and grief, respectively).

The Interpersonal Formulation/Role Transitions: The Case of W

W is a 51-year-old woman who presented for treatment of BED. She is college educated, has her own business, and is a divorced mother of one adult son in his early twenties. Prior to treatment, W had a BMI of 42 and had been binge eating approximately 10–15 days per month for the last eight years. Along with her current diagnosis of BED, W struggled with recurrent major depression.

During the *Initial Phase*, W and her therapist began to review her history and the interpersonal events that were associated with her binge eating. W shared that she began over-eating and gaining weight at age 14. When she was age 18 she moved to a foreign country with her parents. Soon after the move, W's father left her and her mother to return to the United States. W was enraged at her father for leaving them, and still gets very tearful and angry when discussing the separation. W and her mother decided to stay abroad since W had started university and W's mother was working. Both had developed strong social ties and felt comfortable in their new home. During this time, W continued to gain weight, and started dieting. Shortly after graduating from university, W met and married a foreign national and at age 28 delivered their only son. Two years later, W and her husband went through a very bitter divorce. Although we described this as a terrible time in her life, she maintained close ties with her friends and her mother. During this time, she began to diet and reached her lowest adult weight. At age 35 when W's mother died of a heart condition, she had her first episode of major depression, which was treated and resolved with antidepressants and a brief course of psychotherapy. Although W had previous cycles of weight loss and weight regain, she did not evidence any sign of eating disturbance at this point. W continued to maintain close social ties and enjoyed her close relationship with her son. When W was in her early forties, an economic downturn in her adopted country forced her to return to the USA. Having lost all of her savings, W struggled financially while she looked for work. During this time, W started binge eating and gaining weight. Within a year of this move, W's son decided to return to live with his father (who was very wealthy). W felt angry and betrayed. Yet, when her son would visit, she would assume a subservient role with him, as she was afraid of losing his affection. He, in turn, became quite demanding and critical of her. Prior to seeking treatment, her heightened feelings of isolation and loneliness were leading to increased binge eating, depression and weight gain.

By session 3 of the Initial Phase, W's therapist began to consider which problem area would be the focus of the remainder of treatment. W had a history of important relationship losses and subsequent grief: the loss of her father, her husband, her mother, and most recently, her son when he went back to live with his father. However, none of these losses were associated with the development of binge-eating problems (although her dieting was clearly linked to her feelings of anger after the divorce from her husband, and her depression was intimately linked with her mother's death). W's anger at her son for returning to live with the enemy was clearly a role dispute, yet her binge eating had begun two years prior to his departure (although it clearly worsened after he left). Since neither of these problem areas were directly linked to the onset of the eating disorder, W's therapist decided that the focus of treatment would be to assist W in managing her role transition. W's move back to the USA, with the subsequent loss of her support and friendship networks, were clearly associated with the onset and continued maintenance of her binge eating. During the fourth session of the Initial Phase, W's therapist shared her formulation of the problem area with her:

> From what you have described, your binge eating really began after you returned to the USA. After that transition, you were more isolated and alone than you have ever been. It seems that binge eating was a way for you to manage that transition and the subsequent feelings of isolation and loneliness. Your transition has also had a negative impact on your relationship with your son. Even though you are a very social person and enjoy the company of others, you have yet to develop the kind of support that you had before you moved. Although you have struggled with some very significant issues over the course of your life your father leaving, the pain of the divorce, and the death of your mother your friends and support systems sustained you. If we work together to help you find and develop more intimate and supportive relationships here, I believe you will be much less likely to turn to food and binge eating as a source of support or comfort.

W agreed with the formulation and worked with her therapist to establish some treatment goals to help her resolve the problem area. First, W was encouraged to become more aware of her feelings (especially isolation and loneliness) when she was binge eating, and how binge eating seemed to be the way she managed those feelings. A second goal was for W to take steps to increase her social contacts and develop more friendships. The third goal, which was identified as a secondary problem area, centered on helping W resolve the role dispute with her son. Specifically, the therapist developed a goal with W to help her establish a clearer parental role with her son.

During the *Intermediate Phase*, the therapist helped W grieve the loss of her previous role and the extensive support that she once had. W and her therapist worked to identify several sources of support and friendships of which she had not been aware. Soon after, W reported significant progress in initiating and establishing relationships with others. This change appeared to help give her confidence in her new roles. In fact, she had begun to receive a few social invitations. She was more attuned to the ways that she would rely on food especially when she felt lonely or felt that she was not receiving enough time from others. The connection between the lack of supportive contacts and binge eating was becoming very clear to her in these intermediate sessions. During this phase, the therapist also assisted W in setting appropriate limits in her relationship with her adult son, and recognizing his adult-like responses in return.

By the *Termination Phase*, W reported that she no longer felt so lonely and isolated and that her binge eating had all but disappeared. She remarked how the quality of her relationship with her son had changed dramatically. He was more supportive and respectful, visited more frequently, and stayed with her for longer periods of time. In the final sessions, she talked about her need to let go of the past and move on to her life as it is now, assuming her new roles more fully. She worked closely with her therapist to develop a plan to maintain the gains that she had made in treatment and used the final session to review the important work that she had accomplished.

Interpersonal Role Disputes: The Case of S

S is a 35-year-old woman who presented for treatment of her BN. S is married to a lawyer and has one child. When she came in for treatment, she was bingeing and vomiting an average of five times per week. Her pattern was to binge and purge when she was alone on the weekend and during the week when husband was at work and her son at school. Although S did not work, she was actively involved in her community church, and attended several extracurricular activities (e.g. dance class, weight lifting) during the week. S indicated that she used to work with her husband as his office manager, but stopped about five years ago. She described her relationship with her husband as cold and passionless. S did not think that her husband really cared that much for her. She did say that he was a great father to her son and that she should love him, but wondered whether or not she did.

During the *Initial Phase*, S and her therapist began to review her history and the interpersonal events that were associated with the onset of her BN. Although S had a history of dieting, her bingeing and vomiting had begun 10 years ago soon after her marriage to her husband. S has strong religious convictions and did not have sexual intercourse with her husband until their honeymoon. Her husband was fairly forceful with her on their honeymoon night and caused her great physical discomfort. She thought that she would enjoy intercourse but since their honeymoon had not been interested in having intercourse with him. She never raised this issue with her husband, and at the time of treatment had not mentioned to him her dissatisfaction with their sex life. Currently, she let him have intercourse with her about two times per month and resented even this limited sexual relationship. When S's therapist explored with her any other significant interpersonal events connected with the onset of her bingeing and vomiting, S related that soon after their marriage, S and her husband began to have financial problems. Specifically, her husband had lied to her about the amount of debt he had accrued during law school. In addition, they had used her savings to establish a private practice for him. When the practice failed, they went even further into debt. S tried to assist her husband by helping him with billing and collection, but her efforts did not help. At that time S felt angry, resentful and trapped. During that time about five years prior to treatment, her bingeing and vomiting were at their worst. Currently, S found herself bingeing and vomiting more frequently when bills came to the house, and when she knew that her husband was going to want to be with her sexually.

Toward the end of the initial phase, S's therapist asked her if she was interested in working on and improving her relationship with her husband. S confessed that she did still have loving feelings toward her husband, and would be willing to work on the relationship. She indicated however, that she did not understand how talking about her relationship with her husband would help her eating disorder. At this point, S's therapist acknowledged her skepticism and then began to conceptualize her bingeing and vomiting in terms of a role dispute with her husband. The therapist speculated that S was binge eating and vomiting as a means to manage her anger and frustration at her husband over their financial woes and his insensitivity to her sexual needs. To punctuate this point, the therapist reminded her of the several examples she had given in which her bingeing and vomiting occurred either before or after these two events occurred. The therapist then suggested that a focus on helping S resolve her resentment and anger toward her husband would help to improve the quality of her relationship with him and to eliminate her BN. Although still somewhat skeptical, S acknowledged the connection and agreed to work on the role dispute with her husband.[2] At this point, S and her therapist developed a set of goals to guide their work through the remainder of treatment.

In the *Intermediate Phase* of treatment, S and her therapist began working on her goals. The therapist concluded that S's relationship with her husband was at an impasse, because they had not discussed the frustration that S was feeling, nor had they talked about their passionless relationship. S's therapist first encouraged her to be honest with her husband about her current bulimic symptoms (she had told him it stopped five years earlier) and her feelings about their sex life—including the experience she had during their honeymoon. This task took place over several sessions in which the therapist worked closely with S on her communication style and delivery. Although S's husband was initially overwhelmed and angry about her feedback (specifically that she had never told him), he soon acknowledged her feelings and apologized for his behavior on their honeymoon and asked her what, if anything, he could do to make things better. During a joint meeting with S and her husband, the therapist was able to help S's husband verbalize his feelings of love and passion for her feelings that he had locked away because he thought she did not care for him. As a result of this meeting, S began to take more control of their sexual encounters and found herself enjoying intercourse with him for the first time. Her therapist also encouraged her to talk more with her husband about her concerns over their finances, since this was another goal that she had set for herself. As a result, S and her

---

[2] In our clinical experience, we have found that approximately one-fifth of patients are initially skeptical of the interpersonal approach. Nonetheless, most of these patients do agree to work on the identified problem area and typically end up profiting from treatment.

husband began to seek financial advice and developed a concrete plan to decrease their debt. As S and her husband began to engage with one another more actively, S's bingeing began to dissipate.

By the beginning of the *Termination Phase* of treatment, S's bingeing had ceased. During the final sessions with her therapist, S noted the improvements she had made. Specifically, she cited the importance of being able to make the connection between her eating disorder and her relationship difficulties with her husband. She also shared how talking with her husband about her feelings and sharing the distress she felt during their honeymoon was an important breakthrough for her. S realized that as she took more control over her feelings and her relationship with her husband, their marriage improved and her eating disorder resolved. In the final sessions, S and her therapist developed a plan for her to identify and manage periods when she might have an urge to binge. Specifically, her therapist encouraged her to keep sharing with her husband, and to maintain open communication about their relationship.

Interpersonal Deficits: The Case of C

C is a 45-year-old woman who presented for treatment for binge eating. C is a hairdresser and was currently in a live-in relationship with a boyfriend of three years. She was bingeing on average 5-6 times per week. Her pattern was to binge on fast food which she purchased and ate during her drive home, after spending 12 to 14 hour days at work. During her work days, she would often work through lunch and stay late to accommodate her clients' busy schedules. When she arrived home, she would also eat dinner with her boyfriend. She described her relationship with him as okay, but stressful as he keeps telling me that I spend too much time at work and not enough time with him. She indicated that she wanted this relationship to be a perfect one. Therefore, she tried to keep the peace and did her best to please him so he would not be mad at her.

During the *Initial Phase*, C and her therapist began to review her history and the interpersonal events associated with the onset of her binge eating. C had a history of conflict avoidance and a fear of criticism. At the age of 15, she began a series of failed relationships that she hid in order to appear as the perfect daughter and to not disappoint her parents. Accordingly, she binged when she was alone to numb out as a way of managing the feelings that she kept private. Her attempts at secrecy and use of food to disconnect from her feelings continued throughout C's marriage at age 20. Although her husband was cruel and verbally abusive, C worked hard to fool everyone for 15 years into believing that she had a perfect, fulfilling relationship because she did not want anyone to think that she had failed in her marriage. Prior to her divorce at age 35, C's bingeing and weight gain were at their worst. In discussing her current relationship, C indicated that she really liked her boyfriend, but she was always worried that he was angry with her about her work. Consequently, she went out of her way to please him so he would not be upset with her. Similarly, she put in 14-hour days because she felt uncomfortable saying no to her customers' requests to see her before and after their business hours.

Toward the end of the initial phase, C and her therapist began to examine the link between her binge eating and her use of food as a way to avoid the conflicted feelings of wanting to please her boyfriend and clients, but at the same time resenting them for the demands they made on her. Given her history of unfulfilling relationships and an inability to manage her current interpersonal relationships effectively, the therapist identified interpersonal deficits as C's primary problem area. C found it very difficult to see how her eating was related to her difficulties in managing relationships. She shared with the therapist that she did not have problems with relationships. 'I have millions of friends.' Given her history, C's therapist chose not to challenge that perception, but instead talked with her about how she seemed to have a difficult time managing the stress of her work life and her current relationship. The therapist speculated to C that her binge eating might be a way to manage this distress. To highlight this, C's therapist shared some examples that C had discussed in previous sessions. C was able to see this link and, along with her therapist, developed specific goals to guide her work during the remainder of treatment.

In the *Intermediate Phase* of treatment, C and her therapist began working on C's goals. C's therapist used the context of the therapeutic relationship to encourage C to notice that specific behaviors—maintaining a perfect façade, glossing over problems, and avoiding conflict—might be preventing her from having more satisfying relationships. Moreover, they were connected to her episodes of binge eating. In session, the therapist used the IPT techniques of clarification, communication analysis, and encouragement of affect to assist C in finding ways of negotiating the conflicts at work and with her boyfriend. After several attempts, C was finally able to resolve conflicts effectively. In addition, C began to share more with her boyfriend and her sisters, communicate more effectively with coworkers, and set limits with customers by refusing some of their requests. As a result, she reported that her relationships were more satisfying, her binge eating had ceased, and that she and her boyfriend had become much closer.

During the *Termination Phase* of treatment, C was able to reflect on the progress that she had made during treatment. Specifically, C shared that when she began treatment, she did not have good relationships. She noted that glossing over problems and trying to maintain a perfect image had actually hindered her relationships with others, and perpetuated her binge eating. She talked about and reviewed with her therapist ways that she had learned to attend to conflict without feeling as if the world was coming to an end. During the final sessions, C and her therapist outlined a plan for C to stay binge free. That is, she would try to share more with others during times of increased work stress, take steps to decrease her work load, and continue sharing her fears and concerns about conflict with her boyfriend.

Grief: The Case of G

G is an overweight 39-year-old man who presented for treatment for binge eating. He is married and has two young children. For the last 10 years, he had worked as a physician in an intensive care unit (ICU). Growing anxiety about the family finances and his children's welfare had pushed G to begin working the 11 p.m. to 7 a.m. shift approximately five years prior to beginning treatment. When he came for treatment, G was bingeing on average 10 times per week. His pattern was to come home in the morning after work and eat a large breakfast with his children. After taking his children to school and his wife to work, he would binge eat by himself when he got back home. He was also binge eating prior to returning to work after his wife and children had gone to bed. G was an excellent doctor, but, he found the ICU stressful. It was quite upsetting for him to lose any of his patients. G also indicated that his relationship with his wife and children had become more distant in the past several years, although he still loved them.

During the *Initial Phase*, G and his therapist reviewed his history and the interpersonal events associated with the onset of his binge eating. At age 16 following the death of his father, G began to over-eat and struggle with weight gain. Because his mother was incapacitated by grief, G began, on his own, to assume the primary care of his younger sister, who suffered with a degenerative muscle disease. At age 29, G finished his residency, was married, and began working in the ICU. Shortly after he assumed these new responsibilities, his younger sister passed away. It was during this time that he began to binge eat and experienced his largest weight gain.

Toward the end of the initial phase, G and his therapist examined the link between his binge eating and weight gain with two very significant life events: the death of his father and the death of his younger sister. The therapist explored with G that he may not have had the opportunity to grieve his father's death because of his mother's grief and his decision to assume responsibility for his sister's care. Instead, he began to use food as a way to comfort himself. Similarly, when his younger sister died, G had the responsibility of a new wife and job and was unable to appropriately grieve the loss of his sister. Consequently, G began to binge eat as a way to regulate his feelings. At the time he initiated treatment, G's work was compounding his distress because he was taking care of critically ill patients, a number of whom would die. G's therapist speculated that this might be one of the reasons why he was bingeing prior to and after work. Prior to receiving IPT, G had never made the link between his grief and his binge eating. As a result of this insight, G and his therapist developed goals to guide G's work during the remainder of treatment.

In the *Intermediate Phase* of treatment, G and his therapist began working on G's goals. Specifically, G's therapist helped to facilitate G's delayed mourning for his father and sister. During the first session of this phase, G needed a lot of reassurance from the therapist that he would not lose it if he began to feel strong emotions or cry. With his therapist's help, G reconstructed his relationship with both his father and sister. When he began to do this, G really noticed the connection between his unresolved grief and his binge eating. As treatment progressed, G brought in pictures of his father, letters his sister had written to him when G was away at college, and a book of poetry that was written by his sister. In reliving the memories these documents evoked, G expressed the grief and pain of the deaths and began to work through his guilt about not being a better caretaker for his sister. He expressed some unresolved anger at his mother for abandoning him and leaving him to care for his sister. During this process, G began to see how his unresolved grief, as manifested in his binge eating, hindered his relationship with his wife and children. As a result of this work, G began to share more with his wife (including the feelings about his father and sister) and worked to develop a stronger relationship with her and with his children. This improvement in his family relationships was a secondary benefit of the work on his grief-related goal. Toward the end of the intermediate phase, G had dramatically reduced his binge eating, and had substantially improved his relationship with his wife and children. In addition, he began to explore the possibility of transferring to a less stressful area in the hospital.

During the *Termination Phase* of treatment, G reviewed the changes he had made in his eating, especially as it related to the improvement in his grief. He shared with his therapist how helpful it had been to talk about and express his feelings of loss. He became aware that his work environment had intensified his feelings of grief, leading him to engage in more out-of-control eating. G acknowledged how helpful it had been to share with his wife the grief and loss that he had experienced. He realized that keeping those feelings to himself created more stress and a rift between him and his wife. To prevent a recurrence of binge episodes, G made a plan to decrease his work stress and to continue sharing his thoughts and feelings about his losses with his wife.

EFFECTIVENESS OF IPT FOR EATING DISORDERS

In comparative research studies, IPT has demonstrated successful long-term outcomes that compare favorably with those of CBT for BN and BED. Indeed, IPT is the only psychological treatment for BN that has demonstrated long-term outcomes comparable to CBT. All controlled studies of IPT have been comparison studies with CBT. Early findings with BN indicated similar short- and long-term outcomes for binge eating between CBT and IPT (Fairburn et al., 1993, 1995). A more recent multi-site study (Agras et al., 2000) that also compared CBT and IPT as treatments for BN found that patients receiving CBT evidenced higher rates of abstinence from binge eating, and lower rates of purging behaviors, at post-treatment. However, these rates were equivalent by long-term follow-up (8 months and 1 year following treatment). Moreover, IPT patients rated their treatment as more suitable, and expected greater success, than did CBT patients. This finding suggests that bulimic patients perceive the interpersonal focus of IPT as more relevant to their disorder and treatment needs than the CBT focus on cognitive distortions concerning weight and shape.

For BED, group IPT has been shown to be significantly more effective than waitlist control at reducing binge eating (Wilfley et al., 1993). In two randomized-controlled trials that examined the efficacy of group IPT as compared to group CBT, IPT showed similar results as CBT, proving to be an effective treatment achieving marked short-term and long-term reductions in binge eating (Wilfley et al., 1993, 2002), with 62% of the patients evidencing abstinence from binge eating at 1-year follow-up (Wilfley et al., 2002). Moreover, the time-course of almost all outcomes with IPT was identical to that of CBT. In addition, IPT (similar to CBT) had significant short- and long-term impact on wide-ranging areas of psychosocial functioning, including improvements in eating disorder and general psychopathology, self-esteem, social adjustment, and interpersonal problems. For BED patients, IPT was rated as credible as CBT, and 53% of the patients actually rated, prior to randomization, a preference for being assigned to IPT over CBT.

Although no studies have yet demonstrated the efficacy of IPT for the treatment of AN, McIntosh and colleagues (2000) are currently conducting a randomized clinical trial comparing IPT, CBT, and routine clinical management for a large sample of young women with AN. This research may support the efficacy of IPT for the treatment of AN, similar to its demonstrated efficacy for BN and BED. Because IPT does not focus directly on disturbed attitudes regarding eating, weight, and shape, it may be a more efficacious treatment than CBT, since CBT and other symptom-focused treatments sometimes encounter resistance from AN patients. However, given the severity of the illness, it is likely that IPT for AN will not be a sufficient stand-alone treatment and instead will need to be delivered in the context of other adjunctive treatments (e.g. pharmacological, nutritional). Moreover, it will be important to determine whether IPT is most well-suited to *bring about* remission of AN or to *prevent relapse or recurrence* of the illness.

FUTURE DIRECTIONS

Several key areas are in need of further investigation. First, data from ongoing clinical trials will be critical to determine whether IPT can be effective for AN, and if so, to document the clinical considerations necessary when delivering IPT for AN. Second, although outcome studies have clearly documented the efficacy of IPT for BN and BED, little is known about the mechanisms by which IPT exerts its effects. A greater understanding of these mechanisms would assist in making further refinements of the treatment and yield insights about the nature of those factors that maintain eating disorder symptoms. Third, increased efforts to improve the effectiveness of IPT are warranted. Because IPT for eating disorders has been exclusively tested as an alternative to CBT, the manualized versions examined in research studies have had no symptom focus during the second and third phases of treatment, which is in stark contrast to IPT as tested for depression. Now that studies of BN and BED have demonstrated that IPT and CBT have equivalent long-term effects, it may be productive to test more symptom-focused versions of IPT to see if its effectiveness could be strengthened. Fourth, there exists a need to translate IPT efficacy data to effectiveness studies and routine clinical practice. Fifth, IPT has been used with specific subgroups of eating-disordered individuals, including adolescents with BN (Robin et al., 1998) and individuals with BN and diabetes mellitus (Peveler & Fairburn, 1992). Given IPT's demonstrated effectiveness with BN and BED, empirical tests of IPT with subpopulations of these disorders is an exciting potential direction for future research. Because BN patients often seek treatment in late adolescence, a time when interpersonal factors play an important role, IPT may prove to be particularly useful for eating-disordered adolescents. Finally, data to date have not identified predictors of response to IPT for eating disorders; this is a high-priority area for continuing research.

SUMMARY

IPT is a focused, goal-driven treatment which targets interpersonal problem(s) associated with the onset and/or maintenance of the eating disorder. There is a strong empirical basis for the use of an interpersonal approach to understand and treat eating disorders. IPT has resulted in significant and well-maintained improvements for the treatment of BN and BED, and it is currently under investigation for the treatment of AN. IPT has also been successfully delivered for eating disorders in both individual and group formats (see Wilfley et al., 1998 and 2000 for considerations and techniques in adapting IPT for group). Further research is needed regarding the mechanisms by which IPT achieves its effects, predictors of treatment outcome, and dissemination of IPT for eating disorders in clinical settings outside of controlled trials. In addition, IPT may be successfully adapted in the future for additional subgroups of BN and BED patients. A viable alternative to CBT, IPT's brief, time-limited nature is consistent with the aims of health care delivery systems to limit costs and maximize delivery, while its interpersonal focus is appealing to therapist and patient alike.

REFERENCES

Agras, W.S., Walsh, T., Fairburn, C.G., Wilson, G.T. & Kraemer, H.C. (2000) A multicenter comparison of cognitive-behavioral therapy and interpersonal psychotherapy for bulimia nervosa. *Archives of General Psychiatry*, **57**, 459–466.

Calam, R. & Waller, G. (1998) Are eating and psychosocial characteristics in early teenage years useful predictors of eating characteristics in early adulthood? A 7-year longitudinal study. *International Journal of Eating Disorders*, **24**, 351–362.

Cattanach, L., Phil, M., Malley, R. & Rodin, J. (1988) Psychologic and physiologic reactivity to stressors in eating disordered individuals. *Psychosomatic Medicine*, **50**, 591–599.

Fairburn, C.G., Jones, R., Peveler, R.C., Carr, S.J., Solomon, R.A. O'Connor, M.E., Burton, J. & Hope, R.A. (1991) Three psychological treatments for bulimia nervosa: A comparative trial. *Archives of General Psychiatry*, **48**, 463–469.

Fairburn, C.G., Peveler, R.C., Jones, R., Hope, R.A. & O'Connor, M.E. (1993) Predictors of 12-month outcome in bulimia nervosa and the influence of attitudes to shape and weight. *Journal of Consulting and Clinical Psychology*, **61**, 696–698.

Fairburn, C.G., Norman, P.A., Welch, S.L., O'Connor, M.E., Doll, H.A. & Peveler, R.C. (1995) A prospective study of outcome in bulimia nervosa and the long-term effects of three psychological treatments. *Archives of General Psychiatry*, **52**, 304–312.

Fairburn, C.G. (1997) Interpersonal psychotherapy for bulimia nervosa. In D.M. Garner & P.E. Garfinkel (Eds), *Handbook for Treatment of Eating Disorders*. New York: Guilford Press.

Fairburn, C.G., Welch, S.A., Doll, H.A., Davies, B.A. & O'Connor, M.E. (1997) Risk factors for bulimia nervosa. *Archives of General Psychiatry*, **54**, 509–517.

Fairburn, C.G., Doll, H.A., Welch, S.L., Hay, P.J., Davies, B.A. & O'Connor, M.E. (1998) Risk factors for binge eating disorder: A community-based, case-control study. *Archives of General Psychiatry*, **55**, 425–432.

Frank, E., Kupfer, D.J., Wagner, E.F., McEachran, A.B. & Cornes, C. (1991) Efficacy of interpersonal psychotherapy as a maintenance treatment of recurrent depression: Contributing factors. *Archives of General Psychiatry*, **48**, 1053–1059.

Garner, D.M., Vitousek, K.M. & Pike, K.M. (1997) Cognitive-behavioral therapy for anorexia nervosa. *Handbook for Treatment of Eating Disorders* (2nd edition; pp. 94–144). New York: Guilford Press.

Ghaderi, A. & Scott, B. (1999) Prevalence and psychological correlates of eating disorders among females aged 18–30 years in the general population. *Acta Psychiatrica Scandinavica*, **99**, 261–266.

Greeno, C.G., Wing, R.R. & Shiffman, S. (2000) Binge antecedents in obese women with and without binge eating disorder. *Journal of Consulting and Clinical Psychology*, **68**, 95–102.

Grissett, N.L. & Norvell, N.K. (1992) Perceived social support, social skills, and quality of relationships in bulimic women. *Journal of Consulting and Clinical Psychology*, **60**, 293–299.

Heatherton, T.F. & Baumeister, R.F. (1991) Binge eating as escape from self-awareness. *Psychological Bulletin*, **110**, 86–108.

Herzog, D.B., Keller, M.B., Lavori, P.W. & Ott, I.L. (1987) Social impairment in bulimia. *International Journal of Eating Disorders*, **6**, 741–747.

Horesh, N., Apter, A., Ishai, J., Danziger, Y., Miculincer, M., Stein, D., Lepkifker, E. & Minouni, M. (1996) Abnormal psychosocial situations and eating disorders in adolescence. *Journal of the American Academy of Child and Adolescent Psychiatry*, **35**, 921–927.

Kenardy, J., Wilfley, D.E., Wiseman, C.V., Stein, R.I., Dounchis, J.Z. & Arnow, B. (2001) *The phenomenology of binge eating precursors and consequences in a prospective examination*. Unpublished manuscript.

Klerman, G.L., Weissman, M.M., Rounsaville, B.J. & Chevron, E.S. (1984) *Interpersonal Psychotherapy of Depression*. New York: Basic Books.

McFall, R.M., Eason, B.J., Edmondson, C.B. & Treat, T.A. (1999) Social competence and eating disorders: Development and validation of the Anorexia and Bulimia Problem Inventory. *Journal of Psychopathology and Behavioral Assessment*, **21**, 365–394.

McIntosh, V.V., Bulik, C.M., McKenzie, J.M., Luty, S.E. & Jordan, J. (2000) Interpersonal psychotherapy for anorexia nervosa. *International Journal of Eating Disorders*, **27**, 125–139.

McManus, F. & Waller, G. (1995) A functional analysis of binge-eating. *Clinical Psychology Review*, **15**, 845–863.

O'Mahony, J.F. & Hollwey, S. (1995) The correlates of binge eating in two nonpatient samples. *Addictive Behaviors*, **20**, 471–480.

Peveler, R.C. & Fairburn, C.G. (1992) The treatment of bulimia nervosa in patients with diabetes mellitus. *International Journal of Eating Disorders*, **11**, 45–53.

Powell, A.L. & Thelen, M.H. (1996) Emotions and cognitions associated with bingeing and weight control behavior in bulimia. *Journal of Psychosomatic Research*, **40**, 317–328.

Robin, A.L., Gilroy, M. & Dennis, A.B. (1998) Treatment of eating disorders in children and adolescents. *Clinical Psychology Review*, **18**, 421–446.

Rorty, M., Yager, J., Buckwalter, J.G. & Rossotto, E. (1999) Social support, social adjustment, and recovery status in bulimia nervosa. *International Journal of Eating Disorders*, **26**, 1–12.

Schmidt, U., Tiller, J., Blanchard, M., Andrews, B. & Treasure, J. (1997) Is there a specific trauma precipitating anorexia nervosa? *Psychological Medicine*, **27**, 523–530.

Schupak-Neuberg, E. & Nemeroff, C.J. (1993) Disturbances in identity and self-regulation in bulimia nervosa: Implications for a metaphorical perspective of 'body as self'. *International Journal of Eating Disorders*, **13**, 335–347.

Segrin, Chris. (2001) *Interpersonal Processes in Psychological Problems*. New York: Guilford Press.

Spurrell, E.B., Wilfley, D.E., Tanofsky, M.B. & Brownell, K.D. (1997) Age of onset for binge eating: Are there different pathways to binge eating? *International Journal of Eating Disorders*, **21**, 55–65.

Steiger, H., Gauvin, L., Jabalpurwala, S., Seguin, J.R. & Stotland, S. (1999) Hypersensitivity to social interactions in bulimic syndromes: Relationship to binge eating. *Journal of Consulting and Clinical Psychology*, **67**, 765–775.

Stice, E., Akutagawa, D., Gaggar, A. & Agras, W.S. (2000) Negative affect moderates the relation between dieting and binge eating. *International Journal of Eating Disorders*, **27**, 218–229.

Striegel-Moore, R.H., Dohm, F., Pike, K.M., Wilfley, D.E. & Fairburn, C.G. (2001) Childhood sexual abuse: A risk factor for binge eating disorder? Manuscript submitted for publication.

Tanofsky-Kraff, M., Wilfley, D.E. & Spurell, E. (2000) Impact of interpersonal and ego-related stress on restrained eaters. *International Journal of Eating Disorders*, **27**, 411–418.

Telch, C.F. & Agras, W.S. (1994) Obesity, binge eating and psychopathology: Are they related? *International Journal of Eating Disorders*, **15**, 53–61.

Telch, C.F. & Agras, W.S. (1996) Do emotional states influence binge eating in the obese? *International Journal of Eating Disorders*, **20**, 271–279.

Thelen, M.H., Farmer, J., McLaughlin Mann, L. & Prutit, J. (1990) Bulimia and interpersonal relationships: A longitudinal study. *Journal of Counseling Psychology*, **37**, 85–90.

Thelen, M.H., Kanakis, D.M. & Farmer, J. (1993) Bulimia and interpersonal relationships: An extension of a longitudinal study. *Addictive Behaviors*, **18**, 145–150.

Tiller, J.M., Sloane, G., Schmidt, U., Troop, N., Power, M. & Treasure, J.L. (1997) Social support in patients with anorexia nervosa and bulimia nervosa. *International Journal of Eating Disorders*, **21**, 31–38.

Troop, N.A., Holbrey, A., Trowler, R. & Treasure, J.L. (1994) Ways of coping in women with eating disorders. *Journal of Nervous and Mental Disease*, **182**, 535–540.

Tuschen-Caffier, B. & Vogele, C. (1999) Psychological and physiological reactivity to stress: An experimental study on bulimic patients, restrained eaters and controls. *Psychotherapy and Psychosomatics*, **68**, 333–340.

Van Buren, D.J. & Williamson, D.A. (1988) Marital relationships and conflict resolution skills of bulimics. *International Journal of Eating Disorders*, **7**, 735–741.

Weissman, M.M., Markowitz, J.C. & Klerman, G.L. (2000) *Comprehensive Guide to interpersonal Psychotherapy*. New York: Basic Books.

Welch, S.L. & Fairburn, C.G. (1994) Sexual abuse and bulimia nervosa. *American Journal of Psychiatry*, **151**, 402–407.

Wilfley, D.E., Agras, W.S., Telch, C.F., Rossiter, E.M., Schneider, J.A., Cole, A.G., Sifford, L. & Raeburn, S.D. (1993) Group cognitive-behavioral therapy and group interpersonal psychotherapy for the nonpurging bulimic individual: A controlled comparison. *Journal of Consulting and Clinical Psychology*, **61**, 296–305.

Wilfley, D.E., Pike, K.M. & Striegel-Moore, R.H. (1997) Toward an integrated model of risk for binge eating disorder. *Journal of Gender, Culture, and Health*, **2**, 1–32.

Wilfley, D.E., Frank, M.A., Welch, R., Spurrell, E.B. & Rounsaville, B.J. (1998) Adapting interpersonal psychotherapy to a group format (IPT-G) for binge eating disorder: Toward a model for adapting empirically supported treatments. *Psychotherapy Research*, **8**, 379–391.

Wilfley, D.E., Welch, R.R., Stein, R.I., Spurrell, E.B., Cohen, L.R., Saelens, B.E., Dounchis, J.Z., Frank, M.A., Wiseman, C.V. & Matt, G.E. (2002). A randomized comparison of group cognitive-behavioral therapy and group interpersonal psychotherapy for the treatment of binge eating disorder. *Archives of General Psychiatry*, **59**, 713–721.

Wilfley, D.E., MacKenzie, K.R., Welch, R.R., Ayres, V.E. & Weissman, M.M. (2000) *Interpersonal Psychotherapy for Group*. New York: Basic Book.

Wonderlich, S.A. (1995) Personality and eating disorders. In K.D. Brownell & C.G. Fairburn (Eds), *Eating Disorders and Obesity: A Comprehensive Handbook* (pp. 171–176). New York: Guilford Press.

Woodside, D.B., Shekter-Wolfson, L.F., Brandes, J.S. & Lackstrom, J.B. (1993) *Eating Disorders and Marriage: The Couple in Focus*. New York: Brunner/Mazzel Inc.

CHAPTER 10

Dialectical Behaviour Therapy

Bob Palmer

Brandon Mental Health Unit, Leicester General Hospital, Leicester, UK

and

Helen Birchall

Brandon Mental Health Unit, Leicester General Hospital, Leicester, UK

The treatment of people with eating disorders complicated by comorbid personality disorder is often unsatisfactory (Dennis & Samsone, 1997). The usual treatments, such as manual-based cognitive-behavioural therapy (CBT) for bulimia nervosa, are worth a try but are commonly insufficient. In particular, patients with borderline personality disorder (BPD) may do poorly. The therapeutic relationship often breaks down or becomes so complex as to render such therapies difficult or impossible. Most clinicians are aware of a minority of such patients who consume substantial therapeutic resource with little apparent benefit. Typically they will have other problem behaviours such as repeated self-harm and substance abuse together with affective instability and may be called 'multi-impulsive'. Such patients lead unhappy and chaotic lives with much suffering and substantial risk. Too often those who would help them come to feel that their efforts are overwhelmed by this chaos and distress.

Dialectical behaviour therapy (DBT) is a treatment that has some claim to proven efficacy in the management of women with BPD and recurrent self-harm and/or substance abuse (Linehan et al., 1991, 1999), and may be useful as an approach for people with eating disorders and comorbid BPD.

DIALECTICAL BEHAVIOUR THERAPY

DBT is a complex treatment. It was devised by Marsha Linehan of Seattle and is set out in her book and in the accompanying skills training manual (Linehan, 1993a, 1993b). It is based upon a provisional 'Biosocial Theory' that sees BPD as arising from a probable biological tendency towards emotionality that is shaped by an invalidating environment.

The Essential *Handbook of Eating Disorders.* Edited by J. Treasure, U. Schmidt and E. van Furth.
© 2005 John Wiley & Sons, Ltd.

DBT is usually an outpatient treatment although it has been adapted for inpatient or day patient use (Bohus et al., 2000). Typically it runs for one year although the programme may be repeated. It has four main elements. Three of these are therapeutic activities which involve the patient, namely weekly sessions with an individual therapist, weekly skills training in a group and telephone contact for skills coaching between sessions. DBT is a team treatment and the fourth element is a weekly consultation group in which the team meets together to discuss the patients and the programme. Arguably, one of the strengths of DBT is the clear supportive framework that it supplies for patients and clinicians alike. However, the conceptual underpinnings of DBT are varied. It is a strange hybrid.

Much of the basic thinking of DBT comes from the cognitive-behavioural tradition. DBT espouses the scientific ethos. There is an emphasis on the need for open and explicit collaboration between clinician and patient and there is substantial use of such techniques as self-monitoring. Furthermore, the language of DBT is often very commonsensical or even folksy. It is full of aphorisms. Thus, patients are thought of as 'always doing their best'. The therapist is urged to seek the 'kernel of truth' in the assumptions of the patients. It is said that the patients 'may not have caused all of their own problems but they have to solve them anyway'. Trying to gain something out of a setback or a disaster is described as 'making lemonade out of lemons'.

In contrast, the 'dialectical' in DBT refers to a broad way of thinking that substitutes 'both/and' for 'either/or' and sees truth as an evolving product of the opposition of different views. Its relevance arises from clinical observation of the shifting and non-linear character of human emotion and experience in general and that of the borderline patient in particular. Such thinking pervades the overall style of the therapeutic interaction in DBT. This is sometimes compared to that of a dance to rapidly changing music in which the clinician and patient react to each other. What the 'right' step should be can be judged only in the context of the overall dance. It is important to keep on the move. Humour and irreverence are invoked to this end.

Dialectical thinking emphasises the wholeness and interconnectedness of the world and the potential for the reconciliation of opposites. A further novel element of DBT is the inclusion of ideas and techniques drawn from Zen Buddhism. The key concept is that of mindfulness. The person with BPD is seen as having difficulty in being at all detached from her experience and as being frequently overwhelmed by it. Developing the capacity for mindfulness and living in the moment increases the potential for feeling appropriately in charge of the self. Paradoxically, greater mastery is achieved through an increased ability to be detached. A related idea is that of the balance between acceptance and change. Zen is full of paradox and again there is something paradoxical in the idea that acceptance—for instance, of unchangeable traumatic events in the past—may be necessary for change to be possible.

The overall stance of the therapist in DBT is that of being a 'consultant to the patient'. Although the posture is not rigid, the DBT therapist tends to work with and advise the patient but does not take over except in extreme circumstances. If other professionals become involved then the therapist will tend to help the patient to deal appropriately with them rather than the other way around. The relationship between the patient and the therapist should be quite explicitly a working partnership. The need to cherish and often to repair the therapeutic relationship is seen as central. Time is spent getting explicit commitment and when necessary recommitment from the patient. And, of course, the therapist has reciprocal commitments.

INDIVIDUAL THERAPY

Typically the patient and therapist meet once each week for about an hour. The patient fills in a diary card for the preceding week and this may be used as an initial focus of discussion. Attention is paid to topics according to a hierarchy in which life-threatening behaviours come top, followed by therapy interfering behaviours. Quality of life-impairing behaviours and other issues are dealt with only if these other two topics are satisfactory. In practice, the style of the sessions may vary between therapists. However, there is an overall aim of validating the experience of the patient and encouraging her to become more skilful in the management of her feelings, behaviours and her relationships with others. Detailed chain analysis may be used to explore the antecedents and consequences of troublesome feelings or actions.

Skills Training

The patient is taught skills in a weekly group which typically lasts for two hours or so. The style of the group is didactic. The room may be set out as a classroom with the skills trainers—usually two—facing the patients. Process issues or evident emotion are dealt with only if they threaten the running of the group. Sometimes a skills trainer may also be the therapist of one or more of the patients but this dual relationship is not dealt with in the group. The training is organised around a manual that contains handouts that may be copied freely for this purpose (Linehan, 1993b). There are four modules, *emotional regulation, distress tolerance, interpersonal effectiveness* and *mindfulness.* Each module takes several weeks to teach. Often, the mindfulness module is repeated in brief form between each of the other modules. Typically, each meeting of the group begins and ends with a mindfulness exercise.

Telephone Contact

Patients receiving full DBT may contact their individual therapist between sessions by telephone. Such contact may be planned but is usually in response to crises. The calls are typically quite brief and used to coach the patients in the use of skills to survive and weather their emotional storms. The hours during which such contact is available are agreed between the therapist and the patient. What the therapist can manage is an explicit determinant of the arrangement and is usually the limiting factor. The aim is to provide an alternative to self-harm and the patient is banned from telephoning for 24 hours after such an act.

DBT AND EATING DISORDERS

DBT has been tried out by a number of centres working with eating-disordered patients. However, full DBT has yet to be adequately evaluated. The main work has been conducted by the group at Stanford and has involved the assessment of brief outpatient therapies that have been informed by DBT but which are much abridged compared to the full treatment as described by Linehan (1993a, 1993b). Thus, the group have reported the use of skills training as a treatment for binge eating disorder (Welch & Telch 1999; Telch, Agras & Linehan, 2000). The same team have conducted a trial of an individual outpatient treatment described as DBT for women with bulimia nervosa (Safer, Telch & Agras, 2001a, 2001b). The treatment was found to be superior to a waiting list comparison condition in respect of reduction of binge eating and purging behaviour. The treatment was individual and brief, lasting only 20 weeks. The patients were not selected for comorbid personality disorder. The results of this trial suggest that short treatment based upon affect regulation may be useful in the outpatient treatment of bulimia nervosa. However, it has less relevance to the question of the utility of full DBT in helping people with eating disorders complicated by borderline personality disorder.

Other reported work has been purely descriptive and uncontrolled. Marcus, McCabe and Levine (1999) from Pittsburgh have described a DBT treatment programme for eating-disordered patients. In Leicester, we ran a full DBT programme for 18 months. The seven patients on the programme all had eating disorder and comorbid BPD. Most of them had displayed life-threatening self-harming behaviour and two also had comorbid diabetes mellitus. All of the patients stayed in therapy, all survived and all were improved at 18 months follow-up (Palmer et al., 2003). However, although the improvement of the patients was impressive, formal pre-post measures were not available because of lack of cooperation of several of the patients at the outset. Furthermore, there was no comparison group and improvements may have reflected the settling down of a group of patients initially recruited at the peak of their disturbance. Thus the efficacy and effectiveness of full DBT in the treatment of eating-disordered people has yet to be properly evaluated.

A feature of our programme was the development of an additional skills training module called 'Eatingness' (Gatward, McGrain & Palmer, 2003). This contains psycho-educational material presented in the style of DBT. It was acceptable to the patients and has been used in a number of centres. However, it, too, remains to be formally evaluated.

Case Example

The following case history is fictional. It is included as illustration and not as evidence. However, the story accords broadly to those of women who might be predicted to be suitable for full DBT. Issues set in *italics* are mentioned in the story as illustrations of ideas or techniques characteristic of DBT.

The Story of Jane

Jane is a 28-year-old woman with borderline personality disorder, who had been in touch with psychiatric services since the age of 15. She was born in Scotland, and her parents separated when she was 5 years old. Jane stayed with her mother, who was alcohol dependent and often neglected the physical and emotional care of the children. The mother remarried when Jane was 8, and Jane suffered sexual abuse from her step-father from this time until she left home at 16. Subsequently, Jane had a relationship with a physically abusive man from the age of 17, but left him when she was 22 and moved to England.

Jane began to restrain her eating at the age of 12, and probably fulfilled criteria for anorexia nervosa at this time. When she was 14, Jane began to binge eat, vomit and take amphetamines, in addition to self-harming, which included cutting, burning and pulling her hair out. Soon she was drinking heavily and was truanting from school. This prompted a referral to the local child and adolescent psychiatric services. She had several admissions to the local inpatient unit to try to deal with the eating and self-harm. At 17, she graduated to the Adult services, but continued her chaotic life with multiple admissions.

In her mid-twenties, Jane moved to England. After a year or so, she again came into contact with psychiatric services after a serious overdose that had involved resuscitation and treatment in the Intensive Care Unit. At this time, her body mass index was 18, and she was found to be hypokalaemic. She was found to be actively eating disordered, and was referred to the Specialist Eating Disorders Team, where she was offered psychodynamically informed psychotherapy. However, the therapy did not go smoothly. Jane became abusive and critical of her therapist's efforts to help. After a year or so, the therapeutic relationship broke down, repeating the pattern of other relationships. She continued to self-harm, necessitating recurrent medical admissions sometimes followed by lengthy admissions to the psychiatric unit for containment. Despite attracting many offers of help from concerned professional and lay people, Jane had little sustained support in the community. Typically any relationships were soon damaged beyond repair by her demanding and aggressive behaviour. Her hospital admissions followed a similar pattern, with ward staff feeling angry and frustrated at Jane's behaviour and lack of progress.

Jane said that 'no one can handle me'. This sounded like defiance and a challenge, but superficially covered a desperate fear. Jane was scared, angry, miserable, unable to trust and felt life to be not worth living. The clinical team, too, had problems. There was splitting and disagreement, with some staff members wanting to rescue the patient, and others feeling that she was indeed impossible to manage and was wasting resources that might otherwise have been used for 'people who wanted help'. There was no progress with either the eating or the self-harm and there was the familiar despair and demoralisation.

The Eating Disorders Team decided to offer Jane treatment on their DBT programme, which was a new venture. Jane's problems were seen as her eating disorder, which flipped between partial syndrome AN and BN, and her interpersonal difficulties and self-harm. She was introduced to a new therapist who, although an experienced clinician like the other members of the team, had just finished his DBT training. Jane was his first DBT patient. He met with Jane, and took a history and the *invalidating environment* of Jane's childhood was quickly apparent. The diagnosis of borderline personality disorder was formally reviewed and confirmed. The therapist explained the diagnosis to Jane together with *the biosocial theory*. To his surprise, this made sense to Jane, and she seemed quite relieved that there was some explanation for the way life was for her. Over several weeks, the therapist and patient worked on *committing* to therapy. The therapist said that he would be available from 9am to 9pm seven days a week for *telephone contact*. Jane initially refused the group skills training, but was told this was an integral part of the treatment although she was reminded that she was, of course, under no obligation to accept the *treatment package*.

Jane acknowledged how awful life was for her, and that she did want to improve things, but had no faith that anything could be any better. She finally decided to start DBT.

For the first five months, each session was spent going through the self-harm of the week in great detail. Jane filled in *diary cards* and these were used in *chain analyses* of the antecedents, behaviour and consequences (ABC). She was attending *skills training*, but found this difficult and often missed group. This was discussed within the group as *therapy interfering behaviour* but Jane felt attacked and complained bitterly to her therapist during *individual sessions*, saying she would never return. The therapist was able to say what a pity this was, as he felt she was beginning to make some headway. He said that he would really feel sorry if she were to leave the programme and he was not able to see her any more. Jane was quick to say that she did not want to quit individual therapy, so the therapist coached her on how to address her problems with the group leaders. Here the therapist was being a '*consultant to the patient*'.

Throughout the DBT programme, the professionals involved met weekly in the *consultation group*. Six months into therapy, other members of the team expressed concern that Jane's therapist was overburdened by telephone contact. Jane was ringing him two to three times most days, and although these calls were in general appropriate—dealing with crises by skills coaching—they were interfering with the therapist's working and personal life. The team helped the therapist to look at ways he could manage this, by constructing a *behavioural programme* of reducing phone contact in a planned manner over the coming months. The therapist was able to put this to Jane, saying that in order for him to carry on working with her effectively, this would have to happen. She agreed to this, but on the next phone call, the therapist was unable to respond immediately. He called as soon as practicable, and found the patient to be slurred in speech, having taken an overdose in the interim. He made sure that Jane was not alone, and that she was going to accident and emergency department, before ending the call. The next session was spent dealing with this *therapy interfering behaviour*, and Jane could see that it would be impossible for the therapist to work under the pressure of having to be immediately available, while he validated her distress, which often felt unbearable.

After eight months, Jane began to reduce her self-harming behaviour. She said that she was fed up with doing nothing in sessions but talk about self-harm, and the only way she could get to talk about other things that distressed her was to stop cutting and overdosing. The therapist said he was relieved she had realised this, because it did seem a shame to waste so much session time on 'the same old stuff' (*irreverence*). Group was going better, and Jane was beginning to be able to use the skills to communicate in a more useful way, and was contributing ideas to other group members.

After ten months of treatment, Jane was mugged while in town. The experience frightened her, and brought back memories of past violence she had suffered. She took a large overdose, and was readmitted to hospital, where the long-suffering staff clearly remembered her previous admissions. Jane continued with therapy while in hospital, and the therapist coached Jane on how to manage her interactions with ward staff. Jane began to be able to talk to various members of the ward team, who commented on how she had changed over the last few months. Jane and her primary nurse decided to try to do some work on her eating while she was on the ward, and Jane brought her homework sheets from the 'Eatingness' module to work on with this nurse.

Jane continued in full DBT for 18 months, but finished the skills training group after she had been through each module twice. She remained in weekly therapy for a further nine months and negotiated with her therapist to cut down telephone contact gradually. In sessions they began to explore issues from her past now that the present produced fewer demanding crises. In her life, she began tentatively to build up more social links and Jane used her therapy sessions to discuss problems in doing this. Jane continued to binge and vomit occasionally, but managed to give up her self-harming. She reduced her alcohol intake, and stopped taking illicit drugs.

Towards the end of the third year after entering DBT, Jane moved away to start a degree course and was discharged. However, she would sometimes write to her therapist to say how things were going. She commented upon some of the things that she felt had helped her. She described how contained the therapy had made her feel. She also said that she had valued her therapist's belief in her. She mentioned his comments that she was *trying her hardest* and how this—together with his straight talking when she had behaved unacceptably—had helped her to keep going in the bad times.

CONCLUSION

Full DBT is a complex and expensive treatment. It requires that a team be especially trained. Furthermore, the treatment is personally demanding of the clinicians involved. Nevertheless, it may well have a place in the management of that small group of eating-disordered patients who suffer from comorbid BPD and, furthermore, show a range of highly problematic behaviours. Such patients are familiar to most clinicians working within the field. Helping such unfortunate people within a DBT programme is likely to be more satisfactory and satisfying than trying to do so in an unplanned and reactive manner. It may even be more effective although efficacy has yet to be formally demonstrated for eating-disordered patients. Furthermore, it is unclear how DBT would compare with other special treatments for this patient group (Lacey 1995; Dennis & Samsone, 1997). However, such evaluation and comparison would seem to be warranted by the limited experience currently available.

REFERENCES

Bohus, M., Haaf, B., Stiglmayr, C., Pohl, U., Bohme, R. & Linehan, M. (2000) Evaluation of inpatient dialectical-behavioral therapy for borderline personality disorder—a prospective study. *Behaviour Research and Therapy*, **38**, 875–887.

Dennis, A.B. & Samsone, R.A. (1997) Treatment of patients with personality disorders. In D.M. Garner & P.E. Garfinkel (Eds), *Handbook of Treatment for Eating Disorders*. New York: Guilford Press.

Gatward, N., McGrain, L. & Palmer, R.L. (2003) Eatingness—a new DBT skills training module for use with people with eating disorders (submitted for publication).

Lacey, J.H. (1995) Inpatient treatment of multi-impulsive bulimia nervosa. In K.D. Brownell & C.G. Fairburn (Eds), *Eating Disorders and Obesity: A Comprehensive Handbook*. New York: Guilford Press.

Linehan, M.M. (1993a) *Cognitive-Behavioral Treatment of Borderline Personality Disorder*. New York: Guilford Press.

Linehan, M.M. (1993b) *Skills Training Manual for Treating Borderline Personality Disorder*. New York: Guilford Press.

Linehan, M.M., Armstrong, H.E., Suarez, A., Allman, D. & Heard, H.L. (1991) Cognitive-behavioral treatment of chronically parasuicidal borderline patients. *Archives of General Psychiatry*, **48**, 1060–1064.

Linehan M.M., Schmidt H., Craft J.C., Kanter J. & Comtois K.A. (1999) Dialectical behavior therapy for patients with borderline personality disorder and drug-dependence. *American Journal on Addictions*, **8**, 279–292.

Marcus, M.D., McCabe, E.B. & Levine, M.D. (1999) Dialectical behavior therapy (DBT) in the treatment of eating disorders. Paper presented at the 4th London International Conference on Eating Disorders, London, April 1999.

Palmer, R.L., Birchall, H., Damani, S., Gatward, N., McGrain, L. & Parker, A. (2003) Dialectical behaviour therapy (DBT) programme for people with eating disorder and borderline personality disorder—description and outcome. *International Journal of Eating Disorders* (in press).

Safer, D.L., Telch, C.F. & Agras, W.S. (2001a) Dialectical behavior therapy for bulimia: A case report. *International Journal of Eating Disorders*, **30**, 101–106.

Safer, D.L., Telch, C.F. & Agras, W.S. (2001b) Dialectical behavior therapy for bulimia nervosa. *American Journal of Psychiatry*, **158**, 632–634.

Telch, C.F., Agras, W.S. & Linehan, M.M. (2000) Group dialectical behavior therapy for binge eating disorder: A preliminary, uncontrolled trial. *Behaviour Therapy*, **31**, 569–582.

Welch, S. & Telch, C.F. (1999) Dialectical behavior therapy for binge-eating disorder. *Journal of Clinical Psychology*, **55**, 755–768.

CHAPTER 11

Family Interventions

Ivan Eisler

*Adolescent Eating Disorder Service, Maudsley Hospital and
Psychotherapy Section, Institute of Psychiatry, London, UK*

Daniel le Grange

Eating Disorders Program, The University of Chicago, USA

and

Eia Asen

Marlborough Family Service, London, UK

SUMMARY

- Family therapy is an effective treatment for anorexia nervosa.
- The majority of adolescents suffering from anorexia nervosa, even when severely ill, can be managed on an outpatient basis providing the family has an active role in treatment.
- Family interventions are best viewed as treatments that mobilize family resources rather than treat family dysfunction (for which there is little empirical evidence).
- Brief, intensive multiple family interventions provide an important alternative to engaging families in treatment and are viewed very positively by families.

FAMILY THERAPY: TREATING DYSFUNCTIONAL FAMILIES OR HELPING FAMILIES TO FIND SOLUTIONS?

Over the past 25 years family therapy has gradually established itself as an important treatment approach in eating disorders, particularly with adolescent anorexia nervosa. The growing empirical evidence for the effectiveness of family-based treatments (reviewed later in the chapter) has added weight to the earlier clinical and theoretical accounts of some of the pioneer figures of the family therapy field, such as Salvador Minuchin (Minuchin et al., 1975) and Mara Selvini Palazzoli (1974) and has undoubtedly been one of the important factors in the major changes in the treatment of eating disorders that the field has witnessed in the past 10 to 15 years.

Paradoxically, alongside of the data for the effectiveness of family therapy, there has also been growing evidence that the theoretical models, from which the family treatment of eating

The Essential *Handbook of Eating Disorders.* Edited by J. Treasure, U. Schmidt and E. van Furth.
© 2005 John Wiley & Sons, Ltd.

disorder was derived, are flawed. Minuchin et al.'s (1978) model of the 'psychosomatic family' which has probably been the most influential, hypothesized that there was a specific family context within which the eating disorder developed. The authors argued that a particular family process (characterized by rigidity, enmeshment, overinvolvement and conflict avoidance or conflict non-resolution) evolved around the symptomatic behaviour in interaction with a vulnerability in the child and the child's role as mediator in cross-generational alliances (Minuchin et al., 1975). Although they were clear that this was not simply an account of a 'family aetiology' of eating disorder and emphasized the evolving, interactive nature of the process, they saw the resulting 'psychosomatic family' as a necessary condition for the development of an eating disorder. The aim of family therapy then was clearly to alter the way the family functioned. This is well illustrated by the following quote: 'The syndrome of anorexia nervosa is associated with characteristic dysfunctional patterns of family interaction. The family therapist conceptualizes anorexia nervosa in relation to the organization and functioning of the entire family [. . .] and plans the therapeutic interventions to induce change in the family' (Sargent et al., 1985, p. 278).

In spite of a considerable amount of research endeavour, the evidence for the existence of the so-called psychosomatic family is unconvincing, as there is growing indication that families in which there is an eating disorder are a heterogeneous group not only with respect to sociodemographic characteristics but also in terms of the nature of the relationships within the family, the emotional climate and the patterns of family interactions (see Eisler, 1995, for a detailed review). While there is some evidence that effective family therapy is, in some families, accompanied by changes in family functioning (Eisler et al., 2000; Robin et al., 1995) the observed changes are not readily explained by the psychosomatic family model. The fact that families in which there is an eating disorder are heterogeneous and do not necessarily change in predictable ways, inevitably raises the question about the targets of effective family interventions and the nature of the underlying process of change.

Whether or not the family environment has a causal role in the aetiology of eating disorders, it is undoubtedly the case that the presence of an eating disorder has a major impact on family life (see Chapter 5 by Nielsen and Bará-Carril in this volume). As time goes on, food, eating behaviours and the concerns that they give rise to begin to permeate the entire family fabric, every relationship in the family, influencing daily family routines, coping and problem-solving behaviours. Steinglass and colleagues have described a similar process in families with an alcoholic member (Steinglass et al., 1987) and in families coping with a wide range of chronic illnesses (Steinglass, 1998). They developed a conceptual model that describes the process of family reorganization around alcohol-related (or illness-related) behaviours. They propose that families go through a step-wise reorganization in response to the challenges of the illness in which illness issues increasingly take centre stage, altering the family's daily routines, their decision-making processes and regulatory behaviours, until the illness becomes *the central organizing principle* of the family's life. They argue that families, in trying to minimize the impact of the illness on the sufferer, as well as on other family members, increasingly focus their attention on the here-and-now, making it difficult for them to meet the changing developmental needs of the family.

The model proposed by Steinglass and colleagues is readily applicable to eating disorders. Families trying to cope with an eating disorder in their midst will often say that they feel as if time had come to a standstill and that all of the family's life seems to revolve around the eating disorder. The way families respond to this invasion into their family life will vary depending on the nature of the family organization, the family style of each individual family and the particular lifecycle stage they are at when the illness occurs. However, like with other illnesses, what may be more predictable is the way in which the centrality of the eating disorder magnifies certain aspects of the family's dynamics and narrows the range of their adaptive behaviours. The following case example illustrates this process:

Jenny, a 16-year-old adolescent, was referred to our service with a 14-month history of anorexia nervosa. From the referral letter we knew that Jenny's parents had divorced when she was 9 and that she was living with her mother, Ann, and mother's new husband, Tom. There was also a 3-year-old sister from the second marriage. Although Tom had been living in the family home for over four years, Jenny did not get on with him and did not consider him as a father figure. As is our customary practice we invited the whole family to attend the first meeting, but only Jenny and her mother attended. Throughout the first interview we were struck by the close, at times even clingy, relationship between Jenny and her mother. Jenny tended to let her mother speak for her, but from time-to-time would angrily contradict any inaccuracy in Ann's description of her problem. Ann would invariably back away from the potential conflict. When the therapist inquired about Tom, Jenny quickly answered that he did not understand and in any case would probably not come. The therapist asked if that was because he did not care or because he did not believe that he might be of any help. Jenny and Ann agreed that Tom did care and that if he thought that he could be of help but Ann hinted that there were difficulties between her and her husband (particularly in how they dealt with Jenny's problem) that might make things more difficult if he was involved. The therapist responded by acknowledging that it might be difficult if Tom was there but that Jenny's problem was far too serious for them not to make use of every resource they had. The fact that he was less involved and had a different perspective on things could be useful, although he probably needed the opportunity to learn more about the problem as well.

It would be relatively easy to construct a hypothesis which would 'explain' Jenny's anorexia as arising out of and/or being maintained by a dysfunctional family system. The very close, intense relationship between Jenny and her mother, Jenny's awkward relationship with Tom and the role that she seemed to play in mediating the marital relationship, the avoidance of overt conflict could all be seen as representing the features of the 'psychosomatic family' described above. However, it would ignore the fact that much of what we observed was also clearly connected with the transitional lifecycle stage that the family was going through (i.e. reconstituting itself as a new family)—or more accurately, because of the presence of anorexia was finding it hard to negotiate. The usual difficulties of a step-father becoming part of the new family were magnified by anorexia and at the same time any uncertainty that Tom had in trying to make sense of Jenny's illness, simply confirmed that he did not understand her and did not belong. Ann's occasional doubts whether she had done the right thing in leaving her first husband, and the effect this might have had on Jenny, turned into feelings of guilt that she might somehow be responsible for the illness.

Trying to work out which of these processes were cause and which effect and which were just incidental is, of course, difficult to disentangle and from a clinical point of view perhaps not very useful in any case. It is more important to explore with the family where things have got stuck and to help them to rediscover some of the resources that they have as a family so that they can become 'unstuck' and start looking for new solutions for the problem at hand. The most important step in engaging the family in treatment, therefore, is to be clear that the family is not seen as the problem but as a resource. In coming together to tackle their daughter's problem, families may sometimes find that there are aspects of the way they function as a family that they want to change. That is, however, not the primary aim of the treatment, which has to be the overcoming of their daughter's eating disorder.

EVIDENCE FOR THE EFFECTIVENESS OF FAMILY THERAPY FOR EATING DISORDERS

Uncontrolled Follow-up Studies of Family Therapy for Adolescent Anorexia Nervosa

The first family therapy study of patients with anorexia nervosa was conducted by Minuchin and his colleagues at the Philadelphia Child Guidance Clinic (Minuchin et al., 1975, 1978). In a follow-up of 53 anorexic patients, for whom family therapy had been the main intervention, Minuchin et al. (1978) reported a very high rate of successful outcomes. The treatments were mixed in that just over half of the patients started out receiving inpatient treatment in conjunction with family therapy, and some of the adolescents were also seen individually while engaged in family therapy. The Philadelphia team reported a remarkably high recovery rate of 86% with their treatment approach, which was in stark contrast to most previous accounts of treatment outcome with children and adolescents suffering from anorexia nervosa (Lesser et al., 1960; Blitzer et al., 1961; Warren, 1968; Goetz et al., 1977). The patient population was mainly adolescent with only three patients being over the age of 18, and the mean duration of illness was just over eight months (range = one month – three years). The very positive results reported by Minuchin et al. (1978), together with the clear and persuasive theoretical model that underpinned their treatment approach, has made the work of the Philadelphia team highly influential even though the study has been criticized for methodological weaknesses (the evaluations were conducted by members of the clinical team, the length of follow-up varied from 18 months to 7 years, there was no comparison treatment).

There have been two other very similar studies, one in Toronto (Martin, 1985) and one in Buenos Aires (Herscovici & Bay, 1996). Both studies were of adolescent anorexia nervosa, with family therapy being the main treatment, but used in combination with a mixture of individual and inpatient treatment. The study reported by Martin (1985) was of a five-year follow-up of 25 adolescent anorexia nervosa patients (mean age 14.9 years) with a short duration of illness (mean 8.1 months). At treatment termination there had been significant improvements although only 23% of patients would have met the Morgan/Russell criteria for good outcome, 45% intermediate outcome and 32% poor outcome. The outcome at follow-up was comparable to Minuchin's results with 80% of patients having a good outcome, 4% intermediate outcome, with the remaining either still in treatment (12%) or relapsed (4%). Herscovici and Bay (1996) report the outcome in a series of 30 patients treated by a pediatrician and family therapist, and followed-up 4–8.6 years after their first presentation. The mean age of these patients at the start of treatment was 14.7 years with a mean duration of illness of 10.3 months. More than 40% of patients were admitted to hospital during the study. They report that 60% of patients had a 'good' outcome, 30% an intermediate outcome, and 10% a poor outcome.

Three other studies have been reported in which family therapy was the only treatment used. The first two (Dare, 1983; Mayer, 1994) were small studies of 12 and 11 adolescent patients respectively, who were seen in outpatient family therapy at the Maudsley Hospital in London and at a General Practice based family therapy clinic in North London. In both studies the treatment was brief (usually less than six months) and 90% were reported to have made significant improvements or were recovered at follow-up.

The third is a larger study from Heidelberg (Stierlin & Weber, 1987, 1989). The sample consisted of families seen at the Heidelberg Centre over a period of 10 years. After excluding male patients, bulimics and those whose treatment had ended less than two years before the follow-up study took place, 42 families were included in the follow-up. The study differs from the other studies in several ways. In the first place the patients were older (mean age when first seen, 18.2 years) and had been ill for an average of just over three years. Approximately two-thirds were still at school, the rest were either at university or were working. All but two of the patients had had previous treatment (56% of whom as inpatients). The therapy lasted on average just under nine months but used relatively few sessions (mean = 6). At follow-up (the average duration of which was $4^{1}/_{2}$ years) just under two-thirds were within a normal weight range and were menstruating. The study makes no distinction in the reporting of the findings between adolescents and adults and is not therefore directly comparable to the other studies described. Nevertheless, it adds to the evidence that adolescents, and probably also young adults, do well in family therapy.

Randomized Clinical Trials of Family Therapy in Adolescent Anorexia Nervosa

There have been few randomized trials in anorexia nervosa and all have been relatively small. The first study by Russell and colleagues (1987) compared family therapy with individual supportive therapy following inpatient treatment. This study included patients of all ages and covered 80 consecutive admissions to the inpatient unit at the Maudsley Hospital in London. Twenty-six of these patients were adolescents with anorexia nervosa, 21 with an age of onset on or before 18 years and a duration of illness of less than three years. All patients were initially admitted to hospital for an average of 10 weeks for weight restoration before being randomized to outpatient follow-up treatment. Adolescent patients with a short duration faired significantly better with family therapy than the control treatment (individual therapy), although the findings were inconclusive for those with a duration of illness of more than three years who mostly had a poor outcome. A five-year follow-up of this study (Eisler et al., 1997) showed that in the adolescent subgroup with a short history of illness those who received family therapy continued to do well with 90% having a good outcome. Although the patients who had received individual therapy had also continued to improve, nearly half still had significant eating disorder symptoms, showing that even five years after the end of treatment it was still possible to detect benefits of the family interventions.

Four studies have compared different forms of family intervention. Le Grange et al. (1992) and Eisler et al. (2000) compared conjoint family therapy (CFT) and separated family therapy (SFT) in which the adolescent was seen on her own and the parents were seen in a separate session by the same therapist. Both treatments were provided on an outpatient basis although 4 out of 40 in Eisler et al. (2000) required admission during the course of treatment. The overall results were similar in the two studies, showing significant improvements in both treatments (at the end of treatment two-thirds were classified as having a good or inter-mediate outcome), but relatively small differences between treatments in terms of symptom improvement. Both studies also showed that families in which there was raised maternal criticism tended to do worse in CFT. On the other hand, the Eisler et al. (2000) study showed that on individual psychological measures and measures of family functioning there was significantly more change in the CFT group. Similar to other studies the patients continued to improve after the treatment ended. Preliminary results from the five-year follow-up show that 75% have a good outcome, 15% an intermediate outcome and 10% have a poor outcome.

Robin et al. (1999) in Detroit also compared two forms of family intervention in a study with a similar design to that of the Maudsley group. They compared a conjoint family therapy (described as behavioural family systems therapy—BFST) with ego-oriented individual therapy (EOIT) in which weekly individual sessions for the adolescent were combined with fortnightly meetings with the parents. Robin et al. (1998, 1999) in describing the features of BFST, point out the similarities with the Maudsley CFT. Both treatments emphasize the role of the parents in managing the eating disorder symptoms in the early stages of treatment with a broadening of focus to individual or family issues at a later stage. Robin et al. have also argued that while EOIT is superficially similar to SFT, the aim is quite different. While in SFT there is again an emphasis on helping the parents to take a strong role in the management of the symptoms, the work with the parents in EOIT aims to help them to relinquish control over their daughter's eating and to prepare them to accept a more assertive adolescent. The parents are 'instructed not to be controlling about eating but rather take a proactive, supportive role, for example, planning menus, shopping for food, arranging meals that are eaten together as a family, supervising lunch preparation, providing snacks during activities and quietly monitoring the progress of the anorectic's food intake in a supportive, nonjudgmental manner' (Robin et al., 1998, p. 434). However, while there may well have been significant differences between the Detroit EOIT and the Maudsley SFT, the similarities between the treatments are equally important. In both treatments the adolescent received regular individual therapy in which she had the opportunity to address her own personal and relationship issues as well as matters directly connected with her eating problems. The parallel sessions with the parents may have had a somewhat different focus in the two studies but in both treatments the parents were encouraged to have an active role in providing support for their daughter in the process of recovery and to reflect on some of the family dynamics that might have got caught up with the eating disorder.

There are some important differences between the Maudsley and Detroit studies which could have had a bearing on outcome. One difference was that Robin et al. hospitalized patients whose weight was below 75% of ideal weight (43% of their sample) at the start of the treatment programme until their weight rose above 80% of ideal, whereas in the le Grange et al. (1992)/Eisler et al. (2000) studies, the protocol allowed for admission only if outpatient therapy failed to arrest weight loss (none of the 18 patients in le Grange et al. and 4 out of 40 in Eisler et al. were admitted during the study). A further difference concerns the length of treatment which was 6 months in the le Grange et al. study, 12 months in Eisler et al. study and 12–18 months (with an average of 16 months) in the Robin et al. study. There were also apparent differences between the patient groups in that the patients in the Maudsley studies tended to have a longer duration of illness, the majority had had previous treatment and a higher percentage were suffering from depression.

The end of treatment findings (Robin et al., 1999) showed significant improvements in both treatments with 67% reaching target weight by the end of treatment and 80% regaining menstruation. By the 1-year follow-up, approximately 75% had reached their target weight and 85% were menstruating. BFST led to significantly greater weight gain than EOIT both at the end of treatment and at follow-up and there was also a significantly higher percentage of girls menstruating at the end of treatment in the BFST group. Both treatments produced comparably large improvements in eating attitudes, depression, and self-reported eating-related family conflict although, interestingly, neither group reported much general conflict before or after treatment. Robin et al. (1995) have also reported the results of observational ratings of family interaction in a subsample of their study which showed a significant decease in maternal negative communication (and a corresponding increase in positive communication) in the BFST group which was not found in the EOIT group.

A further study by Geist et al. (2000) compared family therapy with family group psychoeducation (FGP). The effects of the family interventions are difficult to evaluate as nearly half of the family treatments occurred during inpatient treatment and 76% of the weight gain took place before discharge from hospital. There were no differences between the two family interventions. Two other controlled treatment studies in anorexia nervosa included adolescent patients and used family intervention as part of the treatment (Hall & Crisp, 1987; Crisp et al., 1991). In both studies, however, the family interventions were part of a larger treatment package and it is unclear how central the family was in the treatment. Moreover, both studies also included adult patients, and the results are not reported separately for the adolescent subgroup. This makes it difficult to evaluate the effects of family treatment on outcome in adolescent patients in these two studies.

Summary of Family Therapy Studies in Adolescent Anorexia Nervosa

Table 11.1 summarizes the results from the various family intervention studies in anorexia nervosa. The overall findings from these studies are remarkably consistent, showing that adolescents with anorexia nervosa respond well to family therapy, often without the need for inpatient treatment. By the end of treatment between half and two-thirds will have reached a healthy weight, although most will not yet have started menstruating again. By the time of follow-up between 60–90% will have fully recovered and no more than 10–15% will still be seriously ill.

Conclusions about the comparisons between different kinds of family interventions have to be more cautious, given the small size and small number of comparative studies. Treatments that encourage the parents to take an active role in tackling their daughter's anorexia seem the most effective and may have some advantages over involving the parents in a way that is supportive and understanding of their daughter but encourages them to step back from the eating problem. One study (Russell et al., 1987; Eisler et al., 1997) has shown that not involving the parents in the treatment at all leads to the worst outcome and may considerably delay recovery. Seeing whole families together appears to have some advantages in addressing both family and individual psychological issues but may have disadvantages for families in which there are high levels of hostility or criticism. Such families can be difficult to engage in family treatment (Szmukler et al., 1985) and this may be particularly true when the whole family is seen together. There is some evidence that this is associated with feelings of guilt and blame being increased as a consequence of criticisms or confrontations occurring during family sessions (Squire-Dehouck, 1993) and our clinical experience suggests that with such families conjoint family sessions may be more useful at a later stage in treatment when the concerns about eating disorder symptoms are no longer central. It is important to stress, however, that while there may be advantages and disadvantages between different types of family interventions, these differences are relatively small in comparison with the overall improvements in response to any of the family interventions studied.

Table 11.1 Studies of family therapy for adolescents with anorexia nervosa

	Sample	Treatments	End of treatment results	Follow-up results
Open follow-up studies				
Minuchin et al. (1978)	N = 53 Age = 14.8 yrs Duration = 8.6 mths	Average of 6.8 mths FT (2–16) 57% admitted for mean of 2.4 wks	Not reported	FU 2.7 yrs (1.5–7) Recovered 86%; fair 4%; Unimproved or relapsed 10%
Dare (1983)	N = 12 Age = 14.7 Duration = 11.6 mths	Outpatient treatment only FT for mean of 6 mths (1–6)	Not reported	FU 10 mths 33% recovered; 58% fair; 8% unchanged
Martin (1985)	N = 25 Age = 14.9 yrs Duration = 8.1 mths	Average of 11 mths FT (2–39) 72% admitted for mean of 8 wks	23% good; 45% inter; 32% poor	FU 5.1 yrs (2.5–7) 80% good; 4% inter; 16% poor
Stierlin & Weber (1987) Stierlin & Weber (1989)	N = 42 Age = 18.2 Duration = 3.3 yrs	Outpatient treatment only Average of 8.7 mths FT (1–40)	21% > 85% abw; 17% menst	FU 4.4 yrs (2.2–8.8) 57% above 85% abw; 60% menst
Mayer (1994)	N = 11 Age = 17 yrs Duration = 9 mths	Outpatient treatment only FT for 1–9 mths. Mean no. of sessions 6.3 (1–18)	Not reported	Mean FU 1.7 yrs 57% good 29% inter; 14% poor
Herscovici & Bay (1996)	N = 30 Age = 14.7 yrs Duration = 10.3 mths	FT for 24 mths 43% admitted for mean of 4 wks	Not reported	FU 6.1 yrs (4–8.6) 60% good; 30% inter; 10% poor
Randomized treatment trials				
Russell et al. (1987) Eisler et al. (1997)	N = 21 Age = 15.3 yrs Duration = 14.4 mths	10.3 wks inpatient + 1 yr FU of: (a) family therapy (b) individual supportive therapy	(a) 60% good; 30% inter; 10% poor (b) 9% good; 9% inter; 10% poor	FU 6.3 yrs (3.1–9.8) (a) 90% good; 10% poor (b) 36% good; 18% inter; 46% poor
Le Grange et al. (1992) Squire-Dehouck (1993)	N = 18 Age = 15.3 yrs Duration = 13.7 mths	6 mths outpatient FT: (a) conjoint family therapy (b) separated family therapy	(a) 20% good; 50% inter; 30% poor (b) 50% good; 40% inter; 10% poor	FU 2 yrs (a) 33% good; 33% inter; 33% poor (b) 87% good; 13% inter
Robin et al. (1999)	N = 37 Age = 14.2 yrs Duration < 12 mths	1–1.5 yrs FT/IT (43% admitted): (a) behavioural family systems therapy (b) ego-oriented individual therapy	(a) 59% good; 6% inter; 35% poor (b) 38% good; 31% inter; 31% poor	FU 1 yr (a) 73% good; 7% inter; 20% poor (b) 64% good; 29% inter; 7% poor
Eisler et al. (2000)	N = 40 Age = 15.5 yrs Duration = 12.9 yrs	1 yr FT (10% admitted): (a) conjoint family therapy (b) separated family therapy	(a) 26% good; 21% inter; 53% poor (b) 48% good; 28% inter; 24% poor	FU 5 yrs[a] (a) 61% good; 17% inter; 22% poor (b) 76% good; 19% inter; 5% poor

[a] Preliminary unpublished data.

The evidence for the effectiveness of family therapy for adolescent anorexia nervosa is clearly compelling as several reviewers have recently concluded (e.g. Wilson & Fairburn, 1998; Carr, 2000) and on current evidence is probably the treatment of choice. It is important to recognize, however, that this may be, at least in part, due to the lack of research on other treatments. Cognitive or psychodynamic treatments are described in the literature (Bowers et al., 1996; Jeammet & Chabert, 1998) but have not been systematically evaluated with adolescent anorexia nervosa and their relative merits in comparison with family therapy are not known. Similarly, the multiple-family day treatment, described in some detail later in this chapter, is a promising new treatment development but as yet there is no systematic evidence for its effectiveness.

ADULT ANOREXIA NERVOSA

Randomised Treatment Trials

The Russell et al. (1987) controlled trial, described earlier, included 31 adult patients with anorexia nervosa (19 years of age or older) who were randomly assigned to either family therapy or the individual control treatment, following discharge from hospital. There were no differences in outcome between treatments for the group as a whole. However, in the subgroup of patients with an adult onset of the illness ($n = 14$) the results favoured individual therapy in which there was significantly greater weight gain (20%) than family therapy (6%). At five-year follow-up, there were no differences in eating disorder symptoms in this subgroup although there was some evidence that the patients in individual therapy had made a somewhat better psychological adjustment, particularly in the area of psychosexual attitudes and behaviours (Eisler et al., 1997).

Dare et al. (2001) conducted an outpatient study to assess the effectiveness of specific psychotherapies, including family therapy, in the outpatient management of adult patients with chronic anorexia nervosa. Eighty-four patients were randomized to four treatments: (1) focal psychoanalytic psychotherapy, (2) cognitive analytic therapy, (3) family therapy and (4) routine treatment that served as a control. At the end of one-year follow-up, the group of patients as a whole showed modest symptomatic improvements with the specialist treatments proving to be significantly more effective than routine treatment. Of the patients allocated to family therapy or focal psychotherapy, 35% were categorized as recovered or significantly improved at the end of treatment compared to 5% of those in the control treatment. There were no significant differences between the three specialist treatments.

Summary of Studies of Family Therapy in Adult Anorexia Nervosa

The data on the use of family therapy (or indeed other psychotherapies) with adults suffering from anorexia nervosa is still quite limited. Moreover, the existing data comes from studies of mainly chronically ill patients with whom positive treatment results are difficult to achieve in general, which makes it more difficult to demonstrate specific effects of particular treatments. The finding by Dare et al. (2001), that specialized psychotherapies were more effective than routine treatment but did not differ from one another, is worthy of further investigation. The similarity of outcome between the different psychotherapies may be simply another example of the so-called 'Dodo' effect (different psychotherapies leading to similar results) (Luborsky et al., 1975) but it may also be that different subgroups respond differently to particular treatments. Larger studies with greater power than the Dare et al. (2001) study are needed to address these questions.

BULIMIA NERVOSA

Although there have been many accounts in the literature of the use of family therapy in the treatment of bulimia nervosa (e.g. Dare, 1997; Johnson et al., 1998; Fishman, 1996; Garner, 1994), there is very little research data to support the clinical accounts. Schwartz et al. (1985) reported on a follow-up of 30 cases of bulimia nervosa who were treated in family therapy. At the end of treatment 66% were rated as being nearly always in control, with at most one bulimic episode per month. These results were maintained at follow-up (the average length of which was 18 months). In the only study of family therapy with adolescents with bulimia nervosa, Dodge et al. (1995) reported on a small series of eight bulimic patients receiving family therapy on an outpatient basis. Significant improvements in bulimic behaviours were reported at the end of treatment. In terms of the Morgan–Russell outcome scores, one patient achieved a good outcome, five achieved an intermediate outcome, and two a poor outcome. Although these results are encouraging, the results must be viewed with caution given the uncontrolled nature of the study and the very small number of cases. Two centres are currently exploring the efficacy of family therapy for adolescent bulimia nervosa. At the University of Chicago, a controlled treatment study is underway in which bulimics aged 19 or younger are randomized into one of two manualized treatments, family therapy or individual supportive therapy. A multicentre RCT study is also being conducted by the Maudsley team of family therapy and guided self-help CBT.

The only randomized trial of family therapy in bulimia nervosa is the Russell et al. (1987) study described earlier. This trial included a subgroup of 23 adult bulimia nervosa patients. As was the case with the three other subgroups in this trial, bulimic patients were randomly allocated to either family therapy or to individual supportive therapy. In terms of general outcome at the end of the one-year outpatient treatment, patients in neither groups faired well and the distribution for the two treatment groups between the outcome categories did not differ significantly. Five-year follow-up data were obtained for 19 patients in this subgroup (Eisler et al., 1997). On the whole, these patients showed a disappointing outcome with only 16% being asymptomatic and a further 32% bingeing and/or vomiting less than once a week. There were no differences between the two follow-up treatments. The results from this study do not easily compare with other studies of bulimia nervosa in that nearly two-thirds of the patients were significantly underweight and by today's diagnostic criteria would be more appropriately classified as bulimic type anorexia nervosa.

The other, albeit indirect, evidence for the possible value of family interventions in bulimia nervosa comes from studies of interpersonal therapy (Fairburn et al., 1991; Agras et al., 2000). Interpersonal therapy is an individual therapy but, like family or systemic therapies, focuses on the way that symptomatic behaviours become entangled in interpersonal relationships. Interpersonal therapy is comparable in effectiveness in the medium to long term with cognitive-behaviour therapy (although less effective in the short term) which suggests that further study of the possible role of family therapy in bulimia nervosa are warranted.

MULTIPLE-FAMILY THERAPY IN THE TREATMENT
OF ADOLESCENT EATING DISORDERS

The effectiveness of family interventions with adolescent eating-disordered patients and the need to develop more intensive forms of family based treatments for those who do not respond to outpatient family therapy alone has recently led to the development of multiple-family therapy day programmes in Dresden (Scholz & Asen, 2001) and at the Maudsley Hospital in London (Dare & Eisler, 2000). Preliminary results from these programmes are very promising and offer an additional approach for helping adolescents with eating disorders and their families. The experience from these programmes also offers new perspectives on the processes underlying family interventions.

The idea of treating a number of families together was first pioneered in the early 1960s by Laqueur (Laqueur et al., 1964). He saw this as a way of providing a context where the resources of all family members could be used more successfully when several families were treated together in one group in order to improve inter- and intra-family communication (Laqueur, 1972). In addition, by identifying with members of other families and learning by analogy (Laqueur, 1973) patients and key relatives could expand their social repertoires. The multiple-family therapy model has been further elaborated over the past three decades (Strelnick, 1977; Steinglass, 1998; Asen, 2002) and applied to various psychiatric populations including drug and alcohol abuse (Kaufman & Kaufman, 1979), chronic medical illness (Gonsalez et al., 1989; Steinglass, 1998), Huntingdon's disease (Murburg et al., 1988), child abuse (Asen et al., 1989), as well as eating disorders (Slagerman & Yager, 1989; Wooley & Lewis, 1987).

In England, Cooklin and his team at the Marlborough Family Service in London (Cooklin et al., 1983, Asen et al., 1982) pioneered a unique multiple-family approach in the late 1970s, creating a day hospital where up to 10 families would attend together for five days a week for eight hours a day. Bringing a whole number of families together for intensive days or weeks creates a hothouse effect. Interactions are necessarily more intense in a group setting where children and parents are participating in different tasks and where they are required to examine not only their own but also other families' communications and behaviours. This increased intensity can lead to rapid growth—change is more likely to take place as familiar coping and defence mechanisms cannot be employed. Being part of a multiple-family setting requires families constantly to change context, requiring each family member continuously having to adapt to new demands. Such intensity cannot easily be created in individual family sessions.

The therapeutic factors that are described as important in multiple-family work, such as reducing social isolation, de-stigmatization, enhancing opportunities to create new and multiple perspectives, neutralizing chronic staff–patient relationships, etc. (see Asen, 2002), are strongly enhanced by the intensity of the day programme setting.

The Dresden and London projects are very similar (unsurprisingly, since both units have shared their experiences and inspired one another) even though the starting point for each programme was quite different. The Dresden service is based around a large inpatient unit which over the years admitted about 60 anorectic and bulimic teenagers per year, often in rather severe physical states. In addition to other treatments, fortnightly family therapy sessions had been used routinely during admission, and following discharge from hospital (after an average of 12 weeks) the young person would usually continue to attend as a daypatient or outpatient, receiving individual and family therapy and, occassionally, medication. The impetus for developing the experimental multiple-family day treatment (MFDT) was the repeated experience of patients who tended to lose weight rapidly after discharge from hospital, particularly if the parents had not been involved in learning to manage the eating routines of their children.

It seemed obvious that, in order to address this, the parents had to be involved much more centrally in the treatment programme, possibly right from the outset. However, parents are not always welcome visitors on adolescent inpatient wards, particularly when staff believe, consciously or unconsciously, that they are to blame for the eating disorder of their child. There are doctors and nurses who think that the eating-disordered young person needs to be separated from her parents and that an inpatient spell would be extremely useful to help her to cut the umbilical cord and individuate. Moreover, parents might also be experienced as interfering with the well-worked-out ward routines. Rivalries between staff and parents are not uncommon, particularly when it comes to who is the 'best' carer, with the young person inevitably getting caught up in such dynamics. The frequently observed rapid weight loss following discharge from the inpatient unit only serves as confirmation that the hospital staff are 'better' than the parents and seem to confirm the failure of the latter. Parents increasingly feel demoralized and sanction their child's readmission to hospital, more keen to have her discharged later rather than sooner, with an ever-increasing risk of the young person becoming a chronic patient. In this situation the MFDT paradigm seemed highly relevant, since it addresses directly the parents' sense of struggling away in isolation and having to rely heavily on the input of nurses, doctors and therapists. Connecting these parents with other parents seemed a logical step to overcome this isolation. Moreover, involving parents directly in the eating issues of their child seemed another step for them to become expert themselves rather than leave that expertise remaining with the nursing and medical staff.

The starting point of the London group was quite different. The team has for a number of years provided both a local and a national specialist outpatient family therapy service for children and adolescents with an eating disorder. The specialist nature of the service is reflected in the nature of the referrals which are often complex and follow previous attempts at treatment elsewhere. Because of the previous failures and the severity of the illness many of the referrals are requests for inpatient treatment. In spite of this, relatively few cases are admitted to the inpatient eating disorder unit (5–10%) even though more than 70% of the referrals meet recommended criteria for inpatient treatment (APA, 2000). However serious the illness, an attempt is nearly always made to engage the family actively in the treatment, to try to avoid hospitalization. Sometimes the referral is at a point when the child has already been admitted to a general paediatric ward. Providing the physical condition can be stabilized and the medical staff agree that it is safe for the child to be away from hospital at least for a few days, it is often possible to use the crisis to engage the family in effective outpatient work without the need for further admission. The idea of developing a MFDT programme was attractive because it offered a more intensive form of treatment than the standard outpatient family therapy, while at the same time was in keeping with the general principle underlying the outpatient treatment that the most effective help in the long term is to help the family to find its own solutions. While it was initially envisaged that the MFDT programme would be needed mainly for the complex referrals that might otherwise require inpatient treatment, the positive experiences (of both the families and the staff) of taking part in the group suggested that it might be beneficial for all the families referred to the service.

In common with the outpatient family therapy model (Dare & Eisler, 1997), MFDT aims to help families rediscover their own resources by exploring ways in which parents can take an active role in their daughter's recovery. At the same time the families are encouraged to explore how the eating disorder and the interactional patterns in the family have become entangled, making it difficult for the family to follow the normal developmental course of the family lifecycle. The sharing of experiences among families and the intensity of the treatment programme makes this a very different experience for the families than outpatient family therapy. The emphasis on helping families to find their own solutions is much more readily apparent in this context and is an aspect of the treatment that the families themselves frequently comment on.

Although each group develops its own unique dynamic, nearly all the groups very quickly establish a sense of identity which generally evolves around discussions of the shared experience of living with anorexia or bulimia and the effect it has on family life. Given that most parents with an anorectic child have a complex set of feelings—including failure, guilt, anger, fear and embarrassment—having the opportunity to meet with other families who experience similar feelings allows for these to be shared. This has strong destigmatizing effects and creates a sense of solidarity. In a multiple-family setting professional staff are in a minority and this contributes to a 'family' rather than 'medical' atmosphere. Being in the presence of other families also has the effect of making the adolescents and their parents feel less central—they are part of a large group and the feeling of being constantly watched and observed by staff is less intense. This process often quite quickly allows the families to 'externalize' the eating disorder as the enemy or intruder in their family life which they have to join forces to overcome.

The presence of other families also highlights the very real differences between them, which illustrates for the families better than any number of statements by staff, that there is no specific family constellation which leads to the development of an eating disorder. This makes it easier for families to start making comparisons, for example, how other parents handle the food refusal of their teenager—as much as young persons cannot help comparing their own parents' responses to those of other eating-disordered teenagers. The effect of all this is that new and different perspectives are introduced, so important since eating-disordered families tend to have distorted self-perceptions while being often very precise and intuitive about other families. Many people find it easier to use feedback from fellow-sufferers than from staff—it seems more 'credible' because these families all have painful direct experiences around food, hospitalization and dieting. Such feedback gets generated during a whole range of different activities throughout the day, both formal and informal. The role of the therapists is that of a catalyst, enabling families to connect with one another and encouraging mutual curiosity and feedback.

The structure of the Dresden and London programmes is quite similar with a mixture of whole family group discussions, parallel meetings of parents and adolescents and occasional meetings with individual families (see Appendix 11.1 for examples of the day structure). Group discussions are interspersed with a variety of activity techniques including role-plays, family sculpting, body image work, symbolic food preparation, creative art work such as clay modelling, etc. (Appendix 11.2 gives examples of a variety of activities used in the programme). At other times individual families will work with a member of staff, e.g. preparing a genogram which they then bring to the whole group for discussion. The ensuing discussions are usually stimulating all round, providing ample opportunity for cross-family discussion. Information giving—sometimes in the form of psychoeducational talks explaining the facts about eating disorders, their physical risks and psychological side-effects, etc., but more often informally, as part of general group discussions—is an important component of the programme.

Lunch is in many respects the central event of the day—at least in the initial stages of MFDT. In London families go shopping to the local supermarket and here major confrontations may ensue between the teenager and her parents as to what is nutritious food. Once the food has been bought, families are in charge of preparing and serving it. The situation is different in Dresden where food is provided by the hospital, with a fixed menu within which there are a few choices. Each family decides what and how much their daughter or son should eat. Needless to say, soon familiar battles will flare up, with the anorectic making out the best possible arguments for not eating anything, and with the parents determined to impose their will. The staff's role is to comment on and, if appropriate, challenge these interactions around food 'in vivo' and to question the parents' tolerance and their willingness to compromise. Sometimes this is videotaped so that parent–child interactions can be viewed and analysed in subsequent video-feedback sessions. Group discussions of the lunch time sessions is a useful time for families to reflect on the 'possibles' and 'impossibles' of managing eating.

Other sessions are also videotaped with the families' permission so that there is opportunity to record interactions which can then be reviewed jointly by families and staff later that day or at some other suitable time. One-way screens can also be used creatively, for instance to facilitate an uninterrupted discussion between the adolescents that the parents can observe (or vice versa).

Since its inception in 1998, the staff of the Dresden Eating Disorder Unit have experimented with a whole range of different lengths and frequencies of the programme (Scholz & Asen, 2001)—from two block days per month, to whole weeks in two-monthly intervals. The team is multidisciplinary, consisting of nurses, occupational therapists, teachers, social workers, psychotherapists, psychologists and psychiatrists. The minimum staff for each multiple-family group is four, with the various different professionals having different functions and tasks, be that direct therapeutic work, observation or supervision. The structure of each day is discussed and decided by the staff, although families also have an opportunity to discuss the programme for the day and their ideas are often used to create a new daily structure.

The London team at the Maudsley has used a less variable time structure, starting generally with a four-day block running from 09.00 to 17.00 hours which is followed by 4–6 one-day follow-ups (the first being within one or two weeks and the rest at longer intervals) and some individual family attendances in between as necessary. The London team makes regular use of family therapy or clinical psychology trainees who are 'assigned' to different families and will, when needed, do specific pieces of work with them such as helping them to complete a genogram, accompanying them on the daily supermarket shopping trip, etc.

Preliminary Findings

To date over 85 eating-disordered teenagers and their families have been seen in MFDT in Dresden and some 40 in London. In Germany both the more traditionally oriented psychiatric practices as well as the more generous funding structure have resulted in there being many more inpatient beds available than in the UK. Clinicians are under pressure to fill these beds as they are otherwise at risk of having these, as well as staff, cut. This means that in effect quite a few adolescents get admitted who would not be considered for admission in the UK. This makes comparisons difficult. Preliminary observations show that the drop-out rate from the MFDT is very low in both centres (2–3%). In Dresden there has been a 30% reduction in admission rates, a 25% shortening of the duration of inpatient treatment for those who have been admitted and a 50% reduction in readmissions (Scholz et al., in preparation). In London, one patient who dropped out of the programme was shortly afterwards admitted to hospital; one patient completed the programme but continued to lose weight and was admitted; and a third patient had been admitted a few weeks before the start of the MFDT programme and was discharged back to the care of her family soon after completing the day programme. We do not as yet have systematic follow-up data to demonstrate the effectiveness of the treatment in bringing about symptomatic improvement. While in many of the adolescents there has been considerable change in weight, stabilization of eating, reduction of bingeing and vomiting, decreased laxative abuse, etc., probably the most immediate and most striking change has been in the way that families have rediscovered a sense of hope and a belief in their own ability to help the patient. This is accompanied by significant reductions in family tension and disputes, and a cooperative and supportive atmosphere and working environment has been created for the young persons and their families.

A user satisfaction survey revealed that, in Dresden, some 93% of parents, 84% of patients and 100% of staff were in favour of a combination of inpatient and multiple day-patient treatment. All parents and 80% of the adolescents regarded working together with other families jointly in a day hospital setting as helpful and desirable (Scholz & Asen, 2001). In London, Lim (2000) found that the MFDT was experienced generally as helpful, with parents in particular commenting on the collaborative nature of the treatment and the value of being able to exchange ideas with other families on how to cope with their common predicament.

CONCLUSIONS

Proponents of different models of psychotherapy are often prone to make exaggerated claims for their own particular therapeutic approach, both in terms of its ability to explain particular disorders and to provide effective treatment. This leads to a polarization between treatment models, that is hardly justified by empirical evidence, which suggests that differences between treatments is generally much less than we would like to believe. For instance, Asay and Lambert (1999), in summarizing many years of psychotherapy research in a variety of disorders, have estimated that, when different psychotherapies are compared, as little as 15% of the outcome variance is accounted for by factors that are unique to a specific mode of psychotherapy, with the rest being divided between individual therapist factors (30%), patient and environmental factors (40%) and a general placebo or expectancy effect (15%). This should not be taken to mean that it does not matter what therapeutic approach we adopt. There are many studies that have shown that while more than one treatment may be effective, there are also treatments that are ineffective. For instance, the study by Fairburn et al. (1991, 1993), which showed a similarity in outcome between cognitive-behaviour therapy (CBT) and interpersonal therapy (IPT), also showed that behaviour therapy was ineffective in the long term, despite initial positive responses to the treatment. Similarly, our own study of outpatients psychotherapies in adult anorexia nervosa (Dare et al., 2001) showed little difference between family therapy, focal psychodynamic therapy and cognitive analytic therapy, but highlighted the greater effectiveness of these specialized treatments in comparison with routine treatment.

The relative similarity in outcome between different treatments has a more important implication, however. Every model of treatment assumes that there is a particular mechanism of change (e.g. cognitive restructuring, changes in interpersonal relationships, etc.) that is specifically targeted by the treatment. The fact that apparently very different treatments can lead to quite similar outcomes suggests that our understanding of the mechanisms which bring about change is limited. When one takes a look at the history of family therapy for eating disorders much of the above is readily applicable. The pioneering work of Selvini Palazzoli (1974), Minuchin (Minuchin et al., 1975, 1978) and others made very strong claims for the approach. While the empirical evidence for the effectiveness of family therapy, particularly for adolescent anorexia nervosa, is strong, the theoretical models from which it derives are almost certainly flawed and our understanding of the way in which family interventions bring about change has required (and will require further) major revision. Our close involvement with the families in the intensive atmosphere of the MFDT programme has highlighted to us the limitations of our understanding of the process of change during effective family interventions. Just as families vary in the way they respond to having a member with an eating disorder so they vary in the way they make use of family treatment interventions. For some families this is an opportunity for the parents to re-stake their claim to parenting and parental authority in a very literal way, by taking very firm charge of the patient's eating until she is out of physical danger. Other families seem to do the same but only very briefly, or in a fairly symbolic way. In yet other families group meetings serve as an opportunity for the adolescent and the parents to start renegotiating the role the parents are going to have not just in relation to eating but in other areas of life as well. What all these solutions seem to have in common is that the family is able to step back and begin to disentangle itself from the way they have been caught up with the symptomatic behaviour and, perhaps even more importantly, that they have regained their belief that they can find a way of overcoming the problem, even though it may take some time.

APPENDIX 11.1

An Example of a Day Programme

9.00–10.15	Each family (separately): 'Plan the year ahead.' Month by month: critical events and threats; planned achievements, goals, and weight of patient. (At a later session the charts are pinned up and each family presents the chart to the whole group.)
10.15–10.45	Morning snack.
10.45–12.15	Dietetic psycho-education.
12.15–1.15	Parents and offspring buy food at supermarket (each family accompanied by a trainee).
1.15–2.30	Family meals: observed and videoed by trainees and family supported by staff.
2.30–3.00	Offspring: spend time with paper plates and food magazines to cut out food to be put on their parents plate: 'What your parents should eat this evening.' Parents: exchanging experiences of 'tricks of the anorexic trade'.

3.00–3.45   Each patient has to feed the meal designed for their parents to
             one of the parents, who has at all costs to resist being fed.
3.45–4.15   Afternoon snack.
4.15–5.00   Public planning of supper and breakfast.

APPENDIX 11.2

Examples of Exercises used in the Programme

Sculpting the family with and without the eating disorder.

Drawing a family tree.

'Externalising' the problem with a 'speaking' anorexia.

Sculpting the family and the future patterns of family life.

Drawing a 'life line' for the next year. (On the one hand, month by month critical events
   and threats on the other achievements goals, and weight of patient month by month.)

Offspring spend time with paper plates and food magazines to cut out food to be put on
   their parents plate: 'What your parents should eat this evening.' Followed by role reversal
   exercise with the person with the eating disorder 'feeding' one of the parents.

'Opposition' activities, e.g. 'fending off', 'tug of war'.

'Control' activities, e.g. 'following hands', 'leading the blind'.

Role-playing specific problems (using alternate voices, changing roles and other psy-
   chodrama techniques).

Clay/Plasticine modelling (the family as I see it and as I would like it to be).

Drawing the family.

Drawing the shape of the person with the eating disorder.

Observing VTR of previous lunchtime.

Body image work (me as I would like to be, as I see me, as you see me; in clay, drawing).

Parents discus what they had learned of the nature of their daughter's problems; what they
   have been able to change and the ways that they had been unable to change; what could
   be different.

Offspring discuss what's the use of being anorexic and are there better things to do with
   life.

Discussion (parents and offspring separately and then together): What would there be to
   deal with if there were to be no anorexia?

Siblings Group: Discussion of what are the advantages and disadvantages of their sister
   being/not being anorexic followed by patient group commenting on what they had heard.

REFERENCES

Agras, W.S., Walsh, B.T., Fairburn, C.G. & Kraemer, H. (2000) A multicenter comparison of cognitive-
   behavioral therapy and interpersonal psychotherapy for bulimia nervosa. *Archives of General
   Psychiatry*, **57**, 459–466.

APA (2000) Practice Guideline for the Treatment of Patients with Eating Disorders (revision). *American Journal of Psychiatry*, **157** (Supplement), 1–39.

Asay, T.P. & Lambert, M.J. (1999) The empirical case for the common factors in therapy: Quantitative
   findings. In M.A. Hubble, B.L. Duncan & D.M. Scott (Eds), *The Heart and Soul of Change. What
   Works in Therapy*. Washington, D.C., American Psychiatric Association.

Asen, K.E., Stein, R., Stevens, A., McHugh, B., Greenwood, J. & Cooklin, A. (1982) A day unit for families. *Journal of Family Therapy*, **4**, 345–358.

Asen, K.E., George, E., Piper, R. & Stevens, A. (1989) A systems approach to child abuse: Management and treatment issues. *Child Abuse and Neglect*, **13**, 45–57.

Asen, K.E. (2002) Developments in multiple family therapy. *Journal of Family Therapy* (in press).

Blitzer, J.R., Rollins, N. & Blackwell, A. (1961) Children who starve themselves: Anorexia nervosa. *Psychosomatic Medicine*, **23**, 369–383.

Bowers, W.A., Evans, K. & Van Cleve, L. (1996) Treatment of adolescent eating disorders. In M.A. Reinecke, F. M. Dattilio, et al. (Eds), *Cognitive Therapy with Children and Adolescents: A Casebook for Clinical Practice*. New York: Guilford Press.

Carr, A. (2000) Evidence-based practice in family therapy and systemic consultation. I: Child-focused problems. *Journal of Family Therapy*, **22**, 29–60.

Cooklin, A., Miller, A. & McHugh, B. (1983) An institution for change: Developing a family day unit. *Family Process*, **22**, 453–468.

Crisp, A.H., Norton, K., Gowers, S., Halek, C., Bowyer, C., Yeldham, D., Levett, G. & Bhat, A. (1991) A controlled study of the effect of therapies aimed at adolescent and family psychopathology in anorexia nervosa. *British Journal of Psychiatry*, **159**, 325–333.

Dare, C. (1983) Family therapy for families containing an anorectic youngster. In *Understanding Anorexia Nervosa and Bulimia*. Report of the IVth Ross Conference on Medical Research. Ohio, Columbus: Ross Laboratories.

Dare, C., Eisler, I., Russell, G.F.M., Treasure, J. & Dodge, E. (2001) Psychological therapies for adult patients with anorexia nervosa: A randomised controlled trial of out-patient treatments. *British Journal of Psychiatry*, **178**, 216–221.

Dare, C. (1997) Chronic eating disorders in therapy: Clinical stories using family systems and psychoanalytic approaches. *Journal of Family Therapy*, **19**, 319–351.

Dare, C. & Eisler, I. (1997) Family therapy for anorexia nervosa. In D.M. Garner & P.E. Garfinkel (Eds), *Handbook of Psychotherapy for Anorexia Nervosa and Bulimia* (2nd edition). New York: Guilford Press.

Dare, C. & Eisler, I. (2000) A multi-family group day treatment programme for adolescent eating disorder. *European Eating Disorders Review*, **8**, 4–18.

Dodge, E., Hodes, M., Eisler, I. & Dare, C. (1995) Family therapy for bulimia nervosa in adolescents: An exploratory study. *Journal of Family Therapy*, **17**, 59–78.

Eisler, I. (1995) Family models of eating disorders. In G.I. Szmukler, C. Dare & J. Treasure (Eds), *Handbook of Eating Disorders: Theory, Treatment and Research*. London: John Wiley & Sons.

Eisler, I., Dare, C., Russell, G.F.M., Szmukler, G.I., le Grange, D. & Dodge, E. (1997) Family and individual therapy in anorexia nervosa. A 5-year follow-up. *Archives of General Psychiatry*, **54**, 1025–1030.

Eisler, I., Dare, C., Hodes, M., Russell, G.F.M., Dodge, E. & le Grange, D. (2000) Family therapy for adolescent anorexia nervosa: The results of a controlled comparison of two family interventions. *Journal of Child Psychology and Psychiatry*, **41**, 727–736.

Fairburn, C.G., Jones, R., Peveler, R.C., Carr, S.J., Solomon, R.A., O'Conner, M.E., Burton, J. & Hope, R.A. (1991) Three psychological treatments for bulimia nervosa. *Archives of General Psychiatry*, **48**, 463–469.

Fairburn, C.G., Jones, R., Peveler, R.C., Hope, R.A. & O'Conner, M.E. (1993) Psychotherapy and bulimia nervosa: The longer-term effects of interpersonal psychotherapy, behavior therapy and cognitive behavior therapy. *Archives of General Psychiatry*, **50**, 419–428.

Fishman, H.C. (1996) Structural family therapy. In J. Werne (Ed.), *Treating Eating Disorders*. San Francisco: Jossey-Bass Inc.

Garner, D.M. (1994) Bulimia nervosa. In C.G. Last & M. Hersen (Eds), *Adult Behavior Therapy Casebook*. New York: Plenum Press.

Geist, R., Heineman, M., Stephens, D., Davis, R. & Katzman, D.K. (2000) Comparison of family therapy and family group psychoeducation in adolescents with anorexia nervosa. *Canadian Journal of Psychiatry*, **45**, 173–178.

Goetz, P.L., Succop, R.A., Reinhart, J.B. & Miller, A. (1977) Anorexia in children: A follow-up study. *American Journal of Orthopsychiatry*, **47**, 597–603.

Gonsalez, S., Steinglass, P. & Reiss, D. (1989) Putting the illness in its place: Discussion groups for families with chronic medical illnesses. *Family Process*, **28**, 69–87.

Hall, A. & Crisp, A.H. (1987) Brief psychotherapy in the treatment of anorexia nervosa. Outcome at one year. *British Journal of Psychiatry*, **151**, 185–191.

Herscovici, C.R. & Bay, L. (1996) Favourable outcome for anorexia nervosa patients treated in Argentina with a family approach. *Eating Disorders: the Journal of Treatment and Prevention*, **4**, 59–66.

Jeammet, P. and Chabert, C. (1998) A psychoanalytic approach to eating disorders: The role of dependency. In A.H. Esman (Ed.), *Adolescent Psychiatry: Developmental and Clinical Studies*, Vol. 22. *Annals of the American Society for Adolescent Psychiatry*. Hillsdale: The Analytic Press, Inc.

Johnson, S.M., Maddeaux, C. & Blouin, J. (1998) Emotionally focused family therapy for bulimia: Changing attachment patterns. *Psychotherapy*, **35**, 238–247.

Kaufman, E. & Kaufman, P. (1979) Multiple family therapy with drug abusers. In E. Kaufman & P. Kaufman (Eds), *Family Therapy of Drug and Alcohol Abuse*. New York: Gardner.

Laqueur, H.P. (1972) Mechanisms of change in multiple family therapy. In C.J. Sager & H.S. Kaplan (Eds), *Progress in Group and Family Therapy*. New York: Bruner/Mazel.

Laqueur, H.P. (1973) Multiple family therapy: Questions and answers. In D. Bloch (Ed.), *Techniques of Family Psychotherapy*. New York: Grune & Stratton.

Laqueur, H.P., La Burt, H.A. & Morong, E. (1964) Multiple family therapy: Further developments. *International Journal of Social Psychiatry*, **10**, 69–80.

Le Grange, D., Eisler, I., Dare, C. & Russell, G.F.M. (1992) Evaluation of family therapy in anorexia nervosa: A pilot study. *International Journal of Eating Disorder*, **12**, 347–357.

Lesser, L.I., Ashenden, B.J., Debuskey, M. & Eisenberg, L. (1960) Anorexia nervosa in children. *American Journal of Orthopsychiatry*, **30**, 572–580.

Lim, C. (2000) *A pilot study of families' experiences of a multi-family group day treatment programme*. MSc Dissertation. Institute of Psychiatry, Kings College, University of London.

Luborsky, L., Singer, B. & Luborsky, L. (1975) Comparative studies of psychotherapies: Is it true that 'Everybody has one and all must have prizes?' *Archives of General Psychiatry*, **32**, 995–1008.

Martin, F.E. (1985) The treatment and outcome of anorexia nervosa in adolescents: A prospective study and five year follow-up. *Journal of Psychiatric Research*, **19**, 509–514.

Mayer, R.D. (1994) *Family therapy in the treatment of eating disorders in general practice*. MSc Dissertation, Birkbeck College, University of London.

Minuchin, S., Baker, L., Rosman, B.L., Liebman, R., Millman, L. & Todd, T.C. (1975) A conceptual model of psychosomatic illness in childhood. *Archives of General Psychiatry*, **32**, 1031–1038.

Minuchin, S., Rosman, B.L. & Baker, L. (1978) *Psychosomatic Families: Anorexia Nervosa in Context*. Cambridge, MA: Harvard University Press.

Murburg, M., Price, L. & Jalali, B. (1988) Huntington's disease: therapy strategies. *Family Systems Medicine*, **6**, 290–303.

Robin, A.L., Siegel, P.T. & Moye, A. (1995) Family versus individual therapy for anorexia: Impact on family conflict. *International Journal of Eating Disorders*, **4**, 313–322.

Robin, A.L., Gilroy, M. & Dennis, A.B. (1998) Treatment of eating disorders in children and adolescents. *Clinical Psychology Review*, **18**, 421–466.

Robin, A.L., Siegel, P.T., Moye, A.W. Gilroy, M., Dennis, A.B. & Sikand A. (1999) A controlled comparison of family versus individual therapy for adolescents with anorexia nervosa. *Journal of the American Academy of Child and Adolescent Psychiatry*, **38**, 1482–1489.

Russell, G.F.M., Szmukler, G.I., Dare, C. & Eisler, I. (1987) An evaluation of family therapy in anorexia nervosa and bulimia nervosa. *Archives of General Psychiatry*, **44**, 1047–1056.

Sargent, J., Liebman, R. & Silver, M. (1985) Family therapy for anorexia nervosa. In Garner. D.M. & Garfinkel, P.E. (Eds), *Handbook of Psychotherapy for Anorexia Nervosa and Bulimia*. New York: Guilford Press.

Scholz, M. & Asen, K.E. (2001) Multiple family therapy with eating disordered adolescents. *European Eating Disorders Review*, **9**, 33–42.

Schwartz, R.C., Barrett, M.J. & Saba, G. (1985) Family therapy for bulimia. In D.M. Garner and P.E. Garfinkel (Eds), *Handbook of Psychotherapy for Anorexia Nervosa and Bulimia*. New York: Guilford Press.

Selvini Palazzoli, M. (1974) *Self Starvation: From the Intrapsychic to the Transpersonal Approach to Anorexia Nervosa*. London: Chaucer Publishing.

Slagerman, M. & Yager, J. (1989) Multiple family group treatment for eating disorders: a short term program. *Psychiatric Medicine*, **7**, 269–283.

Squire-Dehouck, B. (1993) *Evaluation of conjoint family therapy versus family counselling in adolescent anorexia nervosa patients: A two year follow-up study*. Unpublished MSc Dissertation, Institute of Psychiatry, University of London.

Steinglass, P. (1998) Multiple family discussion groups for patients with chronic medical illness. *Families, Systems and Health*, **16**, 55–70.

Steinglass, P., Bennett, L.A., Wolin, S.J. & Reiss, D. (1987) *The Alcoholic Family*. New York: Basic Books.

Stierlin, H. & Weber, G. (1987) Anorexia nervosa: Lessons from a follow-up study. *Family Systems Medicine*, **7**, 120–157.

Stierlin, H. & Weber, G. (1989) *Unlocking the Family Door*. New York: Brunner/Mazel.

Strelnick, A.H.J. (1977) Multiple family group therapy: A review of the literature. *Family Process*, **16**, 307–325.

Szmukler, G.I., Eisler, I., Russell, G.F.M. & Dare, C. (1985) Parental 'Expressed Emotion', anorexia nervosa and dropping out of treatment. *British Journal of Psychiatry*, **147**, 265–271.

Warren, W. (1968) A study of anorexia nervosa in young girls. *Journal of Child Psychology and Psychiatry*, **9**, 27–40.

Wilson, G.T. & Fairburn, C.G. (1998) Treatments for eating disorders. In P.E. Nathan & J.M. Gorman (Eds), *A Guide to Treatments that Work*. New York: Oxford University Press.

Wooley, S. & Lewis, K. (1987) Multi-family therapy within an intensive treatment program for bulimia. In J. Harkaway (Ed.), *Eating Disorders: The Family Therapy Collections*, **20**. Rockville: Aspen Publ.

CHAPTER 12

Drug Treatments

Tijs Bruna
GGZ Zoetermeer, The Netherlands
and
Jaap Fogteloo
*Department of General Internal Medicine, Leiden University Medical Centre,
Leiden, The Netherlands*

INTRODUCTION

Pharmacotherapy is not the first choice of treatment in eating disorders. The first focus of attention is the physical health of the patient, whether she is suffering from anorexia nervosa, bulimia nervosa, binge eating disorder or other eating disorders. Improvement of the physical condition alone is never sufficient for complete recovery. The dysfunctional attitudes and cognitions towards food, body weight and body size also need to be addressed in treatment. Attention should also be focused on factors contributing to or maintaining the eating disorder.

Psychotherapy is commonly recognised as the treatment of first choice. Individual and family therapy have proved to be effective in the treatment of anorexia nervosa (for a review see van Furth, 1998). Cognitive-behavioural therapy and interpersonal psychotherapy are effective treatment methods in bulimia nervosa and binge eating disorder (for a review see Schmidt, 1998; Agras, 1997; see also Chapters 8 and 9 in this volume). In the treatment of obesity the results of psychotherapy are inconclusive and short lived.

For anorexia nervosa it is striking that, although the treatment results are moderate, relatively few controlled trials with medication have been conducted. New developments within the field of pharmacotherapy make it likely that the number of trials will increase in the coming years. The treatment of bulimia nervosa, with psychotherapy and/or medication, has been studied quite extensively. The results are encouraging but, as with anorexia nervosa, pharmacotherapy is not the first option in treatment. Much is still unknown about the way in which specific drugs contribute to the cessation of bingeing. The quest for new medication which is both more specific and more effective is ongoing and promising. Although binge eating disorder is formally not yet acknowledged as a discrete disorder and questions have been raised about the severity of the disorder (Fairburn et al., 2000), medication has proved to contribute to attaining abstinence of bingeing. In the treatment of obesity the long-term results of pharmacotherapy have been disappointing. However, new developments suggest a more promising role for medication in the treatment of obesity.

This chapter will provide an update of the research (RCTs) and clinical implications in the field of pharmacotherapy of eating disorders. Results of clinical trials and clinical recommendations will be described per DSM-IV disorder and separately for obesity. As obesity is considered a somatic (as opposed to mental) disorder, a short introduction will be dedicated to its therapy in general. In every section attention will be paid to new and promising developments.

ANOREXIA NERVOSA

Research

In the only systematic review of the treatment of anorexia nervosa (Treasure & Schmidt, 2001) authors found no evidence for the improvement of outcome by pharmacotherapy. Medication (neuroleptics, tricyclic antidepressants, cyproheptadine, cisapride) may even be harmful by increasing the sometimes already prolonged QT interval. This does not mean that there is completely no role for pharmacotherapy in the treatment of anorexia nervosa. Although anorexia nervosa has been acknowledged as a discrete disorder for a long time, the number of medication trials has been quite limited. The prevalence of the disease is low, the number of patients that seek help is small, and ethical dilemmas may emerge when doing scientific research with a population with a poor physical health (Mayer & Walsh, 1998; van Furth, 1998).

Although the disturbance in the perception of body shape and the disturbance in thinking about food and weight are akin to psychotic phenomenology, only two double-blind placebo controlled trials with antipsychotic medication have been carried out (Vandereycken & Pierloot, 1982; Vandereycken, 1984). These were two cross-over trials with a modest number of inpatients (18 in both trials) and a short-term perspective (3-week periods) with pimozide and sulpiride respectively. The results not only showed an initial beneficial effect on daily weight gain especially in the first treatment period, but also that the changes in eating behaviour and in attitude towards the body were limited. The authors concluded that their general inpatient treatment method appeared to be effective enough to restore body weight in patients with anorexia nervosa and there was no additional value in adding this type of medication. No controlled trials with antipsychotic medication have been published since.

In the 1980s there was interest in the efficacy of antidepressants, but research came to a halt because of the disappointing results. The selective serotonin reuptake inhibitors (SSRIs) are more tolerated and are relatively safe, and open trials were encouraging. Many patients with anorexia nervosa show features of affective disorders and/or of anxiety disorders and a proportion fulfil the full diagnostic criteria for affective disorder (Halmi, 1995). It is often difficult to determine if these symptoms precede or follow the onset.

Serotonin has a role in the regulation of hunger and satiety. There are signs that serotonin activity is altered in eating disorders, not only during the active phase of the disease, but also after weight restoration and symptom remission. Elevated concentrations of 5-hydroxyindoleacetic acid (5-HIAA), the metabolite of serotonin have been found in the cerebrospinal fluid, suggesting that altered serotonin activity is a trait-related characteristic of anorexia nervosa (Kaye et al., 1991, 2001). Abnormal 5HT function is also consistent with traits as behavioural inhibition, high harm avoidance and perfectionism often seen in patients after recovery from anorexia nervosa.

Some of the older antidepressant drugs have been studied in RCTs. Clomipramine (50 mg daily) did not lead to a faster body weight gain than placebo in a double-blind RCT with 16 inpatients (Lacey & Crisp, 1980). Amitriptyline (Biederman et al., 1985) prescribed up to a maximal daily dose of 175 mg in a small mixed in- and outpatient sample did not show significantly better results in comparison to placebo on any of the outcome measures. In a short-term study (Halmi et al., 1986), inpatients were treated with amitriptyline up to 160 mg daily. The patients who achieved target weight and who received amitriptyline gained weight faster than the patients who received placebo (32 days in comparison to 45 days to target weight). There was no significant effect on treatment efficiency. In the only controlled trial with lithium carbonate (Gross et al., 1981), a significant positive result in weight gain was achieved in the last two weeks of the 4-week trial ($N = 16$). This finding was never replicated, probably because of the increased risk of intoxication with lithium in this population.

In a 7-week study of fluoxetine at a target daily dose of 60 mg in 31 women with anorexia nervosa no significant added benefit to the inpatient treatment was found (Attia et al., 1998). Nevertheless, interesting research has been done by Kaye et al. who demonstrated that there may be a role for fluoxetine in the prevention of relapse in patients who regained weight. Following inpatient weight restoration, 10 of 16 (63%) subjects on fluoxetine remained well over a one-year outpatient follow-up period, whereas only 3 of 19 (16%) remained well on placebo (Kaye et al., 2001). Fluoxetine was associated with maintaining a healthy body weight and with a significant reduction in obsessions and ritualistic preoccupations. These contradictory results may be explained because of the differing nutritional status of the two patient groups. In the starved state there may be reduced synaptic 5-HT, due to reduced availability of tryptophan, the essential amino-acid precursor of serotonin.

Cyproheptadine, a serotonin antagonist, prescribed as an anti-allergic medicine with weight gain as a side-effect, showed some positive results in double-blind RCTs (Vigerski & Loriaux, 1977; Goldberg et al., 1979), although the effect on decreasing the number of days to achieve a normal body weight was marginal (Halmi et al., 1986). No significant differences in weight gain were found. Cisapride, a drug that is prescribed for stomach complaints, did not perform better than placebo in one small RCT (Szmukler et al., 1995). In many countries this drug has now been withdrawn because of the potential to cause arrythmias.

Treatment

At present, a review of the results of RCTs does not justify the prescription of drugs in uncomplicated anorexia nervosa. The benefits do not outweight the harms. An intervention with medication in the starting phase of the disorder, may further be conflicting with therapeutic strategies. The use of medication in this phase may undermine the motivational process. Pharmacotherapy should be reserved for cases in which comorbidity interferes with the development of the therapeutic process, in cases of treatment resistance and perhaps in cases in which relapse is likely.

There is some evidence to suggest that the depressive disorder seen in patients with a very low weight is not easily affected by antidepressants (Ferguson et al., 1999). The mild depressive disorder that develops in the process of weight gain can often be addressed best in psychotherapy. If the low mood is not lifted or the depression becomes more severe, the prescription of antidepressant medication should be considered. It seems reasonable to choose a SSRI given the suggested role of serotonin in the pathophysiology of eating disorders. Furthermore, the clinical picture often shows features of anxiety disorders, on which SSRIs often have a favourable effect. The same arguments for prescribing a SSRI are valid in cases of anxiety disorders that interfere with the process of recovery. If an obsessive-compulsive disorder emerges or persists after weight restoration, antidepressants should also be considered. Because of its side-effect profile and the experience in the treatment of eating disorders (although limited in anorexia nervosa) Mayer and Walsh (1998) recommend fluoxetine.

The clinical assessment of a patient sometimes warrants the prescription of antipsychotic medication. The patient who, in a phase of weight restoration, increasingly reports chaotic thinking, cannot keep her thoughts ordered and increasingly needs rituals and/or compulsions to prevent her from becoming psychotic, can react positively to (low dose) antipsychotics. The relatively new atypical antipsychotics may be of value. Promising results in treatment-resistant patients were described in case studies (La Via et al., 2000) and open label trials are being conducted. It is not yet clear whether there really is a substantial group of patients with anorexia nervosa that can profit from treatment with the atypical antipsychotics, nor is it clear what subgroup this would be. The case studies suggest that there may be a role for these drugs in treatment-resistant patients. A hypothesis about the mode of action of these drugs in patients with anorexia nervosa has not yet been proposed. Do they effect the patient's cognitions, do they reduce the anxiety surrounding weight gain or is the side-effect (weight gain) the main effect? Neither the duration nor the dosage of this new medication have been established in patients with anorexia nervosa, and double-blind placebo controlled trials are needed to provide answers to these unresolved questions. For the time being atypical antipsychotics should be prescribed with reserve, and only in treatment-resistant patients and/or if a psychosis is developing.

BULIMIA NERVOSA

Research

In a recent systematic review (Hay & Bacaltchuk, 2001) the authors found that antidepressants reduce bulimic symptoms in the short term. They found insufficient evidence about the persistence of these effects or about the effects of different classes of antidepressants.

Although bulimia nervosa was only recognised as a discrete disorder in the late 1970s, many controlled psychotherapeutic and pharmacotherapeutic studies have been carried out. Bulimia nervosa is far more prevalent than anorexia nervosa (for a review see van Hoeken et al., 1998) and in general causes less metabolic disturbances (Mayer & Walsh, 1998).

The fact that endogenous opiates play a role in the hypothalamic regulation of hunger and satiety led to a limited number of trials with opiate antagonists. The results were inconsistent (de Zwaan & Mitchell, 1992; Marrazzi et al., 1995) and the risk/benefit ratio is considered unprofitable.

Far more controlled trials tested the efficacy of different types of antidepressant medication. Indeed, many patients with bulimia nervosa show features of a depression or even meet the criteria for a major depression (Halmi, 1995). Furthermore, it has been demonstrated that serotonin function has been disordered in bulimia nervosa, although it is not yet clear whether these psychobiological alterations are trait-related and contribute to the pathogenesis or reflect a state-related abnormality (Kaye et al., 1998; Smith et al., 1999; Wolfe et al., 2000).

All sorts of antidepressant medication (tricyclics, selective serotonin reuptake inhibitors (SSRIs), a monoamineoxidase inhibitor, mianserin and trazodon) have been tried out in double-blind placebo-controlled trials. All of these studies consistently showed a positive effect of the antidepressant medication in comparison to placebo in decreasing the frequency of the binges and the frequency of vomiting. A retrospective analysis of two large multi-centre studies with fluoxetine indicated that the reduction of bulimia-symptoms occurred independently of the presence of depressive symptoms (Goldstein et al., 1999). In earlier (smaller) studies, results in this respect were conflicting (Pope et al., 1983; Walsh et al., 1988). In some studies no significant reduction in depression scores could be found, possibly as a result of low baseline scores (Barlow et al., 1988; Walsh et al., 1991).

However, the results of these trials with antidepressant medication in bulimia nervosa should be put in perspective. Although between 30% and 91% of the patients experience a reduction in the frequency of the binges in the different studies, only 4% to 35%, with one exception of 68%, experience complete remission (Crow & Mitchell, 1994). Moreover, most studies lack a long-term follow-up (most studies last only 6-8 weeks, sometimes 16 weeks). A substantial proportion of the patients relapse despite continuation of the medication (Walsh et al., 1991; Agras et al., 1997). More controlled research is needed to make firm conclusions on the subject of relapse and medication.

Fluoxetine is the most researched drug in the treatment of bulimia nervosa (Fluoxetine Bulimia Nervosa Collaborative Study Group, 1992; Goldstein et al., 1995). It also proved to be effective in a (small) group of patients that didn't respond to cognitive-behavioural or interpersonal psychotherapy (Walsh et al., 2000).

In patients with bulimia nervosa, fluoxetine is effective in a daily dose of 60 mg, which is three times the advised dose in depressive disorders. The high dose and the fact that it is effective regardless of the occurrence of a comorbid depression raises questions about the mode of action, which probably differs from that in depression. Another interesting finding which supports the idea that fluoxetine acts differently to its role in depression is the possible effect of ondansetron on bulimic symptoms. A placebo-controlled randomised, double-blind trial with ondansetron—a peripherally active antagonist of the serotonin receptor 5-HT3 marketed for prevention of vagally mediated emesis caused by chemotherapy—led to a 50% decrease in binge/purge episodes after 4 weeks in patients with severe bulimia nervosa (Faris et al., 2000). Also, there was an increase in the number of normal meals. These results suggest a normalisation of the physiological mechanisms controlling meal termination and satiety, mainly vagally mediated functions. They point also to the possibility of affecting bulimia nervosa through a peripheral point of action.

As for the use in clinical practice, certainly more trials of ondansetron are needed, and certainly more knowledge about the pathophysiological mechanisms in bulimia nervosa before it should be prescribed routinely. Apart from that, cost-effectiveness should be looked at, considering the present price.

Treatment

Most experts and users in the field of eating disorders prefer psychotherapy (CBT or IPT) as their treatment of first choice in bulimia nervosa (Walsh et al., 1997, 2000), because of the superior short- and long-term results, the minimal potential to cause harm, and the better acceptability.

There are some indications that adding psychiatric drugs to a psychotherapeutic treatment leads to a small improvement in the results of treatment (Agras, 1997). On the other hand, adding cognitive-behavioural therapy to treatment with antidepressants also seems to be of value (Agras, 1997). However, it is not yet clear what patient-factors are important in the decision to apply one or the other treatment, or a combination of both.

In everyday clinical practice, such factors as the availability of expertise in psychotherapy with eating disorders and the motivation and preference of the patient will play a role in making a choice. Medication should be considered in patients who do not respond to psychotherapy and in patients with psychiatric comorbidity that prevents improvement in bulimia nervosa. Antidepressant medication should be prescribed in these cases, and it is reasonable to start with fluoxetine at 60 mg daily, given the two large trials that had a beneficial outcome. Moreover, it is generally well tolerated with limited side-effects. Only one controlled trial with another SSRI has been conducted and the negative outcome to fluvoxamine was merely alluded to in a review (Freeman, 1998).

In case of non-response to medication a switch to another drug can be helpful. This was suggested in one study in which desipramine was followed by fluoxetine (Walsh et al., 1997). Compared to a previous study in the same centre, the average binge frequency reduced from 69% to 47%.

In the near future there may be a role for peripherally active agents like ondansetron. For the time being prescribing ondansetron is not warranted in view of the limited evidence and the overall expense.

BINGE EATING DISORDER

Research

In 1994 research criteria for Binge Eating Disorder (BED) were described in Appendix B of DSM-IV (APA, 1994). These criteria made it possible to carry out treatment studies (de Zwaan, 2001).

No systematic reviews of treatment studies have been published. Four double-blind placebo-controlled trials involving medication were done. In three, SSRIs were prescribed; in one, dexfenfluramine, a serotonin agonist.

Fenfluramine was taken off the market in many countries because of the serious side effects. In the controlled trial dexfenfluramine performed better than placebo in reducing the frequency of binge episodes in overweight women with binge eating disorder, but no effect was left after follow-up and it did not lead to weight loss (Stunkard et al., 1996).

Fluoxetine (60 mg daily) improved dietary intake in overweight women with and without BED, but it did not affect their binge frequency or mood (Greeno & Wing, 1996).

Fluvoxamine, to a maximum of 300 mg daily, reduced body weight and the frequency of binges significantly better than placebo in a multicentre trial (Hudson et al., 1998).

The intent-to-treat-analysis did not reveal a significant difference in the level of response. There were significantly more drop-outs because of adverse medical events in the group with the active medication. These events included nausea, sedation and lightheadedness. Compared with the placebo group, a significantly greater percentage of fluvoxamine-treated patients experienced insomnia, nausea and abnormal dreams. No serious medical events were observed.

Sertraline, to a maximum of 200 mg/day, was significantly more effective than placebo in decreasing the frequency of binges, clinical global severity and the body mass index in a 6-week trial with 34 BED subjects (McElroy et al., 2000). Eight patients withdrew for several reasons. No patients withdrew because of an adverse medical event. More sertraline-treated patients ($N = 7$) than patients given placebo ($N = 1$) experienced insomnia. Among the patients who completed the study sertraline was associated with a higher response level than placebo, but the difference did not reach statistical significance.

Treatment

There are clear indications that SSRIs decrease binge-eating symptoms in patients with BED, at least in the short term. Given the remarkably high response on placebo in the first week(s) of the three studies, the lack of a long-term follow-up, the possible mild course of the disorder (Fairburn et al., 2000) and the positive results of other kind of treatments, there only seems to be a modest role for drugs in the therapy of binge eating disorder. Cognitive-behavioural therapy, also in self-help format, and interpersonal therapy have proved to be effective, even at follow-up (Carter & Fairburn, 1998; de Zwaan, 2001).

Medication should be considered in patients with resistance to these treatments or in patients with serious comorbidity. Outcome measures used in the studies with SSRIs were different and none of the studies was replicated. It is not even clear what the primary outcome should be. A lot of patients with BED suffer mainly because of their overweight, but the long-term effects of medication on weight are not known. At present it is not possible to give a clear guideline on what medication should be prescribed for patients with BED.

OBESITY

Introduction

The main therapeutic intervention for patients with obesity is to make sure that their daily energy intake is less than their total energy expenditure. This always implies an energy-restricted diet and, if possible, an increase in the energy expenditure. However, an energy-restricted diet is difficult to maintain and induces a decrease in resting energy expenditure, thus diminishing the efficacy of the diet. As a consequence, there is often a demand from patients for the supplementation of their dietary therapy with medication. More generally, at the local health food store, a large and increasing selection of herbs is available for the treatment of obesity.

Unfortunately, the choice of regular medication is limited, and the efficacy is low. In combination with an energy-restricted diet, all available medication when compared to placebo, results in an additional weight loss of 4 kg after six months or one year of treatment. Also, when medication is discontinued, most patients return to their original weight (NIH Conference, 1993; Pi-Sunyer, 1993). However, an additional weight loss of 4 kg would mean a significant risk reduction in the complications of obesity, such as cardiovascular disease or type II diabetes. For example, a weight loss of 10% significantly improves the glycemic control in type II diabetes (Wing et al., 1987), and for every kilogram lost, blood pressure decreases by 1 mmHg and LDL cholesterol by 1% (Schotte, 1990; Wolf & Grundy, 1983). Cosmetically this additional weight loss is not significant, so the additional weight loss is only advantageous for those patients who are at risk of the complications of obesity and for whom every kilogram of weight loss is significant: i.e. patients with a body mass index >27 kg/m^2 and additional risk factors or patient with a body mass index > 30 kg/m^2.

There are several ways in which medication, whether or not in combination with an energy-restricted diet, could reduce body weight. Medication could (1) reduce energy intake, (2) reduce the absorption of nutrients in the gastrointestinal tract or (3) increase the (total) energy expenditure. Theoretically, stimulation of the local fat mobilisation or decreasing the synthesis of triglycerides could also lead to weight loss. The first three possibilities were tested in research, the fourth possibility is only a hypothesis. Perhaps new developments will arise from the research with leptin, the hormone produced by fat cells.

Research

The drugs in the group that reduces energy intake also decrease appetite. Although there are differences in the mechanisms in which they reduce appetite, these differences are not clinically relevant. Because of their side-effects most of these medications are no longer legally available. Amphetamines are effective; in studies they show an additional weight loss when compared to placebo. The main side-effect is their stimulating effect, but they also have addictive properties (Bray, 1993), and for this reason amphetamines are not legally prescribed. Related to amphetamines are the phenylethylamines, which are not available in every country in Europe. Mazindol is comparable to the amphetamines with regards to effects and side-effects, but their efficacy is limited and no recent clinical studies are available.

Another important and, until 1997 (especially in the USA), frequently prescribed group are the serotonin releasers and reuptake inhibitors. The increase in the level of serotonin stimulates receptors in the paraventricular nucleus of the hypothalamus, and so reduces appetite. Well-known compounds are the fenfluramines and sibutramine. Fluoxetine in higher dosages also reduces appetite. The fenfluramines (fenfluramine and dexfenfluramine) were withdrawn from the market in 1997 because of serious side-effects. The first side-effect that became apparent was pulmonary hypertension (Abenhaim et al., 1996) but it was the second side-effect, the increase in the incidence of cardiac valve abnormalities, that finally led to the withdrawal of fenfluramines. Although the absolute risk was low, their limited efficacy was sufficient reason to withdraw them from the market (Devereux, 1998; Jick et al., 1998).

Sibutramine decreases appetite by inhibition of the reuptake of serotonin but it also slightly decreases the reuptake of noradrenalin (norepinephrin). The latter mechanism slightly increases the resting energy expenditure, and in combination with an energy-restricted diet, sibutramine can result in an additional weight loss of 4.8–6.1 kg (depending on the dosage used). The side-effects of pulmonary hypertension or cardiac valve abnormalities were not seen in the clinical studies. An important side-effect is hypertension, probably caused by the slight adrenergic effect of sibutramine (Lean, 1997). With a dosage of 15 mg. daily the diastolic blood pressure rises with an average of 2 mmHg.

In a higher dosage (60 mg daily) fluoxetine can reduce appetite. In at least one study fluoxetine was shown, as compared to placebo, to give an additional weight loss of 3.6 kg, but other studies have failed to demonstrate the effect of fluoxetine on body weight (Wise, 1992). Fluoxetine is not registered for the treatment of obesity.

Another approach to achieving weight loss is to influence the absorption of nutrients in the gastrointestinal tract and so to reduce the daily energy intake. Paraffin, for example, has been tried for a long time; a more recent development is the non-absorbent fat-substitute Olean®. Olean® is available in the USA but not in Europe. Olean® may only be used in snacks.

Orlistat is a relatively new drug that specifically inhibits the enzyme pancreatic lipase. Orlistat reduces the total dietary fat absorption by 30%. In studies orlistat proved to give an additional weight loss of 3.1% (Hill et al., 1999). The side-effects, especially if the dietary compliance to fat restriction is poor, are steatorrhoea and a decrease in the absorption of fat-soluble vitamins. In the case of longer usage or frequent diarrhoea it is advised to substitute the fat-soluble vitamins. In the first clinical studies with orlistat a higher incidence of mamma carcinoma was seen; this could not be confirmed by additional studies and was caused by a statistical artefact. Orlistat is registered in Europe but not all health insurance companies reimburse the use of this drug.

Another possibility for the reduction of body weight is by medically inducing an increase in total energy expenditure. Many well-known compounds (thyroxin, caffeine or ephedrine) do in fact increase the total energy expenditure but are not acceptable as prescription drugs because of their (mainly cardiac) side-effects or addictive properties. The promising results with β_3 agonists in animal studies, showed a poor efficacy and serious side-effects in studies with humans (Carruba et al., 1998).

A recent development is the research into leptin as a possible therapy for obesity. Leptin is produced by white fat cells and passes the blood brain barrier by active transport. The ventro median nucleus of the hypothalamus has leptin receptors. Stimulation of these receptors leads to inhibition of neuro peptide Y and so decreases appetite and increases resting energy expenditure. In all genetic normal mammals, including humans, there is a strong correlation between the body mass index (or total body fat) and serum leptin levels. But with an increase in total body fat the intracerebral leptin levels rise relatively less and the ratio between intracerebral and serum leptin levels decreases (Zhang et al., 1994; Considine et al., 1996). Possibly the transport of leptin over the blood brain barrier is saturable and this might be the explanation for the resistance for higher leptin levels in obese subjects. Exogenous leptin substitution leads to a dramatic increase in serum leptin levels and possibly to an increase in intracerebral levels. This increase might overcome the leptin resistance and subsequently lead to weight loss. However, there is another physiological mechanism which could explain the way in which leptin substitution can lead to weight loss. As a response to fasting or energy restriction, leptin levels drop sharply. This decrease might be the cause of the well-known neuro-endocrine response on fasting. This response results in the stimulation of the appetite and a decrease in resting energy expenditure. In this setting exogenous leptin substitution could prevent the neuro-endocrine response. The appetite will not be stimulated and the resting energy expenditure will remain stable. This could improve dietary compliance and also the efficacy of an energy-restricted diet. The activity of leptin substitution seems to be dose dependent. Leptin needs to be administered by subcutaneous injection; the main side-effect is erythema of the injection site. Leptin is as yet only available for research purposes. Randomised double-blind placebo-controlled trials (Heymsfield et al., 1999; Huckshorn et al., 2000) have not (yet) given positive answers to the questions on the usefulness of leptin in the treatment of obesity.

Treatment

Because of the limited efficacy and the side-effects of the current medication, the pharmacotherapy of obesity is problematic. On the other hand, many patients ask for medication as they have often had poor results with energy-restricted diets. Also they are often frustrated by the quick return to their original body weight after the period of dieting is finished. Because of this, but also because of the reports on television and internet (there are over 800 websites on orlistat), patients often have great expectations of medication. The current medication has proved to give no more than an additional weight loss of 4 kg. This will not result in the often desired cosmetic effect, so patients wanting to lose weight purely for cosmetic reasons will have little success through medication. However, this additional 4 kg can be significant for the reduction of health risks associated with obesity.

If a reduction of the total alimentary fat intake is indicated (e.g. if the daily intake is high) treatment with orlistat can be considered, but to prevent steatorrhoea, good compliance to the fat restriction is essential.

Sibutramine is effective, but the side-effect of hypertension is a potential problem. At this moment it is not yet clear if there will be a role for leptin in the treatment of obesity.

The perfect drug for obesity does not yet exist. Ideally it should combine a good therapeutic effect (preferably more weight loss than the average additional 4 kg) with minimal side-effects. Treatment of obesity primarily means a reduction of the (obesity associated) risks of cardiovascular disease or type II diabetes. From this perspective, hypertension as a side-effect of drug treatment is a potential problem.

Like type II diabetes, obesity is a chronic metabolic disease. Without additional therapy, weight loss is often followed by a subsequent weight gain. This implies that the ideal drug for obesity has to be suitable for chronic (possible lifelong) treatment.

REFERENCES

Abenhaim, L., Moride, Y.,Brenot, F., Rich, S., Benichou, J., Kurz, X., Higenbottam, T., Oakley, C., Wouters, E., Aubier, M., Simonneau, G. & Begaud, B. (1996) Appetite-suppressant drugs and the risk of primary pulmonary hypertension. *New England Journal of Medicine*, **335**, 609–616.

APA (1994) *Diagnostic and statistic manual of mental disorders.* (4th edition) Washington, D.C.: American Psychiatric Association.

Agras, W.S. (1997) Pharmacotherapy of bulimia nervosa and binge eating disorder: Longer-term outcomes. *Psychopharmacology Bulletin*, **33** (3), 433–436.

Attia, E., Haiman, C., Walsh, B.T. & Flatter, S.R. (1998) Does fluoxetine augment the inpatient treatment of anorexia nervosa? *American Journal of Psychiatry*, **155**, 548–551.

Barlow, J., Blouin, J., Blouin, A. & Perez, E. (1988) Treatment of bulimia with desipramine: A double blind crossover study. *Canadian Journal of Psychiatry*, **33**, 129–133.

Biederman, J., Herzog, D.B., Rivinus, T.M., Harper, G.P., Ferber, R.A., Rosenbaum, J.F., Harmatz, J.S., Tondorf, R., Orsulak, P.J. & Schildkraut, J.J. (1985) Amitriptyline in the treatment of anorexia nervosa: A double-blind, placebo-controlled study. *Journal of Clinical Psychopharmacology*, **5**, 10–16.

Bray, G.A. (1993) Use and abuse of appetite suppressant drugs in the treatment of obesity. *Annals of Internal Medicine*, **119**, 707–713.

Carruba, M., Tomello, C., Briscini, L. & Nisoli, E. (1998) Advances in pharmacotherapy for obesity. *International Journal of Obesity*, **22**, S13–S16.

Carter, J.C. & Fairburn, C.G. (1998) Cognitive-behavioral self-help for binge eating disorder: A controlled effectiveness study. *Journal of Consulting and Clinical Psychology*, **66**, 616–623.

Considine, R.V., Sinha, M.K., Heiman, M.L., Kriauciunas, A., Stephens, T.W., Nyce, M.R., Ohannesian, J.P., Marco, C.C., McKee, L.J., Bauer, T.L. et al. (1996) Serum immunoreactive-leptin concentrations in normal-weight and obese humans. *New England Journal of Medicine*, **334** (5), 324–325.

Crow, S.J. & Mitchell, J.E. (1994) Rational therapy of eating disorders. *Drugs*, **48**, 372–379.

Devereux, R.B. (1998) Appetite suppressants and valvular heart disease. *New England Journal of Medicine*, **339**, 765–766.

McElroy, S.L., Casuto, L.S., Nelson, E.B., Lake, K.A., Soutullo, C.A., Keck, P.E. & Hudson, J.I. (2000) Placebo-controlled trial of sertraline in the treatment of binge eating disorder. *American Journal of Psychiatry*, **157**, 1004–1006.

Fairburn, C.G., Cooper, Z., Doll, H.A., Norman, P.A. & O'Connor, M.E. (2000) The natural course of bulimia nervosa and binge eating disorder in young women. *Archives of General Psychiatry*, **57**, 659–665.

Faris, P.L. Kim, S.W., Meller, W.H., Goodale, R.L., Oakman, S.A., Hofbauer, R.D.,Marshall, A.M., Daughters, R.S., Banerjee-Stevens, D., Eckert, E.D. & Hartman, B.K. (2000) Effects of decreasing afferent vagal activity with ondansetron on symptoms of bulimia nervosa: A randomised, double-blind trial. *Lancet*, **355**, 792–797.

Ferguson, C.P., La Via, M.C., Crossan, P.J. & Kaye, W.H. (1999) Are serotonin selective reuptake inhibitors effective in underweight anorexia nervosa? *International Journal of Eating Disorders*, **25**, 11–17.

Fluoxetine Bulimia Nervosa Collaborative Study Group (1992) Fluoxetine in the treatment of bulimia nervosa. *Archives of General Psychiatry*, **49**, 139–147.

Freeman, C. (1998) Drug treatment for bulimia nervosa. *Neuropsychobiology*, **37**, 72–79.

Goldberg, S.C., Halmi, K.A., Eckert, E.D., Casper, R.C. & Davis, J.M. (1979) Cyproheptadine in anorexia nervosa. *British Journal of Psychiatry*, **134**, 67–70.

Goldstein, D.J., Wilson, M.G., Thomson, V.L., Potvin, J.H., Rampey Jr, A.H. and the Fluoxetine Bulimia Nervosa Research Group (1995) Long-term fluoxetine treatment of bulimia nervosa. *British Journal of Psychiatry*, **166** (5), 660–666.

Goldstein, D.J., Wilson, M.G., Ascroft, R.C. & Al-Banna, M. (1999) Effectiveness of fluoxetine therapy in bulimia nervosa regardless of comorbid depression. *International Journal of Eating Disorders*, **25**, 19–27.

Greeno, C.G. & Wing, R. (1996) A double-blind, placebo-controlled trial of the effect of fluoxetine on dietary intake in overweight women with and without binge eating disorder. *American Journal of Clinical Nutrition*, **64**, 267–273.

Gross, M.A., Ebert, M.M., Faden, U.B., Goldberg, S.C., Lee, L.E. & Kaye, W.H. (1981) A double-blind controlled trial of lithium carbonate in primary anorexia nervosa. *Journal of Clinical Psychopharmacology*, **1**, 376–381.

Halmi, K.A., Eckert, E.D., La Du, T.J. & Cohen, J. (1986) Anorexia nervosa: Treatment efficacy of cyproheptadine and amitriptyline. *Archives of General Psychiatry*, **43**, 177–181.

Halmi, K.A. (1995) Current concepts and definitions. In G. Szmukler, C. Dare & J. Treasure (Eds), *Handbook of Eating Disorders. Theory, Treatment and Research*, (pp. 29–42). Chichester: John Wiley & Sons.

Hay, P.J. & Bacaltchuk, J. (2001) Extracts from 'clinical evidence': Bulimia nervosa. *British Medical Journal*, **323**, 33–37.

Heymsfield, S.B., Greenberg, A.S., Fujioka, K., Dixon, R.M., Kushner, R., Hunt, T., Lubina, J.A., Patane, J., Self, B. & McCamish, M. (1999) Recombinant leptin for weight loss in obese and lean adults: A randomized, controlled, dose-escalation trial. *JAMA*, **282** (16), 1568–1575.

Hill, J.O., Hauptman, J., Anderson, J.W., Fujioka, K., O'Neil, P.M., Smith, D.K., Zavoral, J.H. & Aronne, L.J. (1999) Orlistat, a lipase inhibitor, for weight maintenance after conventional dieting: A 1-y study. *American Journal of Clinical Nutrition*, **69**, 1108–1116.

Huckshorn, C.J., Saris, W.H., Westerterp-Plantenga, M.S., Farid, A.R., Smith, F.J. & Campfield, L.A. (2000) Weekly subcutaneous pegylated recombinant native human leptin (PEG OB) administration in obese men. *Journal of Clinical Endocrinology and Metabolism*, **85** (11), 4003–4009.

Hudson, J.I., McElroy, S.L., Raymond, N.C., Crow, S., Keck, P.E. Jr, Carter, W.P., Mitchell, J.E., Strakowski, S.M., Pope, H.G. Jr, Coleman, B.S. & Jonas, J.M. (1998) Fluvoxamine in the treatment of binge-eating disorder: A multicenter placebo-controlled, double-blind trial. *American Journal of Psychiatry*, **155**, 1756–1762.

Jick, H., Vasilakis, C., Weinrauch, L.A., Meier, C.R., Jick, S.S. & Derby, L.E. (1998) A population-based study of appetite suppressant drugs and the risk of cardiac-valve regurgitation. *New England Journal of Medicine*, **339**, 719–724.

Kaye, W.H., Gwirtsman, H.E., George, D.T. & Ebert M.H. (1991) Altered serotonin activity in anorexia nervosa after long-term weight restoration: Does elevated cerebrospinal fluid 5-hydroxyindoleacetic acid level correlate with rigid and obsessive behavior? *Archives of General Psychiatry*, **48**, 556–562.

Kaye, W.H., Greeno, C.G., Moss, H., Fernstrom, J., Fernstrom, M., Lilenfeld, L.R., Weltzin, T.E. & Mann, J.J. (1998) Alterations in serotonin activity and psychiatric symptoms after recovery from bulimia nervosa. *Archives of General Psychiatry*, **55**, 927–935.

Kaye, W.H., Nagata, T., Weltzin, T.E., Hsu, L.K.G., Sokol, M.S., McConaha, C., Plotnicov, K.H., Weise, J. & Deep, D. (2001) Double-blind placebo-controlled administration of fluoxetine in restricting- and restricting-purging-type anorexia nervosa. *Biological Psychiatry*, **49**, 644–652.

Lacey, J.H. & Crisp, A.H. (1980) Hunger, food intake and weight: The impact of clomipramine on a refeeding anorexia nervosa population. *Postgraduate Medical Journal*, **56** (1), 79–85.

La Via, M.C., Gray, N. & Kaye, W.H. (2000) Case reports of Olanzapine treatment of anorexia nervosa. *International Journal of Eating Disorders*, **27**, 363–366.

Lean, M.E.J. (1997) Sibutramine: A review of clinical efficacy. *International Journal of Obesity*, **21**, S30–S36.

Marrazzi, M.A., Bacon, J.P., Kinzie, J. & Luby, E.D. (1995) Naltrexone use in the treatment of anorexia nervosa and bulimia nervosa. *International Journal of Clinical Psychopharmacology*, **10**, 163–172.

Mayer, L.E.S. & Walsh, B.T. (1998) The use of selective serotonin reuptake inhibitors in eating disorders. *Journal of Clinical Psychiatry*, **59** (15), 28–34.

NIH Technology Assessment Conference Panel (1993) Methods for voluntary weight loss and control. Consensus Development Conference, 30 March to 1 April 1992. *Annals of Internal Medicine*, **119** (7, Pt 2), 764–770.

Pi-Sunyer, F.X. (1993) Medical hazards of obesity. *Annals of Internal Medicine*, **119** (7, Pt 2), 655–660.

Pope, H.G., Hudson, J.I., Jonas, J.M. & Yurgelun-Todd, D. (1983) Bulimia treated with imipramine: A placebo-controlled, double-blind study. *American Journal of Psychiatry*, **140**, 554–558.

Schmidt, U. (1998) The treatment of bulimia nervosa. In H.W. Hoek, J. Treasure & M.A. Katzman (Eds), *Neurobiology in the Treatment of Eating Disorders*. (pp. 331–361). Chichester: John Wiley & Sons.

Schotte, D.E. (1990) The effects of weight reduction on blood pressure in 301 obese subjects. *Archives of Internal Medicine*, **150**, 1701–1704.

Smith, K.A., Fairburn, C.G. & Cowen, P.J. (1999) Symptomatic relapse in bulimia nervosa following acute tryptophan depletion. *Archives of General Psychiatry*, **56**, 171–176.

Stunkard, A., Berkowitz, R., Tanrikut, C., Reiss, E. & Young, L. (1996) D-Fenfluramine treatment of binge eating disorder. *American Journal of Psychiatry*, **153**, 1455–1459.

Szmukler, G.I., Young, G.P., Miller, G., Lichtenstein, M. & Binns, D.S. (1995) A controlled trial of cisapride in anorexia nervosa. *International Journal of Eating Disorders*, **17**, 347–357.

Treasure, J. & Schmidt, U. (2001) Anorexia nervosa. *Clinical Evidence*, 5, 0–12.

Van Furth, E.F. (1998) The treatment of anorexia nervosa. In H. Hoek, J. Treasure & M. Katzman (Eds), *Neurobiology in the Treatment of Eating Disorders* (pp. 315–330). Chichester: John Wiley & Sons.

Van Hoeken, D., Lucas, A.R. & Hoek, H.W. (1998) Epidemiology. In H. Hoek, J. Treasure & M. Katzman (Eds), *Neurobiology in the Treatment of Eating Disorders*, (pp. 97–126). Chichester: John Wiley & Sons.

Vandereycken, W. & Pierloot, R. (1982) Pimozide combined with behavior therapy in the short-term treatment of anorexia nervosa: A double-blind placebo controlled cross-over study. *Acta Psychiatrica Scandinavica*, **66** (6), 445–450.

Vandereycken, W. (1984) Neuroleptics in the short-term treatment of anorexia nervosa: A double-blind placebo-controlled study with sulpiride. *British Journal of Psychiatry*, **144**, 288–292.

Vigerski, R.A. & Loriaux, D.L. (1977) The effect of cyproheptadine in anorexia nervosa: A double-blind trial. In R.A. Vigerski (Ed.), *Anorexia Nervosa*. New York: Raven Press.

Walsh, B.T., Gladis, M., Roose, S.P., Stewart, J.W., Stetner, F. & Glassman, A.H. (1988) Phenelzine vs placebo in 50 patients with bulimia. *Archives of General Psychiatry*, **45**, 471–475.

Walsh, B.T., Hadigan, C.M., Devlin, M.J., Gladis, M. & Roose, S.P. (1991) Long term outcome of antidepressant treatment for bulimia nervosa. *American Journal of Psychiatry*, **148**, 1206–1212.

Walsh, B.T., Wilson, G.T., Loeb, K.L., Devlin, M.J., Pike, K.M., Roose, S.P., Fleiss, J. & Waternaux, C. (1997) Medication and psychotherapy in the treatment of bulimia nervosa. *American Journal of Psychiatry*, **154**, 523–531.

Walsh, B.T., Agras, W.S., Devlin, M.J., Fairburn, C.G., Wilson, G.T., Kahn, C. & Chally, M.K. (2000) Fluoxetine for bulimia nervosa following poor response to psychotherapy. *American Journal of Psychiatry*, **157**, 1332–1334.

Wing, R.R., Koeske, R., Epstein, L.H., Nowalk, M.P., Gooding, W. & Becker, D. (1987) Long-term effects of modest weight loss in type II diabetic subjects. *Archives of Internal Medicine*, **147**, 1749–1753.

Wise, S.D. (1992) Clinical studies with fluoxetine in obesity. *American Journal of Clinical Nutrition*, **55**, 181S–184S.

Wolf, R.N. & Grundy, S.M. (1983) Influence of weight reduction on plasma lipoproteins in obese subjects. *Arteriosclerosis*, **3**, 160–169.

Wolfe, B.E., Metzger, E.D., Levine, J.M., Finkelstein, D.M., Cooper, T.B. & Jimerson, D.C. (2000) Serotonin function following remission from bulimia nervosa. *Neuropsychopharmacology*, **22**, 257–263.

Zhang, Y., Proenca, R., Maffei, M., Barone, M., Leopold, L. & Friedman, J.M. (1994) Positional cloning of the mouse obese gene and its human homologue. *Nature*, **372**, 425–432.

De Zwaan, M. & Mitchell, J.E. (1992) Opiate antagonists and eating behavior in humans: A review. *Journal of Clinical Pharmacology*, **32**, 1060–1072.

De Zwaan, M. (2001) Binge eating disorder and obesity. *International Journal of Obesity and Related Metabolic Disorders*, 25, S51–S55.

CHAPTER 13

Day Treatments

Paul Robinson

Department of Psychiatry, Royal Free Hospital, London, UK

SUMMARY

- Anorexia nervosa has a high mortality and safety must not be compromised.
- High-quality outpatient and day care may make expensive inpatient care unnecessary.
- A team costing £1m (€ 1.63m) with a whole time consultant psychiatrist can treat eating disorders over 16 years of age arising in a population of around 1m.
- Key quality issues for an effective multidisciplinary team for eating disorders are a broad range of skills including family interventions, effective physical monitoring, good support and supervision for staff and access to a wide range of services including inpatient beds.

INTRODUCTION

Anorexia nervosa is a significant cause of morbidity and mortality with a Standardised Mortality Ratio among the highest of all psychiatric conditions (Harris & Barraclough, 1998). It can therefore result in very high levels of anxiety in families and health care professionals. This anxiety often leads to the demand for inpatient care, and, in some life-threatening situations, admission cannot be avoided. However, inpatient treatment may not be necessary or even desirable for most patients.

There is some inconclusive evidence that hospital inpatient care may adversely affect outcome in young patients (Gowers et al., 2000) while evidence for the advantage of inpatient over outpatient care is lacking, or suggests no significant advantage (Crisp et al., 1991, Gowers et al., 1994). In this chapter, the relative advantages and disadvantages of inpatient versus community care will be described, and a new active model of community care in use at the Royal Free Hospital described.

HOSPITAL VERSUS COMMUNITY

Anorexia Nervosa and the Illusion of Control

The causes of anorexia nervosa remain obscure, while the effects of the illness are profound. The young person, struggling with this serious illness, often gives up social contacts,

---

The Essential *Handbook of Eating Disorders.* Edited by J. Treasure, U. Schmidt and E. van Furth.

becomes depressed and at risk for physical complications which can prove fatal. It has been suggested that weight control reflects the individual's need for control more generally (Fairburn et al., 1999). Such control is, in fact illusory. The patient becomes surrounded by people who take a great interest in her eating, including family members, doctors, nurses and therapists. Her health may deteriorate to a point at which control over her life is completely removed and she is admitted to hospital involuntarily. In other words, the more successful she is at exerting control over her food intake, the less control she actually has. By asserting her absolute independence (of food) she brings about complete dependence. Her behaviour parodies the adolescent's quest for independence. It is possible that people with anorexia nervosa (like many adolescents) are seeking to be contained by authority figures, while protesting independence and a rejection of such containment.

The Anorexic Pseudo-Conflict

By asserting her independence of food, she often brings herself into conflict with her family. This conflict, like the illusion of control, parodies the healthy conflict that occurs when adolescents challenge their parents, for example, concerning smoking or staying out late. The anorexic's conflict is, however, a fight to the death and is a lethal challenge to the ability of the mother and father to nurture and provide. When this conflict is addressed early in its course, using family approaches to treatment, parental coherence can be reinstated and the patient may recover (Eisler et al., 1997, and Chapter 18 in this volume). However, if the process becomes chronic, or if the patient is removed from home for a prolonged period, the opportunity for the family to organise in a way that finds alternatives to the anorexic lifestyle may be lost.

'Parentectomy': Family Surgery for Anorexia Nervosa

Prolonged admission for anorexia nervosa speaks to both the illusion of control and the anorexic pseudo-conflict. Admission to an inpatient anorexic unit removes control from the patient or the family and places it in the hands of the clinic; but this would appear counter-intuitive, if our aim as therapists is to increase the autonomy and responsibility of the patient and family. Admission can be an enormous relief to all parties, because it appears to provide a solution to the struggle, and to the family conflict. The latter, however, is merely displaced. The struggle between the patient and the parents becomes the struggle between the patient and a set of strangers whose job it is to impose nutrition upon the patient. The family dilemma, which is 'How do we live with a person on a hunger strike?' is hardly solved by moving the 'hunger striker' to another 'family' and persisting with encouragement, until she eats. The family dilemma still remains, and needs to be solved when the patient, now heavier, leaves the clinic. Little wonder that the weight so often falls off in the few months after discharge (Russell et al., 1987). Admission to hospital, while it may be necessary because of physical deterioration, or exhaustion on the part of family, patient and therapist, decreases the patient's control and autonomy and transforms the anorexic's conflict with her family into a pseudo-conflict with hospital staff that can never be resolved.

USE OF COERCIVE METHODS OF TREATMENT

The inpatient unit for anorexia nervosa could have a sign above its doors 'We will make you put on weight'. Many patients respond to this implicit aim with an implicit 'Let me see you try!' of their own. The investment of the unit in weight gain is so great that it will occasionally go to extreme lengths to achieve it. Such measures include 'assisted feeding', in which the patient is held and food pushed into her mouth by a nurse, and 'peer pressure' in which the person refusing to eat may be forced to eat by other patients. Coercive methods are, in the view of the writer, usually counterproductive, and can only be ethically justified when the patient's life (and not just her welfare or her bone density) would be at risk if she were not forced to accept nutrition. The case for coercive treatment would be better if backed by solid evidence of benefit in controlled studies. No satisfactory study has, however, been reported.

Inpatient Units: Systemic Considerations

In some ways, the structure of the inpatient unit (and, to a lesser extent, the day unit) mirrors a family, albeit a dysfunctional one. The nurses, mostly female, have the task of encouraging the person to eat. The consultant, usually but now less often male, may see the team once a week during the archaically named ward round. The father/consultant hears from the mother/nurse how their child/patient has performed. If she has not gained weight, the nurse feels she has failed and a dynamic is set up echoing that of the parents. The mother feels responsible for the child's weight, spends much of her time with her and may become as obsessed with food as her daughter, while the father lives more and more in the world of work, becomes distant from the problem, and cannot understand why his wife is unable to get their daughter to eat properly. On the ward, the nurses, like mothers, spend, collectively, all the time with the patient and a conflict can be set up between medical and nursing staff which is curiously reminiscent of the commonly observed family conflict.

Inpatient psychiatric units often become rigidly hierarchical. This is necessary because of the role such units have in the enforcement of compulsory treatment under legal sanctions, particularly in relation to the care of patients with psychoses who have a history of violence either to themselves or to others. In the UK, The Mental Health Act (1983) enshrines the authority of the Responsible Medical Officer (RMO) who has to sign a paper to allow a detained patient even to leave the ward for a walk. When a patient with anorexia nervosa (or any other problem) is admitted to a psychiatric ward, she already gives up some rights because, even if she enters the ward freely, she can be detained, if she tries to leave, by the signature of only one doctor or one nurse.

Inpatient care is therefore overshadowed by the immense authority of the psychiatrist and the covert threat of detention, and a staff group that wishes to engender a cooperative atmosphere has to overcome these two very significant influences. It is difficult to overestimate the significance of legal sanctions as an influence on the treatment of a person with a mental illness. They organise not only the patient, but also the ward staff and the patient's family. The result is a rigidly hierarchical system, which, it seems to the author, is most unlikely to be able to help the patient to become more autonomous.

Case Examples

A patient was admitted to an inpatient unit with severe anorexia and bulimia nervosa. The consultant demanded of her that she put on 0.5 kg weekly and she was strongly encouraged to finish meals by the nurses. Her weight gradually rose but her appearance and muscle power suggested decline. A spot weighing on one occasion demonstrated a loss of over 3 kg in one morning, and she admitted to water loading prior to weighing. A second patient in the unit began to have suspicious changes in weight suggestive of water loading.

This patient responded to increased supervision by an equivalent increase in her own dysfunctional behaviour, and passed her skills on to another, less experienced, patient.

A patient placed a waste-bin upside down by her door, stood on it and put her head in a noose attached to the door frame, at a time that she knew a particular nurse would open the door to check on her, thereby pushing over the bin. She survived but the nurse was traumatised.

This case demonstrates the way patients who are willing to risk death can engage destructively with nurses deputed to protect them.

FINANCIAL INVESTMENT IN CUSTODIAL TREATMENT

In many European countries, specialist care for eating disorders can be arranged either through the country's national health service or through health insurance. This provides a mechanism whereby specialist care can be provided for patients with eating disorders who would, otherwise, not have been able to obtain such care from the local psychiatric service. However, the funds generated from inpatient admissions are far in excess of those charged for outpatient care and some clinicians have been aware of pressure from hospital authorities to admit patients in order to fill beds, and generate income. An illustrative example will be provided:

A 15-year-old patient was admitted to a private residential eating disorders service for anorexia nervosa. Funding was from the local health authority. She regained a healthy weight, but refused to eat on her return home. She was immediately rehospitalised and spent the following 12 months as an inpatient, with attempts at returning her home thwarted by her refusal to eat. She was transferred to another residential unit, and spent nearly two more years as an inpatient. The cost to her health authority was around £¹/₄m (€ 0.4m). At no time following her initial admission did her weight fall much below the normal range. After her eighteenth birthday she was transferred to the adult service and has required no further admissions.

This case raises questions about prolonged admissions for adolescents with eating disorders. It is not clear that hospitalisation for nearly three years, irrespective of the cost, was the most appropriate treatment for her. At least, it can be argued that those responsible for funding such health care would be well advised to commission their own experts in eating disorders to determine whether treatment they are funding is being appropriately provided.

AVOIDING HOSPITALISATION IN SEVERE ANOREXIA NERVOSA

The problems that occur among patients and staff of an inpatient unit appear proportional to the degree of restraint and coercion applied. This is unsurprising, as the more a patient's will is directly challenged, the more she will retaliate in order to defend her position. The clinician faced with a severe eating disorder has a very difficult dilemma. It is probable that useful change is only likely to occur when the patient concludes that improvement in health brings advantages, which outweigh the sacrifices she would have to make. Weight loss, itself, however, may produce cognitive changes, which may militate against rational thought, and the doctor may be forced to admit a patient whose physical deterioration threatens her survival.

Alternatives to hospitalisation have been developed in a number of centres in diverse parts of the world. The best described are the Day Hospital Program at the Toronto General Hospital (Piran et al., 1989), the Therapy Centre for Eating Disorders in Munich (Gerlinghoff et al., 1998), Our Lady of the Lake Eating Disorders Program in Baton Rouge, Louisiana (Williamson et al., 1998) and the Cullen Centre in Edinburgh (Freeman, 1992). Outcome data from each of these programmes suggest clinical efficacy, although no satisfactory controlled study has been reported from the centres. A comparison of day and inpatient treatment at the Cullen Centre found no significant difference in outcome between the two treatments, but unfortunately the study was curtailed prematurely due to the overwhelming preference of referrers for the Day Programme (Freeman et al., 1992).

Given that hospital admission, under compulsion if necessary, is mandatory for patients who would otherwise die, what can be done for the remainder? Experience at the Royal Free Eating Disorders Service demonstrates that a service which offers intensive outpatient, day hospital and domiciliary management can avoid most admissions. In five years the service has utilised approximately 1 hospital bed per million residents served.

ESSENTIAL ELEMENTS OF THE SERVICE

Referral

Referrals are welcomed from primary and secondary care and referrers are asked to provide the patient's height and weight, in addition to the provisional diagnosis and any other relevant information. If a referral is marked 'Urgent' the referrer is contacted and the case discussed. Assessment can be immediate or within a few days, although in most cases the wait of 6–8 weeks is acceptable. The assessment interview is done by a staff member who may be a doctor, nurse, psychologist or occupational therapist, or a medical student, using a checklist which indicates the areas to cover. The staff members who have seen patients that morning then meet with the consultant and each person recounts the history of the patient he or she has assessed. In the third hour, each patient is then interviewed by the consultant in the presence of the interviewer and other relevant team members, necessary physical examination and tests are arranged and treatment options are explored. In this way, up to five new patients are seen in a three-hour session, and all are seen by the consultant. Moreover, staff learn how to interview and present patients and hear about a number of patients in each session.

Outpatient Treatment

Following the psychiatric and medical assessment, most patients are seen within a few weeks by a psychologist, and then allocated to one or more of the following:

1. *Individual supportive therapy.* This is provided to patients with a variety of eating disorder diagnoses. Nurses, after joining the team, are trained by more experienced nurses, and begin to attend supervision sessions, before taking on patients. Treatment is eclectic and includes physical monitoring, cognitive-behavioural techniques and supportive and educational approaches. The focus of these sessions is on weight gain and reduction of self-destructive symptoms. Other issues including family and relationship difficulties may also be discussed. We have found that nurses with basic mental health training, when properly supervised, can provide extremely helpful therapy to this group of patients.

2. *Individual psychotherapy.* A limited number of patients, with more serious disorders (e.g. eating disorders complicated by self-harm or substance misuse) are taken on for individual psychodynamic or cognitive-behavioural psychotherapy by clinical psychologists.

3. *Cognitive-behavioural therapy (individual (nurse) or group (nurse + psychologist).* CBT, either individually or in a group, is the first line therapy for patients with normal weight bulimia nervosa.

4. *Family therapy.* Patients with anorexia nervosa, and patients with eating disorders who also have children, are offered family therapy using an eclectic mix of structural, Milan-systemic and other systemic approaches. Supervision of family therapists in training is facilitated by a video link. The approach to families is as supportive and collaborative as possible, as long as the patient aggrees for her family to be involved. Initial sessions may be conducted in the home, or in the family doctor's surgery.

5. *Multiple family groups.* This recent development utilises four workshops per day, on three and a half days over three months, for four or five families with a child suffering from anorexia nervosa. Various styles of work, including 'Goldfish Bowl' discussions (in which one group, such as all the children, discuss a topic while their parents look on), task planning discussions, family sculpts, and art and movement therapy, are used. The techniques are promising and have been reported in detail elsewhere (Colahan & Robinson, 2002).

Day Programme

The Eating Disorders Day Programme takes place within the Royal Free Hospital and consists of the following elements:

1. Supported meals on four days per week, which can be increased to seven days, if necessary. These meals are intended to be educational and therapeutic. Patients generally have only a proportion of their meals at the Unit, and if a patient is eating inappropriately, the intervention by the nurse or other team member present is confined to advice, and a post-meal discussion with other patients. This approach is quite stressful for staff, because they have to be able to handle a group of patients, all eating in differently dysfunctional ways. The aim is to foster a culture of recovery, rather than one in which patients compete to be the most eating-disordered person at the table.

2. A variety of groups led by occupational therapy, creative therapy and nursing staff. (Pre- and post-meal, psychodynamic, nutrition, art therapy, drama and dance-movement therapy and current affairs groups.) Individual massage and dance-movement therapy is also provided.

3. Individual key nurse monitoring and therapy.
4. Participation in team meeting.
5. All therapies which are available to outpatients.

Outreach Care

A small team of a senior nurse, family therapist, doctor and other professionals provide an outreach service. Patients who continue to deteriorate in spite of a full day programme can be supported at home with visits from EDS staff at weekends. Staff can also be employed to spend nights at the patient's home to help the family to cope with a severely ill family member.

Less dramatically, family assessments are often conducted at home, by the key nurse, together with a family therapist, in order to engage new families in outpatient or day patient care.

Patients admitted to other hospitals are visited regularly in order help the staff in the other unit and to engage the patient with the aim of attendance at treatment sessions at the Royal Free. The outreach team also supports staff at other hospitals that treat patients with eating disorders.

Persuading Patients to Gain Weight

This is the main aim of most treatment services, and it is self-evident that without weight recovery the anorexia nervosa remains. The nurse providing individual therapy to the patient has a supportive and accepting role, and, most importantly, eliciting the trust of the patient. At the same time, the nurse will be firm and persistent about the need for improvements in diet and weight, and often asks the dietician to provide a session to emphasise the importance of weight recovery. The family sessions are also intended to be supportive, particularly the family support group sessions, but family therapists will also aim to address dysfunctional patterns, for example withdrawal of the father from family life or a parent defending the *status quo* and preventing therapeutic change. Families are invited to team meetings to discuss treatment with the consultant and the rest of the team, and this can prevent unhelpful splits in the team, for example when one team member is seen by patient or family as good and another bad.

In general, patients are encouraged to find their own route to weight gain, and some may gain weight while clearly under-eating within the unit. This would be commented on and discussed in the post-meal group. The patient is finding her own way to a healthy body weight, but has to do so in private.

Management of the Severely Ill Patient with Anorexia Nervosa

Patients who lose weight to a dangerously low level are monitored closely for signs of physical collapse. It is important to measure several variables, as only one or two of them may change in any one patient whose physical state is deteriorating.

- *Body mass index.* If BMI is changing, physical collapse may be imminent. This is particularly the case at levels below 13, although rapid weight loss at higher BMIs can also be dangerous. BMI, if falling, should be measured once or twice weekly. Patients who sense that they may be liable to compulsory hospitalisation may falsify their BMI in a number of ways, particularly by water loading, as in the case described above.
- *Muscle power.* Muscle weakness is a common sign of physical deterioration.

A patient who brought breakfast to her mother each morning was losing weight and began placing the breakfast tray on each step, sitting on the stair and dragging herself up to the next step, once she was unable to climb the stairs.

The SUSS Test of Muscle Power in Anorexia Nervosa

We have chosen two measures of muscle power, the stand-up and the sit-up (SUSS: Sit-Up, Stand Straight). For the stand-up, the patient is asked to squat and to rise without using her hands, if possible. The scale used is as follows:

0: completely unable to rise
1: able to rise only with use of hands
2: able to rise with noticeable difficulty
3: able to rise without difficulty.

For the sit-up, the patient lies flat on a firm surface such as the floor and has to sit up without, if possible, using her hands. The scoring is just as for the stand-up (see Figure 13.1).

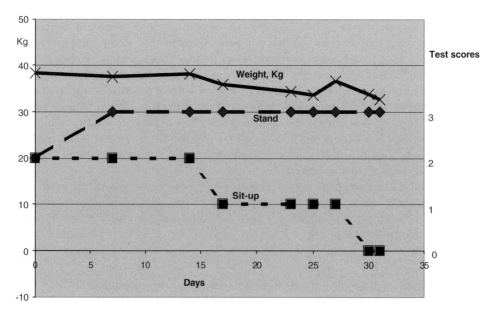

Figure 13.1 Use of the SUSS test in a patient with falling weight. The stand-up test is satisfactory, but the sit-up declines with reduced weight. The transient increase in weight on day 27 was due to water loading. The patient was admitted to hospital on day 31 (BMI 11.4)

Postural Dizziness

This is usually due to fall in blood pressure caused by dehydration and cardiac dysfunction. It is an important sign because it suggests that cardiovascular collapse may occur if further weight or fluid are lost. The scale used for this symptom, tested by asking the patient to stand up after lying down, is:

0: no postural dizziness
1: transient dizziness
2: sustained dizziness
3: unable to stand due to dizziness.

A patient who scores 1 or above should have standing and lying blood pressure monitored.

Blood Tests

These are of limited value, but at times precede other clinical signs of impending collapse. Serum Creatine Kinase may be raised in a patient with anorexic myopathy (Alloway et al., 1988), especially, in our experience, if the patient continues to exercise while losing weight. White blood count and platelets may decline with weight loss, and electrolytes, especially potassium, may fall in a patient with self-induced vomiting or laxative abuse. Thinner patients (i.e. those with anorexia nervosa) are more at risk for hypokalaemia, because of poorer body stores. Liver function tests are also worth monitoring, with rises in transaminase levels indicating liver dysfunction due to malnutrition. A chart suitable for monitoring physical state in this way is provided (Appendix 13.1).

APPENDIX 13.1

The form shown as Figure 13.2 is used to monitor medical state in a patient with anorexia nervosa judged to be at high physical risk. The decision about admission must be taken by the

Name		DOB		Address	Phone	Number
GP (Phone/fax/email)				EDS Contact (Phone/ fax/ email)		
Date	BMI	Stand up^a	Sit-up^b	Postural dizziness^c	Other symptoms/ signs (e.g. oedema)	Tests (K, Na, etc)

^{a}Ability to rise from squatting (0, unable to rise even with help from hands; 1, can only rise with help from hands; 2, some difficulty; 3, no difficulty).
^{b}Ability to sit up from lying flat (no pillow, firm surface). Scale as for stand-up.
^{c}Dizziness on standing up from a lying posture (0, no symptoms; 1, transient; 2, persistent; 3, unable to stand because of dizziness).

Figure 13.2 Medical monitoring of high-risk AN patient

individual clinician and team, and information derived from monitoring several parameters allows a more informed decision than one taken purely on weight. The direction and rate of change are also important. If a patient has a BMI of 12, and is known to have collapsed at a BMI of 10, then it is inappropriate and dangerous to wait until weight goes down, until she is *in extremis*. These decisions are best made in a team context, with contributions from the nurse and therapist who know the patient well, medical staff, family and, if the Mental Health Act might be involved, the social worker.

Where to Admit, and What to do Then

In a service such as that at the Royal Free, with no dedicated beds, a flexible budget is essential. A patient who requires admission because of physical deterioration has the following options:

1. A Medical Bed

In areas in which there are shortages of medical beds, a medical admission may only be only possible for a patient who is very severely ill. Contact between the senior psychiatrist and the consultant physician is essential, and a certain amount of persuasion and diplomacy may be needed in order to secure a medical bed. Once the patient has negotiated Accident and Emergency (ER), and been placed in a bed, a meeting is rapidly arranged between the medical ward staff and the eating disorders team. The patient's key nurse spends time on the ward negotiating between the patient, the nurses and doctors, the catering department and the eating disorders team in what is an exhausting and at times thankless task. The nurse's other duties should be reviewed and shared with other team members in such a crisis. A medical member of the eating disorders staff attends whatever medical meetings are arranged (often in the early morning) and hopes to be involved in treatment planning, particularly around discharge.

A patient with anorexia nervosa lost weight and was admitted to a medical bed, unable to walk due to myopathy. After three days she was deemed no longer to need an intravenous infusion and was discharged by a senior registrar (senior resident) as no longer needing medical services. She was still unable to raise her legs to walk, although she was able to move by sliding her feet along the floor. After two days she collapsed and was readmitted, following a formal complaint by her parents.

In this case, a 'sweep' by the senior registrar (senior resident) in order to clear beds the day before the ward was on take for emergency admissions led to the patient being discharged prematurely without reference to psychiatric medical staff. Her next admission was dealt with much more collaboratively.

2. A Psychiatric Bed

Acute psychiatric wards are often inappropriate for someone with severe anorexia nervosa. However, as long as the ward is reasonably calm, and the patient not too medically unwell, such a bed remains a possibility to be explored. Again, it is very important that eating disorder staff provide support to the general psychiatry staff so that various issues such as lack of information about eating disorders, fears about physical frailty and adverse attitudes to eating disorder patients among staff can be addressed. At the Royal Free Hospital, a women's unit has recently been established, and has provided excellent care to patients with anorexia nervosa requiring admission.

3. A 'Traditional' Inpatient Eating Disorders Bed

Once a patient has been through outpatient, day-patient, medical inpatient and, perhaps, psychiatric inpatient care, the patient should be admitted to an inpatient eating disorders service.

A 19-year-old patient with anorexia nervosa had been treated, initially, with psychoanalytic psychotherapy, then family therapy, day care and two inpatient medical admissions for severe malnutrition. She had developed symptoms of anorexia and bulimia nervosa, and latterly, frankly psychotic symptoms in relation to food. She was admitted to an inpatient eating disorders service for several months, where she made some progress, although her weight fell again rapidly on discharge.

This patient suffers from severe anorexia and bulimia nervosa, together with a paranoid psychosis of uncertain aetiology. Her treatment has proved to be a major challenge to all services with which she has had contact.

Team Structure Support and Supervision

In the last 50 years, psychiatric beds all over the world have given way to community approaches to treatment. In many places, this has proved very successful (Trieman et al., 1999) with hitherto incarcerated patients living freer and more independent lives. However, many patients remain vulnerable, both to self-neglect and self-harm, and to urges to harm others. These patients naturally raise concerns, and society has looked around for systems to replace the asylum walls and contain anxiety. The response has been to charge community staff with responsibility for care and to back that demand with paperwork that can prove oppressive and can, at times, militate against provision of care by engendering a 'tick box' approach to the provision of care. In the eating disorders field, patients are mostly at risk for self-neglect, and the resulting anxiety raised in a service without dedicated beds is absorbed by the staff. It is necessary, therefore, to have a team with sufficient breadth of skill, depth of experience and density of support to cope with the demands. These three essential elements will be addressed individually:

(1) *Breadth of skill.* The skills required are for the administration and management of the service, medical diagnosis and monitoring of patients and the provision of therapy to individuals, groups and families. Specific skills required cover the areas of administration, management, medicine, nursing, psychotherapy, group therapy, family therapy, dietetics and creative therapies.
(2) *Depth of skill.* It is also essential to have a range of depth of skill (usually signifying seniority). Thus, recently qualified staff in any field may be able to take on the care of patients, as long as they are backed by senior medical, nursing and therapeutically

trained staff. In the Royal Free team, 9–11 nurses are employed at five different levels of seniority, providing significant within-profession support while doctors are at all levels from junior psychiatric trainee to consultant. Other professions, including psychology, dietetics, and art, movement and family therapy, do not have multiple levels of seniority, although they do have professional and management structures both within and outside the team.

(3) *Density of support and supervision.* This indicates the amount, variety and frequency of types of communication among team members that occur in relation to patient care and to service development.

    (a) Management structures provide three levels at which information is shared:

        (i) Service manager meets consultant weekly and both liaise with psychiatric service manager monthly.

        (ii) Service manager and consultant with senior administrative and clinical staff (monthly management meeting).

        (iii) All staff on unit (monthly business meeting).

In addition, twice yearly 'away days' provide opportunities for staff to contribute to service planning, informal team outings provide opportunities for interaction outside the work setting, Each professional head meets with his or her staff regularly for appraisal and the consultant meets with all staff members twice yearly for an informal career discussion.

    (b) Clinical supervision takes the form of weekly team meetings, peer support meetings, group and case discussions, and supervision from a consultant psychiatrist in psychotherapy and an eating disorders specialist psychiatrist. There are weekly training sessions provided by team members and outside speakers.

Financial and Managerial Considerations

The service provides assessment and treatment of patients with eating disorders to an area containing 1 100 000 people. Out of area patients are not seen. The lower age limit is 18, although 16–17 year olds will be seen following a referral by a child and adolescent psychiatrist.

Within the budget, which is managed within adult mental health and is designated for eating disorders, is a flexible element, which can be used at the discretion of clinical and managerial staff. Examples of the use of this budget have included:

1. Inpatient care in a private hospital for a patient unresponsive to community approaches.
2. Provision of private analytic psychotherapy when this is unavailable within a reasonable time, and when the Royal Free Clinicians believe that such treatment would be likely to be beneficial.
3. Provision of nurses to work in the home at the weekends, and, if necessary, at night, to help families with the care of their eating disordered family members.
4. Provision of taxis to allow patients to attend the day and outpatient programme.

All treatment for eating disorders under the National Health Service in the designated area is provided through the Royal Free. Any requests for public funding of care outside the

Royal Free service are scrutinised, and appropriate treatment provided by the Royal Free if possible.

This style of service requires a substantial team (Appendix 13.2). The staff budget at 2001 costs, amounts to £800 000 (€ 1.3m). The author suggests that a budget of £1 (€ 1.63) per adult in the community should purchase a satisfactory service for a local population, which should probably not exceed one million. This accords with recent guidelines from the Royal College of Psychiatrists (2001).

APPENDIX 13.2 STAFF RESOURCES AVAILABLE TO THE ROYAL FREE EATING DISORDERS SERVICE

Results in the First Three Years

Of the first 500 patients seen in the service, between 1997 and 1999, the vast majority were treated as outpatients: 25 (5%) were treated as day patients and 5 (1%) were admitted—3 to medical wards, 2 to psychiatric beds (women only unit) and 1 to an inpatient unit for eating disorders. On average, 0.6 beds were used at any one time, and this figure translates to a requirement of 1 bed per million population. (The catchment area population up to 1999 was 650 000.) Over the five years since the service was established, patients with severe, relapsing illness have, however, tended to accumulate, and the eventual need for beds might be a little higher. The service is audited using weight, BMI, and a range of standardised measures of eating disorder and depressive symptoms. Preliminary audit results in the first 81 patients with anorexia nervosa (restrictive or bulimic subtype) followed up at one year showed significant improvements in BMI, eating disorder symptoms and depression. Of these 81 patients, 50 (62%) had gained weight to a BMI over 17.5, the criterion level for anorexia nervosa. Comprehensive audit will extend findings to all diagnostic groups, and a comparison with other services will give some information on relative efficacy of different approaches.

Table 13.1 Staff resources available to the Royal Free EDS

Staff	Grade/Profession	Whole-time equivalent
Medical	Consultant	2
	Psychiatric Trainee	0.5
Nursing	Team leaders	2
	Staff nurses	11
Management	Clinical service manager	1
Therapy	Psychologists	1.5
	Family therapists	1.5
	Occupational therapist	1
	Dietician	1
	Creative therapists	0.4
Administration	Secretaries	2
Total		23.90

Dangers of Avoiding Admission

The approach to service provision is not without drawbacks. When patients are very unwell, managing them in the community, even with high levels of support, can be exhausting and frightening for staff. We have learned, in crisis situations, to try to protect the key worker, as far as possible, from the strain of looking after a very ill patient while managing less acutely needy patients. Liaising with medical and psychiatric units, especially if they are unused to dealing with eating-disordered patients, can be difficult, and requires ready access to senior staff, both clinical and managerial, on both eating disorder and medical or psychiatric teams. Staff in our unit do not get training on how to manage an inpatient eating disorders unit, although they do have contact with patients, generally one at a time, who have been admitted. This problem can be addressed by seconding staff for a period of training to an inpatient unit. There is no evidence that mortality has been increased by the service model. In five years no patient seen and treated by the service has died, although in 2000 one patient who presented to the service in terminal renal failure died in hospital shortly after beginning treatment.

A National Service

If our approach were to be replicated around the UK, a team with responsibility for outpatients, day patients, and for organising brief medical or psychiatric inpatient when appropriate would be provided for every million people. In urban areas, this could be provided from one or two centres, while in rural areas, three or four clinics may need to be set up, according to local needs. The total budget for such a service would amount to 0.5–1% of the general adult psychiatry budget, a reasonable outlay considering that eating disorders are common (1–2% of young women), serious (Ratnasuriya et al., 1991) and treatable, especially if identified early.

REFERENCES

Alloway, R., Shur, E., Obrecht, R. & Russell, G.F. (1988) Physical complications in anorexia nervosa. Haematological and neuromuscular changes in 12 patients. *British Journal of Psychiatry*, **153**, 72–75.

Colahan, M. & Robinson, P.H. (2002) Multi-family Groups in the treatment of young adults with eating disorders. *Journal of Family Therapy* (in press).

Crisp, A.H., Norton, K., Gowers, S., Halek, C., Bowyer, C., Yeldham, D., Levett, G. & Bhat A. (1991) A controlled study of the effect of therapies aimed at adolescent and family psychopathology in anorexia nervosa. *British Journal of Psychiatry*, **159**, 325–333.

Eisler, I., Dare, C., Russell, G.F., Szmuckler, G., le Grange, D. & Dodge, E. (1997) Family and indvidual therapy in anorexia nervosa. A 5 year follow-up. *Archives of General Psychiatry*, **54**, 1025–1030.

Fairburn, C.G., Shafran, R. & Cooper, Z. (1999) A cognitive behavioural theory of anorexia nervosa. *Behaviour Research and Therapy*, **37**, 1–13.

Freeman, C. (1992) Day patient treatment for anorexia nervosa. *British Review of Bulimia and Anorexia Nervosa*, **6**, 3–8.

Freeman, C. P., Shapiro, C., Morgan, S. & Engliman, M. (1992) Anorexia nervosa: A random allocation controlled trial of two forms of treatment. Paper Presented at Fourth International Conference on Eating Disorders, New York.

Gerlinghoff, M., Backmund, H. & Franzen, U. (1998) Evaluation of a day treatment program for eating disorders. *European Eating Disorders Review*, **6**, 96–106.

Gowers, S., Norton, K., Halek, C. & Crisp, A.H. (1994) Outcome of outpatient psychotherapy in a random allocation treatment study of anorexia nervosa. *International Journal of Eating Disorders*, **15**, 165–177.

Gowers, S.G., Weetman, J., Shore, A., Hossain, F. & Elvins, R. (2000) Impact of hospitalisation on the outcome of adolescent anorexia nervosa. *British Journal of Psychiatry*, **176**, 138–141.

Harris, E.C. & Barraclough, B. (1998) Excess mortality of mental disorder. *British Journal of Psychiatry*, **173**, 11–53.

Piran, N., Kaplan, A., Kerr, A., Shekter-Wolfson, L., Winocur, J., Gold, E. & Garfinkel, P.E. (1989) A day hospital program for anorexia nervosa and bulimia. *International Journal of Eating Disorders*, **8**, 511–521.

Ratnasuriya, R.H., Eisler, I., Szmukler, G.I. & Russell, G.F. (1991) Anorexia nervosa: Outcome and prognostic factors after 20 years. *British Journal of Psychiatry*, **158**, 495–502.

Royal College of Psychiatrists (2001) Council Report 87: Eating disorders in the UK: Policies for service development and training. See www.rcpsych.ac.uk

Russell, G.F.M., Szmukler, G.I., Dare, C. & Eisler, I. (1987) An evaluation of family therapy in anorexia nervosa and bulimia nervosa. *Archives of General Psychiatry*, **44**, 1047–1057.

Trieman, N., Leff, J. & Glover, G. (1999) Outcome of long stay psychiatric patients resettled in the community: Prospective cohort study. *British Medical Journal*, **319**, 13–16.

Williamson, D.A., Duchmann, E.G., Barker, S.E. & Bruno, R.M. (1998) Anorexia nervosa. In Van Hasselt and Hersen (Eds), *Handbook of Psychological Treatment Protocols for Children and Adolescents* (pp. 423–465). London: Lawrence Erlbaum Associates.

CHAPTER 14

Inpatient Treatment

Anthony Winston

Eating Disorders Unit, Warwick Hospital, Warwick, UK

and

Peter Webster

Eating Disorders Unit, Institute of Psychiatry, London, UK

HISTORICAL PERSPECTIVE

The inpatient treatment of anorexia nervosa has undergone major changes since the illness was first identified and treated in the 1860s (Lasègue 1873; Gull, 1874). Although prolonged admission was originally the sole recommended treatment (Marce, 1860), early management was pragmatic and both Lasègue and Gull were appropriately reticent about aetiology. They recommended the withdrawal of the patient from the family environment, together with refeeding ' . . . at regular intervals and surrounded by persons who would have moral control over them' (Gull, 1874). By the end of the nineteenth century, this had extended to total isolation during treatment (Charcot, 1889), and this approach continued in some centres up to the 1970s. Another early treatment was the use of medication to correct secondary hormonal deficits and promote weight gain; drugs used included thyroid hormone (Berkman, 1930), ovarian and anterior pituitary extracts (Reifenstein, 1946) and insulin with chlorpromazine (Dally & Sargant, 1960; Bhanji and Mattingly, 1988).

In the 1970s, particularly through the influence of Gerald Russell, the approach to treatment started to change. This coincided with a growth in behavioural psychology and an increasing understanding of the role of individual psychological, family and social factors in the cause and maintenance of anorexia nervosa. Initially, there was disagreement between those who advocated psychological treatment prior to weight gain (Bruch, 1970) and those who aimed for weight gain before psychological treatment (Russell, 1970). The latter often employed operant conditioning techniques to increase weight gain (Garfinkel et al., 1973). Over time a multifaceted approach has evolved, which starts with weight gain in an emotionally supportive setting and is then followed by more specific psychotherapy when the patient has reached a weight at which she is able to make use of it (Russell, 1981). Furthermore, the patient's family and environment have come to be seen as supportive tools to be used in therapy, rather than necessarily as maintainers of the illness.

The Essential *Handbook of Eating Disorders.* Edited by J. Treasure, U. Schmidt and E. van Furth.
© 2005 John Wiley & Sons, Ltd.

In the UK, for example, the increased emphasis on community psychiatric care over the last two decades has led to a move away from inpatient care for anorexia nervosa. Concerns have arisen about the harmful effect of removing the patient from her usual environment and the risks of institutionalisation. Furthermore, previous motivational treatment may be compromised by the greater emphasis on controlled refeeding during inpatient treatment. It has been suggested that admission may actually be harmful, perhaps because it disrupts long-term treatment (Morgan et al., 1983; Gowers et al., 2000). However, this may not be the case if inpatient treatment forms part of a comprehensive and integrated treatment programme, delivered by a consistent clinical team. Alternative models of management which have been developed include outpatient, daypatient and home treatment (Piran & Kaplan,1990).

THE CURRENT PLACE OF INPATIENT TREATMENT

The present role of inpatient care in the treatment of anorexia nervosa varies enormously across the world. In Germany and the USA most patients are still treated as inpatients, whereas the trend at present in the UK is towards a 'stepped care' approach employing outpatient, day patient and inpatient care in sequence. Unfortunately, this model is significantly compromised by a lack of specialist units and the variation in services nationally. This often leads to admissions to distant units which are delayed and expensive and are not coordinated with a local treatment programme extending over a longer period. A more rational approach may be the 'hub and spoke' model of service organisation (Audit Commission, 1997), in which a central, specialist unit (the 'hub') provides inpatient care, research and training and local units (the 'spokes') provide outpatient care in collaboration with the 'hub'.

INDICATIONS FOR ADMISSION

Despite its potential disadvantages, it is generally agreed that admission is sometimes necessary as a life-saving treatment. In some cases it may also be a positive therapeutic intervention, particularly if it forms part of a longer term management strategy. The American Psychiatric Association (2000) has summarised in detail the specific indications for admission. These reflect both the life-threatening nature of the illness and the need to provide an alternative approach to treatment when motivation is inadequate or facilities are not available for treatment at home. The indications for admission are summarised in Table 14.1. Severely ill patients, such as those with profound electrolyte disturbance or cardiac dysfunction, may need a period of stabilisation on a medical ward before being transferred to the eating disorders unit.

STRUCTURE OF THE INPATIENT PROGRAMME
FOR ANOREXIA NERVOSA

While the structure of admissions varies somewhat between units, there is a general consensus on several basic aspects of management. Clinical experience strongly suggests that

Table 14.1   Indications for inpatient admission

Life threatening
Medical
Body Mass index <13.5 kg/m² or rapid fall > 20% in 6 months
Cardiovascular compromise
• Bradycardia ≤ 40 bpm
• Hypotension ≤ 90/60 mmHg (<16 years ≤ 80/50 mmHg)
• Orthostatic drop ≥10–20 mmHg
• Severe dehydration
Proximal myopathy
Hyoglycaemia
Poor diabetic control
Severe electrolyte disturbance (e.g. K + < 2.5 mmol/L; Na + < 130 mmol/L)
Petechial rash and significant platelet suppression.
Organ compromise—hepatic, renal, bone marrow

Psychiatric
High risk of suicide
Severe comorbidity, e.g. severe depression or OCD
Very low motivation/insight

Compromised community treatment
Intolerable family situation (e.g. high expressed emotion; abuse; collusion)
Social situation (e.g. extreme isolation; lack of support)
Failure to gain weight as outpatient

patients with anorexia nervosa should be treated in specialist units whenever possible and that those treated on general psychiatric or medical wards tend to have a poorer outcome. There are a number of possible reasons for this. Firstly, effective treatment depends on an integrated team which shares a common philosophy and understanding of the disorder. Secondly, anorexia nervosa is a rare disorder and it is difficult for non-specialists to develop sufficient expertise in its management. Thirdly, it is unlikely that a non-specialist team will be able to offer the range of skills needed for effective treatment.

The Multidisciplinary Team

Successful inpatient treatment requires contributions from a number of professional disciplines, who need to work closely together as an integrated team. Nursing patients with anorexia nervosa requires a high level of skill and is most likely to be effective when carried out by a nursing team with experience and training in this area. It is important that nursing staff have an understanding of the complex and ambivalent feelings which patients have about gaining weight and the way in which these reflect fears of psychological change (George, 1997). Nurses need to strike a difficult balance between firmness and sensitivity; this requires an ability to understand the patient's dilemmas and must be based on a firm therapeutic alliance. Developing this alliance is one of the crucial tasks in nursing eating disordered patients. Patients are likely to respond badly to staff whom they perceive as rigid and authoritarian, but at the same time are unlikely to feel safe unless those caring for them are able to set clear and appropriate boundaries. The patient's perception of staff is likely to reflect a disturbed attachment history (Ward et al., 2000) and staff may come to function as good attachment objects. Although this experience of 'reparenting' potentially has many positive aspects, the development of an excessively dependent relationship may hinder the development of a sense of autonomy in the patient.

In most teams, a consultant psychiatrist provides clinical leadership, supported by one or more junior doctors. The psychiatrist's specific contributions include the diagnosis of eating disorders and secondary psychiatric illnesses, the management of medical complications and the prescription of medication. In many units, psychologists play a major role in the assessment and treatment of the primary illness. They may also take the lead in the assessment and treatment of comorbid disorders such as depression, obsessive-compulsive disorder (OCD), social phobia and self-harm. However, it may be necessary to wait until a sufficient degree of weight gain has been achieved before instituting specific psychological treatments for these disorders.

Psychotherapy is essential to the treatment of patients with anorexia nervosa and may be provided by professionals from a variety of disciplines. In some units, a family therapist is included in the team. The dietitian has a central role in supervising the patient's nutritional rehabilitation and may also play a part in nutritional education. The occupational therapist may contribute to the patient's dietary rehabilitation, for example supervising her in buying, preparing and cooking meals. She may also have a role in running groups on the ward. Many inpatients have long histories of anorexia nervosa and the disorder may be complicated by social isolation and delayed psychosocial development. These problems need to be included in the treatment programme and the patient may benefit from 'rehabilitation' in terms of social function, education or employment, sexual relationships and other areas.

It is essential that the multidisciplinary team meets regularly to review the patient's progress. Patients with anorexia nervosa are likely to provoke strong feelings in those who care for them. These may include powerful feelings of frustration and anger on the one hand and a wish to protect and rescue the patient on the other. These feelings should be understood as counter-transference responses to the patient's difficulties and staff need to be able to resist the temptation to 'act out' their feelings. Such 'acting out' can result in ostensibly 'therapeutic' responses which are in fact punitive or humiliating and are ultimately counterproductive. Not uncommonly, the patient will 'split' the therapeutic team, viewing one member as sympathetic and helpful and another as authoritarian and cruel. This can lead to conflict within the team and undermine the therapeutic process. Team members need to develop the ability to reflect on their own emotional responses to the patient and this can be facilitated by the provision of regular supervision.

Length of Admission

The primary aim of admission is to achieve significant weight gain while at the same time providing appropriate psychotherapy and support. Although restoration of a normal weight can be achieved relatively quickly, the pace of psychological change is likely to be much slower. There is little empirical evidence on which to base recommendations about the optimum rate of weight gain or length of admission, and units vary in these respects. Moreover, due to the complexity of the illness, patients have to be treated individually.

This results in considerable variation in the length of admission, both between and within units.

One observational study found that people with a longer duration of illness had a higher likelihood of a good outcome with a longer duration of inpatient treatment, while those with a shorter duration of illness had a higher likelihood of a good outcome with briefer inpatient treatment (Kächele, 1999).

Preparation for Admission

Admission to an eating disorders unit represents a major commitment for both the patient and the hospital. Good preparation can be very helpful in facilitating admission and may increase the chances that the patient will remain in treatment. Every admission must involve a full psychiatric, physical and social assessment, as well as an assessment of the patient's capacity. This should include the patient's understanding of and insight into her illness, its current risks, and the treatment involved and her attitude to hospitalisation. The nature and likely duration of the treatment programme should be explained in detail and, if possible, the patient should have the opportunity to visit the unit before admission. Issues such as meals may need to be discussed in some detail at this point.

Treatment Philosophy

There is always a tension during inpatient treatment between enhancement of the patient's sense of responsibility for herself and the necessity of weight gain. This creates a paradox in the treatment: a behavioural approach to feeding goes hand in hand with psychological work aimed at increasing motivation and autonomy. In many units, the former takes precedence early in treatment and the latter becomes more important as weight and insight increase. This can be a source of confusion for both patients and staff, particularly if these issues are not addressed openly. Over the last century the management of anorexia nervosa has transferred from medical to psychiatric settings, which is an implicit marker of the recognition that psychosocial processes are important in the process of recovery.

Historically, inpatient treatment was based on strict behavioural principles in which privileges were removed and returned as a reward for weight gain. However, such an approach is likely to be experienced by the patient as degrading and thus damaging to the therapeutic alliance (Anonymous, 1995). There is no evidence that such programmes are more effective in promoting weight gain than those which are based on more collaborative principles (Eckert et al., 1979; Touyz et al., 1984). It is our view that programmes based on strict operant conditioning can no longer be recommended. However, the issue of control is central to the psychopathology of anorexia nervosa and this needs to be reflected in the structure of the inpatient programme. Admission to hospital entails giving up the rigid dietary control of anorexia nervosa, which many patients experience as equivalent to emotional control. In order for the patient to feel safe enough to relinquish this control, the treatment programme needs to provide a degree of external control, and a clear treatment structure is therefore essential. However, as the patient develops a greater capacity to tolerate and integrate emotion, this external control can be relaxed and the patient can take progressively more responsibility for her own eating.

Meals and Weighing

In one model meals are taken as a group as this encourages socialisation and can provide additional support, as well as making supervision easier. All meals are supervised by a nurse and are treated as a form of group therapy as well as refeeding; difficulties can be discussed and abnormal eating behaviour challenged by the nurse. Nursing staff can also model normal eating by sharing the meal with patients. Strict boundaries are maintained around finishing meals on time and eating everything provided. These boundaries may be maintained in a variety of ways—for example, by substituting calorific drinks if food is not consumed and only allowing patients to leave the dining room when all have completed the meal. In many units, patients are also supervised for a defined period after meals in order to prevent them concealing food or vomiting. At a later stage in treatment, they may eat their meals without supervision.

Patients should be weighed at least twice weekly; staff need to be aware that some patients will attempt to increase their weight artificially by drinking large quantities of water or concealing heavy objects in their clothes. The regular weighing session is likely to be a difficult time for the patient and one at which staff should be able to offer support. Exercise also needs to be regarded as part of the nutritional equation and should therefore be 'prescribed', particularly during the early stages of treatment. During inpatient treatment, exercise should ideally be under the supervision of a physiotherapist.

Target Weight

It is a common practice in many units to set a 'target weight' at the beginning of treatment. This gives definition to the treatment programme and may help to allay the patient's anxieties that she will be allowed to become overweight. There is no clear consensus as to how the target weight should be determined; it may be set at a specific point within the normal range (BMI of 20–25 kg/m^2) or negotiated with the patient. A reasonably common practice is to base it on a low normal body weight, such as a BMI of 19 or 20 kg/m^2. This is, of necessity, an arbitrary figure and may have to be modified in the light of individual circumstances, for example if the patients' premorbid stable weight was significantly higher or lower than this. It may sometimes be appropriate to agree a lower target weight, for example as part of a specialised treatment plan or in intractable cases where the patient has repeatedly failed to attain a normal weight.

Although setting the target at a normal weight results in lengthy admissions, clinical experience suggests that discharge before this point may allow the patient to avoid the difficult psychological transition to a normal weight. There is limited research evidence that discharge at a low weight is associated with a poorer outcome and a higher readmission rate (Baran et al., 1995; Howard et al., 1999). It should be emphasised that the target represents a minimum healthy weight rather than an ideal. In some units a target weight range is used in preference to a single weight. The return of menstruation may be used as a physiological marker of adequate weight restoration, although patients should be informed that this may be delayed for several months after attaining a normal weight.

Maintenance Treatment

There are advantages, if circumstances allow, in providing a further period of inpatient or day patient treatment after the patient attains a normal weight. It is at this point that the patient is forced to relinquish the psychological safety of the anorexic position and face the prospect of life at a normal weight. In many ways, the most difficult psychological work begins at this point. A period of stabilisation—both psychological and dietary—may help to reduce the chances of relapse after discharge. At this point in treatment, it may be appropriate for the patient to eat meals without supervision and to take responsibility for maintaining her own weight within an agreed range. During the maintenance phase, staff can help the patient to learn how to shop, cook and eat meals in a social situation, while supporting her in working through the feelings that these activities generate.

Other Forms of Inpatient Treatment

Although most inpatient admissions will be directed towards full weight restoration, admission may occasionally be required in other circumstances. These include shorter admissions for those whose physical health is in immediate danger but are not able to commit themselves to full weight restoration, and crisis admissions precipitated by comorbid psychiatric disorders.

SPECIAL GROUPS

Younger Patients

This section describes the treatment of adults—that is, those aged 18 or over. Those below the age of 18 are usually best treated in a specialised adolescent eating disorder unit, although this may not always be possible. Patients between the ages of 16 and 18 are frequently admitted to adult eating disorder units in the UK. In those below the age of 16, the effect of malnutrition on growth needs to be taken into account and developmental psychological issues assume even greater importance. Family therapy is likely to play a larger role in the treatment of this age group than in adults, and various models of integrating the family into treatment have been used, e.g. the use of family flats or partial hospitalisation. Another important aspect is the adolescent's educational needs.

Concern has been expressed about the disruption to a young person's life by admission, and indeed Gowers et al. (2000), in a naturalistic study, showed a poorer outcome in patients who had been admitted. However, as with adult patients, admission is necessary if there are life-threatening risks or if the family situation is profoundly detrimental. Medically, this is particularly so, as younger patients can dehydrate extremely rapidly and prepubescent cases have very low fat stores. In this age group, deterioration can therefore be sudden and severe.

Male Patients

The needs of male patients, who represent a significant minority of those with anorexia nervosa, require special consideration. Issues of self-care and body image may be significantly different in men, as may those related to sexual relationships.

Parents

In the relatively infrequent case of a patient who has children, the parental role needs to be acknowledged and the treatment programme may need to be modified accordingly. Depending on the circumstances, it may be appropriate to involve child and adolescent mental health services or social services in the treatment plan.

COMPULSORY TREATMENT

Provision for compulsory treatment of psychiatric disorders, including anorexia nervosa, varies from country to country. Due to the nature of anorexia nervosa, many patients have impaired insight despite an apparent understanding of the nature and consequences of the illness. This compromises their capacity to make an informed choice about treatment. Until relatively recently, there was uncertainty about the legality of compulsory treatment for anorexia nervosa in the UK but the position has recently been clarified by guidance from the Mental Health Act Commission:

> In certain situations, patients with severe anorexia nervosa whose health is seriously threatened by food refusal may be subject to detention in hospital and...there are occasions when it is necessary to treat the self-imposed starvation to ensure the proper care of the patient...naso-gastric feeding can be a medical process, forming an integral part of the treatment for anorexia nervosa. (Mental Health Act Commission, 1997)

The European Court of Human Rights has ruled that compulsory feeding does not constitute inhuman or degrading treatment; it therefore appears to be consistent with the European Convention on Human Rights, which has been substantially incorporated into British law as the Human Rights Act (Radcliffes Mental Health Law Briefing, No. 34, 2000).

Although it is always preferable to engage ambivalent patients through the gradual development of a therapeutic alliance (Goldner et al., 1997), compulsory treatment may be appropriate for the small minority of patients who refuse treatment despite life-threatening risk. The case for compulsory treatment is strengthened by the evidence that apparently intractable cases can recover fully even after 10 years (Theander, 1992). However, involuntary patients appear to take longer to achieve weight gain than voluntary patients and have a mortality rate about five times higher (Ramsey et al., 1999).

THE INPATIENT TREATMENT OF BULIMIA NERVOSA

This is a complex area and differs from that of anorexia nervosa. As with anorexia nervosa, there are national variations: for example, inpatient treatment appears to be used more

Table 14.2 Recommended investigations on admission

Essential	Additional
Full blood count	Vitamin B12, folate levels
Urea and electrolytes ,	Erythrocyte transketolase (thiamin)
Glucose	Serum zinc
Serum calcium, magnesium, phosphate	DEXA scan
Serum proteins	Creatine kinase
Liver function tests	
ECG	

commonly in some other European countries than in the UK. Unlike anorexia nervosa, specific indications for admission have not been clearly defined but it is useful to follow the same pattern, i.e. admitting when there is a severe medical, psychiatric or social risk or a failure of outpatient treatment. The main aim of admission is usually to stablilise the patient's eating pattern and support her in giving up vomiting or laxative abuse. Treatment is likely to be of shorter duration than in anorexia nervosa and may be based more clearly on cognitive-behavioural principles (Tuschen & Bents, 1995).

However, the proportion of patients with bulimia nervosa who require admission is relatively small and is likely to consist mostly of those with the 'multi-impulsive' form of the disorder (Lacey & Evans, 1986; Lacey, 1995). These patients are difficult to treat and can be extremely disruptive to the ward routine. Admission to hospital can precipitate a deterioration, in which the patient's behaviour becomes more disturbed and problematic behaviours such as self-harm more frequent. Clinical experience suggests that such patients tend to respond poorly unless treated in specialised programmes, but there are few outcome data available.

PHYSICAL ASSESSMENT AND MONITORING

Patients require a detailed physical assessment on admission to hospital. This should include a full medical history and a thorough physical examination. A range of screening investigations should be carried out, including blood tests and an electrocardiogram (ECG) (American Psychiatric Association, 1993; Sharp & Freeman, 1993; Carney & Andersen, 1996; Winston, 2000). Detailed recommendations for routine investigations are given in Table 14.2; further investigations may be required, depending on the patient's condition. If significant abnormalities are detected, expert advice may be needed from an appropriate specialist.

NUTRITIONAL MANAGEMENT

Weight restoration in hospital is generally considered to be best carried out under the supervision of a dietician, due to the medical risks involved in refeeding at very low weights. Due to the fact that patients with anorexia nervosa have delayed gastric emptying (Robinson et al., 1995), small and frequent meals are preferable to infrequent but larger meals. Patients should have three meals a day and this may be supplemented with snacks in between. Vegetarianism and other special diets may be allowed, but dietary restrictions based on anorexic thinking should be challenged. An average rate of weight gain of 0.5–1.0 kg per week is generally considered appropriate; most patients require a daily calorie intake of around 2500 kcal per day to achieve this but a higher intake may occasionally be required, particularly in men. Recent preliminary research suggests that a minimum weight gain of 0.5 kg per week results in greater weight gain by the time of discharge from hospital than adoption of a higher minimum (Herzog et al., in press).

Weight gain may be relatively rapid during the first week or two of treatment as a result of rehydration and glycogen deposition; this can be minimised by starting refeeding gradually. A progressive increase in calorie intake in the early stages of treatment will also allow the patient time to adjust to the idea of weight gain; a rapid increase in weight early in treatment is likely to alarm her and jeopardise the therapeutic alliance. Conversely, calorie intake may need to be increased in the later stages of treatment as the basal metabolic rate increases (Salisbury et al., 1995) and the patient becomes more active.

Nasogastric Feeding

Artificial means of feeding such as nasogastric tubes should be used only as a last resort. In most cases, a combination of sensitive exploration of the patient's fears and skilled nursing is sufficient to enable the patient to begin to take food normally. The enforced use of enteral feeding may be very damaging to the therapeutic alliance and may reactivate previous experiences of physical or sexual abuse. However, there is a small number of patients who do require nasogastric feeding. These include those who are being treated against their will and those who have life-threatening medical complications. Enteral feeding should always be carried out under the supervision of a dietician. Parenteral feeding should be avoided if at all possible as the risk of medical complications is high and in most cases it is unlikely to have significant advantages over the enteral route.

Nutritional Supplements

The use of nutritional supplements in place of food is generally avoided as re-feeding patients with a normal diet usually provides adequate renutrition; it also encourages normalisation of eating patterns and a return of normal gastrointestinal function. However, a number of micronutrient deficiencies have been identified in anorexia nervosa (Hadigan et al., 2000; Casper et al., 1980; Philipp et al., 1988; Thibault & Roberge, 1987; Beaumont et al., 1981; Rock & Vasantharajan, 1995). Although the clinical significance of many of these deficiencies is at present unclear, it is probably wise to prescribe a multi-vitamin/multi-mineral supplement in oral form.

Deficiencies of zinc and thiamin (vitamin B1) may be of clinical significance (Lask et al., 1993; McClain et al., 1992; Humphries et al., 1989; Katz et al., 1987). It has been suggested that the use of zinc supplements increases the rate of weight gain (Birmingham et al., 1994), but this finding has yet to be confirmed and the routine use of zinc supplements cannot currently be recommended. A significant proportion of patients with anorexia nervosa are deficient in thiamin (Winston et al., 2000) and the increase in carbohydrate metabolism which occurs during refeeding may exhaust inadequate thiamin reserves. The use of prophylactic thiamin supplements may therefore be appropriate.

COMPLICATIONS OF REFEEDING

A number of complications may occur during the course of refeeding, some of them serious. Clinical experience suggests that many of the untoward consequences of refeeding can be minimised or avoided by starting the patient on relatively small amounts of food and increasing progressively.

Electrolyte Disturbances

A range of electrolyte disturbances can occur during refeeding and these are sometimes referred to collectively as the 'refeeding syndrome' (Solomon & Kirby, 1990). It should be borne in mind that serum measurements of electrolytes may be misleading as they may mask a significant total body deficit (Powers et al., 1995). The metabolic demands of refeeding can unmask hidden deficiencies and complex shifts of electrolytes between intracellular and extracellular compartments may further complicate the biochemical picture (Warren & Steinberg, 1979). The use of intravenous fluids may compound the problem.

Hypokalaemia, hypocalcaemia and hypomagnesaemia occur and hypokalaemia appears to be particularly common in those who purge (Palla & Litt, 1988; Koh et al., 1989; Greenfield et al., 1995; Connan et al., 2000). One of the most serious biochemical complications in the short term is hypophosphataemia. Malnourished patients are likely to be phosphate deficient and ingestion of large quantities of carbohydrate, such as occurs during refeeding, may result in a precipitate drop in serum phosphate levels (Fisher et al., 2000; Winston & Wells, 2002). It is essential to monitor the serum potassium, calcium, magnesium and phosphate closely, particularly during the first week or two of treatment. If significant biochemical deficiencies are identified, the patient may require supplementation, either orally or intravenously.

Gastrointestinal Dysfunction

Gastrointestinal symptoms are common. Delayed gastric emptying results in early satiety and sensations of abdominal fullness or bloating in a significant number of patients. Promotility agents such as metoclopramide and cisapride have been used to increase gastric emptying but cisapride has recently been withdrawn from use in the UK due to concerns about cardiac arrythmias. Metoclopramide may be used in a reduced dose of 5 mg t.d.s. but is often only of limited effectiveness.

Many patients complain of colicky abdominal pain. This rarely responds, in our experience, to antispasmodic drugs such as mebeverine and is generally best managed with explanation and reassurance. A shift of fluid into the gut after eating may cause symptoms such as nausea, diarrhoea and faintness, particularly if the patient is given large quantities of carbohydrate; limiting the amount of sodium in the diet may help. Constipation may be a problem in some patients, particularly those who have abused laxatives. Constipation can usually be managed adequately with a combination of sufficient fluid and dietary fibre together, if necessary, with stool softening agents or bulk laxatives. The use of stimulant laxatives is best avoided.

Refeeding Oedema

Some patients develop peripheral oedema in the early stages of refeeding; this appears to be particularly common in those who have abused laxatives or induced vomiting prior to admission. In severe cases, it can lead to rapid weight gain of several kilograms, which is alarming to the patient. Refeeding oedema should be distinguished from cardiac failure, of which other signs are absent. The aetiology of this problem is at present obscure. It may be related to dysregulation of the renin–angiotensin–aldosterone system but this hypothesis has yet to be substantiated (Jonas & Mickely, 1990; Mitchell et al., 1988; Fujita et al., 1991; Mizuno et al., 1992). There is some preliminary evidence that abnormal sensitivity to vasopressin may also be implicated (Kaye et al., 1983; Nishita et al., 1989). Hypoproteinaemia does not appear to be a major factor in most cases.

Some clinicians believe that the use of a low sodium diet during the early stages of treatment is helpful in preventing refeeding oedema; although rational, there is no research evidence to support this practice. The use of diuretics to treat refeeding oedema is probably best avoided, as the short-term benefits are likely to be offset by intravascular dehydration, which may perpetuate the problem. The most appropriate management in most cases is to reassure the patient that the oedema and weight gain are transient and that they will resolve as the body's homeostatic mechanisms return to normal. In cases where the use of diuretics is unavoidable, the most logical choice would appear to be the aldosterone antagonist spironolactone.

Cardiac Complications

Cardiac failure does occasionally occur and is most likely when patients are fed artificially, particularly parenterally. Patients with severe anorexia nervosa have evidence of impaired cardiac function and loss of left ventricular muscle (Gottdiener et al., 1978; Moodie & Salcedo, 1985; St John Sutton et al., 1985). In this situation, a large salt, water and protein load (such as occurs in parenteral feeding) can overload the circulation and result in cardiac failure. Other factors which may predispose to cardiac failure include hypophosphataemia and thiamin deficiency. Specific care should be taken when using antidepressants and antipsychotics, due to the already heightened risk of arrythmias and the need for lower therapeutic doses at low weight. As QT interval prolongation can occur at very low weights, drugs which prolong this interval should be avoided due to the risk of arrythmias.

PSYCHOTHERAPY

As discussed in other chapters, psychotherapy plays a central role in inpatient and day-patient treatment. Despite the fact that there is a more intense focus on refeeding in inpatient treatment, and the patients are generally of lower weight, psychotherapy should still form an integral part of the inpatient treatment programme. Effective treatment depends on weight gain and psychological change going hand in hand (Agras, 1987). Appropriate psychological interventions enable the patient to gain weight and, conversely, weight gain generates further psychological issues which need to be addressed in therapy. However, patients who are severely underweight have evidence of cognitive impairment (Szmukler et al., 1992; Kingston et al., 1996; Lauer et al., 1999) which may reduce their ability to make use of psychotherapy. Individual psychotherapy during the early stages of treatment may therefore need to be focused primarily on the development of a therapeutic alliance and exploration of the patient's anxieties about change. It should be emphasised to the patient that inpatient treatment is only the beginning of the therapeutic process and that therapy and psychological change are likely to continue for some considerable time after discharge from hospital.

There is at present little evidence on which to base recommendations about the type of therapy for adults with anorexia nervosa, although both psychoanalytic psychotherapy and family therapy appear to be beneficial in out-patients (Dare et al., 2001). Some units adopt a cognitive-behavioural approach (Andersen et al., 1997) whereas others use a predominantly psychodynamic model (Crisp et al., 1985). Therapy may consist of any combination of individual, group and systemic therapy. Family therapy appears to be particularly beneficial for younger patients (Russell et al., 1987; Dare et al., 1990; le Grange et al., 1992; Eisler et al., 1997, 2000).

Whatever approach is adopted, it is important that there is a coherent theoretical model underpinning all aspects of patient care. Ideally, inpatient psychotherapy should form part of a continuum with both pre-admission and post-discharge therapy. There are significant advantages in having the same therapist working with the patient throughout all three phases of treatment. Although the primary focus of treatment is on issues related to food, psychotherapy will need to focus on more complex underlying issues. In this sense, attaining a normal weight should not be seen as an endpoint but rather as the beginning of a new phase in the patient's life, which will bring new challenges and opportunities. It may be helpful to frame this transition as leaving the safety of anorexia nervosa and facing the psychological difficulties from which the illness had previously offered protection.

A group culture is likely to develop among the patients on the unit, which can be supportive or destructive depending on the group dynamics. Relationships within the patient group and between patients and staff may come to recapitulate aspects of family dynamics and transference issues are often prominent. Recovery from anorexia nervosa entails change for both the patient and those around her. The family or partner may require help to adapt to these changes and family or couple therapy should be available if required.

DRUG TREATMENT

Although a number of drugs have been used in the treatment of anorexia nervosa, the place of medication remains unclear at present. Cyproheptadine (Halmi et al., 1986) and pimozide (Vandereycken & Pierloot, 1982) have been shown to increase weight gain when compared to placebo. However, weight gain seems to be restricted to the short term and these drugs are not generally considered cost-effective methods of treatment. Some research suggests that fluoxetine might be effective in reducing the risk of relapse following inpatient treatment (Kaye et al., 1991); however, a more recent study indicates no benefit (Strober et al., 1997). There have also been case reports of olanzepine causing resolution of anorexic cognitions (Hansen, 1999; Jensen et al., 2000). These findings, however, are confounded by weight gain and the concurrent use of other therapies and thus only present a case for further clinical trials.

Symptomatically, medication may be used to reduce the patient's level of arousal and agitation; this can be achieved with standard anxiolytics. Moderate to severe depression occurs in a significant number of patients (Corcos et al., 2000) but often does not respond to antidepressants until weight is significantly restored. This is also generally true of OCD; as both disorders are often present together it is often useful to prescribe an antidepressant which is effective for both, such as a selective serotonin reuptake inhibitor. In general, if depressed mood persists after weight gain it should be managed in the conventional way. Patients with anorexia nervosa may be very sensitive to the effects of drugs and a reduced dose may be necessary; calculating the dose on the basis of body weight is generally best. Prescribers should also be aware of potential contra-indications arising from physical complications such as compromised bone marrow or liver function or an abnormal ECG.

DISCHARGE AND FOLLOW-UP

Preparation for discharge and subsequent follow-up treatment are essential if improvement is to be maintained and admission is to serve a purpose beyond weight gain alone (Crisp et al., 1991). Before discharge the patient should be helped to optimise her skills in managing her own illness; this may be addressed particularly during the maintenance phase of treatment. Concurrently, it is important to educate carers, such as the patient's family, in providing the appropriate level of support. This often needs to be negotiated between the therapist, patient and family in order to achieve an appropriate balance between patient responsibility and external support.

Once discharged, the patient should be offered appropriate help in managing her own eating, while continuing to work on underlying psychological issues. In practice, the type and intensity of care provided after discharge will depend on a number of factors including: the patient's level of insight and motivation, the extent of comorbidity and the availability of services in the area. Eating disorder day units and psychotherapeutic supported accommodation can offer a useful 'half-way house' between inpatient care and independent living. Another important area is planning for any possible relapses or 'crises' and the use of a 'crisis card' may be helpful.

OUTCOME OF INPATIENT TREATMENT

Although it is well established in clinical practice, data on the effectiveness of inpatient treatment are sparse. Published studies have yielded confusing results. Crisp et al. (1991) found no difference in one-, two- and five-year outcome in a randomised trial comparing four treatment modalities: inpatient treatment; a combination of individual and family therapy; group therapy; and assessment only. However, methodological difficulties reduce the impact of this study and leave the question still open (Gowers et al., 1988). A later study indicated significant differences in mortality between areas with and without specialised eating disorder services (Crisp et al., 1992).

As mentioned a naturalistic study found that adolescents treated as inpatients had a considerably worse outcome at 2–7 years than those who received outpatient treatment alone. The authors of this study argue that inpatient treatment may actually be damaging to treatment in the long term (Gowers et al., 2000). However, it should be noted that no adjustment was made for case mix and that these conclusions may not be applicable to adults. Furthermore, the results of Kächele's study in adults do not support the conclusions of Gowers et al. (Kächele, 1999). A recent review concluded that at present there is no clear evidence of any significant outcome difference between in- and outpatient treatment. (Meads et al., 2001).

Drop-out rates of patients with anorexia nervosa from inpatient treatment are high and concerning. Kahn and Pike (2001) found that one-third of inpatients dropped out early, the only predictors being length of illness and bulimic subtype. Early drop-out is a risk factor for relapse in the first year post-hospitalisation (Baran et al., 1995), as well as a predictor of the illness progessing to a severe, chronic course (Strober et al., 1997). Thus, more research is needed to identify predictors of drop-out and reduce the chance of relapse post-discharge.

CONCLUSION

Despite limited and sometimes conflicting research evidence, inpatient treatment has a well-established place in the treatment of severe anorexia nervosa and a less clearly defined place in that of bulimia nervosa. It is increasingly recognised that it must form part of a package of care that extends well beyond discharge from hospital. Further research is needed to determine the essential components of effective treatment, to clarify who is most likely to benefit from it and to establish whether some aspects may actually impede recovery.

Keypoints

- Inpatient treatment has progressively played a smaller role in the management of eating disorders.
- Admission should generally be limited to life-threatening situations, intolerable social situations, and failure of extensive community management.
- Management involves refeeding and psychotherapy and should be multidisciplinary.
- Clear evidence is still lacking for outcome measures compared to community treatment.
- Engagement in treatment and relapse prevention is essential in improving prognosis.

REFERENCES

Agras, W.S. (1987) *Eating Disorders; Management of Obesity, Bulimia and Anorexia Nervosa.* Elmsford, NY: Pergamon Press.

American Psychiatric Association (1993) Practice guideline for eating disorders. *Am. J. Psychiat.*, **150** (2), 207–228.

American Psychiatric Association (2000) Practice guideline for eating disorders. *Am. J. Psychiat.*, **157** (1 Supplement).

Andersen, A.E., Bowers, W. & Evans, K. (1997) In-patient treatment of anorexia nervosa. In D.M. Garner & P.E. Garfinkel (Eds), *Handbook of Treatment for Eating Disorders* (pp. 327–348). New York: Guilford Press.

Anonymous (1995) *Br. Med. J.*, **3111**, 635–636.

Audit Commission (1997) *Higher Purchase; Commissioning Specialised Services in the NHS*. London: Audit Commission.

Baran, S.A., Weltzin, T.E. & Kaye, W.H. (1995) Low discharge weight and outcome in anorexia nervosa. *Am. J. Psychiat.*, **152**, 1070–1072.

Berkman, J.M. (1930) Anorexia nervosa, anorexia, inanition and low metabolic rate. *Am. J. Med. Sci.*, **180**, 411.

Bhanji, S. & Mattingly, D. (1988) *Medical Aspects of Anorexia Nervosa*. London: Wright.

Birmingham, C.L., Goldner, E.M. & Bakan, R (1994) Controlled trial of zinc supplementation in anorexia nervosa. *Int. J. Eat. Disord.*, **15**, 251–255.

Bruch, H. (1970) Instinct and interpersonal experience. *Compr. Psychiat.*, **11**, 495–506.

Carney, C.P. & Andersen, A.E. (1996) Eating disorders: Guide to medical evaluation and complications. *Psychiat. Clin. N. Am.*, **19**, 657–679.

Casper, R.C., Kirschner, B., Sandstead, H.H., Jacob, R.A. & Davis, J.M. (1980) An evaluation of trace metals, vitamins and taste function in anorexia nervosa. *Am. J. Clin. Nutrit.*, **33**, 1801–1808.

Charcot, J.M. (1889) *Diseases of the Nervous System*. London: New Sydenham Society.

Corcos, M., Guilbaud, O., Speranza, M., Paterniti, S., Loas, G., Stephan, P. & Jeammet, P. (2000) Alexithymia and depression in eating disorders. *Psychiat. Res.*, **10** (93), 263–266.

Crisp, A.H., Callender, J.S., Halek, C. & Hsu, L.K.G. (1992) Long-term mortality in anorexia nervosa: A twenty-year follow-up of the St. George's and Aberdeen cohorts. *Br. J. Psychiat.*, **161**, 104–107.

Crisp, A.H., Norton, K.R.W., Gower, S., Halek, C., Bowyer, C., Yeldham, D., Levett, G. & Bhat, A. (1991) A controlled study of the effect of therapies aimed at adolescent and family psychopathology in anorexia nervosa. *Br. J. Psychiat.*, **159**, 325–333.

Crisp, A.H., Norton, K.R.W., Jurczak, S., Bowyer, C. & Duncan, S. (1985) A treatment approach to anorexia nervosa—25 years on. *J. Psychiat. Res.*, **19**, 399–404.

Dally, P.J. & Sargant, W. (1960) Treatment and outcome of anorexia nervosa. *Br. Med. J.*, **2**, 793.

Dare, C., Eisler, I., Russell, G.F.M. & Szmukler, G.I. (1990) Family therapy for anorexia nervosa: Implications from the results of a controlled trial of family and individual therapy. *J. Marital Family Ther.*, **16**, 39–57.

Dare, C., Eisler, I., Russell, G., Treasure, J. & Dodge, L. (2001) Psychological therapies for adults with anorexia nervosa: Randomised controlled trial of out-patient treatments. *Br. J. Psychiat.*, **178**, 216–221.

Eckert, E.D., Goldberg, S.C., Halmi, K.A., Casper, R.C. & Davis, J.M. (1979) Behaviour therapy in anorexia nervosa. *Br. J. Psychiat.*, **134**, 55–59.

Eisler, I., Dare, C., Russell, G.F.M., Szmukler, G.I., le Grange, D. & Dodge, E. (1997) Family and individual therapy in anorexia nervosa: A 5 year follow-up. *Arch. Gen. Psychiat.*, **54**, 1025–1030.

Eisler, I., Dare, C., Hodes, M., Russell, G., Dodge, E. & le Grange, D. (2000) Family therapy for adolescent anorexia nervosa: The resuts of a controlled comparison of two family interventions. *J. Child Psychol. Psychiat.*, **41**, 727–736.

Ferguson, C.P., La Via, M.C., Crossan, P.J. & Kaye, W.H. (1999) Are serotonin reuptake inhibitors effective in underweight anorexia nervosa? *Int. J. Eat. Disord.*, **25**, 11–17.

Fisher, M., Simpser, E. & Schneider, M. (2000) Hypophosphatemia secondary to oral refeeding in anorexia nervosa. *Int. J. Eat. Disord.*, **28**, 181–187.

Garfinkel, P.E., Kline, S.A. & Stancer, H.C. (1973) Treatment of anorexia nervosa using operant conditioning techniques. *J. Nervous Mental Disord.*, **157**, 428–433.

George, L. (1997) The psychological characteristics of patients suffering from anorexia nervosa and the nurse's role in creating a therapeutic relationship. *J. Adv. Nursing*, **26**, 899–908.

Goldner, E.M., Birmingham, C.L. & Smye, V. (1997) Addressing treatment refusal in anorexia nervosa: Clinical, ethical, and legal considerations. In D. Garner & P. Garfinkel (Eds), *Handbook of Treatment for Eating Disorders* (2nd edn; pp. 450–461). New York: Guilford Press.

Gottdiener, J.S., Gross, H.A., Henry, W.L., Borer, J.S. & Ebert, M.H. (1978) Effects of self-induced starvation on cardiac size and function in anorexia nervosa. *Circulation*, **58**, 425–433.

Gowers, S.G., Weetman, J., Shore, A. et al. (2000) Impact of hospitalisation on the outcome of adolescent anorexia nervosa. *Br. J. Psychiat.*, **176**, 138–141.

Gowers, S., Norton, K., Yeldham, K., Bowger, C., Levett, G., Heavey, A., Bhat, A. & Crisp, A. (1988) The St. George's prospective treatment study of anorexia nervosa: A discussion of methodological problems. *Int. J. Eat. Disord.*, **8**, 445–454.

Greenfield, D., Mickley, D., Quinlan, D.M. & Roloff, P. (1995) Hypokalemia in outpatients with eating disorders. *Am. J. Psychiat.*, **152**, 60–63.

Gull, W.W. (1874) Anorexia nervosa (apepsia hysterica, anorexia hysterica). *Trans. Clin. Soc. Lond.*, **7**, 22.

Hadigan, C.M., Anderson, E.J., Miller, K.K., Hubbard, J.L., Herzog, D.B., Halmi, K.A., Eckert, E., LaDu, T.J. et al. (1986) Anorexia nervosa. Treatment efficacy of cyproheptadine and amitriptyline. *Arch. Gen. Psychiat.*, **43**, 177–181.

Hansen, L. (1999) Olanzepine in the treatment of anorexia nervosa (letter). *Br. J. Psychiat.*, **175**, 592.

Herzog, T., Zeeck, A., Hartmann, A. & Nickel, T. (in press) Lower targets for weekly weight gain lead to better results in inpatient treatment of anorexia nervosa. *Eur. Eat. Disord. Rev.*

Howard, W.T., Evans, K.K., Quintero-Howard, C.V., Bowers, W.A. & Andersen, A.E. (1999) Predictors of success or failure of transition to day hospital treatment for in-patients with anorexia nervosa. *Am. J. Psychiat.*, **156**, 1697–702.

Humphries, L., Vivian, B., Stuart, M. & McClain, C.J. (1989) Zinc deficiency and eating disorders. *J. Clin. Psychiat.*, **50** (12), 456–459.

Jensen, V.S., Mejlhede et al. (2000) Anorexia nervosa: Treatment with olanzepine (letter). *Br. J. Psychiat.*, **177**, 87.

Kächele, H. for the study group MZ-ESS. (1999) Eine multizentrische Studie zu Aufwand und Erfolg bei psychodynamischer Therapie von Eßstörungen. *Psychother. Med. Psychol.*, 49, 100–108.

Kaplan, A.S. & Olmstead, M.P. (1997) Partial hospitalisation. In D.M. Garner & P.E. Garfinkel (Eds), *Handbook of Treatment of Eating Disorders* (2nd edn; pp. 354–360). New York: Guilford, Press.

Kahn, C. & Pike, K.M. (2001) In search of predictors of dropout from inpatient treatment for anorexia nervosa. *Int. J. Eat. Disord.*, **30**, 237–244.

Katz, R.L, Keen, C.L., Litt, I.F., Hurley, L.S., Kellams-Harrison, K.M. & Glader, L.J. (1987) Zinc deficiency in anorexia nervosa. *J. Adolesc. Health Care*, **8** (5), 400–406.

Kaye, W.H., Gendall, K. & Kye, C. (1998) The role of the central nervous system in the psychoneuroendocrine disturbances of anorexia and bulimia nervosa. *Psychiat. Clin. N. Am.*, **21**, 381–396.

Kaye, W., Weltzin, T.E., Hsu, L.G. & Bulik, C.M. (1991) An open trial of fluoxetine in patients with anorexia nervosa. *J. Clin. Psychiat.*, **52** (11), 464–471.

Kingston, K., Szmukler, G., Andrewes, D., Tress, B. & Desmond, P. (1996) Neuropsychological and structural brain changes in anorexia nervosa before and after refeeding. *Psychol. Med.*, **26**, 15–28.

Klibanski, A. & Grinspoon, S.K. (2000) Assessment of macronutrient and micronutrient intake in women with anorexia nervosa. *Int. J. Eat. Disord.*, **28**, 284–292.

Koh, E., Onishi, T., Morimoto, S, Imanaka, S., Nakagawa, H. & Ogihara, T. (1989) Clinical evaluation of hypokalemia in anorexia nervosa. *Japan. J. Med.*, **28** (6), 692–696.

Lacey, J.H. & Evans, C.D.H. (1986) The impulsivist: A multi-impulsive personality disorder. *Br. J. Addict.*, **81**, 641–649.

Lacey, J.H. (1995) In-patient treatment of multi-impulsive bulimia nervosa. In K.D. Brownell & C.G. Fairburn (Eds), *Eating Disorders and Obesity*. New York: Guilford Press.

Lasègue, C. (1873) De l'anorixie hysterique. *Arch. Gen. de Med.*, **21** (April), 385–403.

Lask, B., Fosson, A., Rolfe, U. & Thomas, S. (1993) Zinc deficiency and childhood-onset anorexia nervosa. *J. Clin. Psychiat.*, **54** (2), 63–66.

Lauer, C.J., Gorzewskie, B., Gerlinghoff, M., Backmund, H. & Zihl, J. (1999) Neuropsychological assessments before and after treatment in patients with anorexia nervosa and bulimia nervosa. *J. Psychiat. Res.*, **33** (2), 129–138.

Le Grange, D., Eisler, I., Dare, C. & Russell, G.F.M. (1992) Evaluation of family therapy in anorexia nervosa: A pilot study. *Int. J. Eat. Disord.*, **12**, 347–357.

Meads, C., Gold, L. & Burls, A. (2001) How effective is outpatient care compared to inpatient care for thetreatment of anorexia nervosa? A systematic review. [Journal Article] *Eur. Eat. Disord. Rev.*, **9**, 229–241.

Marcé, L.V. (1860) Note sur une forme de délire hypochondriaque consécutive aux dyspepsies et caractérisée principalement par le refus d'aliments. *Annales Médico-Psychologiques*, **6**, 15–28.

McClain, C.J., Stuart, M.A, Vivian, B., McClain, M., Talwalker, R., Snelling, L. & Humphries, L. (1992) Zinc status before and after zinc supplementation of eating disorder patients. *J. Am. Coll. Nutrit.*, **11** (6), 694–700.

Moodie, D.S. & Salcedo, E. (1985) Cardiac function in adolescents and young adults with anorexia nervosa. *J. Adolesc. Health Care*, **4**, 9–14.

Morgan, H.G., Purgold, J. & Welbourne, J. (1983) Management and outcome in anorexia nervosa: A standardised prognostic study. *Br. J. Psychiat.*, **143**, 282–287.

Nishita, J.K., Ellinwood, E.H., Rockwell, W.J.K. et al. (1989) Abnormalities in the response of arginine vasopressin during hypertonic saline infusion in patients with eating disorders. *Biol. Psychiat.*, **26**, 73–86.

Palla, B. & Litt, I.F. (1988) Medical complications of eating disorders in adolescents. *Pediatrics*, **81** (5), 613–623.

Philipp, E., Pirke, K.-M., Seidl, M., Tuschl, R.J., Fichter, M.M., Eckert, M. & Wolfram, G. (1988) Vitamin status in patients with anorexia nervosa and bulimia nervosa. *Int. J. Eat. Disord.*, **8**, 209–218.

Piran, N. & Kaplan, A.S. (Eds) (1990) *A Day Hospital Treatment Programme for Anorexia Nervosa and Bulimia Nervosa.* New York: Brunner/ Mazel.

Radcliffes Mental Health Law, Briefing No. 34 (2000) London: Radcliffes Solicitors.

Ramsey, R., Ward, A., Treasure, J. & Russell, G.F.M. (1999) Compulsory treatment in anorexia nervosa. *Br. J. Psychiat.*, **175**, 147–153.

Reifenstein, E.C. (1946) Psychogenic or 'hypothalamic' amenorrhea. *Med. Clin. N. Am.*, **30**, 1103.

Rock, C.L. & Vasantharajan, S. (1995) Vitamin status of eating disorder patients: relationship to clinical indices and effect of treatment. *Int. J. Eat. Disord.*, **18**, 257–262.

Russell, G.F.M. (1981) Comment: The current treatment of anorexia nervosa. *Br. J. Psychiat.*, **138**, 164–166.

Russell, G.F.M., Szmukler, G.I., Dare, C. & Eisler, I. (1987) An evaluation of family therapy in anorexia nervosa and bulimia nervosa. *Arch. Gen. Psychiat.*, **44**, 1047–1056.

Salisbury, J.J., Levine, A.S., Crow, S.J. & Mitchell, J.E. (1995) Refeeding, metabolic rate and weight gain in anorexia nervosa: A review. *Int. J. Eat. Disord.*, **17** (4), 337–345.

St John Sutton, M.G., Plappert, T, Crosby, L., Douglas, P., Mullen, J. & Reichek, N. (1985) Effects of reduced left ventricular mass on chamber architecture, load and function: A study of anorexia nervosa. *Circulation*, **72**, 991–1000.

Sharp, C.W. & Freeman, C.P.L. (1993) The medical complications of anorexia nervosa. *Br. J. Psychiat.*, **163**, 452–462.

Strober, M., Freeman, R., DeAntonio, M. et al. (1997) Does adjunctive fluoxetine influence the post-hospital course of restrictor-type anorexia nervosa? A 24-month prospective, longitudinal followup and comparison with historical controls. *Psychopharmacol. Bull.*, **33**, 425–431.

Strober, M., Freeman, R. & Morrell. (1997) The long-term course of severe anorexia nervosa in adolescents: Survival analysis of recovery, relapse and outcome predictors over 10–15 years in a prospective study. *Int. J. Eat. Disord.*, **22**, 339–360.

Szmukler, G.I., Andrewes, D., Kingston, K., Chen, L., Stargatt, R. & Stanley, R. (1992) Neuropsychological impairment in anorexia nervosa before and after refeeding. *J. Clin. Exp. Neuropsychol.*, **14**, 347–352.

Theander, S. (1992) Chronicity in anorexia nervosa: Results from the Swedish long-term study. In W. Herzog, H.-C. Deter & W. Vandereycken (Eds), *The Course of Eating Disorders*, (pp. 214–227). Berlin: Springer Verlag.

Touyz, S.W., Beumont, P.J.V., Glaun, D., Phillips, T. & Cowie, I. (1984) A comparison of lenient and strict operant conditioning programmes in refeeding patients with anorexia nervosa. *Br. J. Psychiat.*, **144**, 517–520.

Tuschen, B. & Bents, H. (1995) Intensive brief in-patient treatment of bulimia nervosa. In K.D. Brownell & C.G. Fairburn (Eds), *Eating Disorders and Obesity.* New York: Guilford Press.

Vandereycken, W. & Pierloot, R. (1982) Pimozide combined with behaviour therapy in the short-term treatment of anorexia nervosa. A double-blind placebo-controlled cross-over study. *Acta Psychiat. Scand.*, **66**, 445–50.

Ward, A., Ramsay, R. & Treasure, J. (2000) Attachment research in eating disorders. *Br. J. Med. Psychol.*, **73** (1), 35–51.

Warren, S.E. & Steinberg, S.M. (1979) Acid-base and electrolyte disturbances in anorexia nervosa. *Am. J. Psychiat.*, **136** (4A), 415–418.

Winston, A.P. (2000) Physical assessment of the eating disordered patient. *Eur. Eat. Disord. Rev.*, **8**, 188–191.

Winston, A.P. & Wells, F.E. (2002) Hypophosphataemia following self-treatment for anorexia nervosa. *Int. J. Eat. Disord.*, **32** (2), 245–8.

Winston, A.P., Jamieson, C.P., Madira, W., Gatward, N.M., Palmer, R.L. (2000) Prevalence of thiamin deficiency in anorexia nervosa. *Int. J. Eat. Dis*, **28** (4), 451–454.

Index